Invading the Realm of Demons, Disease, and Death

Invading the Realm of Demons, Disease, and Death

The Miracles of Jesus: God with Us

CARL E. ROEMER

WIPF & STOCK · Eugene, Oregon

INVADING THE REALM OF DEMONS, DISEASE, AND DEATH
The Miracles of Jesus: God with Us

Copyright © 2024 Carl E. Roemer. All rights reserved. Except for brief quotations in critical publications or reviews, no part of this book may be reproduced in any manner without prior written permission from the publisher. Write: Permissions, Wipf and Stock Publishers, 199 W. 8th Ave., Suite 3, Eugene, OR 97401.

Wipf & Stock
An Imprint of Wipf and Stock Publishers
199 W. 8th Ave., Suite 3
Eugene, OR 97401

www.wipfandstock.com

PAPERBACK ISBN: 979-8-3852-0175-4
HARDCOVER ISBN: 979-8-3852-0176-1
EBOOK ISBN: 979-8-3852-0177-8

07/18/24

Biblical quotations are excepted from the Revised Standard Version of the Bible, Old Testament Section copyright 1952; New Testament Section, first edition copyright 1946; the Apocrypha, copyright 1957 by the division of Christian Education of the National Council of Churches of Christ in the United States of America.

To Dottie
my wife and companion for 60 years,
and to
the Judaic Studies Department at
the State University of New York at Binghamton
where the contents of this book had its beginnings,
and to
all the pastors and lay people who want to understand
how Jesus' miracles fit into his society.

Contents

Preface | ix

Abbreviations | xi

Introduction | xv

Front Matter Endnotes | xxi

1. Science, Historiography, and Revelation: The Truth is One | 1
2. The Miracles of Jesus: The Exorcisms | 39
3. The Miracles of Jesus: The Healings | 81

    Excurses: The Beloved Son Determines His Hour: The So-called "Messianic Secret" | 105

4. The Miracles of Jesus: Raising the Dead | 154
5. The Miracles: The Theophanies | 171
6. Summary | 207

    Epilogue: Retrospect and Prospect | 246

    Endnotes | 249

    Bibliography | 325

    Index | 331

Preface

Dear reader, this study is the fourth volume in a series of studies on the Jesus of history. This series had its origin in a course that I taught at the State University of New York at Binghamton in the 1990s that I called "Jesus in Context." The "context" I distilled in the first book of this series that I called *What Was the World of Jesus?* The second volume investigated the parables of Jesus as they are found in the New Testament gospels. I placed them in the context that I described in the first volume and strove to hear them as his first-century interlocutors would have heard them.

My overall thesis in writing these books is that Jesus must be understood in terms of the time and place in which he lived and worked. Hearing them in that way they revealed how provocative they indeed were as well as revealing the character of Jesus himself. So I called that second volume *Who in the World Was Jesus?* I prefaced that volume with an overview and critique of the more prominent approaches and conclusions scholars have come to in their investigations of what they call the "historical Jesus." I wanted the reader to understand the broad research context in which my studies were functioning.

In the third volume, *The Beloved Son as Tantalizing Teacher*, I investigated the apothegms or pronouncement stories, that is, sayings of Jesus that are placed within a brief context in the Gospels. I prefaced that examination with a close look at the birth, baptism, and temptation narratives which revealed a surprising way in which Jesus came to identify himself. In these stories we find Jesus interacting with his contemporaries in the land of Israel. They are divided into biographical and controversy and scholastic dialogues. The biographical stories relate incidences in which Jesus reveals something personal and how he interpreted his experiences. The latter stories describe his encounter with individuals and groups who challenged his words and actions.

In this volume I take up again my thesis that the historical context is foundational to understanding Jesus' words and activity. It is clear from all of my studies that Jesus was engaging the realities of his world, the present circumstances of Israel in the Holy Land of the first century. It is that context in which his performance of miracles is to be understood: the miracles were concrete expression of the kingdom of God which Jesus was setting before the people to choose the restorative powers that were now present in it and in him, rather than the way of death to which the present mindset of the nation was surely leading.

In these books my desire is to help pastors and laypeople understand Jesus in a deeper way and how his words and actions related to the actual life of his people. In that way the application to our present circumstances can be made authentically and be true to his intentions.

The works on the "historical Jesus" are extensive and voluminous. I realize I am adding my studies and my words to that vast literature. However, I think my studies are adding an important feature that is often neglected, that is, anchoring Jesus' words and deeds in the well-known conditions of his time and place. That link then provides a vibrant realism and authenticity to those words and deeds. But you, dear reader, judge for yourself. I think when you engage with my study you will find and amazing relevance to what you read in the Gospels.

Abbreviations

SCRIPTURE ABBREVIATIONS

HebrewBible / Old Testament

Gen	Genesis	Song	Song of Solomon
Exod	Exodus	Isa	Isaiah
Lev	Leviticus	Jer	Jeremiah
Num	Numbers	Lam	Lamentations
Deut	Deuteronomy	Ezek	Ezekiel
Josh	Joshua	Dan	Daniel
Judg	Judges	Hos	Hosea
Ruth	Ruth	Joel	Joel
1–2 Sam	1–2 Samuel	Amos	Amos
1–2 Kgs	1–2 Kings	Obad	Obadiah
1–2 Chr	1–2 Chronicles	Jonah	Jonah
Ezra	Ezra	Mic	Micah
Neh	Nehemiah	Nah	Nahum
Esth	Esther	Hab	Habbkuk
Job	Job	Zeph	Zephaniah
Ps / Pss	Psalms	Hag	Haggai
Prov	Proverbs	Zech	Zechariah
Eccl	Ecclesiastes	Mal	Malachi

ABBREVIATIONS

New Testament

Matt	Matthew	Col	Colossians
Mk	Mark	1–2 Thess	1–2 Thessalonians
Lk	Luke	1–2 Tim	1–2 Timothy
John	John	Titus	Titus
Acts	Acts of the Apostles	Phlm	Philemon
Rom	Romans	Heb	Hebrews
1–2 Cor	1–2 Corinthians	Jas	James
Gal	Galatians	1–2 Pet	1–2 Peter
Eph	Ephesians	1–2–3 John	1–2–3 John
Phil	Philippians	Jude	Jude
		Rev	Revelation

The Apocrypha / Deuterocanonical Books

Tob	Tobit	Ep Jer	Epistle of Jerimiah
Jdt	Judith	Sg Three	Song of the Tree Young Men
Add Esth	Additions to Esther	Sus	Susanna
Wis	Wisdom of Solomon	Bel	Bel and the Dragon
Sir	Sirach or Ecclesiastes	1–2 Macc	1–2 Maccabees
Bar	Baruch	3–4 Macc	3–4 Maccabees
1–3 Esd	1–3 Esdras	Pr Man	Prayer of Manasseh

Pseudepigrapha

Enoch	1(Ethiopic Apocalypse of) Enoch
TestSol	Testament of Solomon
Testaments	Testaments of the Twelve Patriarchs
Pss of Sol	Psalms of Solomon

Other Ancient Sources

Flavius Josephus

Josephus, *War*	The Jewish War
Josephus, *Ant.*	Antiquities of the Jews
Josephus, *Life*	The Life of Flavius Josephus

Philo

Life of Moses — *De vita Mosis*
Embassy — *Legatio ad Gaium*
Special Laws — *De specialibus legibus*

The Dead Sea Scrolls

(The scrolls are designated by the cave they were found in, the initial number, followed by "Q" for Qumran, and by the type of literature using the initial letter of the Hebrew name for the scrolls. S="Serek" (rule); H=Hodayoth ("hymns"); p="pesher" ("interpretation" or "commentary").

The Community Rule	1QS
The Thanksgiving Hymns	1QH
Commentary on Habakkuk	1QpHab

The Mishnah

The various tractates of the Mishnah are preceded by an *m*.
The names of the tractates are always spelled out and translated in the footnotes.

The Talmuds

The tractates of the Talmuds are preceded by *j.* for the *Jerusalem Talmud* and by *b.* for the *Babylonian Talmud*.

Periodicals and Encyclopedias

ABD	The Anchor Bible Dictionary. New York: Doubleday, 1992.
foz	Friends of Zion. Phoenix: Jerusalem Prayer Team International.
IDB	Interpreter's Dictionary of the Bible. Nashville: Abingdon, 1962.
JBL	Journal of Biblical Literature. Atlanta: Society of Biblical Literature.

Introduction

Dear reader, in this book I am investigating the miracles that are ascribed to Jesus in the Gospels. I divide them into exorcisms, healings, raising from the dead, and theophanies. That latter category refers to manifestation of the divinity in the world. The OT is replete with such stories and like them Jesus manifests the presence of God only privately to his disciples except in the story of the multiplication of loaves.

It is important to see his miracles within the context of his contemporaneous world which I will summarize once again as I have in my previous books on the parables and pronouncement stories. It is especially important to understand his concept of the kingdom of God for it is within that overarching reality of his ministry that his actions and words are to be comprehended.

The majority of the people in Jewish society in the Holy Land of Jesus' time were peasants whose "backs were against the wall."[1] They lived a hand-to-mouth existence and were always on the verge of going over the edge. So the society was fraught with anxiety concerning the necessities of life. It was no wonder that people were attracted to revolution, particularly because of the predations of the Roman procurators. One of the core values of this agrarian society was the perception that life was constricted by "limited good." In other words, the availability of life's needs was a zero-sum game: if you had something, that meant it was not available to me and vice versa. Furthermore, the other social values of patriarchy, honor and shame, cultic purity, and corporate personality made for a somewhat rigid social structure which predisposed people to see the crisis of the society totally in terms of the Roman occupation. So the land was rife with revolutionary movements.[2]

Jesus, along with a few others, saw where such movements would end: the destruction of the nation. Jesus called the nation to a different way by his multi-formed and varicolored ministry. The miracles that he performed, along with his teaching and preaching,[3] announced the presence of the coming kingdom of God which he conceived as imminent. The miracles, his call of an inner circle of twelve disciples, and his open commensality made the presence of the kingdom concrete. The twelve gave structure to this community of the new age and his table fellowship made tangible the life in the kingdom exemplified by love, forgiveness of sin, and mutual concern. The miracles further emphasized the materiality of the kingdom in raiding the realm of Satan in his exorcisms, restoring life and physical well-being in his healings and raising the dead, and manifesting God and therewith his approval of his beloved son, Jesus, in the theophanies.

The kingdom is pure divine gift and comes without any human action or striving but requires human involvement. This paradoxical nature of the kingdom is illustrated by the act of sowing (Mark 4:1–8). Humans must spread the word like seed but God will give the increase (1 Cor 3:5). So being in the kingdom meant both a kind of quietism, waiting for God to act but also an activism which involved preaching, teaching, performing miracles, inviting people to sit at table, to reach out with love and concern for the neighbor, to pray for one's enemies, and to share one's goods. In this way the kingdom upended the cultural value of limited good. It also meant a role reversal of servant attending to the master: the master will minister to the slave (Luke 12:37). The peasant was challenged to forgive as he had been forgiven. So Jesus showed the way to solidarity between all levels of society. His message was directed toward the healing of society.

The kingdom had a double nature: it was both present and future preserving the reality of the God of Israel who was both a part of the world in the sense that he dwelt with his people and also transcendent. The fullness of the kingdom lies in the future. God lays claim to the whole life of a person, and though he is transcendent he is not some far-off god withdrawn into some kind of mythological, unearthly realm. He is active in expanding his kingdom as it is sown by his beloved son and those who follow him. The kingdom can appear among the most unexpected persons and in the most peculiar circumstances. When the kingdom finds a person it provokes the absolute depth of joy. But the kingdom is not only promise and grace. This is also a time of crisis. The kingdom is at the gate, and when it dawns repentance will no longer be possible. People will knock at the door and demand entrance but they will be told, "I don't know you" (Matt 25:1–13). Now is the time to reorient life and enter the kingdom.

In all of this Jesus also reveals himself and his own self-consciousness. Foundational to his self-consciousness was his naming in a theophany at his baptism as the "beloved son." That designation was loaded with evocative associations, namely, the story of the "sacrifice" of Isaac (Gen 22:1–19). The "first fruits" belong to God (Deut 21:17). The life of the first-born belongs to God and is marked for both humiliation and exaltation.[4] So the designation as "beloved son" meant he was to be sacrificed. As the "beloved son" he identifies with the servant of Second Isaiah who represents the people and embodies the nation and so will take upon himself the nation's suffering (Isa 52:13—53:12).

Jesus is not opposed to his people but has a great compassion for them and craves their positive response to his proclamation of the kingdom. His miracles reflect the compassion he felt for the plight of the people. He is not some kind of gnostic who imparts hidden knowledge but stands firmly within Jewish understanding of God. Nor is he an apocalyptist clothed in a sandwich board screaming about disastrous scenarios that are about to befall the people. He, in fact, deconstructs popular apocalyptic in the parable of the unjust steward (Luke 16:1–8). Everyone in the parable acts in a fraudulent way. But in the story's denouement all delight in a partnership of joy. So Jesus asserts a new standard of justice and power: the master abnegates power, lets the scam of the steward stand, and all reap the harvest of the forgiveness of debt. His capacious understanding of the kingdom came to include the gentiles and in his parable of the Great Assize (Matt 25:31–46) shows that they will gain inclusion in the kingdom by how they treat God's people Israel. God's grace and mercy are indeed deep and wide!

So Jesus created a counter version of Israel. Not the Israel that would conquer the nations and bring in the kingdom of God but the kingdom which served headed by the true shepherd of the people who sought out the sinner, the outcast, and the marginalized. Again, this did not mean Jesus was opposed to his own people but quite the contrary, he was giving them an alternative to the path that was leading them to death and destruction. So Jesus' invitation to the kingdom was like part of a lovers quarrel.

INTRODUCTION

This brief summary is the context in which the miracles of Jesus must be understood. In chapter 1 I engage the skepticism regarding the miracles, which is based on our culture's basic materialist understanding of reality. Because of the implications found in contemporary scientific investigations and the results which point to the world of the spirit, the materialist point of view is untenable. So I assume their authenticity and historicity unless my investigations of the miracle stories prove otherwise. In every case I find them as reliable reports of Jesus' activity.

In chapter 2 I examine the exorcisms. They must be understood under the rubric of the parable of the returning demons.[5] The parable is a metaphor for the mindset that had infected Israel and which threatened to lead to the demise of the nation. I characterize the "seven demons" that have possessed Israel as its emphasis on its separation from the rest of the world; its increasing belligerent attitude toward Rome; the exclusive concern on obedience to the Torah to the exclusion of mercy; the fantasizing about an apocalyptic divine intervention that didn't include a sense of also standing under God's judgment; the rebuffing of the prophets that were sent to the nation; the sitting in judgment on one another rather than nurturing brotherly love; and accusing Jesus of demon possession when he was the one who was invading Satan's realm and binding the "strong man" (Mark 3:27).[6]

Demon possession involved ritual uncleanness, so it meant exclusion from the community. In exorcising then Jesus was healing the divisions within the nation. The spiritual aspect of demon possession meant that faith in God was failing. The craving to eliminate Rome's hegemony in the Holy Land overwhelmed faith in God to act on his time schedule and was one of the causes that produced the unprecedented frequent occurrence of demon possession in first-century Jewish society. Demonic powers then take advantage of spiritual vacuums. Anger and hostility provoked by the Roman occupation, especially when these emotions were turned inward, were also opportunities for the invasion of humans by demons. So Jesus' exorcisms were part of his work to save the nation and not mere demonstrations of some supposed divine power. Rather, his ability to exorcize a demon with a simple word derived from his total dependence on and on an unadulterated relationship of trust in his Father-God.

Jesus confronts and conquers Satan in his exorcisms. The nation, and indeed the world, had become enemy-occupied territory which by right belonged to God. God had created the world and chosen his people

Israel. By sin, however, it had fallen into Satan's clutches. Jesus invades Satan's rule and liberates nation and world. This overthrow of Satan was the harbinger of a new creation which the kingdom was establishing. In this way the exile, which was so understood because of the predations of Roman rule, was over, and the glorious promises of Second Isaiah were being realized: Israel will be a newly constituted people with a new covenant relationship with God, and they will increase.[7]

The healing miracles of Jesus resonate with the miracle activity of Elijah and Elisha, which witnessed to their standing before God as truly his prophets. This similarity also suggests that Jesus saw the present rebellious attitudes of the people as idolatry and sabotaging faith in God and the rule of his kingdom, the very issues that these ancient prophets faced. Because of his prophetic connection the healing stories were probably told early on as prophetic stories demonstrating the existence of God's kingdom and concern for his people.

But his healings could also elicit the suspicion that he was practicing magic and therefore came under the condemnation of Torah. So he then would appear as a false prophet working with Satan to deceive and delude the people. So Jesus tries to hinder the spreading reports about his healings. In this he was not successful. Because of his compassion and the demands of the kingdom he could not stop these reports.

Jesus was often opposed and roundly criticized for healing on the Sabbath and breaking the rule not to work on that day. Jesus saw boundary markers such as the temple, purity laws, Sabbath laws, and circumcision as the problem. He never disparages Torah, but he saw the contemporary exclusive focus on Torah obedience, its place at the heart of the nation's existence, and as symbols that define Israel (Deut 13) as misplaced. That, of course, brought about his condemnation by some as disloyal to God and a perverter of the nation (John 7:12.). So Jesus was replacing the kingdom for Israel's traditional symbols and in this way was re-ordering the Jewish symbolic universe. In the kingdom, God was reconstituting Israel around Jesus as the embodiment of the restored Israel. The kingdom's "symbols" achieved victory not by violence but by the ethic of non-retaliation, taking up one's cross, restoration by suffering, forgiveness which included forgiving debts, turning the other cheek, going the extra mile, hospitality, repentance, and realizing the real enemy was within and not in the Roman occupation.[8] So the crisis from the kingdom's perspective was not Rome's paganizing influence sullying the land but Israel's own attitude of aggressive hostility and its failure to nurture its call to be the light and salt of the earth to the nations, a city set on a hill, to restore creation, be a cradle of peace and order in the world, and rid itself of internal corruption. Her sufferings were to be redemptive and she would be ultimately vindicated.

So the healings that Jesus performed were concrete realizations of Israel's vocation and God's compassionate concern for his people. Jesus founded a community which embodied the new Israel and pursuing her real vocation the deep, underlying essence of Judaism.

The stories of Jesus' raising of the dead are all related to women. Women were particularly vulnerable to the vicissitudes of life and without a male head would be acutely subject to going under. These raisings also graphically portray Jesus' compassion, his own powerful and intimate relationship with his Father-God, and his consciousness of being the "beloved son." The raising from the dead stories emphasize too that the kingdom as Jesus saw it was not some kind of "spiritual" entity but a flesh and blood historical reality that was meant to renew Israel as she was in the world.

That there are only three such reports emphasize that early Christians did not artificially multiply such stories.

Finally, I will investigate what I call "theophanies" which most scholars call "nature miracles." Theophanies are manifestations of God. My term seem to me to be more apropos since not all of them fit under that latter rubric. These miracles of Jesus reveal the nature of Jesus as God's "beloved son," that God is present in his works and sets his stamp of approval on him and his works.

Front Matter Endnotes

1. A phrase used by Thurman, *Jesus and the Disinherited* to describe the people of Jesus' day and the situation of African Americans in the early twentieth century in the United States.
2. For a detailed examination of these values see Roemer, *What Was the World of Jesus*, 558–62.
3. See my books on the parables and the pronouncement stories in the bibliography.
4. Levenson, *Death and Resurrection*, 59. Cf., Rom 8:32. See the law of the firstborn, Exod 13:2. This self-consciousness of Jesus is revealed in his passion predictions Mk 8:31, 9:31, and 10:33 and in his prayer in the Garden of Gethsemane 14:36.
5. Matt 12:43–5, Lk 11:24–6. See Roemer, *Who in the World Was Jesus*, 347–50.
6. Roemer, *Tantalizing Teacher*, xxi.
7. See especially chapters 41–54 in Isaiah.
8. See note 5.

CHAPTER 1

Science, Historiography, and Revelation
The Truth is One

The heavens are telling the glory of God and
the vault of heaven proclaims his handiwork.
Day to day pours forth speech, and night to night declares knowledge.

INTRODUCTION

Miracles are a problem for historians, to say nothing of theologians.[1] They do not conform to so-called scientific and modern requirements of a perceivable material cause-and-effect relationship that a scientific historiography demands. Before approaching the idea of miracles themselves I will review the developments in science since Newton developed the laws of mechanics that described how things in our perceivable world interact. Newton himself believed he was discovering the inner workings of the universe as God created it. Subsequently, and especially after Darwin propounded his theory of evolution, scientists gave up any notion about a creator God and saw the universe like a mechanical clock that worked by itself without a creator. It was actually believed if the direction and motion of every particle in the universe was known all subsequent time could accurately be predicted. Historians, especially biblical ones, adopted this model and so found miracles to be but human fantasy invented to provide hope for the dispossessed.

However, with the development of the sciences, especially in the world of atomic and subatomic particles, science has entered a very strange and peculiar world that does not conform to the Newtonian and Darwinian certainties. In the following I will provide an overview of discoveries that have totally altered our understanding of the universe and how it works.

First I will follow the developments in physics and astronomy beginning with Newton. In discovering by experiment the laws of motion he thought he was revealing the mind of God. But the conviction that the universe had a designer was not to last. Under the influence of Hume, Laplace, Darwin, and others, science became a materialist philosophy and method. I will follow subsequent developments, especially in the realm of the physics of the atom, subatomic particles, and the constants which characterize the physical universe. Those discoveries along with the evidence for the "big bang," the biological discoveries of the genome, its complexities, and its information laden structure all point to a designer. In discussing the developments in biology I summarize an online video of three scientists who discuss the mathematical challenges to Darwin's theory of natural selection driving evolution.

Secondly, I summarize the investigation of near-death experiences and demon possession as direct evidence of a world of the spirit beyond the material universe.

These scientific investigations affirm that a mind designed the universe and the human genome and that there is scientific evidence for the existence of the world of the spirit beyond our material universe.

Thirdly, I investigate the biblical creation account in Gen 1:2–24 and establish its form (i.e., its literary type)[2] and setting within its religio-cultural context. This context determined its form as a theological treatise which affirms a scientific understanding of the material universe. The form of the creation narrative conforms to how the creation myths of the ancient near east open their narrative "[When,] in the beginning . . ." But there the resemblance ends.[3] In its distinctiveness from the old ancient Near East mythologies perhaps the first line of the Genesis creation account should read, "This is the real way the world began . . ." So the universe participates in God's sacredness: it provides a material home for us material creatures and is meant to be cared for and nourished.

In the final section I introduce the study of the miracle stories in the Gospels. I define the genre and form of these narratives, how they fit into Jesus' activity followed by an enumeration and division of these stories into exorcisms, healings, raisings from the dead, and theophanies (i.e., divine manifestations).

So I invite you, the reader, to enter into an exciting dialogue between science and faith and to see how the so-called incompatibility between reason and faith is a false dichotomy. The sub-heading of this chapter is "The truth is One." Even to assume that reason and faith have different vocabularies and approaches to the reality of the world cannot support the idea that truth is bifurcated. Truth can only be one. Two polar contradicting opposites cannot coexist. The truth of science and the truth of revealed faith cannot cancel one another out. The review which follows discloses the wonder of science and the beauty of divine revelation as a witness to one truth.

THE WITNESS OF SCIENTIFIC DEVELOPMENTS

Physics and Astronomy

The developments in the hard sciences (physics, chemistry, biology, astronomy, geology) have all led to the point where a truly open mind would conclude that reality has a designer. In fact that was the basis for the development of a scientific worldview and the scientific method at its inception.

Science during the medieval period recognized that the world was filled with instinct and purpose which had an intimate relationship with the person and his or her destiny and engendered an intelligent reason for existing in the light of that destiny. Early scientists like Newton[4] understood God as first cause. Indeed, belief in God and particularly Christianity itself played a crucial part in the growth of science during the sixteenth and seventeenth centuries.[5] Specifically the anthropology of the Protestant Reformation under the influence of St. Augustine held that mankind was created in the image of God but simultaneously was infected with original sin. So human beings could understand the workings of the natural world but were also subject to error and fallibility to say nothing of self-deception. So the results of scientific investigations had to be tested by experiment and observation and always be subject to modification and amendment. Such a procedure is essential to the scientific method. The method always has to be open-ended and capable of integrating new information and new ways to thinking. There is no such thing as "settled science." So the conviction that there was a rational and intelligent designer inspired the development of science.

There are three metaphors which describe this deistic scientific worldview. The clock: God is thought of as initiating the processes of the natural world and then left the universe to develop according to its laws of mathematical necessity; the book: the world is thought of as being able to be "read" and reveal the attributes of God (cf., Ps 19:1–2); nature is a law-governed realm in which the investigator expects to find regularity, the so-called "laws of nature." Early investigators like Boyle, Kepler, and Newton understood their work as revealing the intelligibility of the universe and therefore the mind of its designer.

This conviction, however, was not to last. The events of the Thirty Years' War were an impetus toward a turn of thought. This devastating conflict between Catholics and Protestants with their opposing claims of the sources of religious authority led to an exhaustion that engendered reservations about a transcendent origin of the universe and opened up a search for new ways of thinking. So an enlightenment philosopher like David Hume (1711–76) could reject the reality of God and deny the possibility of miracles particularly because they were perceived as violating the laws of the natural world. He was followed by Pierre Laplace who explained the operation of the solar system in meticulous mathematical detail which required no need of a God hypothesis. His work marked a decisive alteration of thought among many scientists.[6] Then Darwin proposed in his 1859 study *The Origin of Species* his evolutionary theory that attributed life to a blind process of natural selection that required no divine agent. So science became a materialist philosophy limited to "natural" processes, and God was defined out of existence! It was demanded that scientists could only offer materialist explanations of phenomena and any other explanation was defined as illegitimate. Marx and Freud, both atheists, added their voices to this new materialism. They both propounded a thoroughgoing materialistic understanding of human nature.

So the enlightenment idea that human reason could function independently and replace revealed religion, an increasing skepticism about the reality of God, and a materialism that propounded that only matter and energy were real became the new norm.[7] Belief in God then was negatively defined as an illusion if not a mental illness. Science became based on the assumption that only those elements which inform us with the quantitative aspects of the material world are real and objective. The "real" then was identified with the quantitative. If you can't express something in numbers it is unreal.[8] The results of this "revolution" were embodied in the myth of the conflict between science and religion, between reason and faith.[9] The human experience of color, beauty, or mystic communion with God were judged as not objective.[10]

But this has all been found to be insufficient. Science has become more self-conscious and somewhat more humble. The scientific method is no longer thought to be the only valid method of acquiring knowledge. If science is the ultimate reality, man is made an entirely accidental by-product of a huge, mindless, purposeless, mathematical machine (some scientists greet that idea, however, with approbation). But the foundation of the belief that the sole reality is matter and motion has been undermined. The Newtonian mechanical model has now been found insufficient in the light of quantum mechanics and the philosophical implications of the new approach is quite different from the old.[11]

Science, it is now recognized, can only give us partial knowledge of reality and it is no longer tenable to think that everything that science can ignore is illusory. Maxwell[12] demonstrated that light was an electromagnetic phenomenon and could not be described mechanically. So physics had to admit that we know nothing of electromagnetic radiation but its mathematical structure.[13] So physics had to say we are not required to know the nature of a phenomenon but only its mathematical structure. Physics can't handle the qualities of matter (massiveness, substantiality, extension, or duration). The essence of the actual nature of the material of the atomic world is inscrutable. Physics studies "pointer readings" which are observable. So knowledge consists of readings not qualities. The readings, however, "have as much resemblance to the quality of matter as a telephone number has to a subscriber."[14] So scientific knowledge does not demand that the human response to beauty or communion with God have no objective counterpart. Rather, they are clues to the nature of reality.[15]

For James Jeans the universe is a thought in the mind of a supreme mathematician because only mathematical pictures in our mind accord with observation.[16] But these pictures are not anything we can imagine. For example, in the wave theory of matter an electron is a system of waves in a three-dimensional space. But two electrons require six dimensions and so on. These waves are elusive. They may be "probability waves" with no material existence whatever. This is all unimaginable. So Jeans concludes that the universe is more like a thought. He bases his thinking on the concepts which prove to be fundamental to our understanding of nature: that space is finite but expanding, empty, and four-dimensional; that one point differs from another due to the properties of space itself; that events follow the laws of probability instead of causation; and that a sequence of events can only be fully and consistently described by going out of space and time. All these concepts seem to him to be "structures of thought incapable of realization in any sense that could properly be described as material." Nothing material could act so oddly.[17] Eddington came to similar conclusions, observing that the only direct knowledge we possess is knowledge of mental states. All other knowledge is inferred knowledge. All knowledge comes to us in the form of physical stimuli to the brain which give rise to mental states which are of an entirely different nature than the physical stimuli.[18]

All of this has a humanistic importance because it leaves such thinking free to attach significance to aesthetic and religious experiences. It cuts the ground from under such interpretations that deem them as illusory. It shows that science only deals with partial aspects of reality and there is no foundation for believing that everything science ignores is less real than what it accepts. The abstractions of physics form a closed cycle and so are immune from the factors it does not take into consideration.[19]

A cardinal assumption of science has been a strict web of causality. However, it doesn't seem to apply at the atomic level! At that level there seems to be an element of free will. Determinism breaks down and the principle of indeterminacy takes its place. It implies that our intuition of free will is not an illusion, that the natural world is capable of "creative advance," and that the distinction between the natural and the supernatural is diminished. This is a huge revolution in scientific thought: the philosophy based on previous scientific thought made matter and motion the sole reality. This claim now is a huge exaggeration. It had dismissed other elements of experience which seemed to have the greatest significance to human beings making life worth living. It had darkened life.[20]

When mathematicians became conscious of the mental power of mathematical reasoning, mathematical theorems became revelations of fundamental principles on which the universe was constructed. Even thought and emotions are construed as embodying numbers. So it was thought there were "necessary truths" such as the properties of a triangle. But the invention of non-Euclidian geometries show us that such properties depend on the postulates and axioms which are presupposed making these axioms and postulates arbitrary. So the idea has been abandoned that "mathematics gives us access to some external stores of supersensible truths."[21]

Mathematics does not have transcendental significance. Originally the simple, primary mathematical ideas were based on experience but their development was independent of experience. That mathematical theorems could be applied to the real world seems like a lucky accident! On that basis some have concluded that the universe has a mathematical designer. But even at that, the universe is such an "oddity" that science is "not yet in a position to weave a satisfactory mathematical web about it." Sullivan concludes that while mathematics is not purely subjective "it is not, in its nature, a body of truth about the objective physical world."[22]

Originally scientific concepts were suggested by ordinary experience. However, it was gradually discovered natural processes couldn't be accurately described in those terms. For example, the motion of a little hard ball cannot describe the behavior of an electron.[23] Erwin Schrödinger developed an equation that could solve the problem of the position and momentum of an atomic particle such as an electron (its size is measured at 10^{-15} meters = 25 trillionths of an inch) which essentially regarded the particle as a "probability wave."[24] And so it was that Newton's law of gravitation was found to be a generalized and particularized instance of quantum mechanical physics at the macro level of human experience.

So, Sullivan concludes, it is highly probable that all scientific theories are wrong and await further refinement or even overturning. Scientific truth then is pragmatic.[25] Physics can only deal with aspects of the world that can be treated quantitatively. In this way the statements of science are only true within the limits it claims for itself, that is, of mathematical structure. No scientific principles are sacrosanct or held with religious conviction. All of its truths are provisional. This Sullivan calls the "homely air" of science and its "great charm."[26]

The ultimate justification for any intellectual endeavor is to increase consciousness (which also appears to be the purpose of evolution). It introduces new ways of thinking that are, however, based on the conviction that nature is orderly.

Atomic physics has opened up a world that is indeed strange and totally beyond our ordinary experiences. The sizes involved are small beyond our imagination. For example there are 10^{21} molecules in an ounce of water![27] The wavelength of cosmic radiation is 10^{-13} centimeters. The nucleus of an atom is about one hundred thousand times smaller than the atom itself. The physical world discovered by science at both its upper and lower limits is something completely alien to us. There is also reason to suppose that there is a lower limit beyond which the notions of space and time measurements become meaningless.

Another aspect of the atomic world is the Heisenberg uncertainty principle, which means that you cannot determine both the position of a particle and its direction of movement (its momentum) simultaneously.[28] To see a subatomic particle such as an electron requires that you bounce a photon off it and then hope to detect that photon with an instrument. But chances are that the photon will impart some momentum to the electron as it hits it and changes the path of the particle you are trying to measure. Or else, given that quantum particles often move so fast, the electron may no longer be in the place it was when the photon originally bounced off it. Either way, your observation of either position or momentum will be inaccurate and, more importantly, *the act of observation affects the particle being observed*. In other words, to observe anything at an atomic level is to *change* it. So the very operation of measurement introduces an error in the measurement. The implication of this uncertainty is that the idea of causality becomes useless. There is no prediction where both position and momentum cannot be precisely determined. The information to predict then is inaccessible![29] Now because of this uncertainty principle which operates at the atomic level a strict determinism does not operate.

However, on the level of ordinary experience and in the macro world of the universe the measurements one cannot make in the atomic world can be made. Astronomy has greatly expanded our understanding of the vastness of the universe which is expanding at an ever increasing rate. Thus the universe, though finite, has no permanent limit. And Euclid's geometry does not apply to what we now call the space-time continuum because that continuum is curved.[30]

On the other hand the science of chemistry, whose practical value to us is immense, giving us control over nature, has not given us greater insight into nature. However, biology with its discovery of the genome was a staggering intellectual achievement. It could be deduced from this discovery that the living organism is but a mechanical system except that at the molecular level physics has shown there is a great degree of uncertainty and even freedom. Biology has also revealed the amazing panorama of life. It's startling to discover that there are insects with wings, legs, compound eyes, and muscles that are smaller than the human ovum! The varieties in somatic structure, size, and habits of living organisms is stunning. And the utter complexity of even one living cell is astounding. All of this makes it immensely difficult to come up with general principles. There are very few general laws in biology that admit of universal application. So the belief in natural selection has to be stretched and modified in not very convincing ways in order to explain many phenomena. So Sullivan understands that biology is the "most immature" of the sciences while psychology, sociology, and the related "sciences" are hardly sciences at all.[31]

There are twenty-six universal constants[32] which describe the physical universe such as the gravitational constant, the strong nuclear attraction, the cosmological constant that causes the expansion of the universe, and the elementary electrical charge. If any of these constants were to have different numbers the universe as we know it would not be possible.[33] So it seems that the universe has a design and that design leads to the development of life. It appears that these constants were "fine-tuned" and designed for the emergence of human beings. This fine-tuning has been called the "anthropic principle" because these are the absolutely prerequisite values to make the universe capable of producing life.[34] It ran contrary to the usual thinking that the universe was random, impersonal, and mechanistic and that human life came about by accident, merely the "by-product of brute, material forces randomly churning over the eons."[35] So the universe had to know what it was going to be before it got started.[36] "The more physicists have learned about the universe, the more it looks like a "put-up job."[37]

Two other types of fine tuning are the initial conditions at the moment of the big bang and the contingent feature of "entropy." The initial conditions included a heterogeneous distribution of mass and energy which resulted in the development of galaxies and the ensuing huge swaths of empty space. If these initial conditions were different the result would have been just a mass of clumped matter or a highly diffuse condition without any structure. In either case there would have been no stars and no galaxies in which life-producing solar systems could emerge.[38] Entropy refers to the amount of order or disorder in a system. The lower the entropy the greater the order. To have our ordered universe the entropy at the time of the big bang had to be low.[39] These initial conditions are unimaginably improbable, 1 out of 10^{10} again raised to the 123rd power! This number, as Meyer observes, is beyond "exquisite" fine tuning.[40]

Invading the Realm of Demons, Disease, and Death

This is a "teleological" explanation for the universe. That is, the reason or explanation for something is a function of its end and its purpose or goal, an argument used by the ancient and medieval natural philosophers. This line of thinking was abandoned by the rise of modern science which preferred to look not for final causes but for efficient causes, the mechanisms that actually bring things about. So our modern science was the victory of mechanism over teleology and the dethronement of God and the "disenchantment" of the universe. Everything had to be explained by mechanistic causes. Belief in a personal God descended into deism (God as first cause) and finally atheism.[41]

The "anthropic principle" is a very uncomfortable idea for many a modern scientist among whom is Stephen Hawking who came up with the idea of the multiverse, the idea that there are an infinite number of universes and one of them, namely ours, got it right. The only problem with such an idea is that it is incapable of being verified by observation or experimentation, two fundamental underpinnings of proving any scientific theory or endeavor.[42]

In summary, we have seen that science has plumbed the depths of the atomic world and discovered the mathematical structure of the material universe. However, in the long search for the essence of matter science has hit a wall. It can describe how these tiny particles act and their characteristics such as electric charge and mass but cannot describe what they are in themselves. On the level of the atomic world matter stops behaving like matter as we know it. Its essence is inscrutable and beyond explication. At the atomic level these particles can only be described as probability waves without material existence and with a freedom of action that cannot be determined beforehand in an easy cause and effect relationship. So at this level of matter there is no strict web of causality. All of this structure is not realizable in any sense that could be described as material. Determinism has broken down and indeterminism has taken its place. Therefore freedom is built into the material universe and the free will of human beings is confirmed. It is not entirely unreasonable to conclude with James Jeans that this description is more like thought which is held in the mind of a "supreme mathematician." So the human being recapitulates the underlying structure of the universe and all this new science leaves open the attachment of significance to human aesthetic and spiritual experiences. The distinction between the physical world and the world of the spirit is much diminished.[43]

Einstein originally thought the universe was in a steady state and neither expanding or contracting. He added a "cosmological constant" to his equations to make them describe such a static condition. However, in 1927 the Belgian priest and physicist Georges Lemaitre showed that Einstein's equation implied that the curvature of space would change over time. In addition, the so-called Doppler effect revealed that the more distant a galaxy the faster it was receding from the earth.[44] So Lemaitre showed that the universe was expanding and thus space itself. The implication was clear. The universe would have been much smaller in the past and so had a beginning and had to start from some "primeval atom."[45]

But what was causing this expansion? The more powerful telescopes of the 1970s found that stars within individual galaxies were moving at impossible velocities. Why were they not flung off into intergalactic space? This led some astronomers to suspect that stars are but sparks of light embedded in some invisible matter that was the really important substance of the universe.[46] Not knowing what they were dealing with scientists called it "dark matter." They still do not know what this matter is made of: it's not dim stars or cold gas nor anything like the matter that makes up our perceptible universe. Evidence mounts that this "dark matter" governs the motion of stars and galaxies and is even responsible for their actual existence and directed the development of the universe from the very moment of its creation. The existence of this substance explains the stability of our galaxy, the formation of the universe's structure of galaxies, and the contours of space-time itself. Most scientists have accepted this theory of dark matter because it best fits the data. So more than 80% of the matter in the universe is invisible. Now there is reason to believe that even dark matter is dwarfed by "dark energy"!

So particle physicists have discovered neutrinos, antimatter, quarks, bosons; astronomers have discovered the nature of the heavens leading to the evidence for the big bang, nucleosynthesis in the first few minutes of cosmic history, and the cosmic microwave background; the rotation of galaxies have been measured, 3D maps of the universe compiled; the distribution of matter in the universe has been mapped; the accelerating expansion of space has been discovered; supercomputers have simulated the growth of large-scale structures; and hundreds of persistent scientists have generated petabytes of data and thousands of publications but still don't know the identity of more than 80% of the material universe! The nature of dark matter remains a mystery.[47]

What is remarkable in this theoretical construct is that scientists believe in the existence of dark matter without being able to see it. Their belief is based only on the evidence of the data and its observed effects. That is precisely the characteristics by which one believes in the existence of God.[48]

So, at the macro level of the sidereal universe, scientific study has also affirmed that the universe had a beginning in a point in time some fourteen billion years ago in the so called "big bang" and that the constants governing the universe predispose it for the development of life. So the universe came into existence caused by something independent of matter, space, time, and energy. There was a "creation event" and the universe has a design. Science has reached a convergence with the biblical revelation.[49]

Atomic physics also teaches that the universe can end at any moment and that it is a distinct possibility. Physics could not understand how atomic and subatomic particles acquired their mass. Peter Higgs in 1964 hypothesized the existence of a particle, now known as the Higgs boson, which conveyed mass to atomic particles such as the neutron and electron. The Higgs boson was then actually discovered as a new particle in 2012 at CERN (the European Organization for Nuclear Research), confirming Higgs's hypothesis. The new particle was subsequently confirmed to match the expected properties of a Higgs boson. The Higgs bosons create the Higgs field which pervades the universe. This field varies in strength and can exist in two states, the vacuum state and the false vacuum, or higher potential state. The false vacuum state creates a bubble of true vacuum causing a "vacuum decay," that is, as it expanded at the speed of light, it would bring about the disintegration of all matter, ending the existence of the universe as we know it. So the universe is in a "metastable" state and could transition to the vacuum decay state by quantum processes at any time. That is, a quantum fluctuation could occur at any time creating this vacuum bubble.[50] It is as if the universe sat on the edge of an abyss and could tumble over with the slightest irregularity in its structure. Similarly, the universe, according to the scriptural creation account, is called out of the nothingness of the "void" and is constantly threatened by the power of this void to draw the universe back into its nihility.[51]

So scientific discoveries about the nature of the universe affirms the biblical concept of linear time and that the universe is in the process of "running down" and will have an end and even could disintegrate at any time if some quantum fluctuation occurred in the Higgs field. So it also affirms biblical eschatology which tells us that the world can end at any moment when God intervenes and heaven and earth as we know will pass away.

Discoveries in physics are leading to a convergence between itself and the world of the spirit confirming what we, on the basis of biblical revelation, have known all along.[52] As Ralph Waldo Emerson so succinctly observed, "Nature always wears the color of the Spirit."[53]

The Biological Sciences

The following is a summary from an online video featuring a discussion between David Berlinsky, David Gelernter, and Steven Meyer, moderated by Peter Robinson[54] on the theme of "Mathematical Challenges to Darwin's Theory of Evolution." Meyer observes that the fossil record of the "Cambrian explosion" of a half billion years ago, during which an incredible number of new species, including even the first animals, suddenly pops up within a mere ten million years ("mere" because that represents about .22 percent of the history of the earth up to that time). Such a variety, mathematically, biologically, and geologically speaking, would suggest the requirement of a span of hundreds of millions of years on the basis of a theory of evolution. Darwin could not explain this "explosion."[55]

New forms of life require new codes to build molecules that service cells and additional information to arrange cells in the body of a plant. So this "explosion" is also an explosion of biological information. Darwin did not have the knowledge we now have as to what it takes to generate that kind of information. For him, as Robinson observed, the cell was thought to be like a "brick of jello" and quite uncomplicated which could just be put together to create different life forms. In response Berlinsky noted that the cell is an unbelievable, unfathomable, complex piece of machinery and not yet completely understood. In fact, the more it is studied the more complex it is found to be. So investigators are continually behind the curve as this complexity increases and the goal of understanding it completely continues to recede, making it more and more difficult to construct a materialistic theory of its origin.

Gelernter acceded that Darwin was correct in explaining small variations within a species but not the emergence of new species. Darwin thought that explaining those variations within a species also explained the developing of new species. Darwin's problem was the lack of understanding of molecular biology and the cognizance of what generating new forms of life entails. The essence of the development of a new species is generating a new shape of protein which means inventing a new gene. A gene contains a program that spells out a code character by character.[56] The mathematics, Gelernter notes, is simple: each position has to be occupied by one of twenty amino acids, and there are several hundred of these acids in the string. The number of possible combinations grows exponentially as you increase the number in a string.

Meyer elaborated the mathematics. A conference in the 1960s was the first to see the mathematical problem of Darwinism. But it was only early in the twenty-first century by way of a number of experimental measures that the rarity of developing a functional gene and protein was clarified. In a series of twenty amino acids the ratio of a functional gene verses "gibberish" is one out of 10^{77} so that the production of a useful protein is extremely rare. Robinson, quoting from an article by Gelernter,[57] emphasized that there simply is not enough time for the materialistic production of a useful gene. It is all but impossible, added Berlinsky. Supporting that judgment Meyer noted there are 10^{40} organisms that have existed in the history of the earth and that every time an organism replicates there is the possibility of mutation. So 10^{40} possible mutations against the one in 10^{77} that might be successful means but one in 10^{37}, i.e., one in a trillion trillion trillion. So Darwin's theory is more likely to be false than true. Again quoting Gelernter in his article, "Evidently there are a total of no examples in the literature of mutations that affect early development and the body plan as a whole that are not fatal." Adding to that, Berlinsky emphasized, "if a change is made late in the development of an animal it's not going to make a difference. If it comes early it destroys the organism. So if it's late, no good, and if early, no good. The possibilities are exhausted."[58]

Meyer has said that the evidence suggests that an intelligent designer must have been responsible for life, a conclusion that neither Gelernter nor Berlinsky can quite accept as Meyer has presented the idea. Meyer responded that the genetic code, which is like an information storage system, suggests a mind and not a material process and that an undirected evolutionary mechanism that has been proposed as the origin of this information fails. He points out that when we find encoded information such as in hieroglyphics, a paragraph in a book, information in a radio signal, or a section of computer code and trace it back to its ultimate source it always ends in arriving at a mind and not a material process. So that from a materialistic evolutionary standpoint, he argues, we don't have any explanation for the origin of information that is necessary to build new biological forms. But, he says, we do know from uniform and repeated experience, which is the basis of all scientific reasoning, that a source of information implies that intelligence or mind is the origin of that information which further implies the activity of a directing mind in the history of life on earth.[59]

Robinson presents another quotation from Gelernter's article where he questions the strategy and purpose of a supposed intelligent designer. Why would the designer, Gelernter insists, back himself into so many corners, waste energy on so many doomed organisms, and do such a slipshod job? Why are humans so disease and heartbreak prone? Robinson replies with the counter-question of whether Meyer then has to either explain all the mysteries of the human heart or say nothing at all. Gelernter counters that assertion with the observation that the world around us does not meet the standard of intelligence. It is more of a mess as is the mind of man. Is the universe and the world good? He reports that the great Pharisaic masters Hillel and Shammai had said "no."[60] Meyer observes there is both design and decay and suffering. To which Robinson adds that theologically evil is a defect in the good and evil has no independent existence. Furthermore, the Genesis account where God declares his creation "good" contradicts Hillel and Shammai. Gelernter agrees that God's creation was good, but God also created imperfect creatures who botch things up. So he says that those who dismiss intelligent design as a "put up job" have to be dealt with intellectually. Meyer repeats that his argument for intelligent design comes from biological, scientific evidence and so meets that demand.

Gelernter agrees that Darwinism is no longer just a scientific theory but the basis of a worldview and an emergency religion of the many troubled souls who need one. To disagree with and challenge Darwinism is to encounter bitter rejection and anger and even the risk of academic destruction by the scholarly world. This is because you are attacking their "religion" so you can't blame them for being all "het up." This means, quoting again from his article, that "Darwin poses a final challenge, whether biology will rise to this last one as well as it did to the first when his theory upset the apple cart, remains to be seen. How cleanly and quickly can the field get over Darwin and move on? This is one of the most important questions facing science in the twenty-first century."

Meyer, carrying this line of thought further, adds that Darwin was mistaken in his answers but was asking invaluable questions. But he got it wrong by trying to explain something very complex by a bottom-up, undirected process. He compares it to the development of digital machines that bear the hallmark of mind suggesting a top-down approach to explain evolution. Scientists committed to materialism will continue to generate bottom-up mechanisms to explain evolution. This approach is holding science back. Predictions are beginning to be made based on intelligent design. For example, the non-coding part of the genome that was previously identified as "junk" by neo-Darwinism has important functions so that looking at life as a designed system is actually yielding insight as to how life works.

Berlinsky elaborated Darwin's now-antiquated approach by characterizing his local theory of variation within a species as a reasonably successful model for breeders but which entirely failed to explain what he thought he was explaining in accounting for biological complexity on the level of species or higher order levels. It was a pre-mature question about the origin of species. He simply couldn't say anything about what he did not know and could not comprehend. The fact that he did not know reflects what we do not know in the twenty-first century. The question is still premature. We're just beginning to learn about the structure of the intellectual inquiry necessary to understand something like the biological cell—a much harder and fantastically more difficult problem than was ever expected.[61]

In summary, the discussion revealed that the so-called "Cambrian Explosion," which produced an eruption of myriad biological life forms, is inexplicable within the time frame that it occurred.[62] The cell itself is so complex that understanding it completely is still beyond present capability. There is simply no materialistic account of how even a cell could come to exist, let alone an animal containing many billions of cells containing complex organs like the eye. Darwin, it was noted, was good at explaining small variations within a species i.e., he provided good knowledge for breeders. But the formation of new species without a designer is *mathematically impossible*. All mutations are fatal to an organism. The genetic code is also like an information storage system and, like any source of information, it implies a designer. Most importantly, the discussion revealed that all of these arguments are based on mathematics and science. A final flaw among those holding to the old materialistic Darwinism is that it has become a kind of pseudo-religion for its impassioned proponents who, when challenged in their beliefs, give in to irrational antagonism and personal attacks.[63]

Psychology and the Phenomenon of Human Near-Death Experiences

In 1975 Raymond Moody's book *Life After Life*[64] was published, reporting on what 150 people had encountered who had gone through the experience of near-death. These people had suffered heart attacks or gone though some catastrophic event. They described floating above their bodies and witnessing resuscitation procedures that were being performed on them. Part of the experiences included feelings of absolute peace and the ability to travel instantaneously elsewhere merely by thought. Many reported passing through a dark tunnel toward a light where they encountered a heavenly landscape and a "Being of Light" whom they identified as Jesus. This figure emanated an overwhelming love. Some reported conversing with relatives who had died. Others experienced a review of their life which included both their thoughts and actions and how they had affected others.[65]

Glynn in his review of this phenomenon recounts the investigations of Dr. Michael Sabom, a cardiologist and initially a thoroughgoing skeptic of these stories. In 1978 he undertook a more scientific and systematic approach of seventy-one subjects who reported the same kind of experiences as Moody's subjects had. His study included thirty-two patients who reported they had drifted outside their bodies and observed the resuscitation procedures that were performed on their bodies. He called these experiences "autoscopic." In six of these cases the reports were detailed. In every case the reports coincided with medical procedure. In one case the patient's account of his open heart surgery matched perfectly with the post-operative report of the surgeon.

An alternative explanation involves proposing that what a person felt along with auditory cues could have produced mental images even under anesthesia. But that did not explain how one patient observed the aneurysm on his heart and how the surgeon manipulated his heart, something the nerves of the heart are not capable of sensing. Or another man who observed his wife and children outside the theater of the operation.

It was theorized that patients may have been told about the procedure. However, Sabom carefully interviewed one man to determine if he had gathered information about his procedure from another source. But the patient flatly denied ever having seen the resuscitation procedure he had undergone. Because of the meticulous methods of his research and the access he had to patients and their medical records Sabom had to give up his initial skepticism. His genuine scientific investigation confirmed the reality of Moody's reports.

Elizabeth Kübler-Ross reports similar experiences of children who were involved in accidents.[66] They report of family members "waiting for them." She reports that ". . . every single child who mentioned that someone was waiting for them mentioned a person who actually preceded them in death, if only by a few moments. And yet none of these children had been informed of the recent death of the relatives by us at any time."[67] Glynn emphasizes,

> One could imagine finding a purely physiological explanation for any of the visionary elements of the experiences but not for the out-of-body perceptions that have been independently corroborated. At the very least, late-twentieth-century medicine has stumbled on a set of phenomena that raises serious doubts about a purely physiological or materialistic model for the human consciousness or self . . . we seem to be in the presence of at least preliminary evidence of the independent existence of a "soul."[68]

What is remarkable about these experiences are their clarity, detail, and vivacity and this when a person is near death and the state of the brain is apparently fraught under such conditions. A brain should not be able to function in that way given its incapacitated circumstances. These experiences and the autoscopic perception of people who report out of the body experiences then question whether they are totally a function of brain activity.[69]

However, not all of these experiences are positive. Some have reported encounters with hell, the details of which were much more likely to be forgotten. But, like their counterparts, they tend to be morally transforming. Others with positive experiences outlined above were also aware that the world of the spirit was not all love and light. These experiences therefore coordinate with biblical teaching and with a moral vision that is common to all religious persuasions.[70] Confirming their plausibility is that they do not meet the conventional expectations about the afterlife of those who have undergone these experiences. The theme that runs through these experiences is that one is responsible for every thought, word, and deed and that one is judged in light of the universal law of love.

As I've already noted above, the "Being of Light" encountered by those who have experienced these near-death phenomena frequently identify the figure with Jesus. Their sense of this encounter is with a person who radiates unconditional love, compassion, and a non-judgmental stance; however, at the same time they are aware of being in the presence of an uncompromising attitude of right and wrong. Of course, these experiences are filtered through each individual subject who interprets them in the light of his or her own understanding and life experiences. However, the pervasiveness of an enveloping love is universal in these encounters which is, of course, the essence of the moral life and so would not be surprising for anyone regardless of their religious persuasion. Of course, this emanation of love accords perfectly with the attitude and practice of Jesus, who demanded love even for enemies and praying for those under whose persecutions one has to suffer.

Glynn notes that such experiences are recorded over time and across cultures which leads him to conclude that "science has indeed stumbled on data of the soul."[71] He admits that these experiences could be the result of some "accident of evolution" that predisposed the brain to respond to death in this way but it would then be "a very strange accident indeed."[72]

This phenomenon echoes the discovery in evolutionary biology that the human being is not the product of some random, material process but derives from a sphere beyond the material universe.

Demonic Possession

Richard Gallagher, a medical doctor, psychiatrist, and practicing psychoanalyst, has recently published the results of his scientific investigations of demonic possession.[73] In his study he rules out odd seizure disorders and undiscovered brain damage before conducting a full narrative assessment and survey of symptoms. He interviewed friends and family to confirm the details supplied by the purported possessed person. He appreciates that it takes a well-trained psychiatrist to discern how possession differs from psychoses, severe personality and dissociative disorders, and persons susceptible to suggestion. He knows the difference between mental illness and those so afflicted who think they are possessed.[74] As a scientifically trained physician he carefully distinguishes what science and good historical testimony can and cannot demonstrate about episodes of possession.[75] He writes,

> ... I've worked hard to develop a system of investigation based on my psychiatric training and experience. To begin, I never officially "diagnose" someone as being "possessed." I do this for several reasons. First it is not a clinical diagnosis that can be shoehorned into a conventional and scientifically responsible psychiatric diagnostic category. Because possession is a spiritual problem–no laboratory or cognitive or mental status texts exist to register that information using medically established categories. Instead, I ask one basic question: Do the patient's symptoms have a natural or scientific explanation?[76]

Important to the evidence that I've detailed above regarding the existence of the world of the spirit is his affirmation on the basis of his scientific study is that we live in a reality that consists of both the seen and the unseen and "that these two realms can influence each other in unimaginable ways."[77] And of course he recognizes that a part of this unseen world is hostile to human beings and seeks their spiritual ruin. The world of the spirit is not all peace and light as the Bible and Christianity teaches. I will elaborate on this reality in the section below on the tendency for the created order to fall back into nothingness.

Gallagher closes his introduction affirming my thesis in this chapter that truth is one and there is no divide between faith and reason. He closes his introduction with the clear-sighted observation,

> ... one must remain persistent and authentic in pursuit of the truth, unshackled by one's upbringing or cultural preconceptions or what conformist opinion dictates one should believe. At a time when many people have lost all sense of the sacred and of the supernatural,[78] and when institutional authority is viewed with suspicion, that need is more of a personal challenge than ever. I believe that the value of identifying and attending to the reality of this sobering topic is worth the effort and that its implications warrant reflection.

In the following chapter I will present more of Gallagher's research as preparation for investigating the exorcism stories in the ministry of Jesus.

THE BIBLICAL CREATION ACCOUNT

The developments in the physical and biological sciences reveal a tendency toward convergence with intelligent design and the biblical account of creation and its ultimate demise. Physics has discovered a realm of free will in its investigation of atomic-level phenomena, unexplainable connections between separated particles, and non-material aspects of the building blocks of matter which science now can only describe as "probability waves." The mathematics associated with the development of living species indicates the impossibility of the development of one species from another without some kind of directing intelligence, a creating will.

In other words, as Gen 1 reveals, God created all the living forms that have existed and still exist in the world. This does not mean that Gen 1 is some sort of a scientific "historical" narrative. Rather it is written within the thought world of its time and place (during the sixth century BC Babylonian captivity). Against the background of the Babylonian creation myth, the so-called *Enuma Elish* (a title taken from its opening words "When on high"),[79] reveals its sublime, countercultural, and demythologizing character which connects with a modern scientific stance. The *Enuma Elish* is true "myth," i.e., stories of the gods, and it narrates how Marduk, who is made the supreme god, battles with Tiamat (Tablet IV, the name means "ocean" or "the deep," i.e., the chaos monster[80]) and her retinue, kills her, and divides her body half of which he uses to create the sky and the other half the world. He creates man whom he "charges with the service of the gods" (Tablet VI).[81]

In Gen 1 there is no "myth" but resonances with the Babylonian epic: verse 2 refers to "the spirit of God moving over the face of the waters" RSV Heb., על פני תהום *'AL P*ᵉ*N T*ᵉ*HOM*; Gk ὑπάνω τῆς ἀβύσσου (*hypanō tēs abyssou*, "over the abyss" or "bottomless, unfathomable depth"). The Hebrew "TᵉHOM" is related to the Babylonian "Tiamat," the chaotic, menacing ocean whom Marduk conquers and kills. In the Genesis account God brings order out of the chaos. This chaos (Heb., תהו ובהו, *T*ᴼ*HU WAB*ᴼ*HU*,[82] RSV "without form and void;" Ger., "wüst und leer," "a disorderly waste and empty;" Gk., ἀόρατος καί ἀκατασκεύατος, *aoratos kai akataskeuatos*, "invisible and unstructured" i.e., "chaotic") is subdued and order created by the word of God.[83] So God calls order out of darkness, chaos, and a fathomless deep, the "void." But this chaos is not personalized as a goddess as in the Babylonian myth. It is the impersonal, awesome power of the chaotic void of nothingness. The character of this "void" is the absence of God, emptiness and even unreality.[84] So there is a tension between the call of God's Word which creates the universe and the attractive power of the void which continually threatens to draw the created order back into itself.[85] Speaking theologically the biblical cosmology is unlike the ancient Near Eastern mythologies which conceived the universe made out of the body of a dead god. In the Genesis account the only connection between God and the universe is his creative Word. Israel asserts God called the universe out of nothing, out of the "void" (Gen 1:2, Job 26:7). The character of this void, as I have described it, is the absence of God, emptiness, and even unreality. The void, however, has a certain attractiveness which constantly threatens to draw back the creation into its nothingness and chaos.[86]

Sin[87] disturbs this equilibrium. Biblical theology understands that before the fall the direction of the created order was upward toward God. After the fall it is downward toward the void, darkness, death, and the evil one so that now the whole of creation is infected, corrupted, subject to death, and involved in an active and unholy opposition to God. Even so, it still longs for a rebirth and deliverance from these bonds of corruption and death (Rom 8:20–22). This scenario has its counterpart in the scientific discovery that the universe burst out of nothingness, called the "big bang," and that it is rapidly[88] winding down as it expands and depletes. However, there is another factor that can end the universe even before it simply runs down. It is constantly threatened by disintegration due to a possible fluctuation in the status of the Higgs field. So von Rad, is completely spot-on when he asserts that ". . . the Creation story . . . seeks to convey not merely theological, but also scientific knowledge. It is characterized by the fact . . . that here theological and scientific knowledge are in accord with no tension between them."[89]

God confines the water. The "waters" are no longer a personal force hostile to the creator God. There is no battle between the gods. It is only water which is located in one place. The stars too are not deities, as in the myth, and the moon and sun are not designated with deified names. They are called only merely "great lights" and so are depersonalized (the word used here is מאר, *M'OR* a word used elsewhere for the lamps in the Tabernacle).[90] These "lights" are not mythological heavenly beings but are there for a practical purpose "for signs and season . . . and to give light upon the earth" (1:14–15). It is God who creates the creatures of the ocean and the "great sea monsters." So they are not foes to be conquered before the beginning of creation. When it recounts how God brings forth plants and animals each reproducing of itself it expresses a proto-scientific view of the world which is conceived as acting in accordance with certain laws.

The greatest contrast between Genesis and the Babylonian myth, however, has to do with the creation of the human being: in the latter he is created from the dead body of Kingu, Tiamat's general, for the purpose of serving the gods: Marduk says,

> I will establish a savage, "man" shall be his name.
> Verily, savage-man I will create.
> He shall be charged with the service of the gods,
> That they might be at ease![91]

In Genesis, however, the creation of the male and female humans are portrayed in royal terms: they are to have "dominion" over the creation and to bear the very image of God himself. They are equal partners. They are not slaves but rulers. They have royal prerogatives. So the creation story in Genesis is not mere polemic against the Babylonian myth but demythologizes it and sets the creation in an incomparable relationship with God and humanity. Humans are blessed by God, and it is within that blessing that they are to be "fruitful and multiply." So they are not mere slaves of a deity but they themselves are to be royal rulers of and a blessing to the creation.

The creation is overall called out of nothing and all living creatures subsist and multiply on their own, independently from God (cf., Mark 4:28). The multiform creation is not the sacral body of a dead goddess that requires sacral means and manipulation to insure its fecundity. The creation has an independent existence and acts according to its own innate laws. So the narrative had the old Babylonian account in view as it massively demythologized it, sheering it of every last fiber of mythology and revealing the created universe whose mysterious reality science is just beginning to unravel. In the Genesis narrative God calls the creation "good" (Heb., טוב, *TOV*).[92] It is declared "good" six times, and at the end of the sixth day it is declared "very good." This stands in stark contrast to those evaluations of the material world as evil and detrimental to the spiritual nature of humanity.[93] Part of that "good" is its freedom. The Genesis narrative makes clear the created universe is not divine stuff, is not dependent on capricious deities to operate, but operates with its own laws, with an astonishing vitality, profligate reproductive capability, lively profusion, and freedom, all of which flows from the nature of God himself. It is an orderly universe.

Of course, the biblical witness does not understand this God of creation as one who now withdraws and lets everything take its course. The freedom of the created order, its "subject to decay," its fallenness, means it can go awry. So this God of freedom is there to save and rescue. That saving activity is realized in and through people whom he calls. This saving help occurs again by his historically proclaimed word through chosen mouthpieces and even by his continued activity in the created order.

SUMMARY AND CONCLUSION

So there is one truth: science and the demythologizing creation account of the Bible mesh as science finds its investigations pointing to a designer and the biblical account reveals the designer.[94] Atomic physics reveals there is a freedom built into matter and a totally predictable course of future events is not possible. That freedom and the mathematics of biology demanding the active involvement of a designer implies extraordinary events can take place which are not subject to a mechanical law of cause and effect, but the cause of an event may lie outside the confines of time and space. Each account, the scientific and biblical one, has its own vocabulary and methods. They both reveal that there is nothing of chance to this created order but rather a designer who gives purpose, reason, and meaning to it all.

Then there is the burgeoning number of reports, and that across cultures and time, of near-death experiences reporting on the world of the spirit which cannot be explained on the basis of a scientific materialism. The human psyche itself witnesses to a world of the spirit beyond the material world. Of course, this is to say nothing of the religions of the world which have done the same throughout the ages.

Meier repeats at great length that the realm of scientific thought and that of philosophy and theology are two separate and distinct spheres, so that a historian in the capacity of a historian could not affirm that God was active in an event even after ruling out human action, physical forces in the universe, misinterpretation, illusion, or fraud.[95] In view of the discoveries and direction that the sciences have taken, this bifurcation and mutual exclusionary approaches to reality is no longer a tenable proposition.[96] Truth is one, and it must therefore be so that the truths discovered by science must accord with the truths revealed by God. Truth cannot contradict truth. However, at the same time it is so that science has not yet completed the task of investigating material reality nor has theology answered every question about the whole substance of revelation. So, at any time there may be some tension between science and theology. But, as I've elucidated above, there is a growing convergence between the two.[97]

This unity of the world of the spirit and the world of matter has always been intact up until the developments beginning with the Enlightenment.[98] Anthropology, in its studies of primitive communities, has found that the two domains of the sacred and the profane, i.e., both religion and science, were conceived as a unified reality. There were acts and observances regarded as sacred and performed with reverence and awe. Conversely, all the acts associated with life and its sustenance in these communities, such as hunting and farming, were engaged in careful observation of natural processes having a firm understanding of nature's regularity by the use of reason, and confidence in the power of that reasoning.[99]

In this overview of the developments in science, the experiential evidence of near-death experiences, and the confirmation of the existence of demonic spiritual beings all point to a designer. Scientific materialism cannot explain the origin of the universe in the big bang, the fine-tuning of our universe so that it could produce life, nor the functional information that is embedded in the genome. The origin of the universe, life, and the mind and human consciousness remain an unsolved mystery.[100] However, I would add that only a dual approach of science and theology can provide us with a real, thoroughgoing understanding.[101] In the end, the proponents of scientific materialism, shorn of the ability to explain the most important facts of our universe, seems to be glorying in and lusting after human autonomy as it constructs its secular religion of a universe that has "at bottom, no design, no purpose . . . nothing but blind, pitiless indifference."[102] Their adoption then of a morality is a sheer "felicitous inconsistency."[103]

As I now turn to the study of the miracles recorded in the Gospels I will not approach them uncritically. This historian, while understanding the unity of truth as found in both the secularity of science and the sacred world of the spirit, will not accept a priori every claim that a miracle has occurred. Each case must be investigated on its own. This also holds true for the reports in the Gospels. In the following discussion of miracles, I will define what a miracle is, how the Scriptures understand them, and how contemporary interpreters approach them.

MIRACLES

Definition

Most people would say that a miracle was some extraordinary, observable event that was not capable of being explained by the usual cause and effect relationship that we assume in everyday life (which has, of course, developed under the influence of the Enlightenment which excluded any reference to the world of the spirit and gave us a world of an exclusive material reality).[104] So a miracle would be defined by the fact that it finds no explanation by an appeal to known forces that we perceive on the basis of our contemporary scientific outlook to exist in our world of space/time.[105]

What I avoid here in seeking a definition are distinctions between natural/supernatural, God or gods acting, and such events as having some religious significance, or events violating the laws of nature. In the ancient world the antipodes "natural" and "supernatural" did not exist. The world was seen as imbedded in the world of the spirit, and there was a continuous intercourse between them. This was particularly true of the biblical world. Jesus' "miracles," of course, occurred within his proclamation of the kingdom. So they were signs, if not the very reality,[106] of the kingdom of God and that it was in some sense present at least in a proleptic way. In this way the coming kingdom was already acting according to this new reality. Jesus was sent by God and so was working his will. However, it is noteworthy that Jesus in performing these "mighty acts" does not reference an "intervention" by God but rather the faith of the individual healed. And that faith is in Jesus as the source of the power (Mark 5:30).[107]

Of course, the Scriptures do not use such terms either. For what we call "miracles" (the word comes from the Latin *miraculum*, "wonder, marvel, surprise, amazement") the Gospels use the terms δύναμις (*dynamis*, "mighty work" or "deeds of power," Matt 13:58); ἔργα, (*erga*, "works" or "deeds," Matt 11:2); τέρατα (*terata*, "wonders" Mark 13:22). However, this word is never used of Jesus' deeds except in Acts); παράδοξος, (*paradoxos*, "contrary to opinion or expectations, strange, wonderful." This word occurs only once in the NT at Luke 5:26); σημεῖον, (*sēmeion*, "sign." This word is used quite frequently and particularly in John's gospel); and θαυμάζω, (*thaumadzō*, "marvel, wonder." This word is the most frequently used word in the Gospels in its various grammatical forms.) As these terms make plain, ancient people and writers were not thinking of the origin of these events as somehow contrary to nature but were giving voice to their reaction to an uncommon and unexpected occurrence which they would naturally attribute to the working of the world of the spirit.

Biblical thinking was aware of the orderly working of nature as it is described in the creation account: there is order in light and darkness,[108] between the heavens above and earth beneath, between sea and dry land, plants and animals that reproduce according to their own kind, the regular flow of seasons (Gen 8:22), and the greater and lesser lights of sun and moon.[109] Underlying this reality was the distinction between the creator and the creation. Creation had its own kind of autonomy. So, unlike the pagan nations, Israel did not have to appease the deity in order to assure blessing or a good harvest. Conceiving the created world as possessing its own autonomy is at bottom a scientific attitude.[110] That attitude, however, did not exclude the workings of God in history.

The contemporary approach to the miracle stories understands them above all in terms of how they functioned in the context in which they arose. That context is identified with the early Christian community. To arrive at that understanding scholarship has sought to determine their "form"—that is, to determine what kind of stories they are. In this process the characters that inhabit them, the motifs that are expressed in them, and the themes which organize the individual motifs into a compositional whole are all enumerated and described. This investigation of modern scholars places the stories both within their historical context and compares them with other such contemporary stories ("synchronic" analysis) and within the development of such stories over time ("diachronic" analysis). The synchrony of a story, however, is more important to its sense than its diachrony.[111]

A further approach in the interpretation of these stories is the process of determining their function. Theissen identifies three functional aspects of these stories: their social function within Christianity and society, their religious-historical function, and their existential function.

In the first of these functions miracle stories can be understood to integrate people into the community. Contrariwise, they can be understood as reflective of intra-group conflicts. In their religious-historical function they, according to Theissen, do not reproduce history, but are a sign of the transformation of ancient culture as it embraced a "new irrationalism" by which he means a general expansion of belief in miracles.[112]

Nor are they, according to him, "enacted parables"[113] but precisely the opposite of what I have repeatedly observed in my investigation of the parables. Existentially, they provide a way for the individual to transcend the reality of suffering and disease and transform them into a human world of meaning. In this way they provide a way for coming to terms with extremes of human life by demonstrating that there is a divine presence that transforms disease and suffering.[114] They are also a form of revelation that comes from outside and beyond human subjectivity so that ". . . miracle stories are neither mere projections of non-intentional factors nor reflections of divine intervention. They are symbolic actions of human subjectivity in which a revelation of the holy is given shape and 'empirical' reality transcended."[115] That rather complex assertion means that Theissen sees them as providing a way to cope with the suffering imposed by life's blows and overcoming them by placing oneself in the hands of a gracious God who will ultimately conquer all the untowardness of this world.[116]

Scholarship has pursued a meticulous investigation of the miracle stories analyzing their typical form, their varied motifs and themes and how the evangelists each in his own way incorporated them into their Gospels.[117] Overall, however, scholarship understands them as community products, not historical reports. It vaguely bases them on some remembered activities of Jesus that in some way produced healing effects in his contemporaries.[118]

Because of its closed view of reality, modern sensibility brackets out the possibility of miracles. Only the material universe exists, and within it there is only a strict cause and effect relationship between events. There is simply no transcendent reality beyond the empirical, perceivable world of matter. The world of the spirit is denied existence. So miracles are simply written off as fantasy, a lie, or due to deception. The eighteenth century skeptic David Hume argued that when weighing up the evidence for a miracle one had to consider which was more probable—that a person would lie or that a given miracle had taken place. So he writes in *An Enquiry Concerning Human Understanding*, "The plain consequence is . . . 'that no testimony is sufficient to establish a miracle, unless the testimony be of such a kind, that its falsehood would be more miraculous, than the fact, which it endeavors to establish . . .'" In other words, if someone believes a miracle has taken place he is either lying himself or has been lied to. If the claimed miracle is greater than the possibility of a person being deceived or deceiving, then that claimed miracle must be rejected.[119]

So what is meant by a miracle? Meier defines it ably by designating it as (1) an event perceivable by any observer, (2) an event that cannot be explained by reference to any force of power known to exist in time and space, and (3) its only cause is an act of God.[120] Popularly it could be described as an occurrence that happens contrary to the regular processes of nature, "nature" being understood by moderns as material cause and effect. Of course "contrary to" means what is *presently known* about natural cause and effect. It may be that there are processes that we simply are not yet aware of that act in what we call miracle.[121] In my outline of the new physics above people are not generally aware of the strange universe that scientific investigation has discovered about the atomic and subatomic world.

As I've indicated above, the NT uses three words to describe miracles, *dynameis* (δύναμιH, "powers" or "acts of power"), *sēmeia* (σημεῖα, "signs"), and *terata* (τέρατα, "wonders"). The first emphasizes that God is acting, he who is the source of all power.[122] The Bible does not emphasize the merely amazing character of miracles and so uses "wonders" in conjunction with "signs" (e.g., Exod 7:3; Jer 32:20; Matt 24:24; John 4:48; Acts 5:12; 2 Cor 12:12). The greatest miracle in the OT is the exodus, and correspondingly the greatest in the NT is the resurrection, each of which brought the people of God into existence. They are mighty acts of salvation. So God is never an abstraction to be known in his inner being but a God who reveals himself in history and in an event. So the resurrection of Jesus is the touchstone for all the other miracles recorded as done by Jesus in the Gospels.[123] But Jesus did not desire to be known as a miracle-worker as his command not to talk about the cures he effects attests. In the temptation story he is portrayed as eschewing the working of miracles in order to dazzle people (Matt 4:5–7). He refuses to give a sign to skeptics (Mark 8:12). So his miracles are signs but only to those who have the eyes to see and truly understand who he is and what he is all about. They are meaningful only to those who can see what they point to: that God is at work here through the one who stands in a unique relationship to this Father-God, the one who has sent him.

So the miracles are powerful acts of the kingdom of God, the acts of the promised age to come (Luke 11:20; cf., Isa 35:5–6; 61:1). Jesus is the fulfiller of Israel's hope. When John's disciples ask if he was the coming one he told them to report to John these mighty acts (Matt 11:4–5). They are signs of the coming kingdom and that God is active in the world to now fulfill those promises. So these signs are not meant to awe the people but to call them into the kingdom and to repent. In this way the miracles are not "wonder stories" but the presence of the kingdom of God, that is, God asserting and establishing his creative power. The appropriate response is to believe the good news, enter the kingdom, and repent (Luke 10:13).

Jesus' exorcisms in particular are signs that Satan's kingdom has been invaded, this "strong man" bound, and his house plundered (Mark 3:22–30). Mark 2:1–12 suggests that as Jesus healed illnesses, which were associated with sin, he was demonstrating his authority to forgive sin. Forgiveness and freedom from demonic power means God's reign is being enacted.

The Authenticity of the Miracles of Jesus

The miracles of Jesus have elicited perhaps the most skepticism in the traditions related to Jesus and his ministry. Because they seem to lie outside what historians regard as the cause and effect interconnections of events in the world and not following what they perceive as the closed nexus of the material universe. So they have been highly suspect of being the creations of the earliest church, serving its missionary needs by seeking to enhance the character and authority of Jesus.[124] However, as Meier observes, the massive amount of this material and its omnipresence in the Gospels renders highly questionable the assertion that they are the creations of the church.[125] Supporting this judgment is the fact that, for example, the miracle material in Mark derives from unrelated sources: from early collections, individual stories, stray bits, and stories imbedded in the passion tradition. Their style and tone also vary. The Q tradition, even though it reports only one miracle, refers frequently to Jesus' exorcisms and healings. The sources M and L[126] also know of miracles. John too reports miracles of Jesus but in narratives that are much more lengthy than those in the synoptic gospels. He, however, refers to no exorcisms.[127] The apostolic sermons in Acts also witness to this tradition as does Josephus when he refers to Jesus as one who performed "startling deeds."[128]

There are also three different forms of miracle stories: healings, nature miracles (such as the stilling of the storm Mark 6:47–51; however, I prefer to call them "theophanies"), and exorcisms. References to miracles also occur in the pronouncement stories.[129] So multiple attestation involves both sources and forms, a strong witness to their authenticity.

In my previous volume analyzing the pronouncement stories the miracles were anchored firmly in the ministry of Jesus and as a coherent part of it. The kingdom Jesus proclaimed meant the end of Satan's rule and the freeing of Israel bound in the demonic rule of hostility toward Rome. The kingdom was already present in these mighty deeds and displayed in part the meaning of the kingdom: replacing anger with love even for one's enemies by refocusing that anger by resisting the real enemy, Satan and his minions. The healings meant the dawn of the Jubilee (Isa 35:5–6), the time of salvation, being loosed from the bondage of labor, and having a foretaste of the "rest" which accompanied the restoration of community with God. Jesus' pronouncements harmonize with and complement the miracles stories.[130] They are coherent and mutually confirm one another.[131] The many followers he attracted also give witness to the fact that many people were impressed by his mighty deeds.[132]

So it will not do out of hand to reject the historicity of the miracles of Jesus, particularly in light of the scientific evidence that point to the reality of the world of the spirit.

Meier affirms the historicity of the miracles on the basis of the criterion of multiple attestation:[133] they appear in various sources, in various forms (healings, exorcisms, and nature miracles), and he notes, take up a large proportion of the Gospel narratives.[134] The pattern of these stories also vary from being rather long to very short. Sometimes the subject of the miracles is named. Jesus often speaks about miracles and commissions his disciples to carry on that aspect of his ministry. The miracles in John's Gospel are lengthy affairs (e.g., the healing of a blind man, the whole of chapter 9). References to his miracles also appear in the sayings materials.[135] Josephus is an extra-biblical witness to the miracles of Jesus when he describes him as "performing astonishing feats."[136] So multiple sources, forms, and sayings material witness to the fact that Jesus performed deeds reckoned to be miracles by himself and others. That large crowds followed him can also be only explained by the fact that he performed acts and spoke in a way that attracted the attention of people.

The Form of the Miracle Stories

There are three major components of a miracle story: (1) the situation and context in which the miracle takes place and the malady which afflicts the person upon whom the miracle is performed are described; (2)

Invading the Realm of Demons, Disease, and Death

the miracle proper takes place by a word and/or action of Jesus; and (3) the conclusion which usually takes the form of the reaction of the bystanders or the populace to the miracle.

However, this form is absent from the so-called "nature miracles" (labeled below as "theophanies") which do not conform to this taxonomy, and therefore it can be questioned if "nature miracle" is a valid, intelligible category. Furthermore, the language and content of these stories is quite varied. Meier even questions the use of the word "nature" as a relevant biblical category.[137] (However, it is so that the ancient world may not have thought in the bifurcated forms of nature and the divine, but it knew of the regular order that characterized the natural world cf., Luke 12:54–55.) More apropos, he observes a problem with definition. If a "nature miracle" is applied to the stories of the raising of the dead, which is power over inanimate matter, how does that not apply to these stories? They demonstrate power over the inanimate matter of a corpse. Also Jesus' walking on the water involves not only inanimate matter but his own body. Finally, he observes that the group of stories labeled "nature miracles" lack a form common to them all and are absent in one or more of the major components of a miracle story. For example in the feeding stories there is no action or word of Jesus that effects the miracle. These stories also lack any conclusion. On the other hand, the "Stilling of the Storm" contains all three components. So there is even an inconsistency among the constituents of this ostensible category.

These stories do, however, resemble theophanies[138] which are stories of God's self-disclosure and widely attested in the OT appearing in the historical, prophetic, wisdom, and psalmic literature.[139] There are two types of such occurrences: (1) a divine manifestation that is intended for individuals representing for them a demonstration of a special favor; (2) a divine manifestation through the powers of nature.[140] "Theophany" is obviously not a Hebrew term, but it is descriptive of stories in the Bible that relate the manifestation of the presence of God. Israelite theology understood God as wholly other but that he could reveal himself by limiting himself to certain places and in particular forms. So he could, for example, show himself in a thunderstorm (Ps 18:7–15) or as the divine warrior[141] leading the hosts of heaven into battle (Hab 3:3–15).

One of the fundamental characteristics of this form is that they occur in earthly environments that were considered sacred and so favorable to encountering the divine. This is especially true of mountains[142] (Exod 19) but also watery places such as springs (Gen 16:7–14; 21:15–19; 26:24) and rivers (Gen 32:22-32). Other traditions locate theophanies at sacred trees whose roots were thought to reach into the underworld and whose heights reached to the heavens making them natural links between heaven and earth (Gen 11:26-27; 18:1; 21:33-34; Exod 3:1-6; Judg 6:11-24). But not all theophanies are located in this way but occur also in unmarked places (Gen 15:1; 20:3; Judg 13:2-3; Ams 7:4; Job 38:1).[143]

The preeminent mountains in Israel are, of course, Sinai, where God reveals his Torah, and Mount Zion, on which the temple was built. So Israel's law, given by God the king, is not a human creation, but its stipulations bear divine authority.[144] But other mountains are also theophanic sites: Mount Carmel, where God discloses his power over the non-existent Baal; Mounts Tabor, Ebal, and Gerizim also figure prominently as places of theophany.[145]

The temple mount becomes the preeminent place of God's self-revelation and protecting presence.[146] Zechariah 9 and 14 conceive of the eschatological battle against the nations from there and that the temple and Zion would become the center of the world and the goal of universal pilgrimage. It is from there that God judges Israel and the nations and accepts Israel's sacrifices and prayers. Prior to the construction of the temple, the "tent of meeting" was understood as the place of God's presence among the people and from where he communicates with Israel (Exod 25:22; 33:7-11). It was in the temple that Isaiah encountered a theophany of God and received his commission (Isa 6).

YHWH also reveals himself at the sea, where he fights for Israel and saves them from the pursuing Egyptians. He reveals his glory in the pillars of the cloud and fire by which he leads his people. So he manifests and reveals himself as ruler of the universe and of human history and as such issues decrees, reveals his will, judges the nations, answers his people's supplications and inquiries, and commissions his prophetic messengers.

In the theophany God can take on different material forms: the thunderstorm which is both threatening in its power but gracious in that it brings much needed rain and so embodies the sense of both awe and fear and fascination and gracious intent (Ps 18).[147] So terror is a part of the experience of a theophany (Gen 28:17) as well as the fear and threat of death (Gen 32:30).

Human characteristics are also ascribed to God: he has facial features (Exod 158), hands and feet (Exod 15:5), he marches into battle (Hab 3:12-13), rides a chariot (Ps 18:11), he speaks (Deut 33:27), and has human emotions (Exod 17:7). God is a warrior who leads the host of the heavenly armies waging war against cosmic enemies which threaten the order of nature and against Israel's historical enemies.[148] God is king, the supreme power in the universe surrounded by a divine, heavenly council who often appear to human beings as representatives of the divine delivering a message, protecting the righteous, and executing divine justice (Gen 16:7–11). The prophets understand themselves as the earthly counterpart of these heavenly messengers.

Five of what I call the theophany stories, the "stilling of the storm," the two feeding stories, the "shoal of fish," and "changing water into wine" easily, along with the exorcisms and healings, can be identified as miracle stories, even though the feeding stories and the "water into wine" do not conform to the miracle story form. The "stilling of the storm" follows the form and resonates with Ps 84:9 and Ps 107:29 in which God himself stills "the raging of the sea" and "calms the storm." So Jesus then is manifesting divine power and images and exhibits the power of God. Similarly, the feeding stories are redolent of the giving of manna in the desert which again manifested God's power (Ps 78:24). The awe with which Peter reacts to the great shoal of fish resonates with the encounter of the numinous in the story of Jacob and the ladder (Gen 28:17) as he senses the manifestation of the divine. The "water into wine" miracle is evocative of a divine manifestation. In Gen 27:28 God is described as giving "of the dew of heaven, and of the fatness of the earth, and plenty of grain and wine." In each of these stories a divine intervention is portrayed, making of them both miracles and theophanies.

However, the stories of walking on the water, the transfiguration, cursing of a fig tree, and a coin in a fish's mouth seem to fit uneasily into the category of miracle stories because they do not follow the form. The first two, however, are theophanic. In Ps 77:19 God is celebrated as the master of the chaotic power of the sea: "Thy way was through the sea, thy path through the great waters; yet thy footprints were unseen." Jesus' walking on the water then reveals him as imaging the majesty of God. The transfiguration is also a manifestation of divinity like that of the LORD in Exod 24:16: "The glory of the LORD settled on Mount Sinai, and the cloud covered it six days; and on the seventh day he called to Moses out of the midst of the cloud." As for the "cursing of a fig tree," it resembles the "song of the vineyard" in Isa 5. God plants a vineyard, but it brings forth "wild grapes" unfit for consumption. So he destroys it. So the cursing action looks like a prophetic enacted parable by which Jesus is saying so will it be with the nation if it does not turn from the violent path it has chosen in the face of Roman domination.[149] A "coin in a fish's mouth," on the other hand, is a conundrum especially because the story does not relate the actual finding of the coin.[150] The occurrence of the promised "miracle" is not reported! But I include it in the list of "miracles" and will analyze it along with the rest that I enumerate below.

The Miracles and Jesus' Person and Ministry

If the miracles are considered to be nothing but the creations of the early church and were no part of Jesus' activity our understanding of the historical Jesus, his mission, teaching, and self-understanding would be fundamentally altered.[151] They explain his popularity and why he attracted large crowds (see e.g., Mark 6:54-56). It was because of this activity he was undoubtedly also asked for a "sign," that is, some spectacular event in nature or a cataclysmic event in the sky that would authenticate his claims (cf., Mark 8:11-12).[152] That every Gospel portrays Jesus as clashing with the authorities because of his miracle working (cf., Mark 2:1-11) point further in the ubiquity of this activity on Jesus' part. Finally, the use of his name by other miracle workers also points to the intensity of this activity.[153] All of this leads to the conclusion that his miracle working must have taken up a large part of his ministry which is supported by the gathering of crowds and the messianic speculations about Jesus provoking the apprehension of the leadership.

In Luke 10:13 Jesus himself describes his ministry exclusively in terms of the miracles he performed. Again in Luke 7:19 Jesus describes his ministry in terms of healings. In this latter passage the final word is that the poor have the "good news preached to them." The poor here are not the marginalized. The phraseology is drawing on third Isaiah who is speaking of the entire nation as it has returned to Judea and there awaiting salvation.[154] So the nation is described as broken-hearted, captive, imprisoned, and mourning.

The occurrence of this same reference in Qumran as a description of the messiah suggests that Jesus was identifying himself as the fulfiller of prophetic expectations as well as his works as messianic.[155] However, it is not from his miracle working that Jesus derived his consciousness of being God's anointed but rather his baptismal experience as the "beloved son."[156] So miracles and kingdom proclamation were complementary activities of Jesus and constituted the heart of his ministry. They both actualized and made the kingdom present; that is, the kingdom is the presence of God exercising his power in word and deed.[157] So the eschatological presence of God was already being manifested and extant (cf., 1 Cor 10:11). The miracles then are not mere signs of the kingdom no more than Jesus' proclamation of the kingdom in teachings and parables are mere road marks to God's reign. They actualize its presence (Matt 12:28). They are God's power in action (cf., Rom 1:16). And in the exorcisms in particular Jesus was fighting the eschatological battle against Satan and his minions. He historicizes what the apocalyptists projected into the world of the spirit.

Enumeration of the Miracle Stories in the Gospels

In the following chapter I will proceed to examine the miracles attributed to Jesus from the standpoint of the existence of the transcendent world of the spirit and that there is evidence that this world can impinge on our reality, the material universe. Science has led to the logical conclusions that the universe had a beginning and will have an end, that it was designed and created, that the development of life was due to the active involvement of the designer, and that there are mechanisms at work in the world that are beyond explication. So the miracles attributed to Jesus are not to be rejected out of hand as mere fabrications either to further the missionary activity of the church,[158] to enhance the reputation of Jesus, underscore his divinity, or provide courage to the communities that told them. They may have worked in those ways but such a role was secondary to their function in the life of Jesus. So why did these earliest communities tell these miracle stories? Their retelling were a mirror to their function in Jesus' own ministry: to make present the kingdom of God.[159] In voicing these stories the power of God was once again at work in the community of believers and made present his Messiah and his power among the people.[160] The book of Acts records how this same power was exercised by the primitive community and enhanced the acceptance of the gospel of salvation through Jesus as it was proclaimed.[161]

Here is a list of the miracles in the Gospels divided according to the traditional genres: exorcisms, healings, and, rather than using the conventional but inaccurate label of "nature miracles," I use the more descriptive nomenclature of "theophany."[162]

I. Exorcisms

1. A Demoniac in the Synagogue: Mark 1:12–18. Luke 4:33–37
2. The Gerasene Demoniac: Mark 5:1–20. Matt 8:28–34.
3. The Daughter of the Syrophoenician Woman: Mark 7:24–30. Matt 15:21–28.
4. A Demoniac Boy: Mark 9:14–29. Matt 17:14–21. Luke 8:37–43.
5. A Dumb Demoniac: Matt 9:32–34. A Blind and Dumb Demoniac: Matt 12:22–23. Luke 11:14–15.

II. Healings

1. Peter's Mother-in-law's Fever: Mark 1:29–31; Matt 8:14–5; Luke 4:38–39.
2. A Leper: Mark 1 40–45; Matt 8:1–4; Luke 5:12–16.
3. A Paralytic: Mark 2:1–12; Matt 9:1–8; Luke 5 17–26.
4. A Man with a Withered Hand: Mark 3:1–6; Matt 12:9–14; Luke 6:6–11.
5. A Woman with a Hemorrhage: Mark 5:25–34; Matt 9:20–22; Luke 8:43–48.
6. A Deaf Mute: Mark 7:31–6.
7. A Blind Man: Mark 8:22–26.
8. Blind Bartimaeus: Mark 10:46–52; Matt 20:29–34; Luke 18:35–43. (Matt 9:27–31 is perhaps a doublet of this story.)
9. A Crippled Woman: Luke 13:10–17.
10. Ten Lepers: Luke 17:11–19.
11. A Man with Dropsy: Luke 17:1–6.
12. A Paralytic by the Pool Bethsaida: John 5:1–9.
13. A Man Born Blind: John 9.
14. An Official's Servant at the Point of Death: Matt 8:5–13; Luke 7:1–10; John 4:56–54.

III. Raising the Dead

1. Raising Jairus' Daughter: Mark 5:21–24; 35–43; Matt 9:18–19; 23–26; Luke 8:40–42; 49–56.

2. Raising of a Man at Nain: Luke 7:11–17.

3. Raising of Lazarus: John 11

IV. Theophanies

1. Stilling of a Storm: Mark 4:35–41; Matt 8:23–27; Luke 8:22–25.

2. Feeding of the Five Thousand: Mark 6:32–44; Matt 14:13–21; Luke 9:10–17.

3. Feeding of the Four Thousand: Mark 8:1–10; Matt 15:32–39.

4. Jesus Walks on Water: Mark 6:45–52; Matt 14:22–33; John 6:16–21.

5. Cursing of a Fig Tree: Mark 11:12–14; 20–26; Matt 21:18–22.

6. Catching a Shoal of Fish: Luke 5:1–11. (cf., John 21:1–14.)

7. Water Changed into Wine: John 2:1–11.

8. A Coin in a Fish's Mouth: Matt 17:24–27.

9. A Transfiguration: Mark 9:2–8; Matt 17:1–9; Luke 9:28–36.

CHAPTER 2

The Miracles of Jesus
The Exorcisms

But if it is by the finger of God that I cast out demons, then the kingdom of God has come upon you.

THE EXORCISMS OF JESUS RECORDED IN THE GOSPELS

The following five (considering Matt 12:22–23 derivative) pericopae relate the stories of individuals who are described as being possessed by demons that are exorcised by Jesus.

1. A Demoniac in the Synagogue (Mark 1:21–28; Luke 4:31–37)
2. The Gerasene Demoniac: Mark 5:1–20; Luke 8:26–39; Matt 8:28–34.
3. The Daughter of the Syrophoenician Woman: Mark 7:24–30; Matt 15:21–28.
4. A Demoniac Boy: Mark 9:14–29; Matt 17:14–21; Luke 8:37–42.
5. A Dumb Demoniac: Matt 9:32–34; Luke 11:14–15. A Blind and Dumb Demoniac. Matt 12:22–23.

EXORCISM IN THE LAND OF ISRAEL IN LATE ANTIQUITY

Exorcism and possession by evil spirits probably struck the nation's consciousness most markedly with the appearance of the film "The Exorcist" in late December of 1973. In the film, based on the 1971 novel *The Exorcist* by Peter Blatty, two priests are called upon to exorcise Regan, a young girl of twelve. The demon identifies himself as the devil himself. In horrendous scenes the demon is ultimately exorcised only to take over the body of the priest-exorcist who, in a final act of self-sacrifice, defeats the demon by throwing himself to his death.

To affirm the reality of demon possession does, of course, acknowledges at the same time the existence of the transcendent world of the spirit. For those, on the other hand, whose reality encompasses only the physical universe, another explanation must be found for the phenomenon. It must be due to some psychological abnormality. The post-Enlightenment period in the eighteenth and nineteenth century Gospel criticism sought to eliminate the miraculous from an understanding of the Jesus of history.[163] Even today the analysis of the miracles attributed to Jesus are sketchy compared to the investigation of his teachings.[164]

In the following I define what exorcism is and explicate the historical setting of Jesus' exorcisms focusing on the Judaism of the Jewish homeland and the Galilee in particular.

Exorcisms may simply be defined as causing the demons or evil spiritual beings to leave a person that they have entered and "possessed."[165]

There has been a long debate and effort to distinguish Hellenistic Judaism and the Judaism found in the Holy Land.[166] The conquest of the east by Alexander and the subsequent empires that developed after him were not interested in merely establishing political control of these respective empires.[167] Rather they understood themselves as bearers of Greek civilization that constituted a universal norm of culture grounded in the Greek language, political tradition, artistic forms, and intellectual life.[168] But each of these cultures developed their own style shaped by its own cultural inheritance. This was true also locally within the urban complexes within each empire. So "Hellenism" developed in different degrees and styles dependent on historical heritage and local customs.

The Jews in the Holy Land were not immune to this whole process. Within the homeland Jews adopted Hellenistic urban lifestyles, many spoke Greek, the diplomatic protocols of government were adopted according to Greek norms, and patterns of social, economic, and political life were assumed that were known all over the Roman world.¹⁶⁹ A theater and gymnasium with a sports complex, were, for example, established in Jerusalem.

However, Judaism in the homeland also had its own long history of a political expression to say nothing of its monotheistic theology, its central Temple, and covenantal nomism.¹⁷⁰ Jews spoke Aramaic, a language that distinguished them from the lingua franca of the Roman Empire and which language had come to be understood as prototypically Jewish. Jews also were very aware of being under foreign domination which sparked the Maccabean revolt in the second century BC and the war with Rome in the first century AD. In the case of the Maccabean revolt, Hellenism looked like a cultural weapon of Greek domination. So there was a debate between the degree of Hellenization and Judaism, as it had developed in the post-exilic era under the Persians, and which became a focal point of political opposition.¹⁷¹ It was regarded as the pristine tradition and under its banner the Maccabees fomented the successful rebellion against the Seleucid Empire. But then the Maccabean successors themselves became increasingly Hellenized.¹⁷²

So within the land Hellenization remained a problematic policy, program, and practice and Judaism became defined for most Jews there in terms of opposition and antithesis. However, in the diaspora, while the Jews retained their ethnic distinctiveness and traditions, it was comprehended within a thorough mastery of all aspects of Greek civilization. So it is clear that each community no longer lived within the former insular world of the Persian Empire.¹⁷³ The reality is that among both homeland and diaspora Jews the relationship to Hellenism and its thought world was only a matter of degree. Even the Galilee was not an insular "backwater" as some have suggested. Great trade routes passed through it which made even these northern Jews cognizant of the greater Roman world and its Hellenistic culture.¹⁷⁴

But the differences are not trivial. The teachings and practices of the Pharisees and the Essenes demonstrate how deeply embedded many Jews were in the ancient literature and practices of Judaism and its development after the exile.¹⁷⁵ Recognizing the differences between the homeland and the diaspora we must locate Jesus' activity as an exorcist against the background of life in the homeland of the Jews.

Important to our understanding of demon possession and Jesus' exorcistic activity is that they were not a part of Old Testament nor of first-century Jewish expectations regarding healing and the liberation brought about by the coming of the kingdom.[176] Demon possession and its alleviation also was not a prominent part of the activity of the early church.[177] However, it was not uncommon in both early Judaism and in the church. In this way the historicity of Jesus' exorcistic activity and the importance he placed on it (Luke 11:20) is reinforced. So for Jesus exorcisms reflected his battle against the forces of evil at work in his society and liberating it from the disaster that would ensue if Israel was not freed from its courting of violent activity against the Roman occupation and "possession."[178]

On a social level demon possession meant ostracizing by the community.[179] It was another source of ritual uncleanness perhaps of the most extreme sort. So Jesus, by his exorcisms, was healing the body politic and removing another source of friction and division within Israel.

The rabbinic literature refers to a certain Hanina ben Dosa who encountered a demon who had to submit to him because of his standing before God. So his power had to do with his relationship with the divine and not in his personal authority.[180] Another reference mentions Simeon ben Yose whose exorcisms were due to his own charismatic power. The story of Johanan ben Zakkai, however, emphasizes that exorcisms were accomplished by words and actions. The demon is exorcized by the smoke from a burning root and the aspersion of water.[181] Action and the personal force of the exorcists is also involved in the story of the Pharaoh taking Abraham's wife Sarah into his household as it is retold in the Genesis Apocryphon from Qumran. God scourges Pharaoh with an evil spirit which Abraham exorcises by the laying on of hands while he prayed.[182]

Aside from Pharisaism and Qumran and their literature it is clear that other writings from around the time of the first century AD provide access to the world of the Jews during this period and are relevant in determining the thought world of Jesus' time regarding demons, possession, and exorcisms.[183] In the testament of Solomon, Solomon is portrayed in terms of controlling demons and having conversations with demons rather than exorcising them. This power over them is construed as a divine gift.

Cynicism was another factor since there is evidence of wandering Cynic philosophers in the Holy Land which attributed to them wonder-working activity and confronting the sins of the people.[184] Some of their aphoristic teaching and lifestyle may well have circulated among Jesus' and John the Baptist's contemporaries which exerted an influence on both of them: John's austere life resembled that of a Cynic who lived frugally, wore a single garment, ate simple food, and lived in the open. Jesus' peripatetic ministry and teaching often in aphorisms certainly bear a resemblance to these Cynic philosophers.[185] Of course, these make up only two elements in Jesus' activity and do not totally explain his complex ministry.

Twelftree spends some time explicating the reference to the exorcistic activity of some wandering Jewish priests in Acts 19:13-19. They are not active in the Jewish homeland but in Ephesus. That they are Jewish priests on the move witness to an aspect of the world of Jesus. In v. 13 he understands the word ὁρκίζω (*horkidzō*, adjure) to mean not ordering the demon to leave but putting a restriction on it and terrifying it with the name of Jesus. So the exorcist identifies who this Jesus is with reference to Paul's proclamation and used incantations to restrict the demons. However, the translations use either "adjure" (NRS, RSV, KJV, NAS, NJB) or "exorcise" (NKJ). The former seems to be the most accurate translation.[186] So there is much more than merely "restricting" the spirits but exorcising it in imitation of Paul's own actions of exorcizing.[187] That "abjuring" is connected with exorcism is demonstrated by a story told by Josephus of his contemporary, Eleazar. In the presence of Vespasian Eleazar put a ring containing a root mentioned by Solomon under the nose of the demoniac and while reciting incantations "composed by Solomon" drew the demon out through his nostrils "abjuring" it not to enter the man again. To prove his power, Eleazar commanded the demon to knock over a basin filled with water, which it did.[188]

Distinguished from the story of the sons of Sceva, who are rejected, is the reference to the rival exorcists in Mark 9:38-40. The phrase "in your name" raises questions regarding the report's authenticity suggesting the pericope arose within the primitive church. However, the name of a god is usually employed in healing and the phrase without the "in" has been found elsewhere.[189] The word "follow" (v. 38, Gk ἀκολουθέω, *akoloutheō*) is used exclusively in the Gospels and restricted to a relationship with Jesus whereas in the epistles other terms are used.[190] Jesus is tolerant of this activity which distinguishes him from the later intolerance of the church. This tolerance is reflected in his many parables which portray the kingdom of God as appearing under unexpected circumstances, places, and people.[191] Jesus implies that those who use his name have accepted him and are furthering the extension of the kingdom and its invasion of Satan's realm.[192]

These stories which reflect exercising exorcistic power by the personal force and piety of the exorcist rather than their actions find a counterpart in the apocryphal songs of David from Qumran (11QapPs[a]),[193] in which the two ancient royal figures of David and Solomon are portrayed in the same way.

A similar picture emerges in the characterization of the Jewish exorcists in Matt 12:27, Luke 11:19 (cf., Mark 3:22–27) when Jesus answers his critics who accuse him of using "Beelzebul" to cast out demons. He puts a counterquestion to them and asks. ". . . by whom do your sons cast them out?"[194] The "sons" are merely the fellow Jews of Jesus' accusers (Matthew has probably added "Pharisees" to identify them more narrowly).[195] Jesus' counterquestion implies that they, like him, cast out demons by the power of God.

The Greek Magical Papyri[196] provide another source for clarifying the practice of exorcism in the ancient world. Although the age of these papyri extend over several centuries, they still provide a somewhat uniform picture of the practice of exorcism and exorcists as they describe the incantations to be recited along with directions for the actions to be employed. First the exorcist invokes a power authority followed by a descriptive history of the deity so invoked in order to gain its support; then the exorcists used the god or calls upon the god to perform the exorcism. To achieve the exorcism the performer had to know the demon's name which gives power over it. The demons are then sent away to protect the sufferer from further possession. Thus Twelftree finds in the papyri the fourfold pattern of invocation, identification of the god, command, and protection.[197] In this pattern the person of the exorcist fades into the background and his words and actions come to the fore.

In summary we have found two prevailing types for the practice of exorcism: exorcisms are brought about (1) by the power and charismatic force of the exorcist; or (2) by the exorcist's action and words. Sometimes these two types are combined as in the story of Abraham and Pharaoh. Another characteristic of exorcists is they often, like Cynic philosophers, appear as wanderers (e.g., the sons of Sceva, Acts 19:14–16).

The ubiquitous belief in hostile, spiritual powers is expressed by Paul in Eph 6:12:[198] "For we are not contending against flesh and blood, but against the principalities, against the powers, against the world rulers of this present darkness, against the spiritual hosts of wickedness in the heavenly places" (Eph 6:12).

Twelftree's investigation of the NT and the NT apocryphal literature reveals that exorcisms conformed to a pattern as it was practiced in the Jewish homeland of the first century:[199]

1. The exorcist and demoniac confront one another.
2. The exorcist addresses, or even abuses, the demon.
3. The spiritual power of the exorcist effects the exorcism without any mechanical or physical aids.[200]
4. There is a conversation between the demon and the exorcist.
5. The conversion of the demon possessed.

The second and fourth items in this list involved the knowledge of the demon on the part of the exorcist in order to combat the demon while simultaneously identifying with a powerful precursor such as Moses. In this confrontation the demon would often plead for mercy (Mark 5:7).

So across time and space, in the Jewish homeland and in the diaspora, we find exorcistic activity in which both the power of God is invoked or the exorcist operates by his own charismatic power.

In the following section I will present contemporary investigations of exorcistic activity and demon possession which show they are not just phenomena of the past. It will become clear that demon possession is not merely a psychological abnormality that was misinterpreted by ancient cultures which imagined a mythical world of spiritual beings that were capable of possessing a person. In the discussion below I will be following up on the reference I made in chapter 1[201] on the work of the medical scientist Richard Gallagher who has scientifically investigated this phenomenon and affirmed its objective reality.

EXORCISMS IN OUR CONTEMPORARY ENVIRONMENT

I have referred to Richard Gallagher's book *Demonic Foes* in the previous chapter. In the following I will summarize the results of his careful scientific investigations and analysis. Anthropologists have found evidence for demon possession throughout history and all but universally, although some cultural traditions blame these spiritual attacks on other entities such as ancestors, deities, and goblins.[202] Gallagher cites the work of the anthropologist Erika Bourguignon who documented accounts of possession in three-fourths of the 488 cultures she investigated. She found the belief in possession ubiquitous across time and cultures putting the lie to the claims of some poorly informed modern critics who claim that only "credulous members of traditional religious subcultures" experience such a phenomenon.[203]

Great discernment is required in assessing whether a person is truly possessed or suffering from some medical or psychological disorder. There are strict medical criteria for determining whether a person is afflicted by demon possession. One basic question has to be asked: Do the patient's symptoms have a natural explanation? So in each instance of a claim of demon possession he investigates if a person is suffering from some odd seizure disorder, psychosis, or whether a person is prone to suggestibility. Here is a scientist at work ruling out natural explanations. He emphasizes that an exorcism is not mumbo-jumbo. It is a long, demanding, and dreadful struggle involving the cooperation of the victim, a reality that is obvious when we read the story of the Gerasene demoniac (Mark 5:1-20). And it takes a trained and experienced and psychiatrically sophisticated exorcist to effect healing of possessed people.

Gallagher describes briefly four occurrences early on his study to demonstrate that true possessions have no material or scientific explanation: a young woman who is levitated for half an hour; a woman whose hearing was blocked when anyone mentioned a religious topic; another woman who suffered from unexplained bruises; and a tiny woman who, in a possessed state, threw a two-hundred pound man across the room.[204] In subsequent chapters he goes into detail describing specific cases whose subject's symptoms had no natural causes.[205] He is an objective diagnostician and demonstrates the reality of demonic possession. He emphasizes that diabolical attacks are spiritual, not mental, disorders and they are of different kinds.[206]

The experiences of exorcists over the ages led to the creation of taxonomies of the different demonic states and the special spiritual treatment required for each such state. Psychological or medical assistance were (and are) not in and of themselves of any help. There are two major conditions, possession and oppression, which exist on a continuum from relatively minor to severe and disabling effects.

The pattern emerging from the state of possession constitutes what medicine calls a syndrome. A possessed person's body is under the control of the spirit entity; the manifestation of the evil spirit is intermittent; a possession can be temporary and even voluntary; the spirit is aggressive and belligerent, especially in attacking anything of a holy or religious nature; when it speaks it does so in a vile and arrogantly blasphemous manner; accompanying these manifestations are abnormal physical signs: it can speak in an unknown ancient tongue,[207] has awareness of hidden knowledge, demonstrates immense strength, and can cause extreme physical contortions of the possessed person's body including levitation (which, however, is rare); they frequently have the capacity to distinguish blessed objects from ordinary ones such as holy water; they can affect the physical environment including the ability to emit intense and raucous noises, make the room hot or cold, or fill the room with sulfurous smells; and they can produce discomfort if their victim is in a holy place.

Gallagher notes that all of these diagnostic indicators may all be present only during an exorcism which confirms that some spiritual entity has possessed the host and is unequivocally operating. To witness these possessions one can only ascribe their appearance to a distinct creature totally discrete in its identity from the human host and able to exhibit spiritual faculties beyond the human.[208] These spirits hate their hosts and delight in torturing them. They demonstrate their repellant personalities by using their demonic talents in vicious ways.

However, Gallagher emphasizes that no single factor can prove demonic possession; rather clear signs of preternatural activity along with other typical manifestations must be present and documented, i.e., *"the sum of hard evidence"* in order to arrive at a diagnosis of possession.[209] The investigator must also take into consideration the background of the victim and what led to the possession.

As in the possession syndrome there are also a wide variety of oppressions by which evil spirits sow division and discord. Oppressions can be divided into internal and external.[210] In the latter a person can be battered physically and be plagued by scratches and bruises on their skin. The former can take the shape of messages delivered not by sounds or voices heard internally (as in many people who suffer from schizophrenia) but a strong sense of receiving a coherent and comprehensible message which feels like an assault leaving the subject troubled and unsettled. In the example of such oppression that Gallagher describes he observes that evil spirits usually lie about their true nature, feigning to be dead people, angels, or deities of pagan religions. Under the duress of the exorcism process, however, they will reveal their true nature. Their goal in falsely identifying themselves is to stimulate superstitious beliefs in their subjects and create turmoil with true faith.[211] The most common reason a person becomes the target of an oppression is that they have turned to iniquitous or occult practices but usually in less intense ways than a possessed person. It also happens that an oppressed person can develop a full possession.[212]

Gallagher emphasizes the role of trained doctors to monitor the physical health of an individual and, as I have already mentioned, to rule out natural causes before affirming the diagnosis of demon possession. He references Thomas Aquinas, who warned clerics not to jump to diagnosing a supernatural cause when a natural one would suffice. Gallagher sums up:

> ... the Roman Ritual calls for someone not only 'outstanding in knowledge' but also with personal qualities such as maturity and holiness. Overly emotional or poorly educated ministers or priests, just like ill-informed doctors or lawyers, don't make good judges of complex situations, such as demonic states that require patience, caution, and sober judgment. Some astute and experienced exorcists are knowledgeable enough to discern diabolic attacks largely on their own. Still, they are advised to seek a medical professional's opinion whenever any doubt or other medical needs arise—a sacred role passed down in my profession for centuries.[213]

Gallagher notes that these evil spirits have differing personalities and degrees of intelligence which affect how each exorcism proceeds demanding different approaches. They can speak sarcastically, pontificate on theological themes, use ruses, distract and mislead, try to spread confusion, make false predictions, and even assert they have "legal" rights over the possessed.[214]

There have been a growth in the number of possessions. That growth coordinates with the decline in traditional religious practice and the marked increase of occultism in Europe and North America. Consequently, the International Association of Exorcists was founded in the early 1990s, and there are now about one hundred established exorcists in the US, those who are officially sanctioned by their church.

Demons not only take possession of humans but also of locales and objects, called "infestations" which involve the breakup of religious objects, furniture tipping over, unexplained noises, screams, and the smell of sulfur. Gallagher suggests that ghost tales may reflect examples of infestations. He refers to a woman who had recently returned to her faith after a conversion experience in whose house objects were moving and sounds of odd speech and whimpering were heard. She had the house blessed and the phenomena disappeared.[215]

In a final chapter Gallagher deals with hucksterism and false healers and irresponsible ministers who can harm people both spiritually and physically. Physical means, he emphasizes, that involve violence are risky and superstitious. So, characteristically, he promotes the necessity of scientifically literate and well-trained practitioners of exorcism. He emphasizes that there is nothing unscientific about asserting the objective reality of demon possession and "that to the unbiased mind the evidence is compelling." None the less he still has to deal with resistance to a "spiritual" topic because it "goes beyond what our modern and narrower conception of science can legitimately study." He admits that it is "impossible to subject spiritual realities, such as spirits and prayers, to the same kind of scientific scrutiny as metals and clouds . . . and we don't want our scientists pontificating on subjects outside their areas of expertise."[216] So the study of possession requires a multidisciplinary approach involving medical, historical, and spiritual insight and knowledge. While he believes in the separation of science and religion to him that does not mean

> there cannot be a creative, constructive dialogue between the two. Reason and faith can be complementary fields of inquiry and should not contradict one another. Legitimate historical and other religious controversies like religious phenomenological and historical scholarship are subject to nuanced, reasoned discourse. Otherwise we reduce faith to a world outside reason, and we allow science in its more constricted sense to dictate every answer, even about spiritual questions or experiences. This narrower definition is labeled 'scientism,' and its truncated demarcations rule out religious questions from the start as unanswerable in nature.[217]

In his epilogue[218] Gallagher gives his answer to the important question of the why evil spirits exist and our understanding of them. Demons are dedicated to the destruction of people both physically and spiritually. Superficially it can be said that since they are miserable they want human beings to share their misery. The deeper answer is that they hate humanity because of their hatred of God. They want to corrupt people and direct their activity toward sullying the image of God within us and in this way to negate our capacity to love. They know much about us, despise us, and want to mislead and harm us. There is indeed a very dark aspect to the world of the spirit. That world is not all light and goodness!

Invading the Realm of Demons, Disease, and Death

The reality of demon possession also raises the question of why evil exists at all. God allows evil for a limited time. Love without freedom or good without the option of evil is both logically impossible and would deprive both love and goodness of any meaning.

Furthermore, we should not expect that intelligent spirits were any different from us in their ability and willingness to freely choose different moral pathways. However, demons have a greater power and intelligence than human beings and so have a greater capability to create havoc and misery. Only divine power acting through effective exorcists can overcome them and liberate their victims. He believes that evil spirits would kill everyone if not prevented. And there is no evidence that they want to change.

Reflecting on miracles in general he quotes Pascal. ". . . it would not be possible that there should be so many false miracles, if there were none true." Gallagher goes on to comment,

> [Pascal's] point about historical miracles is analogous to the long record of debates about demonic phenomena, too. Pascal knew that the many false or exaggerated reports about miracles derive a borrowed legitimacy from the real ones; they prove confusing to people and stimulate false hopes and superstitious reactions precisely for the reason that these false claims are based on their mistaken parallels with the rare but genuine ones. Possession, true and false ones, are nearly an exact analogue in that sense.

I have gone into some detail in summarizing Gallagher's important investigation and study for the purpose of placing the reports in the Gospels of Jesus' exorcistic and miraculous activity in a context. His scientific study indicates above all that the realm of the demonic is not some ancient, primitive outlook trying to explain psychological phenomena. The world of the spirit is real and impinges upon our material reality in manifestly diverse and sundry ways. So Jesus' exorcisms cannot be dismissed out-of-hand but must be approached with the initial assumption that they took place. Indeed, the dispute about exorcism recorded in the Gospels would never have taken place if Jesus' opponents did not think he was involved in such activity.[219]

As I have emphasized in my first chapter, Gallagher too highlights the unity and complementarity of faith and reason. The truth is one.

THE EXORCISMS OF JESUS

In the following I will summarize Josef Schmid's short but comprehensive overview of the development of belief in and the experience of demons in the OT and Judaism and in comparison with their portrayal in the Gospels.[220]

Belief in demons is not a subject of major importance in the OT and is unrelated to the figure of Satan whose figure appears only as a judicial prosecutor in Zech 3:1–2 and in Job 1. In 1 Chr 21:1 he is characterized as a tempter.[221] An important development appears in WisSol 2:24 which asserts that because of Satan's envy death entered the world, a clear reference to the story of the fall and the figure's equation with the serpent in Gen 2. The basic belief of Israelite religion was that God was the origin of both weal and woe in human life (cf., Amos 3:6). However, in early Judaism under the influence of Persian theology the belief in demons and Satan grew. Now Satan's abode was no longer in the divine council but appears as the opponent of both God and human beings whose goal is the destruction of God's plan of salvation, the apostasy of Israel from God, and the seduction to every kind of sin. Because of the strength of Jewish monotheism, however, this blossoming belief did not lead to a dualism of equals such as was found in Persian Zoroastrianism.[222]

Satan remains a creature of God which led to the understanding that he was a fallen angel and whose hubris was the origin of his fall from his fellowship with God. The other evil spirits, the demons, then became a kingdom of their own under his dominion. In this way the demons were understood as pervading the world, whose dwelling was in the air (cf., Eph 2:2), and who can take possession of people. All kinds of plagues are traced back to them especially sickness, natural catastrophes, poverty, and death. That they can seduce people to commit evil is found only in Jub 7:27, 10:1, 11:4, 12:20 and in TestPatr (Zebul 9, Asher 6). However, they can also appear as in service to God as a divine angel of punishment. So they are bound to God's will and cannot therefore arbitrarily harm people.

Judaism knows of defenses against them such as phylacteries, and amulets, but above all exorcism by incantation and magic. Their final destruction was expected in the messianic age (1 Enoch 69:27). The development of demonology in the time of early Judaism perceived that where faith in God wavered there demonic powers broke in and overpowered people.[223] In this I would also add that one of the psychological aspects of demon possession has to do with the internalizing of anger. Anger was a particularly prevalent aspect of the culture in the time of Jesus because of the growing hostility toward Rome and the hankering to eliminate the Roman occupation by force. This self-absorbed craving to eradicate Roman hegemony obscured the reality that either a person belongs to God by faith or collapses under the evil powers and dominions which develop their own gravity and exercise their own deranging effects. The end result is demonic possession.[224]

Demon possession in the Gospels is characterized by somatic and psychic injury such as dumbness, deafness, blindness, lameness, epilepsy, and delirium. These maladies are seen as a result of demon possession and clearly differentiated from possession itself.[225] However, not all such disabilities are understood as due to possession. Nor are the possessed portrayed as morally bad persons but rather as defenseless victims of satanic power. It is also not said that demonic possession is a result of earlier sins or that the demons want to lead their victims into evil deeds or plunge them into eternal ruin. Their intent is to torment their victims. So they are the enemies of God and man and their baneful effects oppose God's will. In contradistinction to the Judaism of the time they are not portrayed as God's angel of punishment. Jesus' exorcisms are his struggle against the dominion of Satan.

Schmid rejects the modern materialist critique of the exorcism narratives that maintains that had Jesus the knowledge of our psychiatric understanding of natural conditions of this illness he would have had a correct judgment of these cases. Above all, he argues,

> the behavior of the possessed over against Jesus contradicts the psychiatric explanation. In these narratives there is never a case where there is the sense of a double ego at work in the possessed or that the possessed does anything against the will of the demon. The behavior and speech of the possessed is portrayed thoroughly as the utterances of the demon and the possessed as its tool. Particularly noticeable is that they recognize and confess Jesus as messiah and so testify to a higher knowledge of the person of Jesus.[226]

He observes that Jesus never appeals to the will of the possessed but speaks directly to the demon. He finds that the story of the Geresene demoniac especially contradicts a natural explanation: it would not be logical to discard the characteristics of the story that conflicts with a psychiatric explanation as a "later stylizing of the tradition." As I've already noted, absent in the story are the usual magical formulae and practices.

The exorcism is effected by a mere word of Jesus. Further, he observes, that the healing of the Syro-Phoenician woman's daughter occurs at a distance, rendering a direct physical influence impossible. The exorcisms are to be seen in terms of Jesus' other miracles as divine power at work. The exorcisms are not to be understood as a mere power over demons but a component of the struggle between Satan and the proclamation of the kingdom of God.

From the temptation, when Satan seeks to make Jesus defect from his messianic task, to his prompting of Judas's betrayal, he is portrayed as the opponent of God who works to take the word of God out of the heart of people. But Jesus is the stronger. In his environment therefore Jesus' exorcisms are a proof that God's dominion has dawned and Satan's dominion is on the way out.[227]

At this point I would like to summarize Haenchen's more rationalistic reflection on exorcisms and healings because I think that he makes some very important observations on the strictly human level of these phenomena.[228] He clearly rejects the nineteenth century notion that the miracle stories are a creation of superstition and fantasy. He rightly asserts that the Gospels cannot be understood if it is denied that Jesus performed miracles and deeds of power. He introduces his understanding of Jesus' miracle-working by observing that we are now aware of facts that a former time had no access to, namely, of the body-mind connection. Physical illnesses can affect the life of the mind and the reverse. The psyche can actually cause physical illness. For example, a person can escape into illness to avoid difficult challenges. A doctor can heal because of his mental influence.

Trust, he notes, is not just a subjective opinion and an insignificant outlook. It is an indispensable power for human life. Trust can work miracles which was well known in the ancient world (cf., Mark 11:23). He suggests that trust has two senses. Trust can be in one's own power or in the power of another. Trust in self or in God can effect the unimaginable. However, a trust not based on God tends toward a "cramped hubris" which I take to mean a self-restricting arrogance that excludes the possible influence of another. Trust in God remains free of such a "cramped and sick exaggeration of the self." So where Jesus met mistrust there his power was limited (cf., Mark 6:5).

Haenchen emphasizes Jesus' humanity rather than some alleged divine power in effecting his healings. This comports well with my interpretation of his existence in the world which was devoid of any divine power according to Phil 2:7.²²⁹ So Jesus' unsullied trust rested in his heavenly Father and that enabled him to be free and able to work with every afflicted person who reached out to him in trust. This trust of his, according to my understanding of his character based on Phil 2, grew as it can in any person. That trust is best expressed in the conviction he came to that God was his "Father," his "Abba." His experience of God at his baptism where he was called "my beloved son" then was confirmation and intensification of that conviction.

So Haenchen is correct when he observes that Jesus' power unfolded from a pure relationship of trust as it came forth from his own trust and relationship with God. His trust in God was inseparably bound up with his understanding of God as the unbounded will to love. God was merciful love, so he could be unconditionally trusted. He saw in God an almighty love at work where the unbelieving person saw only an incomprehensible, terrible *deus absconditus*.²³⁰

However, Haenchen does not accept the existence of demons as objective reality. He understands a belief in them in this way. Jesus' time was a time of fear which was expressed in the belief in demons. So demons could be seen in a fever as in a wind storm.²³¹ With this as his basic understanding he finds a shift in the gospel tradition, and Jesus is made to appear as the victor over demons like a *theios anēr* (Gk., θειὸς ἀνήρ, "divine man") which he equates with a "magician." Scholars have come up with this designation for types of miracle workers in the Hellenistic environment of the ancient world. However, the concept has come into question and we now know that scholarship has to take considerable care to avoid implying that in the Hellenistic environment of early Christianity. The "divine man" functioned as a technical term for human figures who manifested their divine nature through miraculous deeds.²³² So Jesus cannot be said to portray a "divine man" in the miracles stories of the gospels.

A Demoniac in the Synagogue (Mark 1:21–28; Luke 4:31–37)

Probably Mark added the "immediately" (Gk., εὐθύς, *eythys*) in vss 21 and 23. The word is highly characteristic of his style. The story does not fit the style of miracle stories or even the form of an exorcism. Usually the exorcist demands the demon identify itself which is a protective strategy. Here the demon seeks to protect itself by recognizing who Jesus is!

Bultmann admits being convinced that these words of the demon are not part of the so-called Marcan messianic secrecy motif.[233] However, he understands the phrase "a new teaching with authority" as a Marcan insertion because it conflicts with the point of the story. With his emendations he makes the story conform to the typical form of a miracle story: 1. The demon recognizes the exorcist which begins a struggle between the antagonists; 2. The exorcist threatens and delivers a command; 3. The demon leaves its host making a demonstration; 4. The spectators react.[234] However, Taylor sees these as primitive elements attesting to a more primitive form preceding the form of a popular miracle story and closer to an eyewitness account: Jesus' commanding word alone exorcizes the demon without the use of magical formulae, his authority, and the supernatural aura of his person.[235] Mark has recorded "a tradition which preserves the colour and detail of the actual event."[236]

That Jesus was in Capernaum (כפר נחם, *KFaR NaCHuM*, "Nahum's Village," or more colloquially, "Nahumsville") is not surprising since he made the place a center of his ministry and outreach into the Galilee (Matt 4:13).[237] The remains of the first century synagogue are to be observed as the foundation of the vestiges of the present structure which dates to the second or third century.[238] That the demon charges Jesus' purpose to "destroy us" (vs 24) implies that Jesus had been proclaiming the kingdom of God which involved the "binding of the strong man" (Mark 3:27) and invading the rule of Satan rendering him powerless.[239] Jesus is everywhere in the Gospels characterized as using the synagogue as a place to teach. It was an obvious strategy to reach out to as many people as possible at one time.[240]

The Greek reads "Sabbaths" in the dative plural, which is Semitic usage witnessing to the antiquity of the tradition.[241] The "amazement" at Jesus' teaching occurred because, unlike the scribes who would refer to the line of scribal authority behind what they taught, he taught with personal authority without any such references.[242] Inferred is divine authorization. It was even unlike the authority of the prophets who prefaced their prophecies with "Thus says the LORD . . ."[243] whereas Jesus flatly says "I say to you . . ."! (see Matt 5:22–44). This sense of authority rested on his baptismal experience of being designated God's "beloved son."[244] He spoke then out of his own understanding of God and his will.[245] So he interpreted not the Torah but what the nearness of the kingdom demanded revealing the will of God.[246] These scribes would have been secretaries to the court of Herod Antipas or worked for the affluent, keeping their books and assuring their compliance with the Torah. They had to know the Torah well and its application to present conditions.

We now arrive at the point of the narrative as a man "in an unclean spirit" appears. This prepositional phrase is again Semitic phraseology reproducing the Heb ב = "with." The preposition indicates that it is the unclean spirit who has possessed the man who "shouts aloud."[247] The phrase "What have you to do with us" ("What do you want with us?" RSV and NJB; "Halt, was haben wir mit dir zu schaffen?" Luther, "We have nothing to do with you.") reproduces, according to Taylor, the Hebrew מח לנו ולך "Why do you meddle with us?"[248] The demons live out of their own power so there is no mutuality between them and Jesus.[249] It speaks in the plural (ἡμῖν, 1:24, hēmin, "with us") for the whole world of evil spirits who are opposed to God. The phrase is also an allusion to the story of Elijah and the widow of Sarepta (1 Kgs 17:16). The people consider Jesus as Elijah redivivus (Mark 6:14). So the reference suggest that Jesus exorcisms were a renewed battle against foreign idols and thus implicates the Roman occupation and their introduction of their (demonic) gods into the Holy Land. So Jesus appears here as the messiah whose task was freeing the land of pollution and restoring its holiness (PsSol 17).[250] By casting out demons God's reign is restored (Luke 11:20) and bringing an end to Roman rule is proleptically performed.

But this witness is inadvertent because what the unclean spirit purposes here is that by knowing Jesus' true identity and uttering his name it can gain power over him. So this is a titanic confrontation between the kingdom of God present in Jesus and the assault of the whole world of evil spirits. Consequently, this is not a mere exorcism but the assault of the mighty one on the whole kingdom of Satan.

The unclean spirit applies two appellatives to Jesus: "Nazarene" (Gk., Ναζαρηνέ) and "holy one of God" (vs 24). While all the versions translate the former with "of Nazareth," the two appellations might be coordinated if "Nazarene" is to be derived from "nazir" (i.e., "consecrated").[251] The second appellation, "holy one of God," is not a messianic title. "Holy one" is usually a designation of God in the OT. However, Num 16:7 coordinates a "holy one" with one whom God chooses. Moses is described as God's "holy one" in Ps 106:16, Elisha in 2 Kgs 4:9, and Nebuchadnezzar's dream consists of heavenly visitants, "the watchers" who are described as "holy ones." They proclaim God's universal rule which subjects all the kingdoms of the earth (Dan 4:13–17). So the locution "holy one of God" then is not related to a divine figure but a divine agent. When the demon recognizes Jesus as the "holy one," it is as the one who brings God's kingdom and the concomitant subjection and destruction of Satan, the chief demon, and the plundering of his household.[252] He is exercising the high priestly office.[253] The demon uses the plural thereby including the whole demonic world in recognition of Jesus' kingdom proclamation which is an attack on the whole of Satan's realm. The ultimate destruction of demonic power was expected in the messianic age (1 Enoch 69:27) and by the messianic high priest.[254]

There are two ways to understand the demon's identification of Jesus as the "holy one." The demon may have designated Jesus in this way to sew confusion. Demons were liars, so the people might suspect that the demon is covering the fact that Jesus is not truly the "holy one" at all but, as his enemies are wont to accuse him, of being in league with Satan. So Jesus commands his silence. Or, bearing in mind that demons have preternatural knowledge, this one could be privy to the declaration of Jesus as the "beloved son" at his baptism and his proclamation of and his inaugurating the kingdom of God. What would be remarkable here then is that the demon identifies, or names, Jesus. Usually it is the exorcist who wants to know the name of the demon in order to gain power over it (cf., Mark 5:9). So the demon's naming him, as I've already noted, might be a ploy to gain power over Jesus in order to prevent its expulsion from its victim.[255] Another reason Jesus would command its silence.

Nestle makes a question of the contention that Jesus had come to destroy the evil demons (vs 24). Taylor correctly insists it is "defiant assertion" which would more accord with the character of demons who can insolently claim they have even a legal right to possess people![256] As assertion it coordinates with Jesus as the "holy one of God" who has come to do precisely that. Jesus then commands that the demon be silent and leave the man manifesting his consciousness of having authority and power over the minions of Satan.[257] Jesus' command to the demon to be quiet (φιμώθητι, *phimōthēti* 1:25) does not merely mean to be silent (σιώπα, *siōpa*). It is part of incantational vocabulary and means to render inoperable and could be translated as "muzzle."[258] Mark takes up this silencing in his Gospel structure in 1:34: "He did not permit the demons to speak because they knew him." The full revelation of his identity must await the time when Jesus chooses to reveal himself in the parable of the vineyard as the beloved Son.

Jesus' power is in contrast to contemporary exorcists who frequently have to spend more than one session to effect an exorcism. The demon leaves the man as it "convulses" (Gk, σπαράξαν, *sparaksan*, "throw into convulsions") him.²⁵⁹

As in most miracle stories the crowd's reaction of amazement is noted. Exorcisms were not uncommon in Jewish culture so the reaction has to do with an experience of the numinous as Peter had at the great draft of fish (Luke 5:1–11).²⁶⁰ Contributing to this astonishment is the fact that Jesus does not do any manipulating or use magical formulae. A simple word effects the exorcism. There is also no proof of the exorcism by some activity of the demon after its exorcism such as smashing a pot.²⁶¹ The crowd coordinates the exorcism with Jesus' manner of teaching which did not appeal to any authority to corroborate what he said. His teaching is "new" (καινός, *kainos*) in the sense of quality (as distinct from νέος, *neos* chronologically "new"²⁶²). The final sentence concerning the spread of the witness to Jesus' deed was probably not added by Mark as one of his summaries since the word for "fame" (ἀκοή, *akoē*, "hearing, report, rumor"²⁶³) occurs nowhere else in Mark, and it describes the further effect of his activity of teaching and exorcizing. That Jesus' remarkable activity spread everywhere is totally explicable considering how quickly news passed among people of an oral culture in which he was embedded.²⁶⁴ The ultimate destruction of demonic powers expected in the messianic age (1 Enoch 69:27) added to the excited propagation of Jesus' action. Jesus stands in the service of God's grace and so has come to battle for God and man against the powers that oppose God.

The Gerasene Demoniac: Mark 5:1–20; Luke 8:26–39; Matt 8:28–34.

The place name "country of the Gerasenes" (χώραν Γερασηνῶν, *chōran Gerasēnōn*) has several variant readings in the manuscripts: "Gadarenes" and "Gergesenes."²⁶⁵ Gerasa was a city of the Decapolis and lay over thirty miles from the Sea of Galilee. The place could be identified with Gadara even though it was located some six miles southeast of the southern tip of the Sea of Galilee.²⁶⁶ However, Josephus reports that Gadara possessed territory that extended northward whose boundary lay on the shores of the lake.²⁶⁷ So we are left with Matthew's "Gadarenes" and Mark's and Luke's "Gerasenes." Gerasa, however, is some sixteen miles from the Jordan River half way between the Sea of Galilee and the Dead Sea in the area of Perea, some thirty-seven miles southeast of the lake. "Gergasa" is read by the corrector of Sinaiticus, the eighth-century majuscule Δ, the ninth-century Codex Koridethi, and family 1 manuscripts (dating from the twelfth to the fifteenth century). Origin also preferred the reading "Gergesa" which corresponded with the local (oral) tradition. Oral tradition is not to be easily dismissed.[268] This is the only place that fits the description of a steep cliff on the edge of the lake and is therefore the only possible place where the events described could have taken place.[269]

This narrative has had a myriad of interpretations: it was a psychic event, a symbolic story. Some have interpreted it psychologically; others find a Christian midrash inspired by Isa 65:1–5. Furthermore, sociological analysis has been applied to the story.[270] The story has also been divided into an exorcism and a tale of the destruction of some pigs.[271] So Schmid accurately observes that the story contradicts every kind of natural explanation, and as a whole the interpreter has to conclude that the story is to be understood either as a "genuine eyewitness report or as pure fiction."[272]

Matthew and Luke have reproduced the story in different ways. Matthew's rendition of the story focusses on what could be called the expulsion of Jesus from Gentile territory and underscoring the recounting of Jesus' commission when he sent out the twelve, commanding them not to go to the gentiles (10:5).[273] Luke's rendition, on the other hand, is more faithful to Mark's shape of the account.[274]

The narrative portrays the horror of a poor man who has been taken over by multiple demons: no one was able to bind him in order to control his irrational behavior. The superhuman strength that enabled him to tear off the chains and shackles is certain evidence of possession by an evil spirit, if not evil spirits.[275]

In verse 6 where the demoniac falls down and "worships" Jesus (προσεκύνησεν *prosekynēsen*, "do obeisance to, worship") emphasizing an experience with the numinous and reflecting Jesus' identity as the "beloved Son."[276] The following verse underscores the point: the demoniac calls Jesus "the son of the most-high God."[277] The only other occurrence of the word in Mark is in 15:19 where the auxiliary troops under Pilate, the procurator, conduct a mock worship of Jesus. Mark's verbal resonance implies that these troops were evoking a demonic activity. Conversely, it might be said that the demoniac's confession bears a mocking nuance. The word links the Gerasene demoniac narrative with the passion and suggests that the confrontation between Jesus and the "legion" is part of the victory that he won by his death and resurrection.

Invading the Realm of Demons, Disease, and Death

The man's worship of Jesus is also an attempt by the demons within the possessed man to ward off and protect themselves (cf., vs 10). Their plea not to be "tormented" by Jesus (vs 7) is also a recognition of his surpassing power. The torment which the demons seek to avoid is being driven out of his victim and sent back to Gehenna[278] or banned to a desert place.[279] But vs 8 looks, at first hand, like a Marcan insertion, for if Jesus had already commanded their exit, wouldn't the demon already have been gone?[280] However, in Mark 8:22–26 Jesus' healing of a blind man involves a two-action process, so it is not improbable that a similar process is involved here. This is particularly likely since the man is possessed by a huge number of demons representing a massive force of evil. The verse indicates that Jesus had initially demanded a "demon" to leave the man when actually a "legion" was involved. This is so because the man is at the outset described in vss 2 and 8 as "having an unclean spirit." Having not effected the exorcism, Jesus inquires about the name (vs 9).[281] Discovering the name would bring the demon(s) under Jesus' power which it in fact does, and the exorcism is effected. So there is no discrepancy between the initial reference to one and the final discovery of the many.

The narrative looks like it has been carefully constructed with intended tensions that are only relieved as the narrative progresses. The demoniac is assumed and portrayed initially in terms of what a hearer of the story would expect: the man is possessed by one demon. His incredible strength is then described in terms of his ability to keep himself from being bound by rending the chains and shattering the shackles by which it was sought to bring him under control. This strength is then underscored by the notice that no one could subdue him. What kind of demoniac is this? That is only made clear when Jesus, having encountered him and not initially effected the exorcism, inquires about its name.[282]

To avoid Gehenna the demons ask to be sent into the herd of swine grazing in the meadow above the lake (vs. 12). Noteworthy here is that Jesus does not command silence even though the demons have named him "son of God." So the silencing, as in the narrative of the demoniac in the synagogue, has nothing to do with a so-called "messianic secret." To call God "the most high" (vs 7) is mainly a gentile expression and fits the location of the story in a pagan land.[283]

That the swine charge over the cliff and drown in the lake is not necessarily Jesus' intention. When the people in the city who hear of the incident reported by the herders they rush out to the area and bear witness to the fact that the demoniac had been healed. They're not joyful but rather filled with fear at the power of Jesus and so do not want him to remain there with them.[284] They are not led to belief in him as one who was an agent of a transcendent power. The former demoniac, however, does recognize him as healer and savior. But Jesus doesn't allow him to become a follower perhaps because he did not want to make of him some kind of showpiece and because he was a gentile and would not fit into his mission to Israel where his witness as a gentile might not be accepted.[285] Rather he sends him back to his own people to bear witness to what God has wrought for him. This mission stands in stark contrast to other cases where Jesus expressly forbids healed persons to disseminate his restoration of their health (1:44; 3:12; 7:36; 8:26). The healed demoniac is to proclaim what the true God of Israel has accomplished by sending his healer. And the man obeys, proclaiming the miracle in the whole of the Decapolis.[286]

Human bodies can function as metaphors for the body politic.[287] And not just as metaphors but can actually embody and personify political, cultural, and social realities. That embodiment becomes clear in this narrative. The demons naming themselves "legion" alludes to the Roman military presence and hegemony in the eastern Mediterranean. During the war with Rome the Tenth Legion, named *Fretensis*, was stationed in the Galilee along with other legions. It participated in the sack of Jerusalem and was stationed there and occupied the city after the war. The emblem of this legion was the boar.[288] The number of the demons also limns the six-thousand-man size of a legion. The inability to bind the demoniac (v. 3) and the numerous attempts to do so (v. 4) point to the overwhelming strength of the Roman occupation. So the possessed man embodies the Roman occupation power. The military dominance of Rome is expressed in his person and the experience of that power as death is realized in the demoniac's life among the tombs. It is the antithesis of God's kingdom manifested in Jesus. We meet here a scathing indictment of Rome and its power. But that power is not conquered by force of arms but by the invasion of the kingdom of God.[289] We find Marcan vocabulary in verse 15: ἐφοβήθησαν (*ephobēthēsan*) and in verse 17, ἤρξαντο (*ērksanto*), ἀπελθεῖν (*apelthein*), and ὁρίων (*horiōn*). Verses 18–20 are also redolent of Marcan motifs although drawing on traditional material as Mark is wont to do in many of his summaries throughout the gospel. So the denouement of the story (5:18–20) containing Marcan vocabulary relates the story to the Gospel context. The phrase ἵνα μετ' αὐτοῦ ᾖ (5:18, *hina met autou hē*) is almost the same formula in 3:14 where Jesus has appointed the twelve ἵνα ὦσιν μετ' αὐτοῦ (*hina ōsin met autou*) implying that the former demoniac wanted to join the inner circle of the twelve having been liberated from his "legion." So Mark links the story with the call and mission of the disciples. But the cured demoniac is not allowed to "be with Jesus." In this way Mark separates the mission with which the cured man has been authorized from that of the disciples. The disciples all end up abandoning and denying Jesus and at the end of the Gospel they apparently do not even receive the good news of the resurrection since the women flee from the tomb and "say nothing to anyone." The mention of the Decapolis also forges a link with a missionary motif. The mission, however, takes place in gentile territory, suggesting a dissociation of the gentile mission from any connection with the disciples and with Israel.

The phrase, "Why do you meddle with us?" (τί ἐμοὶ καὶ σοί, *ti emoi kai soi*) occurs again as in the story of the possessed man in the synagogue.[290] So the words are a defense mechanism against Jesus and a recognition of his power to exorcise. The demons then ironically invoke God's authority and use the exorcist's formula for casting out a demon in an attempt to ward off the power of Jesus: "I adjure you by God do not torment me" (verse 7, βασανίσῃς, *basanisēs*). "Torment" has clear eschatological associations and designates the torments of the final judgment. For example, Rev 14:10 uses the word in speaking of the final judgment of the hostile world. "And he also shall drink the wine of God's wrath, poured unmixed into the cup of his anger, and he shall be tormented with fire and sulphur in the presence of the holy angels and in the presence of the Lamb."[291] Mark also employs the word in the story of the calming of the sea (6:47–52): "And [Jesus] saw that they were making headway painfully (Gk., βασανιζομένους ἐν τῷ ἐλαύνειν, *basanidzomenous en tō elaunein*), for the wind was against them." Literally "they were being tormented (or tortured) while they rowed."[292]

In the first story of the calming of the sea, which immediately precedes the Gerasene narrative, Mark says Jesus commanded or rebuked (ἐπιτίμησεν, *epitimēsen*) the sea to be still. It is the same word that he uses against the demoniacs in 1:25 and 9:25 suggesting again that the sea-calming narratives are related by Mark to his passion, death, and the mission that issues from it. The calming of the sea is also related to Jesus' identity. In the psalms it is God who calms the raging sea.[293] So Jesus' calming of the sea identifies him as God present in confronting the chaotic, threatening sea, a form of demonic terror. It also identifies the nation as in a Satanic grasp because they "exorcise" (ἐξέβαλον, *eksebalon* Mark 12:8) the "beloved son" from the vineyard, i.e., declare him satanic and excommunicate him from the nation. The result is God's judgment which turns the vineyard over to others.

The title "the most high God" occurs in the OT where God exercises power over the whole earth (e.g., Deut 32:8; Dan 4:17). God exercises this power as the divine warrior to subdue the nations and Israel's enemies (Pss 9:3-5; 47:1-9). The demons confess that they, as representatives of Rome's power and its assertion of mastery over land and sea, is also subject to God. So Jesus is represented as embodying the power of the all-conquering divine warrior God who alone rightly claims sovereignty over the whole earth. That claim is realized in the mission to the gentiles.

The demons then exhort Jesus "not to send them out of the country," that is, they recognize their subordination to Jesus but still want to limit his power and defend their occupation of the land. The word "send" has military associations and means dispatch, as when a commanding officer dispatches spies (Josh 2:1) or military forces (Josh 8:3).[294] So the demon legion recognizes Jesus' authority as a military officer but seeks to secure its own interest, power, and authority. This same motif is expressed in the legion wanting to be sent into the pigs: to preserve control over the land's production.[295] The request to "let us enter them" or "go into them" also has sexual connotations. So the demon legion's request seeks to maintain imperial control over the land and its production, projects military occupation and the violence associated with war, including rape.[296] But entering into the swine they rush into the sea and drown, just as Pharaoh's army perished in the Reed Sea, utterly deprived of their power.

The rush of the pigs over the cliff also constitutes proof that the demons have indeed left their host.[297] The legion's exorcism is further confirmed by vs 15 when the residents of the area find the man sitting clothed and in his right mind.

So a number of themes of Jesus' ministry arise in the story: his plundering of Satan's house, healing, the mission to the gentiles, and the Roman occupation and its proleptic demise. This is the kingdom of God at work. The passion is also foreshadowed in the aggressiveness of the demons attempting by their opposition to Jesus to ward off their exorcism. To reemphasize: Jesus' power is not divine as exorcisms by any adept exorcist makes plain. His power rests on his sheer and unambiguous trust in his Father-God who pronounced him his beloved son. The métier of that trust is evident in that a "legion" of demons is subject to him. The message of the kingdom again rings strong and clear: the Roman Empire is subject to God, and he will bring an end to its domination of God's people in his own time (Acts 1:7). So the exorcism is a striking demonstration that God's people will eventually prevail and now is the time to exercise total trust in him and not in their own strength and their timetable.[298] This is the time for Israel to exorcise its own demons of violence, revolution, enmity, discord, poverty, and the fantasies of a divine apocalyptic intervention.

The Daughter of the Syrophoenician Woman: Mark 7:24–30; Matt 15:21–28.[299]

Bultmann includes the story as an addendum to his treatment of biographical apothems although he suggests it can also be a sort of controversy dialogue even though Jesus is not the victor. He finds the main point in Jesus' change of attitude.

As Taylor observes this story has more in common with a pronouncement story[300] or a controversy dialogue[301] than a miracle story. His judgment is affirmed by a structural analysis which reveals that the dialogue between Jesus and the woman is central to the story whereas the healing of the woman's daughter is part of the framework:

A. Jesus enters the region of Tyre and into a house and wishes to remain anonymous.

B. An anonymous woman finds him and asks that he exorcise a demon from her daughter.

C. Jesus answers that bread meant for the children should not be thrown to the dogs

C.' She answers that the dogs under the table eat the crumbs from the children's bread.

B.' Jesus commending her for her answer tells her the demon has been exorcized.

A.' The woman finds it so when she returns to her house.

A–A' refer to entering a house. Anonymity also pervades the story beyond Jesus' own desire for it. The woman is not identified by name nor her daughter. In B–B' a request is made for exorcism and it is accomplished.

That leaves C–C' as the central element. So in essence we have in the story a biographical pronouncement story and only incidentally an exorcism.[302] So the main interest is, as Taylor states, the attitude of Jesus toward gentiles.[303]

The details in the story attest to its description of an actual encounter of Jesus, to say nothing of the pejorative portrayal of Jesus in identifying a foreign woman as a dog (which, however, would not have offended Jewish ears). These details include establishing where the incident took place, Jesus' quest for privacy, the woman's clever reply, the satisfaction Jesus derived from her reply, that the woman is portrayed as the victor in the controversy, and the almost incidental reference to the healing which really functions as affirmation of the woman's insistence gentiles also have access to the bread of the people of God.

The word "from there" (Gk., ἐκεῖθεν, *ekeithen*) and the particle "and" (Gk., δέ, *de*) occur rarely in Mark and point to their traditional formulation of the pericope. (The reference seems to refer back to 6:32, the area around Geneseret which lay on the northwest shore of the lake between Capernaum and Magdala).[304] Another Semitism is the use of the redundant "resumptive pronoun" in vs 25 which reads literally "[the woman] whose daughter of her had an unclean spirit."[305] The vocative "sir" (vs 28, κύριε, *kyrie*, "Lord, lord," or "sir") is used in this sense only here in Mark and is quite appropriate in the mouth of a gentile. These details point to Mark faithfully reproducing the tradition and the historicity of this account.

That Jesus wished to hide himself (vs 24) indicates that his fame had indeed stretched far and wide even across the border between the Galilee and Phoenicia. Jesus is frequently depicted as seeking a quiet place to pray.[306] So it is not unreasonable to assume that he crossed the border hoping for a quiet retreat for a time from his frenetic activity in the Galilee (Mark refers to this intense activity in his little summaries e.g., Mark 6:34–36). Foreign soil may have beckoned since his conception of the outreach of his ministry was confined to Israel, and he could have expected to be relatively unknown there and so find some respite and repose.[307] The text says the "region of Tyre" so he may have just crossed over the border which is some twenty-eight miles from Geneseret. He probably chose Phoenicia rather than travel across the lake where, having exorcised the "legion" of demons, his fame would have been widespread. On the other hand, he may have been closer to this border at the time of his crossing. In that case, this narrative would have originally been connected with some other place other than Geneseret.[308]

The woman is described as being a Greek and Syrophoenician.[309] By "Greek" Mark probably means "gentile," emphasizing that she was not Jewish. Josephus indicates there was a large Jewish population in Tyre and many were massacred during the war by the gentile population.[310] Of course, this does not mean the Jewish population was spread throughout the countryside. But because of the large Jewish population there Mark distinguishes the woman as a gentile and not a Jew.[311]

The word "first" (Gk., πρῶτος, prōtos) in the phrase of vs 27a: "Let the children first be fed" has provoked a lot of discussion seeing in it a reference to Christian mission theology which formulated as beginning with the Jews first and then turning to the gentiles.[312] It is quite possible that Mark has added the phrase "let the children be fed first" which rests on his understanding that the vineyard has been "given to others" (Mark 12:9) making it fit precisely into his gospel narrative.[313] Furthermore, the phrase without the word "first" makes perfect sense and prepares what follows in the verse encouraging a reply from the woman.

Jesus referring to this gentile woman as a "dog" has also engendered a plethora of comments trying to mitigate its apparent harshness.[314] No matter. It will not go away, and the harshness only serves to underscore the historicity of the account. The point of Jesus is not that the bread should not be taken from the children to be given to the gentiles but that the gentiles cannot be equated with the children.[315] Jesus is not testing the woman's faith. There is no reference to faith in the story. (It is Matthew who adds the faith dimension to the story, 15:28[316]). Taylor rightly observes the tension in Jesus' own mind involving the boundaries of his ministry and that the woman astutely recognizes this tension.[317] The tension would have involved the universality of the kingdom of God[318] versus Jesus' own ministry, confined as it was in his mind, to Israel.[319] By entering a house in a foreign land Jesus was projecting a rather relaxed attitude toward purity laws (cf., Acts 10:28).[320] This behavior could also have contributed to the woman's insight that there was tension in Jesus' thinking about gentiles. In my previous book on the parables of Jesus I found this encounter to be the "wellspring" of many a parable of Jesus which portrayed the kingdom as participating in corruption which included questionable behavior and questionable people.[321] Some of his parables had a universal aspect to them implying that some event or encounter caused Jesus to expand his concept of the kingdom. That cause is found in this encounter with a gentile woman who, with her shrewd retort, "forces" her way into the kingdom.[322]

Jesus' harsh characterization of the woman underscores how committed he was to his own people, his love for them, and how he longed to save them from the certain fate that awaited them if they would not turn from their present path of growing hostility toward the Roman overlord.

There is no word of exorcism but only the announcement by Jesus that the demon had left the woman's daughter. It is an apparent healing at a distance much like the official's household member. Jesus' cures are usually wrought by contact or by a commanding word. Alternatively, it might be understood that a healing had taken place which was then intuited by Jesus. Such perceptive power would have to derive from his intimacy with and knowledge of the mind of his Father-God (Matt 11:25–27; Luke 10:21–22). In this regard Taylor remarks that such knowledge results from "an incomparable sense of communion with God, sustained by prayer and made possible by an unmatched consciousness of sonship."[323] The woman returns to her home and finds that her daughter has been freed of the demon. The daughter is in bed apparently recovering from the attacks of the demon.[324] Notable here is that there is no "proof" of the exorcism nor a chorus of approval by bystanders, traits that are usually part of a miracle story. Emphasized again is the centrality of vss 27–28.

This encounter between Jesus and the Syrophoenician woman obliges Jesus to do what was always implicit in his proclamation of the kingdom: to open the kingdom to the gentile world (that issue is taken up explicitly in Acts 10). But that then calls into question the necessity of faithfulness to Torah in order to be included in the kingdom.[325] So the kingdom then becomes a matter of faith in Jesus himself, although "faith" is not mentioned explicitly.[326] The humility and persistence of the woman, however, attests to her conviction that God would be merciful to her through Jesus. As is so eminently clear in Jesus' ministry, there are no prerequisites for entering the kingdom.[327] She claims the kingdom by insisting that, though she does not sit at the table of the kingdom (Matt 8:11; Luke 13:29), like a household dog she claims the crumbs that are thrown under the table as refuse.[328] You could easily imagine Jesus' jaw dropping at this self-effacing confession of faith coming from a woman and a gentile yet![329]

Invading the Realm of Demons, Disease, and Death

A Demoniac Boy: Mark 9:14–29; Matt 17:14–21; Luke 8:37–42.

Like the story of the Syrophoenician, the detail in this rather long narrative attest to its historicity: that the father had already inveighed upon the disciples to heal his son and their inability to do so; that Jesus approaches with three of his disciples is not Marcan style; the presence of the crowd of people and scribes; the conversation with the father (lacking in Matt and Luke); and the vivid description of the boy's symptoms.[330] The astonishment of the crowd (vs 15) may be a typical Marcan insertion. The connection with the transfiguration narrative can be suspect in that a variety of manuscripts read the singular for "when they came" (vs 14).[331] However, the connection may witness to being another example of a short collection that Mark found in the tradition.

Bultmann[332] finds two stories combined, the one involving the master and his disciples who are unable to effect a cure and the second, "more of an apothegm," involving the paradox of unbelieving faith. He supports his assertion by noting that there are two descriptions of the boy's illness by the father in vss 18 and 21–22 and that the disciples disappear from the scene in the latter half of the story. However, they are there immediately thereafter (but Bultmann judges vss 28–29 as an editorial insertion). As it is, the figures of the disciples form an *inclusio* in vss 14 and 28 so their presence is assumed (at least by Mark) during the story as it develops.

Taylor makes a creative suggestion. On the basis of this analysis he proposes that two narratives of the same story have been combined: the first 14–19 + 28 which emphasized the inability of the disciples to effect a cure and the miracle story proper in 20–27 which, having lost its original conclusion, is "imaginatively reproduced by Luke in 9:43."[333] This appears to be a good solution considering the anomalies as well as the similarities between the two halves of the story. In this way the whole of it can be regarded as a unity while taking into consideration its disparities. A structural analysis supports the unity that is created out of these apparent two renditions of the story:[334]

- A. vs 14, Jesus finds the disciples disputing with scribes.
- B. vss 15–18a, The crowd is struck with awe at Jesus' presence and gather around him. Jesus asks about the dispute. The father answering from crowd describes his son's plight: he cannot speak and the possessing spirit tries to kill him.

C. vs 18b, Disciples couldn't exorcise the demon.

D. vs 19, Jesus complains about lack of faith and how he has to endure it.

E. vs 20, The boy is brought to Jesus and the spirit reacts to his presence.

E'. vss 21–2a, Jesus asks about how long the demon has possessed the boy. The father answers from childhood and adds how it seeks to destroy him.

D'. vss 22b–24, The father pleads for help if Jesus is able. Jesus throws the words back at him and asks if he is able adding that if one has faith all is possible. The father pleads that he believes and asks Jesus to help his unbelief.

C'. vs 25, The crowd runs together and Jesus rebuked the spirit identifying it as the power that keeps the boy from hearing and speaking commanding it to leave the boy and never enter him again.

B'. vss 26–27, The spirit convulses the boy and the crowd pronounces him dead. Jesus takes him by the hand and the boy is able to stand.

A'. vss 28–29, In the house the disciples ask why they could not exorcise the demon to which Jesus answers that it takes prayer.

Mark may have found the tradition as he records it, but it is also possible that he himself united two traditions and created the form we find it in his gospel whose impressive unity is supported by the structural analysis. A and A' refer to the disciples; in B and B' the condition of the son is described and then the evil spirit actually demonstrates what it does to the boy; in C and C' the disciples are described as not being able to exorcise the demon but Jesus does; in D and D' Jesus complains about the lack of faith and the father asks that his unbelief be helped; and finally, in E and E', the central elements of the structure sets off these verses as the focus and fundamental component of the story: the reality of demon possession and its evil nature that seeks to kill. However, this central element appears sandwiched within the issue of faith in D and D' which then functions as a subsidiary concern of the passage. That the passage is a composite of two traditions is supported by the rather prolix members B and D'.

The central feature and imagery of the piece emphasizes the possession by an evil demon so that the symptoms of inability to speak and hear are not due to a mere illness or epilepsy.[335] The evangelical material makes a distinction between illness and demon possession. The ancients knew the difference. As Gallagher in his analysis of possession makes clear demons are dedicated to the destruction of people both physically and spiritually. They are also capable of producing symptoms of illness and mimic an actual illness. That ability is made clear in this story which is almost medically analytical in its description of the symptoms related to epilepsy.[336] In the last paroxysm that it inflicts on the boy it appears that it has indeed killed him. Perhaps it did and Jesus restores his life.

Jesus reproaches his generation for unbelief (vs 19). It is difficult to understand why this reproof comes at this point. It would be easier to understand if he said it to the father when the latter asked if Jesus was able to cure his son in vs 22. However, it fits well into the chiastic structure of the story and is paired with the father's own unbelief and lack of faith. At any rate Jesus has in mind not just the present crowd and circumstances but the general response of Israel at the time to his proclamation of the kingdom and its rejection. It is not some kind of gnostic expression of a divine redeemer who is for a time caught up in a dark world and soon to return to the world of light.[337] Rather it is an expression of Jesus' sense of his being sent by God as his anointed son, a consciousness awakened at his baptism (cf., Mark 1:38).

The RSV correctly translates the opening of vs 20 with "And when the spirit saw him [Jesus] . . ." The demons always respond when they encounter Jesus (Mark 1:23–24; 5:6–7). That the disciples had not been able to exorcise the demon perhaps leads the father to doubt if even Jesus can help (vs 22, "if you are able"). Taylor finds this suggestion plausible by the fact that the father's appeal to Jesus comes after the demon viciously attacks the boy.[338] There is a close relationship between master and disciple which is particularly poignant here because Jesus had given them the power to exorcise (Mark 6:7). The father's persona comes forward particularly lively and with a vibrant verisimilitude: his doubt about Jesus' power, his affection and concern for his son, the bonds that unite the whole family with this suffering son (the plurals vs 22, "Help us and have compassion for us!"), and admitting to his own vulnerability by professing the limitations of his own faith.

I've already suggested that Jesus, when he repeats to the father his own word "If you are able," is asking the father if he is able to believe. That this is so is supported by Jesus' further word directed to the father, "all things are possible for the one who believes" and by the father who then pleads for Jesus to help his unbelief (vs 23).[339] The father believes but his faith is encumbered with fear and doubt.

Verse 25 then follows with the notice that Jesus saw the crowd, which had already been reported to have run up to Jesus in vs 15 when he arrived on the scene, "come running together" (present tense! ἐπισυντρέχω, episyntrechō) which has led commentators to suppose two stories have been amalgamated in the present form of the narrative. Taylor refers to the suggestion that the word represents the Aramaic rᵉhat 'al, "attack," i.e., the crowd rushed against the boy to attack him.[340] Such an "attack" perhaps would have been brought on by the fact that the evil spirit itself attacked the boy right at that point and scared the crowd into fearing they too might become victims of possession.

The prolix commands of Jesus in exorcising the demon (vs 25) are also unique to this story and correspond to the descriptions of the unclean spirit's torture of the boy. The exorcism then takes place and leaves the boy, after a further demonic attack, appearing to be dead. Remarkable here is that there is no reaction of the crowd reported (but Luke 7:15 provides that detail). The story in complete simplicity says that Jesus takes the boy by the hand, raising him up, and that "he arose." The drama thus ends in complete repose.

The structural analysis above indicates that vss 28–29 are not an appendix but are an integral part of the narrative and rounds out the story as a whole. Jesus, by emphasizing that the exorcism needs to be accompanied by prayer, is saying that the exorcist does not accomplish driving out a demon by his own power but by God's power.[341] So Jesus places the exorcism in a wider context, that of his exorcistic activity as the victory of the kingdom of God over evil. It is also a subtle warning that the "exorcism" of the "demons" of Roman occupation that possess the nation will not be accomplished by force of arms (i.e., a Holy War) but by the power of God as his kingdom manifests itself in the world and the people joyfully enter it.

A Dumb Demoniac: Matt 9:32–34; Luke 11:14. A Blind and Dumb Demoniac: Matt 12:22–23.

These passages have no parallel in Mark but the obviously literal parallels between the three passages would suggest that Q was the source of the story. Twelftree is obviously correct in judging Matt 12:22–23 as a variant of this story.³⁴² The language of the passage follows closely that of Matt 9:32–33 and Luke 11:14. In 11:4–6 Matthew shows a special interest in Isa 35:5–6 where the reception of speech is combined with the reception of sight. He also understands Jesus as fulfilling the messianic hopes of the OT.³⁴³ The word "blind" (τυφλός, *typhlos*)³⁴⁴ also occurs more frequently in Matthew and the description of the reaction of the crowd is also typical of him. I conclude that Matthew has simply added that the man was also blind to 12:22–23.

Matthew's hand is at work in recording that the man was "brought" to Jesus and in his description of the man as a "demoniac." (Luke usually reproduces verbally the traditions that are handed down to him.) The word for "dumb" here is κωφός (*kōphos*) meaning "dull" or "blunt" and is used of both speech and hearing. But the context make clear that the man cannot speak. The exorcism is related in the briefest of descriptions as is the fact that he is healed. Following the healing the expected reaction of the crowd occurs. Matthew's crowd exclaims, "Never was anything like this seen in Israel" while Luke merely reports that "the crowds marveled." Matthew also prefers that kind of response and so the difference from Luke probably comes from his pen.³⁴⁵

Following the crowd's reaction is that of the "Pharisees" which is probably Matthew's hand at work since Luke only reports that "some of them" made the accusation. Again Luke may be closer to Q than Matthew.³⁴⁶ Both evangelists include the reaction so it was a part of Q and serves as an introduction to the Beelzubul controversy.³⁴⁷

So the Q tradition contained a brief story in which a man, possessed by a demon which rendered him dumb, is exorcised by Jesus with a word that heals the man, a deed that amazed the crowd followed by the Beelzubub controversy.³⁴⁸ So it serves also as a brief introduction to the controversy giving it an eschatological dimensions in that in the messianic age the dumb would sing for joy (Isa 35:5–6).³⁴⁹ The simplicity and Q's laconic reproduction of the incident speaks for its historicity as well as fitting well into the ministry of Jesus whose proclamation emphasized the proleptic presence of the kingdom. The connection between the exorcism and the controversy could well be historical since it is highly likely that Jesus' exorcism provoked the accusation that he was in league with Satan. Matthew adds the words "blind" and "saw" then to his introduction to the controversy in 12:22–30 in order to distinguish it from the original shape of the story in 9:32–33. The additions pick up on a

Matthean emphasis on the healing of the blind which for him accents Jesus activity as the sign of the presence of the messianic age.[350]

SUMMARY AND CONCLUSION

The Jews in the holy land of the first century, surrounded as they were by a sea of paganism and Graeco-Roman culture, were aware of their distinctiveness within that milieu not only because of their unique imageless, monotheistic faith but also by their language, political ideals, and law (Torah). Their faith was a powerful critique of all earthly powers which set them over against their religious and political environment. Judaism became defined in terms of opposition and antithesis even while Hellenism had its influence upon the cultural elites, especially the Jewish client kings and the priestly authorities.

Although the Jews of the diaspora maintained their distinctiveness and traditions, they worked at the mastery of all aspects of Graeco-Roman civilization. So the relationship between the homeland and diaspora Jews with the Hellenistic world was one of degree. Of course, groups like the Pharisees and Essenes remained totally embedded in the ancient literature and practices of Judaism and its covenantal nomism.

Exorcistic activity was not a part of the Old Testament and so not a part of Jewish expectation in the first century regarding the kingdom of God. Nor was it prominent in the life of the early church. However, it was not a completely uncommon activity in both early Judaism and Christianity. The prominence of Jesus exorcistic activity against the background of its relative infrequency in Judaism and early Christianity is a strong support for the historicity of the accounts recounting these healings. Jesus' practice also differs strikingly from the pattern of activity in the Jewish homeland and the fourfold pattern of pagan practice.

Since demon possession involved ritual uncleanness it meant shunning by the community. So exorcism was one aspect of Jesus' ministry that contributed to the healing of the body politic.

I supplemented this discussion of the ancient practice with an investigation into the existence of the phenomenon in our contemporary world provided by a modern investigator, Richard Gallagher. He in turn cites the work of another investigator, Erika Bourguignon, who documented the existence of demon possession in three-fourths of the 488 cultures she studied. His investigation is not merely an anecdotal recounting of such purported cases. But he stresses scientific criteria for determining the existence of true demon possession. There is no material or scientific explanation to phenomena exhibited by possessed person such as levitation, unexplainable physical strength, and knowledge to which the victim could not have had any access. To make a diagnosis of possession, typical manifestation must be present—and the sum of hard evidence.

He notes that there are two major conditions involved, possession and oppression, both of which exist on a continuum of relatively minor to severe and disabling effects. In the former the possessed person's body is under the control of a spirit entity. These spirits hate their hosts and take pleasure in torturing them. Oppressions can be divided into internal and external. In either case evil spirits sow division and discord. In the former the victim receives messages not by sound or voices but by the strong sense of receiving a comprehensible message which feels like an assault leaving the subject disturbed and disconcerted. Oppression comes about by a person delving into iniquitous or occult practices, and their symptoms are usually less intense than those of a possessed person.

These spirits lie about themselves, masking their true nature, feigning to be dead people, angels, or pagan deities. The object is to create turmoil and attack true faith. They have different personalities and degrees of intelligence too, demanding different approaches to an exorcism. They can also take possession of physical places called infestations.

Gallagher emphasizes the need for careful discernment in making a diagnosis which requires the definition of a constellation of symptoms, a multidisciplinary approach involving medical, historical, and spiritual insight and knowledge.

In the study of this phenomenon he emphasizes my thesis in chapter 1 that reason and faith can be complementary and do not necessarily contradict one another. Faith, on the one hand, cannot be reduced to a world outside reason. Nor can science, on the other, dictate every answer and rule out religious questions from the start as unanswerable.

He concludes his investigation with the important question of why evil exists. These possessing spirits hate God and so hate humanity. They want to corrupt people and work to defile in us the image of God in which we are made. Secondly, love without freedom and good without the possibility of evil would deprive both love and goodness of any meaning. These spirits have greater power and intelligence than we do so only divine power acting through effective exorcists can overcome them.

Gallagher's scientific investigation demonstrates that the realm of the spirit and the existence there of malevolent entities is actual and that the demonic is not some ancient outlook explaining psychological and medical conditions.

Demons and demon possession do not figure at all in the OT. It was under Persian influence that the theology and recognition of their existence grew. Satan, the prosecutor in the divine council, came to be recognized as a fallen angel and demons were under his dominion. Even so they are not a dominion equal to God but are allowed by him to exist. Their final destruction was expected in the messianic age.

Where faith in God falters these demonic powers find an entry. Anger and hostility and turning them inward is also an opportunity for the work of demons. These emotions were pervasive in the Holy Land of the first century. The craving to exorcise the Roman occupation of Jewish society suppressed faith in God to act in his own time and caused the unprecedented prevalent occurrence of demon possession. So Jesus' exorcisms were part of his work to save the nation from its destruction and are not to be understood as mere power over demons but a component of Jesus' invasion of the demonic realm by the kingdom of God. So it is little wonder that Satan attacks Jesus in his temptation and seeks to divert him from his messianic task. He tries again with Judas's betrayal but Jesus' obedience to the cross becomes not Jesus' defeat but Satan's.

Jesus' power to exorcise derived from his total dependence on and a pure relationship of trust in God and not his exercise of his divine nature of which he had emptied himself. God, his Father, was the unbounded will to love and so could be unconditionally trusted.

Jesus exorcizes by a word and not by magical formulae. It is clear from the Beelzubul controversy[351] that Jesus understands his exorcisms as the invasion of Satan's kingdom and rule. When he exorcises the demon from the man in the synagogue on the Sabbath he excites both a positive and negative response. The people are amazed at his authority but scribal authorities see him as a threat to the Torah and its authority which was the distinguishing marker of the people separating them from the world. Paradoxically, it is the evil spirit that recognizes Jesus as God's agent as he exercises his high priestly authority. Jesus was shifting the foundations from Torah to kingdom which stood opposed to the prevailing revolutionary mood while at the same time breaking down "the wall of hostility" (Eph 2:14) between Jew and gentile.

Invading the Realm of Demons, Disease, and Death

Jesus in many ways was like a Jeremiah who so many years before suffered under the hostility of the authorities and who encouraged the exiles to "seek the welfare of the city where I have sent you into exile, and pray to the LORD on its behalf, for in its welfare you will find your welfare" (Jer 29:7). It was this attitude that Jesus tried to inspire among his contemporaries. At the same time he recognized the prevailing sense among the people that they were, though in their own land, still in exile because of the disrespect, contempt, and predations that the Romans exercised toward their Jewish subjects. God's kingdom would set things right and he was in the vanguard of its establishment as he exorcized, healed, even raised the dead and sat at table with sinners. It was this kingdom and those who accepted the invitation to enter it that was the most effective antidote to Roman occupation and its depredations.

Jesus, in exorcising the "legion" of evil spirits from the Gerasene demoniac, demonstrates that Rome can be conquered not by force of arms but by the invasion of God's kingdom into Satan's stronghold. Here Jesus reveals himself as the messiah, the beloved son, who is charged by God to proclaim and bring in the kingdom. Cf., particularly Zech 4:6, "This is the word of the LORD to Zerubbabel: 'Not by might, nor by power, but by my Spirit, says the LORD of hosts.'" The prophetic book of Zechariah seems to have played a marked role, at least early on, in Jesus' thought and understanding of the character and goal of his ministry. The Temple cleansing episode, for example, was shaped by Zech 14.[352] The prophecies of Zechariah (chapters 1–8 in which Zech 4:6 is embedded) focuses on the promised restoration after the exile. Joshua, the messianic high priest, and Zerubbabel, the prince-messiah, are prominent figures in these oracles. These two men are not just witnesses but they are signs of the restoration that will take place and the carrying out of God's purposes for his people and for the whole world.[353] A new age will be established when the world will live in peace and prosperity. Zechariah 4:6b–10a concerns the rebuilding of the temple and full restoration effected by God's presence.[354]

So Jesus' encounter with the Geresene demoniac becomes the perfect opportunity for him to demonstrate the heart and core of his message and ministry: Rome will be conquered not by "[human] might or power" but by the "finger of God" (Luke 11:20). The restoration of Israel will be God's doing in his own way and time. The restoration, however, is proleptically present in Jesus' proclamation of the kingdom, in his open commensality, in his exorcisms and healings. To follow him, to sit with him at table, is to participate already in the defeat of Rome and Israel's restoration and the end of exile. The "great mountain" of opposition is laid low before the messiah, the Temple cleansing is the sign that God will accomplish his purpose (Zech 4:7), and the nations shall all do obeisance to the God of Israel (Zech 14:16).[355]

Rome is indeed indicted here for its reprehensible "rape" of Israel, while at the same time it loses its power in the face of Jesus as he plunders Satan's house and the demons perish in the waters. So Israel needs, with full faith in the kingdom, to take leave of revolutionary fantasies of some apocalyptic divine intervention when Israel pursued a "Holy War" with Rome.[356]

The encounter of Jesus with the Syrophoenician woman centers in the verbal exchange between the two. The woman argues that gentiles too have a right to the bread of the kingdom. She is convinced that God's mercy would come to her through Jesus. Her faith in him, to fulfill her entreaty, is all-embracing. Up to now his ministry had been confined to Israel. But she detects a certain ambiguity in him due to his entering a pagan house. So he loses his debate with her. There is no "exorcism" but only the assurance of Jesus that it had taken place. The encounter led him to a re-orientation of his thinking about the kingdom. The gentiles were already forcing their way into the kingdom. This state of affairs combined with the widespread lack of faith he found in Israel led him also to give up the Zecharian eschatology (Zech 14:16–21). As a result he predicts the demise of the temple (Mark 13:2).

The demoniac boy is plagued by a demon who mimics the brain disease of epilepsy. But faith is an overarching concern of the story. Jesus emphasizes it because of the lack of a faith response by so many of his contemporaries. So when he encounters lack of faith here he cannot but make a point of it just as he did in the story of the healing of the official's son.[357] Faith is the crux of his ministry: that Israel would respond with faith and trust demanded by the kingdom and by which alone the people would avoid the calamity of the coming disaster in a vain military encounter with Rome. Jesus stresses total dependence in God rather than illusions about driving Rome from the land in his call to prayer when asked by the disciples why they could not exorcize the demon (although it so that in dreaming of a military solution to Roman occupation the revolutionaries would be thinking of a Holy War by which the defeat of Rome would come by an act of God fighting for them, which is also a dependence on God).[358]

Invading the Realm of Demons, Disease, and Death

The story of the (blind and) dumb demoniac limns Jesus' understanding of his ministry to bring about the conditions of Second Isaiah's prophecy to restore paradisiacal conditions in Israel by the kingdom's restorative power.[359] In these chapters (Isa 40–55) the exiles in Babylon are called to leave there, the land of false gods, and return home. YHWH, who is supreme over the "dumb" gods of Babylon, will glorify Israel in their return. In this way YHWH creates a new exodus and a new Israel.

Moreover, Second Isaiah says, there is YHWH's servant who represents or embodies and recapitulates the new Israel and what Israel is to become: first, like the servant, Israel is to accept the exile as just punishment for her sins and, secondly, to join in the new exodus/conquest.[360] The people are described as blind and deaf (42:18–20). They fail to comprehend what God is doing. The prophet links this with idolatry (40:18–20) to which is juxtaposed the faithfulness of God. His people are "engraved on his hand" (49:16). Tied to the assurances of hope that the prophet gives is the anticipation of a renewal of the Davidic dynasty (55:3).[361] People and king were intimately related and the captivity of both belong together.[362] So the release of Jehoiachin, their king, from his Babylonian prison foreshadowed the release of the people.

The acceptance of the exile as proper punishment for its sins is also an act of discipline. In this acceptance God's will can be carried forward and made effective.[363] The longed for hope seemed to be dying among the people so the prophet declares that God is still at work and the people have a part to play in that redemptive work. There will be a "new creation," a new exodus, and the ransoming of Israel from captivity. The overthrow of the hostile forces in the primeval chaos in the creation is coordinated and recapitulated now in the new creation (43:14–21).

Babylon was the instrument of God's punishment of Israel, but it in turn will be subjected to that same divine judgment. The instrument of that judgment would be Cyrus the Persian (44:28, 45:1). Even though he did not realize it, he was fulfilling the will of God who called him and designated him as his messiah. So God is the sole initiator and mover of events working through means.

The restoration will mean fertility of the land (41:17–20); Israel will be a new people of a reconstituted twelve tribes (49:6); they will be re-established in a new covenant relationship with God; they will grow in numbers in a new Jerusalem (54:11–14).[364] But it is not only Israel that is restored but God's saving power will include the whole world (49:6).

The servant has both a political and religious function: as a leader of the people he is loyal to and a lover of God. His task is to lead the people to do God's will. So he stands on YHWH's side both over against the people and simultaneously represents them to the sovereign God. He embodies the divine plan for all the people. He has submitted to the exile and is preparing to return in the new exodus/conquest. He calls the people to be like himself so he works to prepare the people to join him in becoming once again YHWH's people as they join the new exodus/conquest. Unalloyed happiness awaits them if they respond positively.[365]

Jesus explicitly identifies with the servant and his ministry in Luke 4:18 and 7:18-35,[366] and in this story of the dumb demoniac he explicitly enacts the ministry of the servant as he does in all of his healings. Joy is also prominent in Jesus' understanding of the kingdom[367] which is related to his understanding of the kingdom as the Jubilee.[368] However, we cannot suppose Jesus merely concentrated on individual passages of Second Isaiah. There is evidence that the whole message of Isaiah played an important part in his understanding of his mission and his place in it.

In the exorcisms Jesus meets, confronts, and defeats Satan and his minions whose "fortress" he attacks. The world (and the nation!) had become enemy-occupied territory which by right belonged to God for it was his creation as was his people Israel.[369] But by sin it had fallen under the tyranny of Satan. Jesus has now broken into this fortress and liberated it. There can be no truce or neutrality in this struggle. He who does not side with Jesus sides with Satan (Matt 12:30).

The great and glorious hopes of Second Isaiah, however, were never realized nor fulfilled. It is now that his prophecies take on poignancy, and for Jesus they finally achieve realization in the presence of the kingdom and in his ministry and proclamation. The people indeed thought their subjugation under Rome was an exile though they were in their own land. John the Baptist marked the end of the old and the beginning of the new era as he called on the people to recognize their sins, confess them, and be baptized.[370] Jesus (or his disciples) continued John's ministry of baptism.[371] For Jesus repentance and recognition of one's sins began after one entered the kingdom and fellowship with him. In this way the exile really found its end.

The healing of the blind and deaf were a sign that the new age had arrived; the exile was over. These signs were also a call to the people not to be blind and deaf but hear the call and the invitation and see what God was doing in and through Jesus.[372] Jesus places the revolutionary ideology permeating the society in the context of Second Isaiah's assessment of the great world powers as a "drop in a bucket." Compared to God they are but "dust" on the scales of a balance and as "nothing" (Isa 40:15–17). Just as God wrought the return and restoration of the people in their ancestral land so will he restore Israel in his own time and manner.

The overthrow of Satan is the harbinger of the new creation promised by the kingdom. Rome will suffer the fate of Babylon.[373] The exorcisms break the demonic behavior of violence against Rome and set Israel free from such an oppressive state of mind so that Israel may live "as though" finally home from the exile (1 Cor 7:29–31!). But all of this depends on hearing, believing, and entering the kingdom and finding the joy of the proleptic end of the exile in the presence of the kingdom wrought by Jesus' words and deeds and in his open commensality. "Joy" awaits all those who find the kingdom which is already among them.[374] Jesus identifies with the servant of Second Isaiah who in turn is representative of the people and embodies the nation. This also means that he will take upon himself the shame and suffering of the nation (Isa 52:13–53:12) which so characterizes its situation under Roman hegemony. Although he is accused by his opponents of not following God's will he is actually the loyal, obedient son who only appears as one who seems not to follow his will.[375]

CHAPTER 3

The Miracles of Jesus
The Healings

The Spirit of the Lord God is upon me,
Because the Lord has anointed me
To bring good tidings to the afflicted.

THE HEALINGS BY JESUS RECORDED IN THE GOSPELS

The following fourteen pericopae (excluding the seven that were investigated in my previous book[376]) relate the stories of individuals who are described as being healed of various maladies.

Healings

1. Peter's Mother-in-law's Fever: Mark 1:29–31; Matt 8:14–5; Luke 4:38–39.

2. A Leper: Mark 1:40–45; Matt 8:1–4; Luke 5:12–16.

3. A Paralytic: Mark 2:1–12; Matt 9:1–8; Luke 5:17–26.

4. A Woman with a Hemorrhage: Mark 5:25–34; Matt 9:20–22; Luke 8:43–48.

5. A Man with a Withered Hand: Mark 3:1–6; Matt 12:9–14; Luke 6:6–11.
6. A Stammering Man: Mark 7:32–36.
7. A Blind Man: Mark 8:22–26.
8. Blind Bartimaeus: Mark 10:46–52; Matt 20:29–34; Luke 18:35–43; (Matt 9:27–31 is perhaps a doublet of this story.)
9. A Crippled Woman: Luke 13:10–17.
10. Ten Lepers: Luke 17:11–19.
11. A Man with Dropsy: Luke 14:1–6.
12. An Ill Man by the Pool Bethesda: John 5:1–9.
13. A Man Born Blind: John 9.
14. A Centurion's Servant at the Point of Death: Matt 8:5–13; Luke 7:1–10; John 4:46–54.

MIRACLES

The Development, Historiography, and Study of Miracles

There has been a fundamental shift in the attitude of scholarship toward the factuality of miracles. Although academic attitudes have changed toward the existence of miracles, God's action in history, there still remains a virulent skepticism toward the idea that God is active in the world.[377] The classical Deists could not accept miracles because for them they violated reason.[378] If miracles came into their purview at all they were explained in naturalistic ways. Or, more extremely, they thought of the Gospels as myth dressed up as history.[379]

By the end of the nineteenth century a relativist tendency also gripped historiography which asserted that objective history could not be written because the prejudices, outlooks, and moral positions of the historiographer affected how history was understood and perceived. In other words, because of human subjectivity, merely to observe history is to change it. However, this position was softened by the recognition that the use of the tools of historical research and the recognition and consciousness of the subjective factors at play in the historian's analysis could render reasonable, if not provisional, assertions about what "really happened."[380]

In terms of the investigation of the miracles in the Gospels an inevitable critique of a total abandonment of the transcendent followed in the middle of the twentieth century which demanded some openness to God's action in history. Contributing to his new direction was a growing awareness of Jesus' Jewish context and rootedness in his time and place.

So we are left with a number of different approaches to and interpretations of the miracles:[381] the rational (interpreting them naturalistically); the mythical (the whole report is not historical but told in terms of ancient culture's transcendent proclivities); the inadmissible investigation (miracles are outside the historians purview since there is "no empirical access to it."); the uncertainty of interpretation (the correct interpretation of historical facts cannot be known if you are dealing with an act of God); the irrelevance to faith (no historical proof can justify a religious belief which is a subjective affair); the evidential (belief in miracles is rational and a miracle can be asserted to have taken place if the data point to a strong probability).

The collection of essays in Geivett and Habermas begins with David Hume's case against miracles.[382] Hume's basic argument places human experience of the regularity of nature to question miracles which for him require the suspension and violation of nature's laws. The corollary requires the preponderance of evidence coming from experience and observation as a deciding factor. The character and number of witnesses then enters into the equation, the degree of agreement between the witnesses or their contradictions, the degree of involvement of witnesses in what is reported, and whether their testimony is delivered with either too much tentativeness or forcefulness. No miracle can be assumed to occur, though the event be exceptional and unusual, even though it is only occasionally observable in nature. Hume's definition of a miracle is an occurrence that "has never been observed" so that "[t]here must, therefore, be a uniform experience against every miraculous event..."[383]

He posits four criteria by which to approach the veracity of a reported miracle: the number of witnesses must be of unquestioned integrity; by the assumption that nature works everywhere and always in the same way; by the observation that miracle stories are cultivated among "ignorant and barbarous" people; and finally the awareness that reported miracles are opposed by a large number of counter-witnesses. So working with contemporary knowledge of what is probable or improbable the occurrence of miracles is precluded.[384]

It appears to him, after reviewing a number of reports of miracles in the past, that there is no testimony that amounts to any probability miracles have actually occurred. He concludes, "no human testimony can have such force as to prove a miracle" ... and "that the knavery and folly of men are such common phenomena, that I should rather believe the most extraordinary events to arise from their concurrence, than admit of so signal a violation of the laws of nature."[385] Hume concludes that the occurrence of miracles cannot be proved and so cannot be the foundation of a "system of religion." So Hume was a son of the Enlightenment, skeptical and focused on this world as a closed system of cause and effect that admitted of no other causes other than imminent ones, i.e., he was a secular humanist and an advocate of "metaphysical naturalism" (there is nothing outside the physical universe).[386]

For the metaphysical naturalist the material universe was never created but always existed (which is contradicted by the fact that evidence shows that the universe did indeed have a beginning and did not always exist). However, some representatives of this persuasion hold that the universe had a beginning, but there was no cause for its springing into existence. So miracles are impossible. In this view all things and events are interlocked, and no events or thing can claim independence from this "total event" of the universe (= "nature"). So human beings do not have free will; consequently, spontaneity is a phenomenon reserved for nature.[387] In this system there is no God. Everything human—memories, hopes, plans, intentions, thoughts, beliefs, and logical inference—are all caused by something material. All the events in nature are explicable in terms of nature itself, i.e., this system of thought is deterministic: every event is physically necessary and determined by processes within the universe (which is contradicted by the fact that there is at the atomic and subatomic level an indeterminism).[388]

For Hume, when he defines a miracle as "something that has never been observed," he assumes what he wishes to prove so he begs the question. It is also not a useful definition because it would include any unique event that has not yet happened in his day such as landing a man on the moon.[389] So he makes it a matter of past experience and not whether natural law allows for a particular occurrence. Furthermore, Hume's definition asserts that there is no amount of evidence that would be sufficient to confirm that a miracle has occurred. Of course, that is precisely what he wants to affirm: miracles do not exist nor are they possible; they are excluded by the laws of nature. This is congruent with his "metaphysical naturalism" (everything in the universe can be accounted for by physical cause and effect so that there is nothing outside or beyond this physical universe. These natural laws and forces do not allow for any exceptions). Of course, to assert that there is nothing beyond nature is not a scientific statement but a philosophical one.[390]

However, the universe, as I have explicated in chapter 1, witnesses to the existence of God and that the universe has a designer and creator whose design includes the natural order of things (Gen 1: 21; 24–25). Such order does not exclude his interest in and his interaction with his creation. So we can expect miracles to happen, i.e., "an event in which God temporarily makes an exception to the natural order of things, to show that God is acting."[391] Paradoxically, we would have to say that this definition makes the creation of the universe also a miracle because it is quite out of the order of natural occurrences! Given that, we would think that miracles are to be expected and part of the "natural order" of things. So in this view of reality the scientist is free to continue his experiments and the Christian to continue to pray.[392]

Our contemporary culture is imbued with Hume's understanding of the universe and anti-supernaturalism. Even believers would think most immediately of natural cause and effect before they would attribute an event to the working of God in the world. In this materialist spirit our culture finds miracles to be simply incredible and that thoughtful people find belief in them therefore to be irrational. So critical historians find historical reports of them to be scientifically impossible as unrepeatable so, it is argued, the evidence against them is greater than the evidence for them.

This Humean uniformitarian approach to miracles, however, does not have access to all of human experience. Of course human experience also includes claims of person who have experienced miracles. So what you have here is a circular argument: we know the experience against them is uniform only if we know reports of them are false, and we know them to be false only if we already know they have never occurred. Furthermore, a rational evaluation of an event cannot be determined by a majority vote. Facts are not based on odds.[393] If we accept the assumption that the repeatable outweighs the unrepeatable then we should not believe in the historicity of unusual events of the past, since they are not repeatable.[394] Thus to disallow miracles in advance of considering the evidence for their occurrence is not scientific or rational. In this way our contemporary naturalistic way of thinking is neither logical nor reasonable.

Critique of the "Metaphysical Naturalist" Understanding of History

In spite of the logical fallacies which argue against the historicity of miracles historians are reluctant to deal with them like any other event of the past for two reasons: the agent of miracles is "non-empirical" (i.e., God or some other spiritual being), and historians don't have the implements to detect such an agent; historians are limited by their subjectivity which inhibits their ability to render a reliably objective account of the past.[395] Many a historian claims that there are no historically objective facts but only subjective interpretations of events limited by the historian's own historical location in time and space and their beliefs and worldview. Neither of these arguments are trenchant. Historians can examine the context in which an alleged miracle occurs without considering its agency. Historians implicitly reject the second objection because they would not want to give up the possibility of disproving the occurrence of miracles on historical grounds. Historians can also investigate claims that a miracle has taken place. The argument that claims a disqualifying objectivity to historical investigation is self-refuting: the claim then itself is relative and if relative objectivity is possible and cannot eliminate the possibility of describing objective facts of history. And, of course, all historical writing is subject to critical analysis and correction as well as agreement on some basic facts of history.

Just as physical laws are based on repeated regularities observed in the natural world so historical fact is based on trustworthy multiple witnesses and attestation, document analysis, and the connection between data in a simple and coherent way.[396] One of the principles of historiography is continuity between the past and the present. So, if miracles can definitely be corroborated as occurring now then such occurrences in the past are also to be expected. So the historical investigation of miracles in the past is justified as part of the historian's task.[397]

So, how to gauge when a miracle has happened? One criteria is to ask if the occurrence is best explained as a direct act of God and what the outcome would have been had he not acted. However, when someone claims that God has acted by natural means to bring about a result such as being accepted for a position in a certain job the skeptic would say natural causes and effects, though unusual, can never be ruled out. So when an occurrence can be explained on a natural basis, claiming a miracle is not justified. But there are two situations in which a miracle might be said to have occurred. The "constellation miracle," in which a number of natural things happening but their likelihood of all happening in conjunction with one another, is highly improbable. The "violation miracle" in which an event apparently has contravened a natural law.[398] Both these types have in common the coming together of two unusual features whose atypical quality point to divine activity and most plausibly explains the occurrence.

Hypothesizing an event as a miracle means the facts have to be accurate and plausible, taking into consideration the total circumstances and consistency with the worldview of the theorist. For example, when interpreting and denying the miraculous nature of an event, one has to indulge in a series of mental gymnastics to explain it exclusively in terms of the laws of nature such a process, especially if it appeals to some yet to be discovered law of nature, the denial becomes implausible.[399]

In all of this discussion it is clear that our view of the world and reality affects how we interpret our experiences. If one's worldview is not realistic and inaccurate the sense that such a person would make of life and the world would be wrong. A worldview involves five constellations of beliefs: beliefs about God, ultimate reality, knowledge, morality, and human nature.[400] The Christian worldview is theistic: there is a God, eternal, transcendent, non-material, omnipotent, omniscient, loving, and personal, who, out of free choice, designed and created the universe out of nothing which, again according to his design, operates in an orderly fashion; God is Trinitarian—Father, Son, and Holy Spirit; the second person of this Trinity, the Son, became incarnate, taking upon himself our humanity and whose sacrificial death reconciles humanity to God; this Triune God reveals himself to the world.[401]

God is also the ground of moral life, and in obeying that moral order we create the possibility of order between people. This worldview includes that idea that knowledge is attainable by the human mind so that Christianity is not skeptical. We bear the image of God and therefore are capable of rational thought. If not, our so-called knowledge is merely the way our minds have organized our perceptions, and we then have no knowledge. Consequently, there would be no validity to human reasoning and no true science.[402] "Human reason requires something that exceeds the bounds of nature, namely, the laws of logical inference."[403] If this is not so and our human faculties are the result of a purposeless evolution and chance variations then they cannot be reliable guides to any truth but only what can be inferred from their own structure. But if our cognitive faculties are trustworthy then we must conclude they are the result of the work of a purposeful and intelligent agent. Furthermore, if human reason is not valid then no criticism of Christian theism by a metaphysical naturalist would be valid. So the only way the naturalist can provide rational grounds for believing in naturalism is to abandon being a naturalist.

Though we are moral creatures, sin has distorted this image, and we turn from God, are alienated from him, and are capable of evil thoughts, words, and deeds. Therefore, humanity faces judgment if one is not living in reconciliation with God. So we are fundamentally spiritual creatures, and the solution to the disorder of our world is spiritual.

Most opposition to the possibility of miracles is based on naturalistic thinking. Miracles are *a priori* declared to be impossible and lie outside the limits of science. That judgment is based on the worldview of metaphysical naturalism. It insists that science must follow methodological naturalism. In this way science and theology are at best complementary to the same reality but "focus on different levels of description."[404] Moreland's concept of complementarity has it rejecting interaction between science and theology, that is, an interaction that has "roughly the same description of the same reality that can be in conflict or in harmony to varying degrees of strength."[405] The complementarian view can thus reduce the psychological to physically sufficient causes. So it rejects libertarian freedom and agency.

A view that is more in keeping with the reality of both science and theology is the understanding that the relationship of God to the universe, his creation, is one of constant activity in sustaining it, and while for the most part supporting the order which he has created, he also is involved in new acts of creation, or "miracles." So there is an analogy between human and divine acts. When human actions are based on personal reasons they are free and so have a teleological goal or end purpose.[406] Persons are agents and have the power to act as the ultimate originators of their actions. So the laws of nature govern event-event causality whereas the free acts of a person (and by analogy, God) produce "libertarian acts." Thus so-called miracles can be treated not only by a theological examination but also scientifically and "leave *scientifically detectable gaps* in the natural world."[407] Libertarian acts leave gaps in the fabric of natural causation.

Understanding the Literary Nature of the Miracle Stories and their Function within the Community in Which They Arose

Form critics work at understanding the miracle stories as literary productions. Form critical analysis works at distinguishing the situation in life in which a given tradition is passed on. This situation determines its function. For example the context of its transmission may be within a liturgy, the mission concerns of the community, or a part of the catechesis of the community. Involved in this determination is an analysis of the cultural influences, historical development, and social conditions of the community.[408] This process can be further developed by a structural analysis by classifying the subunits of miracle stories by listing their literary elements such as persons, motifs, and themes and then examining the connections between these elements. The "structure" then consists of the relationships between these sub-units.

Characters appear in the role of companion of the person with a malady, the vicarious petitioner, or in the case where the ill person is not present the companion becomes the "opposite" of the miracle worker. The elements of a story usually are arranged in a particular order although it can be varied by the art of the narrator.

Motifs are recurring stereotypical narrative features such as cries for help, prostrating oneself, the exhibition of faith or doubt, acclamation, and rejection.[409] Themes give internal shape to a narrative, to the behavior of characters, and the motifs.[410] For example, an ill person is healed or a person is rescued from a threatening situation. So themes organize the various elements into a compositional whole.

By the lights of this analysis, to fully understand miracle stories they must be set within the historical context in which they arose and how they functioned there. This so-called "functionalism" understands texts as a form of (symbolic) human action and seeks to comprehend them by investigating their social function within the Christian community and their religious-historical and existential function within the ancient world.[411]

The sociology of literature examines the human actions between the tradents of the tradition and their hearers which are preserved in the texts. This interaction can involve various forms such as instruction, entertainment, or persuasion. These three forms of communication constitute the "situation in life" of a text. Factors that influence these forms are the social-ecological environment (urban, rural), social-economic location (social strata), and social-cultural factors (norms and values of those involved).[412]

This form of analysis also investigates the conditions and intentions of texts which follow either of two functionalist models, the integration or conflict model. According to the former the purpose of religious acts is to integrate the individual into the community. The latter model recognizes that there is often conflict within the group. So attempts at integration means there is conflict, and conflicts represent the failure of integration.[413]

So the sociology of literature understands miracle stories as symbolic and as a way for a group to transform social reality into a symbolic world of meaning in which its members can feel at home. This interpretive model then understands the miracle stories as a way for early Christians to contend with existential problems, such as how a person is to cope with life and to deal with and change one's life situation. This happens not only by actions but by reframing one's experience. Experience is transformed by transcending it by symbolic actions in order to find meaning. "The existential function of texts consists in the symbolic mastering of reality."[414] In this interpretation Christian miracle stories witness to a revelation: Jesus, the "Holy One of God" (Mark 1:24), can transform disease and distress and free one from distress.

Theissen then goes completely astray as he rejects the possibility of divine action within our spatial-temporal universe, an untenable position in the face of the discussion in chapter 1 and the further contemporary evidence presented below. He asserts and appeals to Bultmann along the way, quoting his conclusion:

> Today we can no longer regard miracle stories as evidence of divine intervention in the normal course of things. "Diseases and their cures have their natural causes, and do not depend on the action of evil spirits or on their casting out. This puts an end to the New Testament miracles as miracles." Of course there were miraculous phenomena, unlikely cures, and wonder-working charismatics, but it was only symbolic intensifications which transformed these miraculous phenomena into the paradoxical action of divine beings . . . [For the New Testament "e]mpirical"

reality is always seen as containing more than ordinary events. It becomes transparent, revealing the holy. On this interpretation miracle stories are neither mere projections of non-intentional factors nor reflection of divine intervention. They are symbolic actions of human subjectivity in which a revelation of the holy is given shape and "empirical" reality transcended."[415]

The Social Milieu of the Miracle Stories

Theissen traces the belief in miracles back first to social conditions. The ancient Graeco-Roman world was rife with miracle-working activity. There were soothsayers, magicians, oracles, and healing sanctuaries. Obvious is that this Graeco-Roman world recognized the existence of the world of the spirit. So the difference between paganism and Christianity was the nature of that world not the existence of that world. These various forms of achieving desired results of healing were dependent on easily acquired skills and learning the correct formulas and rituals from adepts and practitioners. These healing and magical practices could also be used for nefarious ends, whereas oracles and sanctuaries fulfilled exclusively positive ends. Magicians and soothsayers fall in between these two extremes. So there were six forms of miracle activity: soothsaying, oracles, prophets (forms of divination), magic, healing sanctuaries, and charismatic miracle workers.[416] These activities can serve to integrate (help society to function within accepted norms) or produce conflict (different interpretations given to extraordinary events).

It was the lower classes that sought healing in the sanctuaries of Epidaurus, Canopus, Serapis, and Aesculapius. These sanctuaries were visited largely by the poor due to the fact that the wealthy could afford doctors. However, they also eventually came to be used by the well-to-do. The poor were left to their fate and so in danger then, if they did not quickly recover, of simply working until they died. The healing sanctuaries then functioned to integrate all social classes, but especially the poor, back into society.[417] There was a special affinity between the poor and the god of healing, Asclepius.[418]

The performance of magic was an individualistic affair characterized by its lack of relatedness to a community and its norms. Three main characteristics of magic are its syncretism, individualism, and optimism.[419] In the magical papyri[420] every name for the one God is employed making

Invading the Realm of Demons, Disease, and Death

possible indiscriminately all avenues to power. National religious ideas are individualized but serve the ends of the performer, and so magic had a marked anti-social character. It was used in four ways: to attack and inflict harm, to defend and protect, acquire love and power, and procure knowledge and revelation.[421] So there were attempts to criminalize such behavior. (Magic was also proscribed by the Torah, Deut 18:9–11.) Its optimism in the face of the contemporary expectation of the collapse of the universe was expressed in its conviction that there was power available to people to overcome the vicissitudes of the world. But it also was a subversive art and a sign of social disintegration. It attracted marginalized people and as a survival technique provided powerful weapons to struggle with the politically powerful elite.[422] Knowledge of the future was important to those who lived lives on the edge such as soldiers and gladiators.

There were several levels of magic: *goetia* (the summoning of demons) and *theourgia* (seeking union with the divine). The latter was favored by the elites and involved verbal invocation in contrast to using material objects. However, the inner structure of both were the same.[423] It was under pressure of troubling social, economic, and political conditions that led to embracing these practices. So taking recourse into this occult realm was not religious but a result of the breakdown of the social order. The magician remains in the dark as opposed to the charismatic miracle worker who initiates social movements and founded schools of followers seeking new patterns of social life. In this way they came into conflict with the existing social order.[424] So the power of miracle working legitimated the miracle worker and motivated his followers.

In my description of the prophetic movements in first-century Israel it is clear they all had a typological link with Israel's history: the temple, the conquest of the land, the exodus (cf., the reference in the previous endnote), and that the miracle itself would be executed by God. All of these signs promised by these prophets had to do with the liberation of Israel from Roman occupation (the promised divine miracles, of course, never occurred). The procurators themselves perceived this because of the large numbers of people who joined the prophets so they moved quickly to crush these movements.

Ecological Location of the Miracle Stories

Most of the miracle stories are set in the Galilee and continued to be transmitted there. The gospels do not always specify the place, implying that these stories were told somewhere in the land of Israel and need not be localized only in the Galilee. Jesus is also portrayed as not active in large cities and villages but, for example, that he was in "the region" of Tyre and Sidon" but did not enter those cities (Mark 7:24). Furthermore, the miracle stories themselves are set in the context of the open country outside of settled communities.[425] In conclusion, it can be said that the miracle stories acquired their character in a rural environment and were transmitted there. Theissen thinks Mark perhaps heard them in specific locations and so identified that location for them in his Gospel. I would suggest that members of his community came from these places and so told them in terms of that location.[426]

Socioeconomic Factors

The movement begun by Jesus was largely focused on the peasants but not exclusively (cf., Luke 8:3 where Johanna the wife of the Herodian official Chuza is cited as providing support for Jesus. (Tax collectors, though shunned by polite society, were well-to-do.) Mark's summaries refer to the "crowds" that followed him, which were made up of the lower class. The miracle stories themselves refer to diseases, hunger, impoverishment, and danger, whose conditions do not strike so heavily on the elites.[427]

It seems that demon possession had surged over the land of Israel in Jesus' time. This was partly due to the Roman occupation (or one could say "possession"!). One of the aspects of demon possession is anger turned inward leading to depression and the openness to the hostile forces of evil. Anger was rampant in the society of the time because of the degrading aspects of the Roman occupation such as the building of pagan temples in the land and the constant disrespectful and contemptible actions of many of the procurators.[428]

Miracles too were, like exorcisms, class-specific. Theissen refers to the story of the woman with an issue of blood (Mark 5:25–34) who had spent all she had with doctors who couldn't heal her. So illness was a grave economic threat and could lead to destitution because one could not work.[429] Theissen is certainly correct as far as he goes in seeing how these stories functioned within the church. They assured ill people that they would not be abandoned but cared for. So the church met not only physical problems but the economic and social ones too. In this way the miracle stories are to be understood, but not merely, in terms of "collective symbolic actions by which distress was remedied" and led to combating illness with real action.[430] So the miracle stories also provide us with a window into their social setting: they express the hopes of those whose social position and economic poverty left them no alternative. For Theissen this observation may exhaust their historical location. However, as a fact of the life of Jesus and his ministry, they illuminate the character of how Jesus understood his kingdom proclamation as he enunciated it with his quotation of Isa 61:1–2 in Luke 4:18.

Sociocultural Factors

The stories of the Syrophoenician woman and the centurion from Capernaum[431] indicate the boundaries between Jews and gentiles and the tensions between them. The gentiles in these stories appear in an ambivalent position; the woman is worthless and the centurion a model. But these stories overcome and transcend the boundaries.

Theissen also finds that the use of foreign words in miracle stories witnesses to ethnic conflict as in the story of the Geresene demoniac who declared the name of the demons within him was "Legion."[432] The Roman occupation meant the introduction of foreign gods and the pollution of the Holy Land. But the Aramaic words of Jesus are witness to the superior power of eastern words over against western ones and of Jesus himself. As I've suggested above, political control and oppression can produce demonic possession (a dynamic process indeed and not just a psychological process such as the experience of a profound belief in demons as Theissen would have it.[433]) So the social setting is indeed the tensions between different peoples and their culture, specifically the subjugation of eastern cultures by the west and the promulgation on the part of the east as superior over the west. So charismatic miracle workers and their miracles were a source of legitimation in social conflicts and contributed to the establishment of a new way of life and a new understanding of existence particularly among the lower social groups where traditional ways of life had been abandoned.[434]

Social Intention of Miracle Stories

Miracle stories promise salvation and redemption and are directed outward from the community and so have a missionary intention. The disciples are sent out with a message and the command to heal (Mark 3:15; 6:7-13). Even the mere telling of the occurrence of miracles results in conversions (cf., Acts 9:42; 13:12). The acclamations at the end of miracle stories also point in this direction. Conversions herald the victory of Israel's God and the end of the reign of demons and the pagan gods (Acts 16:16-21), embody the claim of a new way of life, bear witness to a revelation of God, and call on the world to accept that revelation. The situation in life of the miracles, therefore, is the mission of the church. The missionaries were itinerant and miracle workers (2 Cor 12:12). However, miracle workers do not talk about or tell miracle stories; that mission is left to others.[435] These stories do prepare the way for the coming of charismatic missionaries who then perform miracles.

Function of the Miracle Stories

Theissen traces the developments of miracle-working activity in the Graeco-Roman world.[436] In classical Greece and the period of Hellenism medicine and healing was founded on an empirical basis but this scientific mythology increasingly declined during the period of the Roman Empire. The healing centers such as Epidaurus flourished as did divination and oracular activity. Astrology also became popular with the introduction of the Julian calendar in 46 BC. The phenomenon also spread to the upper classes. The first century AD saw the appearance of the charismatic miracle worker, particularly in the east. Apollonius of Tyana and his contemporary Simon Magus in Samaria (Acts 8:9-24) are representatives of this development. In the land of Israel we find the miracle-working Hanina ben Dosa and Eliezer ben Hyrcanus, later contemporaries of Jesus. Miracles, beyond the ones recorded in Exodus, were also attributed to Moses.

Exorcisms must be differentiated from the miracle-working tradition. Exorcism was not charismatic activity but activity based on methods. Matthew 12:27 indicates that the disciples of the Pharisees were exorcists. As regards miracle activity books were studied (Jub 10:12-13) which, it was asserted, were written by Noah after his enlightenment by angels. The end of the first century BC saw a growth of belief in miracles and by the beginning in the third century AD there was a continual increase in the telling of miracle stories in Judaism. The spread of the Roman Empire may have had something to do with this expansion. Part of that expansion meant the concentration of power in Rome and the decline of individual initiative indicating that belief in the miraculous was adopted by subjugated people.[437] So Christianity did not grow up in a culture pervaded with the belief in miracles but rather the intensification of belief in miracles by the end of the first century AD, an intensification catalyzed by Christianity itself.

Historical Intention of the Miracle Stories

Jesus uniquely combined eschatology and his miracle working: he understood the coming kingdom of God and universal salvation as already present in his miracle working. Of course, the kingdom was also seen as present in his meals, his proclamation of the kingdom, and in his mere presence. So his miracles were only one aspect of the "now" of the kingdom's presence.[438] That the miracles functioned within that eschatological horizon made them unique among all the other miracle working of that age.[439] The exorcisms (see chapter 2) are signs of the collapsing of Satan's rule (Luke 10:18; Mark 3:24–26; Matt 12:28). Because the rule of the realm of evil had been broken salvation can come even now to individuals who are held in the bond of sickness, disease, and physical maladies.

However, this eschatological context and interpretation of the miracles is found basically only in the sayings tradition and not in the miracle stories themselves. One exception is Matt 8:29 (however Matthew has added "before the time" to Mark's account in Mark 5:7). Theissen claims that the eschatology has been written out of the miracle stories. That may be so but they were told within the context of a community that was immersed in eschatological expectations and so would have been understood in terms of those expectations. So it has nothing to do with a heightening and enhancing the miracle itself or the figure of Jesus. They are told in a rather sober, conservative, and even terse manner without embellishments.

The Existential Function of the Miracle Stories

Theissen would find miracles as symbolic actions reaching back to the experiences of childhood when adults "magically" conjure up food, giving rise to the idea that the child, as weak as it is, can bring about the satisfaction of its desire by omniscient adults. So miracles are an expression of the human race in its childhood, but adult experience reformulates those childhood experiences. Miracles then become "historical embodiments of wishes in symbolic actions."[440] For Theissen these stories open up a new understanding of human existence and symbolically transform and master reality by transcending the limits of life in the world. The message of the miracle stories is to attest to a revelation of the holy and its power to break into the normal nexus of temporal existence.[441] So he criticizes modern interpreters who see them as "faith's illegitimate child" and primitive. For him these "deeds of power" are signs and, like a parable, convey "the gospel as a whole" but still are "alien visitors in our world." So their "existential meaning" amounts to the miracle stories being symbolic actions which overcomes the negative in human experience by a revelation of the sacred and the shaping and transformation of human desires.[442] They are a protest against the adverse in human experience.

Reflection and Analysis

Theissen's study has provided us with an excellent overview of the environment of the ancient world in which the miracle stories of the Gospels are embedded as well as the various analytical approaches to interpreting them. He seems to understand them as basically reflective of wish-fulfillment but still wants to save them and find a positive understanding for them. In the process, however, he has to jump through so many hoops and push the reader through many a mentally torturous twist and turn in order to achieve his ends. So much of his argument seems ambiguous. He wants to remain a modern and question their historicity but at the same time, though they are but "symbolic actions," to preserve their usefulness as part of theology and find a function for them in the proclamation of the gospel. So they convey the gospel but are also alien to our world.

Applying Occam's razor here, the simplest explanation for the miracles is that they actually occurred as they are recorded in the gospels. No mental gymnastics are then required à la Theissen in order to find meaning in them. Of course, I'm not just making a bald assertion here.

Chapter 1 provides the factual and scientific underpinning that not only suggests but demands that because the world of the spirit exists, that God is the designer of our universe, and the undeniable evidence that he is still active in it. So miracles have occurred and still occur. The following will corroborate this contention.

CONTEMPORARY MIRACLES

Moreland in his study and reporting[443] has provided a thoroughly researched investigation of contemporary miracles. He defines a miracle as "an event or intervention that is caused by the special action of God or some other supernatural being that is an exception to the ordinary, law-governed course of nature for some specific purpose."[444] He explicates questions related to such occurrences: what it means to know something, how to actually know that a miracle has occurred, and how to discern the difference between coincidences and a genuine miracle. He points out that one can know something even without knowing how one knows. There are two factors involved in determining if an event was brought about intentionally for a purpose and by an intelligent agent: it was unlikely to happen and it can be identified as a special occurrence.[445] So small probability plus independent uniqueness means an event was done on purpose by an intelligent agent. He calls this "IAP" (the "intelligent agent principle").[446] So if an event occurs that satisfies the IAP it is a miracle, and that distinguishes it from what is mere coincidence. If an occurrence satisfies the IAP there is solid basis for claiming an event is a miracle.

The miracles recorded in the NT demand, according to critics, extraordinary evidence to establish their veracity. The basis for even entertaining the possibility of these miracles rests on the existence of the world of the spirit and God's existence. I have shown in chapter 1 how the sciences all support and point to the existence of the world of the spirit and of an intelligent designer of the universe and of human beings. The real motivation for critics and atheists is that they don't want God to exist and don't want a universe that subsists in him.[447] I agree with Moreland's approach: not to show that miracles prove the existence of God but the reverse: because God exists, it follows that just as he created the universe and human beings he, along with us, would still be active in the world and effect what we call "miracles." So then we would not expect these miraculous actions of God to be a seldom affair but rather a regular part of human existence. Moreland testifies,

> Over the years I have interviewed around one hundred church leaders and countless Christians to find out whether they have experienced a miracle or know firsthand from credible testimony about a miracle. The numbers are staggering. So many individuals have experienced stunning answers to prayer, undergone miraculous healing, heard specific words form God that later came true, or had encounters with angels or demons that were clearly real, given the evidence.[448]

Moreland then faces the question of witness reliability. A strong case can be made for reliability if the following six criteria are met:[449] 1. How well the witness could perceive the event; 2. How well the witness was capable of remembering; 3. The influence of bias or prejudice on the witness; 4. The reasonableness of the testimony in the context of other evidence; 5. Does the witness's character suggest the truthfulness of the report; 6. Is the witness known to be a person of integrity and known to behave in such a way as to make his testimony believable. He applies these criteria to all of the eyewitness accounts of miraculous answers to prayer which he cites and to cases of miraculous healings.[450] I want to quote one of the miracles he records as an example of the many which he recounts:

> In 2006 I spoke at a Christian education conference. During lunch the first day, I spoke with an American teacher who taught in Brazil with the Association of Christian Schools International. He told me that two of his missionary friends had recently been called into a village to pray for a desperately sick little boy with a softball-sized hernia protruding from his abdomen. They laid hands on the boy and prayed, and before their very eyes, the hernia disappeared and the boy was healed.[451]

You will notice that this report conforms to the six criteria that Moreland has established to assess the reliability and truth of miracle accounts. So he proceeds in a scientific way that can leave little room for doubting the veracity of the events which he recounts.[452] Miracles happen and they are real, they have occurred throughout the history of Christianity, and they obviously, relying only on Moreland's reports, occur frequently in our contemporary world. Metaphysical naturalism is found to be totally inadequate to explain what scientific investigation itself has uncovered about the reality of the universe in which we live.

An example of a miracle from another source: Michael Evans, the founder of an organization called "The Friends of Zion" retells his experience of a miracle because of his prayer.[453] In 1978 he and a group of friends were in the Sinai following the route of Israel on its way out of slavery in Egypt to the Promised Land. As they made their way across the desert they encountered a Bedouin and stopped to visit. They were offered food and drink. When a woman of the family found out there was a doctor in Michael's group she brought her six-year-old daughter out of the tent who had a vile infection on her head that was almost invisible because of the flies which buzzed around her. After the doctor examined her he announced she needed surgery, and he could do nothing there in the wilderness. Michael was moved by her dire need and spontaneously placed his hand on her head imploring God to heal her. The next morning when they awakened the doctor said he would try to set up a makeshift operating room. He was so fearful the girl would not survive. He entered the tent where the girl was and Michael heard him weeping. Michael describes his experience:

> I was afraid he was mourning the death of the little girl. I walked over and stooped down to look inside. I saw him rejoicing with the family. He said, "This is the greatest physical miracle I have even seen!" The girl was lying on a pile of rugs, totally healed! There was no trace of the infection, and the injury was gone.

So as I proceed below to investigate the miracle reports attributed to Jesus in the Gospels I must ask if these reports meet the criteria that Moreland has established to determine the reliability of an account which claims to be a miracle. The accounts themselves report that Jesus was always surrounded by a crowd. That means within the Evangelists' communities there were multiple people who observed these occurrences and consequently would have corrected and refined the reports that circulated within these communities. The reports themselves give evidence of such critical refinement. They are terse, unadorned, and not embellished. They do not aggrandize either the miracle worker or the miracle itself. The culture of the day was an oral culture and inured to memorization. The reports themselves often include the amazed reaction of the bystanders which implies that there would have been a measure of skepticism regarding these reported occurrences. Jewish society was very wary of magicians as potential perverters of Israel's faith[454] which would lead Jewish people to reject these occurrences if they were interpreted as magic. Of course, some would have interpreted them in this way (cf., Mark 3:6). The issue of the character of the witness(es), because these stories were told within a community, has to devolve on the character of the community itself. These early Christian communities would have been bound by demanding two or three witnesses to corroborate truth.[455] Jesus is everywhere characterized by miracle working (Acts 2:22; John 3:2), so it is not unreasonable to accept the reported occurrences as actual events. The word "truth" occurs eighty-eight times in the NT. To tell the truth was fundamental to early Christianity. Christianity rose and fell on whether the gospel was true or not. This was in keeping with the historical veracity demanded by biblical faith. It was not confined to a corner (Acts 26:26) but its very life depended on openness, telling the truth, and the truth of its assertions and claims. So the miracle stories in the Gospels have a robust claim to historical reliability.[456]

JESUS' MIRACLES OF HEALING

The Healing of Peter's Mother-in-Law's Fever: Mark 1:29–31; Matt 8:14–5; Luke 4:38–39

The whole section here (1:21–38) looks like a unity that was handed down to Mark in just this form and suggests that an eyewitness had recounted a day in the life of Jesus and his disciples. A visitor today to the ruins of Capernaum has a vivid experience of the physical context for stories in this section: the synagogue, next door to it a tenement building (one of whose apartments could well have been where Jesus took up his residence), and next to it the foundation of Peter's house.[457] Taylor suggests the section was a reminiscence of Peter and is easily translated into the first-person singular.[458] In Luke's rendition of the story Jesus "rebukes" the fever reflecting the idea that illnesses are due to personal forces and so it is possible that he understood the fever as a result of demon possession. Or it could be reflective of the old belief that God is behind all the exigencies of life. Indeed, in the OT it is God who "creates weal and woe."[459] That is why the healing stories often read like exorcisms.[460]

Jesus is bringing the rule of God which has to do with restoration and healing (Isa 35:5–6). Usually Jesus speaks a word of healing, but here there is only an action: he raises Peter's mother-in-law, taking her by the hand. The cure is performed with ease without any special manipulative techniques. The "lifting up" is the usual expression used in the rabbinic literature meaning to "cure" or heal."[461] That the woman is then described as "serving them" functions to demonstrate that her cure was complete and accomplished with miraculous swiftness. This is no gradual recovery. Serving is the characteristic of women's form of discipleship. The rabbis, on the other hand, disapproved of women serving at the table.[462] Here Jesus' open commensality is already portrayed in a veiled manner. So Jesus concludes, at the end of his first day in Capernaum, with table fellowship with the disciples he had just recently won as companions in his ministry.[463]

The details in the story which enliven its character are omitted by Matt and Luke. The word for fever here (πυρέσσω, *pyressō*, "have a fever") is a rare word (Luke doesn't use the word but refers to her as "having a high" or "great fever" (πυρετὸς μέγαλος, *pyretos megalos*, the language of physicians).[464]

All of this points to a plain retelling of an actual event in the life of Jesus and his ability to heal. It portrays in a nutshell characteristics of his developing ministry of proleptically establishing the kingdom of God including his table fellowship, his assembling of a close band of disciples, and the inclusion of women in his ministry. This little healing story probably was the first of Jesus' healings (when he moved from Nazareth to Capernaum, Matt 4:13), and by it he became aware of the divine gift of healing power within himself.

Critics, as I've elaborated above, insist that the miracles recorded in the Gospels demand extraordinary evidence to verify their historicity. In chapter 1 I've summarized the scientific evidence for an intelligent designer of the universe and of human beings. Since God exists it follows that it would be quite surprising if he were not active in the world and effects what we call miracles (the universe itself is a miracle). So the burden of proof for the Gospel miracles not being historical rests on those who represent this point of view.

Applying Moreland's criteria to this cure it is clear that there were four reliable witnesses present (Peter and his brother Andrew and the two brothers James and John) who would have had no trouble recalling this uncomplicated event. The disciples in general would unlikely to be prejudicial in their witness as Peter's mother-in-law was up and about "serving them." Jesus' healing fits well into the pattern of his healing activity and he sent these same disciples out to do the same (Mark 3:14–15; 6:7, 30). If the disciples were effective in healing it is hardly likely they would need to make up stories about Jesus' healing activities (see Acts 3:1-9).

The Healing of a Leper: Mark 1:40-45; Matt 8:1-4; Luke 5:12-16.

Leprosy[465] was not just a severe and disabling disease; it also rendered a person ritually unclean and demanded that the person live outside the community. So the leper was both socially and religiously isolated. If cured the leper had to be declared clean by a priest.[466] The rabbis held that the cure of leprosy was as difficult as raising the dead.[467] Jesus in Matt 11:5, Luke 7:22 adds the cleansing of leprosy to the list of signs of the coming of the kingdom in quoting Isa 35:5-8.[468] That Jesus "touched" the man would have rendered Jesus himself unclean. This touch conveyed his compassion for the man, his reintegration into society, his acceptance into the kingdom, and the forgiveness of sin (sin being often seen as the cause of disease).

There are some textual anomalies in the pericope, the most pointed of which is the substitution by Codex Bezae of "with anger" for "moved with compassion" in vs 41. This reading would comport better with Jesus expressing "indignant displeasure" with the man in vs 43 and with the fact that Jesus "casts him out" (an expression used for exorcism). The RSV tones down the harshness of the verse by rendering it with "... he sternly charged him, and sent him away at once."[469] Jesus' strong reaction may have been originally against the leprous spirit which had afflicted the man whom he "casts out" (associating disease with demon possession).[470] This strong reaction on Jesus' part (eliminated by both Matt and Luke) with its negative associations points to an accurate historical report. Then in the present form of the story his strong reaction came to be applied to the leper himself. At any rate, a cleansing of leprosy is here performed, an event as "difficult as raising the dead"! For Jesus purity and impurity are not decisive rather the person hence Jesus' compassion for the plight of the man. So he differed from the Pharisees and Essenes: what mattered was not purity before God but what purity or impurity effected in the person.[471] The leper assumes that Jesus is able to heal him as the one authorized by God and as God's agent. So he falls on his knees before Jesus. He, like Peter in Luke 5:8, is conscious of the numinous presence in Jesus. In curing him and declaring him clean, Jesus also appears as a

Invading the Realm of Demons, Disease, and Death

priest who alone had the authority to declare someone clean of leprosy even as he is the cause of healing.

Nineham suggests that the anomalies of the story are due to the conflation of two independent reports. One version reported Jesus' indignation to the work of a demon. In the other Jesus was motivated by compassion by the leper's appeal and by his word and touch healed him and then demanded he keep silence about the healing. So in the conflation Jesus' strong emotion was transferred from the evil spirit to the leper.[472] Yet, the story still preserves the rugged form of early testimony especially the feature of anger.

Jesus commands the cleansed man to do what the law required: to show himself to the priest in order to officially verify his having been cleansed and to offer the prescribed sacrifice (Lev 13). That is, Jesus wants him to be fully reintegrated into society. The command to be silent emphasizes that the man is to make the demands of the Torah his first consideration. These commands are by no means universal in the miracle stories which implies that they pertain to particular cases and persons as well as Jesus' own concerns.[473] Jesus is saying that the man should not delay in being declared cleansed of his disease so that his witness will be believable and fully reliable.[474] So the following phrase "as a witness to them" means to his own family and people in general with whom he would come into contact. It might also mean that the witness is made by the priest to the nation that the man is indeed healed and cleansed so that the priest would appear as a witness for the defense of the man's true healing (Deut 31:26; James 5:3). The declaration of being clean would accuse those of bearing false witness who slander Jesus as one who despises the Torah as well as a witness against their unbelief.[475] In this way Jesus would receive an official corroboration of the miracle. As a matter of course, without the official declaration of the man's healing he would not be allowed to reenter society and the life of his village. The prescription of Leviticus has to be fulfilled. Positively, the healing is a witness for the nearness of the kingdom. Indeed, the following verse indicates the man went out and "proclaimed" (Gk., κηρύσσειν, *kērussein*, which is almost a technical term for proclaiming the gospel) that Jesus had healed him, which was in direct contradiction to Jesus' command "to say nothing to no one" (vs 44). The good news of the kingdom can't be held back in spite of Jesus' command. On his side, perhaps Jesus did not want to be known strictly as a miracle worker and consequently to misunderstand him as a wonder-working magician. The context of his healings within the proclamation of the kingdom means that the healings witnessed to the nearness of and the in-breaking of God's rule and action.[476]

That the story in its present form seems to be a combination of two different reports on the same incident suggests two sources which supports the historicity of the event. That Jesus is portrayed as reacting with anger toward the evil spirit which caused the leprosy also supports this conclusion.[477] No one would make up a story that Jesus acted with indignation (or as Haenchen translates, "imperiously"[478]) toward the leper. Jesus' ability to cure leprosy (whatever the nature of the skin disease which plagued the man), underscores the extraordinary power which Jesus exercised, and his profoundly intimate relationship with God as his beloved son.[479]

Jesus' healing activity was performed openly and publicly which implies there were many witnesses to it. That the telling of them as the stories appear in the gospels was not sensationalized but conveyed in a sober and straightforward manner also witnesses to their authenticity.

Excursus
The Beloved Son Determines His Hour:
The So-called "Messianic Secret"

The idea of the "messianic secret" was introduced in 1901 by Wrede in his book, *Das Messiasgeheimnis in den Evangelien* (*The Messianic Secret in the Gospels*).[480] He purports that it was not until after the resurrection that the messianic dignity of Jesus was affirmed by the early church. So the injunctions to silence in Mark were his literary device to account for the non-messianic character of the traditions about Jesus, although he held that Mark did not invent the idea, but it was current in the community to which he belonged. He referred not only to the silence that Jesus demanded in the miracles and after the transfiguration but his withdrawal from the crowds (7:24; 9:30), giving private instruction to the disciples on the "mystery of the kingdom" (4:10–12),[481] his teaching in private about prayer (9:28–29), his suffering (8:31; 9;31, 10:33–34), and the Parousia (13:3–37). So for Wrede, Mark's gospel is saturated with dogmatic ideas and full of contradictions and improbabilities.

It has been argued that Jesus would not have been understood as the Messiah after his resurrection unless he had been so recognized during his ministry. He was tried and executed as a royal pretender. The titulus on the cross also attests to the cause of his execution. So the idea has been widely rejected but still exercises an influence on Marcan studies and Gospel interpretation in general. So the idea is untenable as Wrede propounded it, but it is still historically and theologically important.

It is not an idea imposed on the material, but it is an integral element of Jesus' own understanding of himself as we can recognize in the miracles and their exposition in this study, not only there but throughout the tradition. However, Jesus' self-understanding was expressed more in terms of being the "son of man" and the "beloved son," terms which he filled with ideas related to the restoration of the world as God created it expressed in his healings, exorcisms, victory over Satan and his minions, and his suffering and resurrection. He reserved for himself the time in which he would reveal himself, that is the time when he was ready to take up the cross and "give his life as a ransom for many." This reservation is expressed in John's gospel in other words: "His hour has not yet come" (8:20); "My time has not yet come" (7:6); "I lay [my life] down of myself. I have the power to lay it down and I have power to take it again" (10:17–18).

Jesus reveals his identity as the beloved son in his parable of the wicked tenants (Mark 12:1–12) and as the rejected stone. So he claims to be the rightful shepherd of God's people and the present leadership of Israel to be usurpers. The psalm quotation in vss 10–11 makes that clear. Jesus' judgment on them leads, as Mark observes in 12:12, to their desire to "lay hands on" Jesus (the phrase means "to kill" see Esth 2:21; 3:6; 9:2). So Jesus is now ready to face his passion. In this he has determined the time and place for his sacrifice to occur. They are the ones who will ultimately be destroyed and deprived of their position as builders and disposers of the vineyard while he, the rejected stone, becomes the cornerstone.[482] In the cross is where his true nature is revealed as the beloved son (or "Son of God").

Healing of a Paralytic: Mark 2:1-12. Matt 9:1-8. Luke 5:17-26.

Standing at the center point of this story is not a miracle of healing but rather the authority of Jesus to declare the forgiveness of sin.

Jesus is probably in the house of Simon Peter in Capernaum. We have to think of the "roof" (στέγη, *stegē*) which those who bore the paralytic to Jesus "unroofed" (ἀποστεγάζω, *apostegadzō*) letting him down through the gap they thus created not as the roof over the house (which would have created a huge amount of debris made up of clay and straw as it was) but as the roof over the courtyard to which the house was attached. The roof over the courtyard would have consisted only of straw. Furthermore, people would have crowded not into a house, into which little daylight would be present to say nothing of the small space which it would provide. A courtyard would have provided sufficient room for a (small) "crowd."[483] Jesus sees "their faith," meaning the four bearers of the pallet[484] on which the paralytic lies. But the paralytic must have been included since he would have been the one to muster some friends to bring him to Jesus.

The thinking of the day presupposed that illness was the result of sin.[485] That conception lies behind this story. Furthermore, forgiveness was understood as God's prerogative.[486] No one could claim to have such power and if they did it would amount to blasphemy (as the scribes declare, vs 7).[487] In this passage Jesus refers to himself as "son of man" as he announces the forgiveness of sins to the paralytic (vs 10). The figure of the "son of man" (Aram., בר אנש "*bar enash*," "son of mankind") occurs preeminently in Dan 7:13 where the writer fuses the figure of "son of man" with a Davidic royal messiah and with Isaiah's "servant of the Lord" and in this way combines the characteristics of those figures: the royal figure wreaks judgment on the rebellious leaders of the world, works for justice, and simultaneously is the exalted servant of God. The figure is further developed in the Similitudes of Enoch and 2 Esdras.[488] The son of man is hidden but is at the same time the transcendent champion who works vindication and salvation for God's people.[489]

However, "son of man" in Jesus' day was a rather neutral term, and he employed it to identify himself but filled it with his own meaning. He uses it in three ways: as the coming one at the eschaton (the "parousia sayings"), as the suffering servant, and he uses it in combination with his earthly activity.[490] Jesus could easily identify with the coming endtime son of man and also apply the concept to his earthly ministry and suffering. Jesus also employs it as what is known as "illeism" and uses the term to refer to himself in the third person (e.g., Matt 17:22).[491] He could be using it in this way in this story of the paralytic and saying "I have the power on earth to declare the forgiveness of sin."[492] So this authority is "given" and Jesus possesses it because he is the "son of man."[493] But he could be identifying himself simultaneously with the eschatological son of man which coordinates with his understanding that in his proclamation, healings, and exorcisms the kingdom of God was already present. But the kingdom was also coming in the future in all its fullness. This double aspect of the kingdom parallels the double aspect of the son of man who was presently active and would return at the eschaton.

The term also included the community of the age to come. The kingdom then is present in the world in the form of the new community of God's people. Jesus also proclaimed the ethics of this kingdom delineating how those who had entered the kingdom were to guide their lives. So eschatology, kingdom, community, son of man, and ethics are all woven together as one piece.

Just as Jesus as the messianic "son of man" has authority over demons and disease he has the authority to declare the forgiveness of sin. He addresses the man affectionately with "my child," which suggests his faith makes him a "son of the kingdom," that is, he is drawn into Jesus' fellowship and to himself personally as the father of this new family.[494] But the declaration is construed in the passive, "Your sins have been forgiven." The passive usually implies God's action. It is also in the aorist tense (punctiliar action) which would bear the meaning "right at this moment God forgives your sin."[495] But the scribes understand it as Jesus own personal declaration. So they judge him a blasphemer (cf., John 10:33). The epithet is pronounced again at his condemnation by the Sanhedrin (Mark 14:64). Jesus speaks with certainty as God's agent endowed and commissioned with divine authority.[496] The scribes show their contempt for him as they refer to him as "this man" (vs 7). If Jesus has the power to heal implied also is the power to announce the forgiveness of the sin that brought the disease about. So Jesus heals the man, which is tantamount to forgiving his sin.[497] He sees that forgiveness is indispensable to the man's total cure.[498]

Jesus employs an illeism by referring to himself in the third person as "son of man" (but implied is his status of "beloved son" destined to be a sacrifice but who will return in glory at the eschaton). Mirrored in the criticism of the scribes[499] is Jesus' passion and cross. They are represented

HEALING OF A PARALYTIC

as "debating" (διαλογίζομαι, *dialogidzomai*, which also means "consider, discuss, argue"[500]). The phrase "in their hearts" implies non-verbal thoughts which Jesus is able to perceive. But there is ambiguity in all of this because the ἐν ἑαυτοῖς (*en eautois*) can mean both "within themselves" or "among themselves." Even if we translate "within themselves" so that we would then understand Jesus as perceiving their thoughts it would not require thinking of some supernatural ability. Anyone present could read their minds by the expressions on their faces.[501]

His ability and claim to forgive sin is then part and parcel of the presence of the kingdom in which God is active as he, through Jesus, calls people into the kingdom where sins are forgiven. Repentance meant being forgiving so that God would forgive them. John the Baptist did the same with his baptism. His message was, come confess your sins, repent, and receive forgiveness. So forgiveness is offered quite outside the official road to forgiveness effected at the temple and its sacrifices and priestly service. Jesus does not then heal the man in order to prove his ability to forgive sin. Rather forgiveness and healing are two sides of the same coin in the kingdom proclaimed by Jesus.[502] He could easily assert their combination because the culture identified sin and disease. This man was no doubt caught up in that identification and needed to know that even before his healing he was a forgiven man who had friends bring him to Jesus because he had faith and knew in Jesus he would find healing. Jesus sensed that forgiveness was important to the paralytic and in declaring forgiveness reflects Jesus' intention from the moment that the man appeared on the scene to heal him. Jesus then had to show the scribes his authority to forgive by doing exactly what he intended to do from the beginning (vs 10). Jesus is not making healing a proof for his declaration of forgiveness. Jesus rejects such "sign seeking" (Mark 8:12). Rather, this is an argument from the lesser to the greater. The easier points to the greater (cf., Matt 7:1; Rom 5:8–10) and are connected so that the more difficult follows from the easier.[503] So Jesus functions here as the high priest of the messianic time. He replaces the high priest who entered the holy of holies on the Day of Atonement offering the prescribed sacrifice. He limns his passion and death that will be a "giving of his life as a ransom for many" (Mark 10:45). And all the bystanders recognized God at work here, not blasphemy: they "glorified God" declaring "we've never seen anything like this." (vs 12. These latter words are not common in Mark.[504]) This praise recognizes that in Jesus God is at work. He is the servant of the Lord. God's eschatological action is praised.[505]

The reproduction of everyday realities of life in the villages of Jesus' day and the fact that this story does not even focus on the miracle but rather the forgiveness of sins speaks for its authenticity. That latter focus would have contributed to the vividness of the account.

Healing of a Woman with a Hemorrhage: Mark 5:25–34. Matt 9:20–22. Luke 8:43–48.

Unusual in this telling of a miracle story is that it is imbedded within another story, that of the raising of Jairus's daughter. The connecting links with that story and the absence elsewhere of such a combination in the gospels implies the two stories were historically associated.[506] Also pointing in this direction are the preparatory words for the woman's action in seeking a cure in vs 24 and the subsequent reconnecting link in vs 35 to the story of Jairus's daughter who is now reported to have died. Such connectives are absent elsewhere in healing stories. It is not like the story of the beheading of John the Baptist which Mark uses to fill in an interval of time (6:14–29).[507] The story is told in the typical form of miracle stories (a description of the sufferer, the failure of finding a cure, and the healing). However, the reaction of the crowd is missing (see e.g., 1:23–28.)

The description of the woman's fear, her bold action, and the rather rough and blunt question of the disciples all reflect a psychological realism and historical actuality. That Matthew and Luke both toned down the disciples' question, which bordered on the censorious, indicate the primitive nature of Mark's rendition of the report. The description of the woman's thoughts (vs 28) can be grounded in the fact that the woman "told the whole truth" to Jesus (vs 33). And Jesus' consciousness that "power had gone out of him" can be inferred from his question, "Who touched my garment?" (vs 30).[508] That Jesus asked this question indicates not supernatural knowledge but rather Jesus' sensitivity toward the fact that the touch of others signified to him that people were wont to touch him in a purposeful manner seeking healing (cf., Mark 3:10; 6:56). Matthew and Luke say the woman touched the κράσπεδον (*kraspedon*), the fringe of his garment, or it might also refer to the "tassel" which the Israelite was required to wear on the four corners of his outer garment (Num 15:38; Deut 22:12, ציצית, *tsitsith*).[509] Why didn't she just ask to be healed? Perhaps she wanted to spare publicly rendering Jesus unclean or to avoid being censured because she, a ritually unclean person, was mingling in a crowd.

That the woman had suffered for twelve years, the same age of Jairus's daughter, may be coincidental and may mean merely a generalized long time.[510] The severity of her hemorrhaging[511] is underscored by the fact that she had "suffered under many physicians and had not improved but gotten worse" (vs 26). So Jesus was her last great hope. She approaches him under cover of the crowd. Her hemorrhaging would have kept her ritually unclean for all those years and made it difficult, if not impossible, for her to have normal social interactions.[512] So the woman by mixing in with the pressing crowd rendered unclean all those who physically came in contact with her and especially Jesus himself. Her boldness is reflected in her willingness to render others unclean for the sake of being healed. How else could she gain access to the healer? Now what of the ruler of the synagogue who had invited Jesus into his house to heal his daughter? Jesus cannot be made unclean (Mark 1:41). He makes clean.[513] She shared the folk belief that merely touching Jesus' clothes would result in her being healed.[514] And she wasn't disappointed. Jesus' power to heal is conceived as a substance which worked by God independently of Jesus' will. In being discovered the woman falls down before Jesus with "fear and trembling." This posture of worship again points to the experience by the woman of the presence of the numinous underscored by describing her reaction with the biblical phrase "fear and trembling." The phrase occurs in contexts of being faced with an emotionally charged setting such as a life-threatening situation, a numinous experience, realizing that one's duty is divinely commanded, and supernatural appearances.[515] The woman then tells "all the truth."[516] Jesus then attributes her healing to her faith which implies not auto-suggestion since faith in the NT derives its substance from its object.[517] Jesus' consciousness that his power to heal has been drawn from him supports this understanding of the woman's faith. The woman had believed the reports about Jesus, had faith in them, and so relied solely on him for healing. Jesus declares the healing as permanent with the words "be restored to health from your sufferings." This phrase, ἴσθι ὑγιὴς ἀπὸ τῆς μάστιγός σου (*isthi hygiēs tēs mastigos sou*), occurs nowhere else in the NT or the LXX.[518] It is hardly a stereotypical phrase suggesting again that this encounter between Jesus and an ill woman is a reliable historical report.

Jesus approves of her actions and bids her "go in peace" because she relied on the reports about him (vs 27), that is, she relied on the good news that he embodied, the presence of the saving power of God.[519] To rely on it is to have faith which means to possess "salvation" or wholeness (σῴζω, *sōdzō*, a comprehensive term that literally means to save or rescue in both a physical and spiritual sense). Biblically the word means, especially in a spiritual sense, to save from sin and its effects and from spiritual death effected and completed by the sacrifice of Jesus and ultimately fully completed in the eschaton.[520] It is personally apprehended by the acknowledgement of sin (implicit in the woman's prostrating herself before Jesus) and trust in him (graphically portrayed in her touching of his garment). So vs 34 can be alternately translated "Your faith has brought you salvation. Go in peace and be whole of your plague."[521] Also in this way Jesus preserves the personal independence of those whom he heals making them responsible for their healing by trusting in the power of God active and available in him.[522]

Healing of a Man with a Withered Hand: Mark 3:1–6. Matt 12:9–14. Luke 6:6–11

This story is more of a pronouncement story and only secondarily a miracle story. The point is Jesus' teaching on doing good and saving life on the Sabbath which is then confirmed by his action.[523] The observers of Jesus' behavior waiting for the opportunity to accuse him of breaking the prohibition of working on the Sabbath, calling the man to stand in the midst of the gathered congregation, and Jesus' grief at their "hardness of heart" suggest the story is based on eye-witnesses reminiscences.[524] Jesus' opponents here are not the Pharisees (which the story makes clear by not specifying who they were). It is only by inference from vs 6[525] that they were Pharisees (Luke adds them to this context based on vs 6). Pharisees would have agreed with Jesus that in terms of human needs and the saving of life the Torah can be set aside. Although they might have argued along with the ruler of the synagogue in Luke 13:14 that the man's healing could have waited a day.[526] So the Pharisees would not have been so stringent and punctilious as the apparently unlearned opponents, but this perspective may not have been necessarily shared by the rest of the congregation gathered in the synagogue, the Galileans being notoriously lax concerning the application of Torah. But Jesus in vs 4 states the issue has to do with whether doing good or evil were permitted suggesting that not doing the good passively permits evil to happen.[527] It would seem that

HEALING OF A MAN WITH A WITHERED HAND

Jesus intentionally chose a Sabbath to heal in order to confront directly the Jewish Sabbath laws and those who represented them most strictly.[528]

This is opposed to Meier who sees the Christological concerns of the early church in vs 4 when the concern expressed here is actually tied to the Jewish environment of the time of Jesus. Torah, its observance, and its application to daily life were lively issues.[529] Jesus was a well-known and popular character in the Galilee of his day. What he did would have engaged popular comment and concern particularly how the Torah was or was not observed. This verse makes clear his activity was well known and so he would be carefully watched by those who had an interest in Torah observance. That does not mean that the average peasant would have interest in the fine points of Torah observance, which I've already noted. Meier has to admit that the average peasant would (I would add "only") have observed some basic rules of the Sabbath.[530] Furthermore the story does not imply that it was peasants who questioned Jesus' action of healing. The Galilee would have been crawling with scribes employed by Herod Antipas's administration who would be very much concerned with the proper handling of agricultural products demanded by Torah.[531]

The scribal point of view is clear: what God has ordered only obedience can follow.[532] Anything else comes of evil. The laws of Torah are not to be questioned. There is no "why" to them or speculation about God's motives. Man's task is to do what God bids. Only in this way is the sacred boundary between God and man kept intact. Jesus' point of view differs, of course. God is the merciful one, an over-flowing well of love. Who doesn't clarify this love and goodness of God fails to do his actual will (Matt 9:13; 17:15; Luke 10:37). So here Jesus speaks out of his consciousness of his relationship to God as his beloved son, the certainty of his fatherly love which illuminates everything. So to forbid the healing is to hold God "hard-heartedly" at a distance. Neither side is dealing on rational grounds but rather it is one belief against another. That is why the struggle is so tough and the conflict so inescapable. Both serve the same God so Jesus in terms of the representatives of Torah is a blasphemer and vice versa. In this little story it comes to the fore how strange Jesus had to appear to his opponents and how that led to the cross. "So the highest treasure which [Jesus] can dispense, is in the eyes of . . . the pious, worthless, yes even worse: it is reprehensible, godless."[533]

This break between Jesus and his opponents lurks behind vs 4. Their ultimate intention in watching his behavior will lead to his elimination. Jesus asks, Will you save or kill? So to save here means that the sick man can be saved and brought into the kingdom of God and those who lie in wait for Jesus to condemn him leads to the death of God's messenger of the kingdom.[534]

Meier is also not quite correct when he says that Jesus actually performs no action but only a word in vs 5 to effect the healing.[535] It does stand in contrast to other healings where Jesus is reported to touch a person. But a word can also be an action. It says in Shabbath 23:3, "A man may not hire labourers on the Sabbath or say to his fellow that he should hire labourers for him."[536] In other words, speaking itself is considered a work that is not permitted on the Sabbath if it promotes or effects a disallowed action.[537]

The meaning of the verb συνλυπέω (synlypeō or συλλυπέω, syllypeō) in the passive means, as it occurs here, "to hurt or be grieved with" (vs 5). The phrase "hardness of heart" in the NT means "obtuseness" or "intellectual blindness" or, as here, to have no compassion for the plight of another.[538] The combination of his grief with "anger" meets the "hardness of heart" of his critics which hinders the good and promotes the bad. The man's malady would have kept him from work and would have contributed to his poverty and perhaps reduce him to begging, a shameful state in a society based on honor.[539] So Jesus' word brings about the restoration of the man, he is included in the work of the kingdom, where the renovation (or "restoration" ἀποκαθίστημι, apokathistēmi, a loaded word describing the healing of the man's hand) of the creation takes place. So his healing is a living sign of the kingdom! The kingdom and its priorities take precedent over the Torah and its requirements. At a deeper level Jesus' healing meets the requirements of the Sabbath law of rest. The rest of the Sabbath was a sign of God's own rest and his just finished, pristine, creation. The creation was, as God created it, a reflection of his kingdom of rest. But it would be sullied and become a place of work and pain by Adam's and Eve's disobedience. The Sabbath rest recreated a time within the fallen world that reflected God's original intention for his creation. So Jesus' opponents don't recognize the deeper meaning of the Sabbath law which made it an actual necessity to heal the man. And that is why Jesus would not wait for the morrow.

Taylor mentions that according to Jerome the Gospel to the Hebrews has a detailed description of the man: he was a mason who asked Jesus to restore his health so that he would not have to turn to begging for his livelihood.[540] This is a perfect example how stories could be embellished in the interest of providing details of the characters involved and satisfying the curiosity of the hearers or readers of the story. These additions serve to accentuate the terseness and brevity of the original Gospel tradition, its primitive historicity as well as witness to its antiquity. This report bears so many subtleties and reflects so deeply the mind of Jesus that it cannot be anything other than a brief, but at the same time, thorough report of an action and word of Jesus.

Healing of a Stammering Man: Mark 7:32–36.

The introductory vs 31 is Marcan redaction fitting the story into the geographical context of his gospel. Verse 37 also looks redactional as a generalized acclamation of the works and deeds of Jesus.[541] Anonymous people bring a stammering man (κωφός καὶ μογιλάλος, kōphos kai mogilalos, meaning both "dumb" and "speaking with difficulty") to Jesus. That vs 35 says he spoke "correctly" after being healed implies that he originally could speak but not normally so he was probably a "stammerer."[542]

Jesus takes the man aside "privately" again to escape the publicity that would ensue because of the presence of the crowd. This is part of Jesus' strategy to choose the time himself for revealing his messianic sonship and thus fulfill his call as the beloved son whose life will be offered to God. The time comes when in Jerusalem he obliquely reveals his status as the beloved son in the parable of the wicked tenants.

That Jesus uses saliva in the healing is also an action he employs in the story of the healing of the blind man in John 8:23. A similar technique is recorded of Vespasian who used his saliva to heal a man.[543] The use of saliva[544] and placing his fingers in the man's ears cannot be construed as using "magic." As already noted, the use of magic was so proscribed in Israel that Jesus would hardly indulge in any techniques that would be identified as magic.[545] Taylor refers to contemporary use of manipulations used by psychotherapy coupled with verbal encouragement in dealing with maladies caused by hysteria (but there's no way of knowing if the man was suffering from a hysterical reaction).[546] Rather, by using saliva in these healings, Jesus was demonstrating that he was indeed a legitimate and firstborn son, the beloved son of God. Jesus also uses the same strategy when it describes him as "sighing" and saying, "Ephphatha." The use of foreign words is prevalent in the miracles stories of the time. But it is hardly the case here as it reproduces the Aramaic that Jesus spoke. Sighing and groaning belong to the techniques of magic but here they reflects Jesus' deep feelings and compassion for the stammering man.[547] That Jesus "looks up" is the common Jewish attitude in prayer and emphasizes again Jesus' dependence on his father God who is active in his ministry of making the kingdom palpable by bringing healing and restoration to the people.

The cure is artlessly noted. The man's ears "are opened" and the "bond of his tongue" loosed. That he can now speak witnesses to the fact that he obviously was not deaf his whole life but had learned to speak. The "bond" may refer to bonds of demonic possession but there is nothing in the rest of the report to suggest that. Jesus by means of this healing, appears as wisdom:

> . . . wisdom opened the mouth of the dumb, and made the tongues of babes speak clearly. (WisdSol 10:21)[548]

Jesus clearly understood his healings as the realization of the proleptic presence of the kingdom and the kingdom, as the new creation:

> Then the eyes of the blind shall be opened, And the ears of the deaf shall be unstopped. Then the lame shall leap like a deer, And the tongue of the dumb sing. For waters shall burst forth in the wilderness, and streams in the desert. (Isa 35:5–6)

Jesus had taken the man and his companions aside from the crowd so he could justifiably demand that he not spread abroad the good news of his cure. The plural "charged them" refers, of course, to the man himself and to the men who had brought him to Jesus. But typically they disobey. They cannot contain the joy they experienced with the healing of their friend and comrade (cf., Isa 35 describing the future restoration and glory of Israel). So the narrative is a unity, from the opening of the story where the men who brought the man to Jesus to the closing of the story when they all are admonished to keep silent about the cure.

Why this demand for silence? In Mark 8:30 Jesus commands the disciples after Jesus' confession of him as the messiah that "they tell no one about him." Again in Mark 9:9, after the transfiguration scene, Jesus charges the disciples not to tell anyone what they had seen until after his resurrection. The reaction of Caiaphas to the report of Jesus' working of "signs" causing people to believe in him generating the fear that Rome would destroy the nation (John 11:45–50) puts these demands for silence in their proper context.[549] Jesus would forestall his death by being in charge of exactly when his "giving his life as a ransom for many" would take place. This command for silence then reflects Jesus' own self-consciousness of being the beloved son.[550] Pointedly, Jesus does not demand silence when he cures blind Bartimaeus (see below, Mark 10:46–52). At that point he is entering Jerusalem and his final days lay before him. Now there is no longer any need for silence.

Healing of a Blind Man: Mark 8:22–26.

This story bears a close resemblance to the previous story of the stammerer with similar linguistic parallels: in each the suppliant is brought by others, saliva is used as a healing agent, Jesus lays his hands on the suppliant, the event occurs privately, and there is a charge not to spread the news of the healing. However, there are also two striking differences: the blind man, after Jesus' first word and the anointing of his eyes with his saliva, describes what he sees with his partially restored sight: people moving about looked like trees and secondly, Jesus laying his hand on the man a second time. The healing in stages does not suggest Jesus' lack of power but rather how difficult the healing was.[551] However, intractability of the man's blindness might question Jesus' miraculous powers in the eyes of some.[552] In that case the story's authenticity would then be bolstered by the criterion of embarrassment. These two details probably explain why both Matthew and Luke omit the story. These similarities along with the differences rather than suggesting a product of invention and an artificial story of a blind man fashioned after the story of the stammerer point to its authenticity.[553] Furthermore, Jesus would have used similar methods from case to case in his healings but would also vary them in accordance with the circumstances of the afflicted person.

The blind man is able finally to see "clearly" (vs 25, τηλαυγῶς, *tēlaugōs*, "to see clearly from afar") meaning the man can now focus on distant objects.[554] This word with its repetitive emphasis on the man receiving his sight is perhaps Mark's interest in making it clear that the man's sight was fully restored by Jesus. (One could translate the sentence with "And he saw sharply and being restored he saw clearly, seeing everything from afar lucidly.") The use of the word "restoration" invokes the presence of the kingdom and its fulsome inauguration in the future. Jesus then commands the man to "go home and not to say anything to anyone (about his cure) nor enter the village."[555]

Anomalous is Jesus leading the blind man out of the village of Bethsaida after he had been brought there and then, after healing him, telling him not to go back into the village but to go directly home.[556] Why doesn't Jesus want him to return to Bethsaida where the men who had initially brought him to Jesus were waiting? It is possible that Jesus had given up on Bethsaida accepting his kingdom proclamation. In Matt 11:21 he pronounces woe on this village: "Woe to you, Chorazin! Woe to you, Bethsaida! For if the mighty works done in you had been done in Tyre and Sidon, they would have repented long ago in sackcloth and ashes." In this way Jesus effects the woe that he had pronounced on it by depriving it of the good news of the healing of the blind man. The incorrigible blindness of Bethsaida's inhabitants is confirmed.

Healing of Blind Bartimaeus: Mark 10:46–52; Matt 20:29–34; Luke 18:35–43.[557]

In the gospel narrative this is the last report of a miracle. Naming Jericho as the region where this story occurred is probably not a Marcan notice but part of the tradition handed down to him along with the name of the blind man.[558] Most of the miracle stories do not mention the name of the afflicted person. This story stands out in that respect. It might be like the story of Simon of Cyrene whose sons are mentioned and who may have been members of Mark's community (Mark 15:21).[559] Like them perhaps Bartimaeus had relatives or acquaintances who were also part of Mark's community. Another peculiarity of the story is that it is told from the point of view of the person healed and therefore does not follow the form of a miracle story.[560] It looks more like a biographical apothegm.[561]

The translation of the man's name from the Aramaic before naming him is not Marcan style who usually gives the translation after the Aramaic word. It points to Mark reproducing faithfully the story and its wording handed down to him. Only here is Jesus called "son of David." The restoration of Israel was coupled with the blind receiving their sight (Isa 35:5; 42:7). This restoration was also coordinated with the arising of the Davidic messiah.[562] It is highly likely that Mark is preserving the tradition since he has Jesus question the usage as applied to himself in 12:35–37.[563] Traditions of this time associated Solomon ("son of David") with exorcisms and healing.[564] If there were rumors that connected Jesus with Davidic descent then the blind man's cry would be natural. Even more so because his fame as a healer and exorcist would have preceded him.⁵⁶⁵ Jesus with an entourage and the imploring shout of Bartimaeus asking for mercy also limns a visiting king entering a city where people line the streets begging for the "mercy" of gifts and having gifts showered on them.⁵⁶⁶ His cry is anticipatory of Jesus' procession into Jerusalem which story occurs in Mark immediately after this one (Mark 11:1–10). The crowd, perhaps irritated by this man's shouting for Jesus' mercy, tries to silence him⁵⁶⁷ which only leads him to shout all the more. So Jesus bids the crowd call the man. He then "throws off" his garment. He could have made a bowl-like receptacle in his lap with his outer garment as he sat cross-legged on the wayside, a pose which enabled him to receive the alms of the passers-by.⁵⁶⁸ Such a posture is suggested by Luke 6:37, "Give, and it will be given to you; good measure, pressed down, shaken together, running over, will be put into your lap."

When Jesus asked what Bartimaeus wished he would do for him he wants the blind man to specify his need, i.e., make explicit his desire and to get the man to express his faith. "Rabbouni" is a stronger appellative than "Rabbi" and means something like "my great master."⁵⁶⁹ His rising from his sitting position and addressing Jesus with this title shows high respect. This word displays the "faith that has saved (healed)" him (vs 52). This title and naming Jesus the "son of David" sets the origin of the story firmly on the soil of the Holy Land.⁵⁷⁰ Remarkably, Jesus says no word and makes no gesture that effects his healing. He merely tells him his "faith has made him well." Mark has probably added "followed him in the way" because it conflicts with Jesus' command "to depart" (ὑπάγω, *hypagō*, "withdraw," or "go on your way") which suggests that he withdraw to his house in Jericho. He no longer needs to be a beggar. To follow Jesus "in his way" is the way of the cross because Jesus, in Mark's narrative, is on his way to Jerusalem (11:1). Bartimaeus becomes a disciple. He's literally following Jesus on his way to the cross.

The historicity of this event is then supported by a number of factors: the healed person is named; the place and time is precisely indicated; the specific place within Jesus' ministry is specified; two Aramaic words are used; and an archaic conception of Jesus as "son of David," a Solomonic miracle worker, is expressed.⁵⁷¹ The primitive Christian community preserved the story of one of its members witnessing to Jesus.

Invading the Realm of Demons, Disease, and Death

Healing of a Crippled Woman: Luke 13:10–17

This story like the two following occur only in Luke's Gospel. The vocabulary is Lucan style and contains phrases that imitate the language of the OT.[572] The woman is described as "having an illness [producing] spirit for eighteen years." This temporal and concrete detail speaks for the historicity of the account since there is no particular motivation for including this number. It does stress the severity of her affliction.

She was not able "fully to stand erect." This description of her infirmity is only in general terms. Perhaps she had something like scoliosis or its symptoms. Jesus later in vs 16 describes this "spirit" as Satan himself who has so afflicted her. Demons, by possessing a person, can produce the symptoms of an illness.[573] There are some resemblances to the story of the healing of the man with dropsy (#11 below) and especially the fact that both stories are a form critical fusion of both a miracle story and a controversy dialogue.[574]

Jesus lays his hand on her and announces her release from her illness. She had not asked for healing. That could be due to the fact that she was possessed and the demonic presence in her life would not want to be exorcised. To the uninformed leader of the synagogue this laying on of hands could have counted as unlawful work on the Sabbath. It is not a Pharisee who challenges Jesus' action this time. A Pharisee could well have agreed with Jesus' argument from the greater to the lesser: if an animal bound for a few hours and is rescued how much more a human being bound for eighteen years! This poor woman not only should be "loosed" but ought to be. It was Pharasaic understanding that the Sabbath law can be suspended where human welfare and life are at stake. Jesus names his disparagers as "hypocrites"[575] because the synagogue leader pretended to criticize the people when he was really censuring Jesus.[576]

That many of these stories occur in a synagogue on the Sabbath are due to the fact that Jesus would be present there because all the people of a given village would be gathered there and so he could catch the ear of more people at once with the proclamation of the kingdom whose presence he would realize by his healing. So it was almost imperative that healing take place at those times to undergird his preaching (See Mark 10:1; Luke 4:16).

The uninformed criticism of the synagogue ruler unfamiliar with Pharasaic humanism and a careful application of the Torah contrasts with Jesus' kingdom proclamation and the presence already of the

Jubilee. The presence of kingdom manifest in this healing, the delight of the people (the ones who rejoice in the glories of the kingdom) are completely congruent with what we know of Jesus' ministry and so manifest historical truth reflecting Jesus' activity as we have come to know it.[577] The kingdom is here! Healing does not have to wait! It is time to celebrate and to glorify! It is time to acknowledge the grandeur belonging to the wonderful works of the kingdom (vs 17)!

Healing of Ten Lepers: Luke 17:11–19.[578]

Curing lepers was part and parcel of Jesus' ministry. He charged his disciples to do that very thing (Mark 6:13) and Jesus in his answer to John the Baptist's question about his identity is to tell John about his healing activity including "cleansing lepers."[579] It is possible that "Simon the Leper," in whose house he shares a meal (Mark 14:3–9), was cured and healed by Jesus. In cleansing leprosy Jesus appears as the eschatological prophet rooting this cleansing of lepers story firmly in history.[580]

The story is a narrative unity although consisting of two parts: as these lepers, obeying Jesus' command to leave and show themselves to the priest so that they can be declared cleansed of their leprosy and return to society (Lev 14:2–8), are healed the story immediately continues with one of them noticing that his healing has taken place turns back to Jesus praising God. The initial healing and the returning man cannot be understood apart from one another. It follows the form of a miracle story in that the healing takes place and there is a praise response to the healing although in this instance only one of the healed responds. This one man, a Samaritan, thanking God, "glorifying him," in this way recognized that God had worked through Jesus to bring about his cure. His thanks was so profound that he "falls on his face" at Jesus' feet. This gesture suggests that the man had sensed that he in his cure had encountered the numinous presence of God.

Jesus reacts with three rhetorical questions (and express his surprise implying the "limitation of his knowledge"):[581] "Were not ten cleansed? Where are the nine? Has only this foreigner returned to give glory to God?" Jesus then declares what he often does after a miracle of healing: "Go, your faith has saved you." Commentators have found that this two-part character of the story makes it difficult to categorize form critically.⁵⁸² So the story's unique form emphasizes that it is describing an event as it happened and therefore witnesses to its historical nature.

Jesus encountered these ten lepers outside of a village into which he was about to enter, which accords with Torah that the leprous person be isolated (Lev 13). Their "standing at a distance" (vs 12) reflects this command. It is not surprising that a Samaritan would be among this group of leprous men because Jesus and his disciples were passing along the border between the Galilee and Samaria (διὰ μέσου, *dia mesou*, "middle, in the middle").⁵⁸³ This notice seems to be difficult geographically in terms of Luke's narrative. Already in 9:52 Jesus and his disciples have entered Samaria. So it could be that Luke added the phrase to make sense of a Samaritan being part of a group of Jewish lepers. That the ten lepers⁵⁸⁴ includes both Jews and a Samaritan (or Samaritans) means that the place in which this miracle had occurred had to be on Jewish soil near Samaria. The Jews in the group certainly would not be living in Samaria since most first-century Jews regarded the Samaritans as ignorant, superstitious, and outside of God's favor and mercy and avoided contact with them.⁵⁸⁵ The Samaritan had joined himself to this group of fellow suffers so that he might enjoy the piles of food that would be left for them outside the villages by sympathetic villagers. That the group, which undoubtedly contained Jews, allowed a Samaritan (or Samaritans) to join their fellowship implies a certain amount of grace and mercy on their part. Part of the dynamic of inclusion was that a common personal calamity had broken down the racial and religious barriers that in common life divided them. It needs to be noted that the text does not say that he was the only Samaritan in the group.⁵⁸⁶

Jesus is surprised that it is only a "stranger," a Samaritan, who returns "to give glory to God" and that "with a loud voice" (which does not imply he was some distance away, but rather that he was so overcome with joy he no longer kept himself some distance from Jesus but "fell at his feet").⁵⁸⁷ Not one of his fellows in the group took the time to follow the Samaritan's example. His return doesn't imply that the others were not thankful. They were no doubt overjoyed and couldn't wait to be declared cleansed and return to their homes and their families. We might even say that the nine praise God for their healing in their own way: first by obeying Jesus without question and secondly, by their haste to be declared whole and return to their loved ones. In this they are like the day laborer in the parable of the treasure in a field who with joy sells all and buys the field to make it legally his own.⁵⁸⁸ But it doesn't say what he did with his treasure. Jesus leaves the parable open-ended, allowing his hearers the freedom to make a decision about how they would respond to the treasure of the kingdom.[589] I'm tempted to think that perhaps Jesus created the parable on the basis of his experience with these ten lepers and similar experiences. So it is not as if the nine received only a physical healing. They have encountered the kingdom and respond in their own way. They too have received salvation![590] This connection with the parable also supports the historicity of the story and we encounter again a development in Jesus' thought.[591]

In a sense, however, the nine did not recognize what the Samaritan had: here God was present and working to establish his kingdom. They were emblematic of the nation that refused to eschew the way of hostility toward their Roman overlord and join in the peaceable kingdom that Jesus was establishing by word and deed. Jesus says to the man that his faith has "saved" (brought him salvation) him and brought him a new relationship with God and his kingdom of peace.[592]

Meier notes the peculiar vocabulary and phrases in this pericope: "leper" used as an adjective (vs 12); ἀπαντάω (vs 12 *apantaō*, "meet") occurs elsewhere only in Mark 14:13; πόρρωθεν (vs 12 *porrōthen*, "from a long distance") occurring elsewhere only in Heb 11:13; the address to Jesus as "master" in the mouth of people who are not his disciples; and ἀλλογενής (vs 18, *allogenēs*, "a person of another race, a foreigner") occurs nowhere else in the NT.[593] This vocabulary may be due to the influence of the language of the LXX which was cultivated in Luke's community and appears therefore in the L tradition which he has incorporated into his Gospel. Meier therefore is inclined to think that this little narrative circulating in his community was reworked by Luke toward his own aims.[594] These peculiarities also point to the historicity of the account.

Healing of a Man with Dropsy: Luke 14:1–6.[595]

The story is similar to two other accounts of curing an illness in a synagogue and eliciting a controversy (Mark 3:1–6 the man with a withered hand and the crippled woman in Luke 13:10–17). They also have a composite form of a miracle story and a controversy dialogue. Form critics may have to designate this combination with a new name such as "controversial miracle story." I described in my previous study the differences between this story and that of the two other controversial miracle stories.[596] Jesus was not frivolously flouting the Torah but was emphasizing the presence of the Jubilee which accompanied his establishing the kingdom of God and which included the restoration of people (Isa 35 and Lev 25). Did the man just wander into the lawyer's house or was he "planted" there to entrap Jesus?[597] Most likely he was a guest too, as was Jesus, at this Sabbath meal.[598] Even before he works the miracle Jesus brings up the issue of his intent to heal a man on the Sabbath, heading his opponents off at the pass. Jesus doesn't say a word but "takes hold of him,"[599] heals him, and then sends him on his way.

In this way the controversy dominates the story and the miracle takes a second place as almost only an illustration of the justification of Jesus' action in healing the man on the Sabbath. Jesus was apparently invited to a Sabbath meal by a "leader of the Pharisees." Luke has added "of the Pharisees" (see below) which leaves simply a "leader" (ἄρχων, archōn) which can refer to a ruler, governor or an official member of a body of elders that leads the Jewish community.[600] Those who kept their eye on Jesus (the "they" of vs 1 apparently refers to the "lawyers and Pharisees" of vs 2) like a cat watches a mouse[601] (vs 1 παρατηρέω, paratēreō) end up with nothing to say (vs 4). Jesus then challenges them with a rhetorical question. "Who of you, having a son[602] or an ox that has fallen into a well, will not immediately pull him out on a Sabbath day?" The argument is an argument *a pari* (i.e., an equal comparison).[603] The Pharisees would argue similarly (so their presence in vs 1 and 2 is probably an addition by Luke or his source).[604] So Jesus' question assumes that most people would agree with him. In this way he, the Pharisees, and the average person were all basically in agreement.[605] The argument is what people allow for themselves and for their benefit must be allowed to Jesus for the benefit of the (ill) people.[606] The question is similar to what Jesus says in the story of the man with a withered hand. Although the argument there is an argument *a fortiori*. No doubt Jesus used this illustration more than once and probably used different language in various cases which would explain the differences in these two miracle stories.[607] Jesus here is enacting the Jublilee which will not wait to be inaugurated. "They could not give (a hostile) reply"[608] (vs 6, ἀνταποκρίνομαι, *antapokrinomai*).[609]

Jesus' rhetorical question has no exact rabbinic parallel and the different symptoms of the man as compared to the similar story of the man with a withered hand indicates a different situation as does the nature of the argument (*a fortiori* as compared to *a pari*).[610] That Jesus is eating a

Sabbath day meal in the house of a "lawyer" and he's not in a synagogue, that he heals with a touch and not a word, and no hostile words or action are said or planned against him all emphasize that this is a different event from other similar stories and reinforces the historicity of this occurrence.

Healing of an Ill Man by the Pool Bethesda: John 5:1–9 (10–15).

Establishing the text of this account is particularly challenging because of the complexity of the manuscript evidence.[611] Both Nestle and Metzger agree on how the passage is to be read so I follow this agreed upon text with one exception. The word προβατική (*probatikē*, "having to do with sheep" hence "sheep market" or "sheep gate") preceded by a preposition meaning "at" or "by" or "near," indicates it has to be taken as a dative and then in connection with "pool" (καλυμβήθρα, *kalymbēthra*) the phrase has to mean "at the sheep gate" or "at the sheep market" (markets were held outside of gates).[612] Nehemiah 3:1 refers to the construction of this sheep gate (Neh 12:39). That it was built by Eliashib the high priest and his priestly associates infers that it was associated with the temple.[613]

There are a number of different readings for the name of the place: Bethesda,[614] Bethsaida (P 66), Bedsaidan (P75),[615] and Bethdzatha (Sinaiticus, L, which the RSV, NET, and NRS read). The name Bethesda would be based on the Aramaic בית אשדא (BETH 'ESDA) "house of outpouring." The Copper Scroll from Qumran also supports the name as Bethesda (see note 226) and can be translated as the "house of the twin pools." The Old Syriac manuscript Curetonian (fifth century, containing only the four Gospels) reads בית חסדא "house of mercy" which transliterates to "Bethesda." The reading of Codex Sinaiticus βηθζαθά (*bēthdzatha*) is adopted by both Metzger and Nestle. The reading in the Copper Scroll בית אשדתיי (*Beth Eshdathayin*) is a Hebrew dual form, a form that was lost in the Aramaic of the Holy Land. If then, the Hebrew dual was replaced by an Aramaic feminine plural form it would read בית אשדתא (*Beth Eshdatha*) and the reading Bethzatha would be its Greek transliteration where the daleth (ד, "D") and the shin (ש "S") were represented by the Greek zeta (ζ "Z").[616] So the tradition is fundamentally coherent. The readings "Bethesda" and "Bethazatha" represent the Hebrew and Aramaic forms of the name of the pool and the Copper Scroll witnesses to the fact that there was a double pool there.[617]

Invading the Realm of Demons, Disease, and Death

This account is not to be seen as a doublet of Mark 2:1–12. The verbal parallels are due to the fact that both stories share the same genre of a miracle-healing story.[618] The setting alone of each story is proof enough of their independence from one another. The archaeological evidence for the existence of the pool of Bethesda supports the historicity of the story[619] as do the various forms of the name. Vs 1 describes the pool as having five porticos (a columned porch) which would be an unusual feature. Many interpreters of the past considered this an unhistorical literary creation. But when the site was excavated it revealed a rectangular pool with two basins separated by a wall and a five-sided pool, and each side had a portico! The southern basin had broad steps leading into it indicating it was a mikveh while the northern basin provided water flowing into the southern pool. It was therefore a reservoir or *otzer* which continually replenished and kept the water in the mikveh fresh and ritually "clean." So this story evidences "a remarkable knowledge of the topography of pre-AD 70 Jerusalem"[620] supporting its historicity. Its semiticized Greek does the same implying the antiquity of the story.[621] After the destruction of Jerusalem and the Temple the Romans turned the site into a pagan city, "Aelia Capitolina." They subsequently constructed medicinal baths there reflecting a continued tradition of the site as a place of healing.

Vs 1 could be redactional fitting the story into the Gospel context (one ninth-century manuscript adds "Tabernacles" after "feast of the Jews"). But then again, the tradition may have known that Jesus was present at the pool during one of the Jewish feasts. He no doubt went there just because many people would be at hand seeking healing. The story indeed indicates there were many people there who sought healing in the pool and that the first person who entered its waters when it was stirred up would be cured. Jesus knows that the man has lain there for many years much like his knowledge of Nathaniel before they meet (John 1:47–48) and of the checkered history of the Samaritan woman at the well (John 4:17–18).

Jesus seems to catch the man's ambivalence about being healed (vs 6) and the man seems to excuse his lack of healing in vs 7 (his exact malady is never specified; he is simply described as ἀσθένεια (*astheneia*, lit., "weak," and so by extension "ill"). Jesus ignores the man's excuse and heals him. After being healed the man also does not thank Jesus although he obeys his command to take up his pallet and walk. Neither does he even ask about Jesus' identity which is emphasized later in 9:13. It is only later when Jesus comes across him again in the temple that he discovers

Jesus' identity. It is again only later that the themes of Sabbath and sin come up (vss 9:10, 14). All of these peculiar characteristics point to the historical nature of the story.

John's Gospel also portrays Jesus as going up to Jerusalem more than once, so it would be expected that he would also perform miracles there.

Healing of a Man Born Blind: John 9

The narrative in vss 1–8 follow the form of a miracle story: the problem is presented, the act of healing takes place, and the reaction of observers affirming the miracle is reported (although in this case the doubt of some observers is also reported questioning the identity of the man). Thereafter follows the controversies regarding the healing (vss 9–41) culminating in the excommunication of the man because of his confession of faith in Jesus. These latter verses do not constitute a part of the miracle story. Furthermore, they are saturated with Johannine theology reflecting the much later break between the church and Judaism (vss 22 and 34) when after the war and the destruction of Jerusalem and Temple the Pharisees seized control of Judaism and their interpretation of it became normative. Historically speaking, the Pharisees had no authority to exclude anyone from Israel and the body of the faithful to say nothing of the synagogue during the time of Jesus.[622] They were just one stream of Judaism in the time of Jesus which was decidedly pluriform. Meier notes another item of the Johannine theology in the so-called "realized eschatology" of vs 39 where Jesus judges not at the eschatological day of judgment but in the present moment of belief or unbelief.[623] Another Johannine theological motif is Jesus as the light of the world (vs 5). So all of this reflects a later time toward the end of the first century in John's own time.

In the following I have included in the left column the narrative of the text of John's Gospel. The words in italics in the left column are deemed to be John's additions. They clearly reflect John's vocabulary and theology of his Gospel. John has intervened by inserting Jesus' reflection on being the sent one who is "the light of the world" in vss 3–5. He has also inserted the temporal reference to the Sabbath which then allows him to import the Pharisees into the narrative. The Pharisees would not have an issue of healing on the Sabbath since for them human needs supersede the Sabbath.[624] Vss 24–34 I have put in brackets, indicating that it might not have been part of the tradition handed down to John.

Invading the Realm of Demons, Disease, and Death

However, these verses do round out the story and bring the narrative to a nice conclusion as a confession of faith in Jesus. I will investigate them in detail below.

In the right column I have restored what I regard to have been the original narrative and the probable form of the tradition as it was received by John. The sentence in bold letters I have added as Jesus' conclusion to his observation about the connection between untoward events and being a sinner adapted from Luke 13:2.

So the basic core of the story consists of vss 1–8 but not vss 4–5. The tradition handed down to John may have read something like the text in the right column.

As he passed by, he saw a man blind from his birth. 2 And his disciples asked him, "Rabbi, who sinned, this man or his parents, that he was born blind?" 3 Jesus answered, "It was not that this man sinned, or his parents, but that the works of God might be made manifest in him. 4 *We must work the works of him who sent me, while it is day; night comes, when no one can work. 5 As long as I am in the world, I am the light of the world."*[625] 6As he said this, he spat on the ground and made clay of the spittle and anointed the man's eyes with the clay, 7 saying to him, "Go, wash in the pool of Siloam" *(which means Sent)*.[626] So he went and washed and came back seeing. 8 The neighbors and those who had seen him before as a beggar, said, "Is not this the man who used to sit and beg?" 9 Some said, "It is he"; others said, "No, but he is like him." He said, "I am the man." 10 They said to him, "Then how were your eyes opened?" 11 He answered, "The man called Jesus made clay and anointed my eyes and said to me, 'Go to Siloam and wash'; so I went and washed and received my sight." 12 They said to him, "Where is he?" He said, "I do not know." 13 *They brought to the Pharisees the man who had formerly been blind.*	As he passed by, he saw a man blind from his birth. And his disciples asked him, Rabbi, who sinned, this man or his parents, that he was born blind?" Jesus answered, "It was not that this man sinned, or his parents. **Do you think they were worse sinners than any others?"** He then spat on the ground and made clay of the spittle and anointed the man's eyes with the clay, saying to him,[627] "Go, wash in the pool of Siloam."[628] So he went and washed and came back seeing. The neighbors and those who had seen him before as a beggar, said, "Is not this the man who used to sit and beg?" Some said, "It is he." Others said, "No, but he is like him." He said, "I am the man." They said to him, "Then how were your eyes opened?" He answered, "The man called Jesus made clay and anointed my eyes and said to me, 'Go to Siloam and wash.' So I went and washed and received my sight." They said to him, "Where is he?" He said, "I do not know."[629]

14 *Now it was a Sabbath day when Jesus made the clay and opened his eyes.* 15 *The Pharisees again asked him how he had received his sight. And he said to them, "He put clay on my eyes, and I washed, and I see."* 16 *Some of the Pharisees said, "This man is not from God, for he does not keep the Sabbath." But others said, "How can a man who is a sinner do such signs?" There was a division among them.* 17 *So they again said to the blind man, "What do you say about him, since he has opened your eyes?" He said, "He is a prophet."*[630] 18 *The Jews* did not believe that he had been blind and had received his sight, until they called the parents of the man who had received his sight, 19 and asked them, "Is this your son, who you say was born blind? How then does he now see?" 20 His parents answered, "We know that this is our son, and that he was born blind; 21 but how he now sees we do not know, nor do we know who opened his eyes. Ask him; he is of age, he will speak for himself." 22 *His parents said this because they feared the Jews, for the Jews had already agreed that if any one should confess him to be Christ, he was to be put out of the synagogue.* 23 *Therefore his parents said, "He is of age, ask him."*[631]

Those who did not believe that he had been blind and had received his sight until they called the parents of the man and asked them, "Is this your son, who you say was born blind? How then does he now see?" His parents answered, "We know that this is our son, and that he was born blind. How he now sees we do not know, nor do we know who opened his eyes. Ask him; he is of age, he will speak for himself."

[24 So for the second time they called the man who had been blind, and said to him, "Give God the praise; we know that this man is a sinner." 25 He answered, "Whether he is a sinner, I do not know; one thing I know, that though I was blind, now I see." 26 They said to him, "What did he do to you? How did he open your eyes?" 27 He answered them, "I have told you already, and you would not listen. Why do you want to hear it again? Do you too want to become his disciples?" 28 And they reviled him, saying, "You are his disciple, but we are disciples of Moses. 29 We know that God has spoken to Moses, but as for this man, we do not know where he comes from." 30 The man answered, "Why, this is a marvel! You do not know where he comes from, and yet he opened my eyes. 31 We know that God does not listen to sinners, but if any one is a worshiper of God and does his will, God listens to him. 32 Never since the world began has it been heard that any one opened the eyes of a man born blind. 33 If this man were not from God, he could do nothing."] 34They answered him, "You were born in utter sin, and would you teach us?" *And they cast him out.*[632]	So for the second time they called the man who had been blind, and said to him, "Give God the praise; we know that this man is a sinner." He answered, "Whether he is a sinner, I do not know; one thing I know though I was blind, now I see." They said to him, "What did he do to you? How did he open your eyes?" He answered them, "I have told you already, and you would not listen. Why do you want to hear it again? Do you too want to become his disciples?" And they reviled him, saying, "You are his disciple, but we are disciples of Moses. We know that God has spoken to Moses, but as for this man, we do not know where he comes from." The man answered, "Why, this is a marvel! You do not know where he comes from, and yet he opened my eyes. We know that God does not listen to sinners, but if anyone is a worshiper of God and does his will, God listens to him. Never since the world began has it been heard that any one opened the eyes of a man born blind. If this man were not from God, he could do nothing."

Not to impugn sin to those who are afflicted is a theme of Jesus' teaching (Luke 13:1–4). Also his understanding of himself as being sent (as a prophet) was part of his consciousness (Mark 1:38). So John has adapted the traditional story to his theology of Jesus. The story did contain the question of the disciples and Jesus' answer that sin was not involved in the man's blindness but was intended, in the original wording of the story, to manifest the kingdom of God and Jesus' own messianic ministry of healing.[633]

The mention of Siloam indicates the story was rooted in the early church whose members were familiar with pre-70 Jerusalem (since Titus destroyed all of Jerusalem in AD 70).[634] Unique aspects of the story are the following characteristics: the use of mud or clay formed by Jesus spitting on the ground and then anointing the man's eyes with it as part of the healing process; the anointing with clay does not immediately effect the healing but it is combined with healing at a distance; in the other stories of healing at a distance Jesus does not come into direct contact with the person healed; and the washing in the Pool of Siloam. These difference leads to Meier's observation: ". . . the precise way in which Jesus brings about this healing is discontinuous with the entire miracle tradition in the Gospels."[635] I have to agree with Meier's conclusion that the discontinuity, the knowledge of Jerusalem, and the lengthy tradition history converge to make a claim for the historicity of the primitive tradition (although he hedges his bets by admitting "certitude is not to be had").[636]

The use of clay is evocative of the creation of Adam when "a mist went up from the earth and watered the whole face of the ground" and God "formed man of the dust of the ground and breathed into his nostrils the breath of life and man became a living being" (Gen 2:6–7). Spittle is mentioned elsewhere in just two of Jesus' healings (Mark 7:13, 8:23) but not mixing it with dirt. So more is involved here than healing a physical infirmity.[637] Implied is the recreation, i.e., the new creation, of the man and that Jesus' healing activity is to be seen in the context of the kingdom of God which he proleptically establishes through his healing ministry. The kingdom of God is therefore a restoration of the creation in terms of God's original creative act.

Washing in the waters of Siloam is also evocative of baptism and that Jesus is the "living water" (John 4:10, 14; 7:38, cf., Jer 17:13) who brings life to the world as people enter the kingdom through him. So the blind man returns from Siloam "seeing" (vs 7, i.e., "believing" cf., John 6:30).[638] In Jesus he becomes a remade—a recreated—man. Underscoring this new reality is when the man is questioned as to whether he was the blind beggar or not says, "I am," ἐγώ εἰμι (*egō eimi*), a loaded phrase. Jesus uses it of himself nine times in John's Gospel.[639] He identifies with Jesus and the kingdom he brings. The washing emphasizes again that the kingdom of God is God's new creation.

That the blind man is described as being "of age" means he was at least thirteen years old. So we may assume he was a young man around that age. During the second questioning he is adjured to "Give God the praise" i.e., "admit the truth" (Josh 7:19). If Jesus is judged to have broken the Sabbath law then he is by definition a sinner.[640] The man really offends his interlocutors when he asks if they want to be disciples of Jesus. They answer that they are disciples of Moses. So they make quite clear what the choice is: will it be Moses and the law or the new creation, the kingdom of God and his grace.[641]

Invading the Realm of Demons, Disease, and Death

In Jesus' context it was the great devotion to the Torah that was leading many to advocate revolution against Rome. The way to avoid the destruction to which that revolutionary devotion would lead was to enter the kingdom. They assert that they do not know where Jesus is from. Apparently people knew quite well from where he came (John 7:27, 41–42). So there is irony in their assertion: they knew from where he came in a geographical sense but not that he was sent by God and his origin divine. They can only affirm that God has spoken through Moses (vs 29). The formerly blind man points out the illogic of their rejection of Jesus as God's representative: if he were an abject sinner how could he do such good by bringing about the miracle of healing a man's blindness (he who now sees in both a physical and spiritual sense).

Remarkable is the length of this healing story. Compared with all the other miracle stories it stands out in this respect and the commentator might surmise that the evangelist has lengthened the story which he indeed has. We are able to discern those verses which John has most certainly added to the story. But what of the rest—and especially vss 24–33? There are some factors and historical circumstances to be taken into account that might indicate that these verses may have been a part of the original tradition.

If the Pharisees were John's addition to the story how can the hostility of just average people (the neighbors of the healed man in this case) against Jesus be explained? The tensions between urban and rural inhabitants stands to the fore in this regard. The urban elites often owned large plantations and were interested in expanding their lands at the expense of rural peasants. These large landholders were often absent and left the running of their plantation to their retainers who would be more interested in serving their master than concern for the poor. It was cities that depended also on the peasants for food and produce and who would manage the markets to which peasants would bring their produce to be sold. The elites would also hold loans granted to the peasantry who could often lose their little farms to them by default on loans. The elites generally held the little people in contempt (see John 1:46!). The sophisticated inhabitants of Jerusalem would especially look down on rural people and particularly those from the Galilee where the finer points of the Torah would hardly be familiar let alone practiced.[642] Indeed, the Pharisees could not get a foothold in this northern province so far removed from the center of Judaism.

The Sadducean exclusive focus on the Torah to the exclusion of the prophetic and other literature of the OT would certainly have had an affect on the populace of Jerusalem and their devotion to the law. A poignant example of this Jerusalamite zeal for the law and the sanctity of Jerusalem was their reaction to the Procurator Pilate's contemptuous action of bringing the Roman standards into Jerusalem by night very early on in his assumption of office in AD 26. A crowd assembled in Caesarea Maritima where he lived in the palace built by Herod the Great petitioning him to remove the standards since they bore the images of pagan deities. Their presence there violated even Roman law. After six days Pilate surrounded them with his troops and threatened them with death. The people threw themselves on the ground and bared their necks saying they would rather die than have the Holy City profaned. Pilate had to relent. He withdrew the standards rather than have the report go out that he attacked innocent and defenseless people.[643]

Jesus appearing again in Jerusalem preceded by his reputation as a lawbreaker would not endear him to the populace. They might have judged him perhaps even a "Galilean heretic." That is especially true because he had previously initiated his action in the temple courtyard clearing it of the purveyors of animal sacrifice and money changers (John 2:14–16). To shut down the temple's economic function and depriving the income that flowed from it to the people of Jerusalem[644] would have engendered the animosity of the inhabitants of Jerusalem whose livelihood depended on the uninterrupted operation of the temple.[645]

So the animosity of the blind man's neighbors is thoroughly understandable given the parameters of the tensions between urban and rural populace and Jesus' own reputation and actions within the Holy City. For them Jesus is a sinner pure and simple. They surely are Moses' disciples and know that God had spoken through him.[646] This "sinner" Jesus is hardly a person through whom God has spoken or could have spoken. They don't know where "he comes from" (πόθεν, *pothen*, is used in John 7:27 to mean place of origin either geographically or parentally). But to know that excludes him in the eyes of his interlocutors as being the Messiah whose origin is not supposed to be known (John 7:27).[647] The formerly blind man's witness, however, is logical, simple, and forceful. That Jesus could make a blind man see is unprecedented and a sure sign that God worked through him and in him. He is "from God."[648] It is remarkable that these people do not know where Jesus comes from in spite of the fact that he gives sight to the blind. His repeating the truism that

God "doesn't listen to sinners" (Ps 66:18) witnesses to Jesus and means that his faith in Jesus is not merely due to the miracle. He is like the one returning leper who gave thanks and praised God for his healing.

This blind man, though unnamed, could have been a member of the earliest Christian community in Jerusalem whose story was preserved in detail as an effective witness to the Gospel. This is suggested by his powerful witness to Jesus.

An Official's Servant at the Point of Death: Matt 8:5–13. Luke 7:1–10. John 4:46–54

This is the only miracle story that appears both in the synoptic tradition and John.[649] The outline below provides a way of comparing the three versions of the story:

AN OFFICIAL'S SERVANT AT THE POINT OF DEATH

Matthew	Luke	John
1. Jesus enters Capernaum and a centurion comes to him pleading for his servant (παῖς, *pais*, "child, boy, girl, servant")[650] who is paralyzed.	1. Jesus enters Capernaum. A centurion's slave (δοῦλος, *doulos*) was sick and ready to die sends elders of the Jews who plead for him to come and heal his slave.	1. Jesus enters Cana of Galilee where a nobleman (βασιλικός, *basilikos*, "royal official") whose son (υἱός, *huios*) was sick at Capernaum hearing that Jesus was in the Galilee came to him and told him that his son was dying and implores him to come to Capernaum.
2. Jesus says he will come and heal him. (Or, "Am I to come into your house?!")	2. These elders emphasize that he is worthy to have the healing done for him for he loves "the nation" and built their synagogue.	2. Jesus says people want signs or they will not believe.
3. The centurion answers that he is not worthy to have him "come under his roof" and says Jesus only needs to say the word because Jesus is like him: his soldiers obey has commands without hesitation.	3. Jesus goes with them. When not far from his house the centurion sends friends (φίλους, *philous*) saying he is not worthy for him to "come under his roof." He needs only say the word because Jesus is like him: his soldiers obey his command.	3. The man begs him to come before his son dies. Jesus says to return for his son lives. The man believes and leaves. As he's on his way his slaves (δοῦλοι, *douloi*) meet him and tell him that his son lives.
4. Jesus marvels at his faith unlike what he has even found in Israel.	4. Jesus marvels at his faith unlike what he has found in Israel.	4. —
5. Jesus adds that many Gentiles will enter the kingdom while the "sons of the kingdom" will be cast out.	5. —	5. —
6. Jesus tells him to go and as he has believed so it shall be done for him. The story then reports that he was healed at that very hour.	6. They return to his house and find the slave healed.	6. He asks when he got better the slaves tell him the hour when the "fever" left him. So the father knew it was the same time that Jesus had said his son lives.
7.—	7.—	7. He and his whole household then "believed."

The chart makes plain that we are dealing with a very complicated tradition. Complicating also the identifying the narrative as a miracle story is the large amount of dialogue material. The apex of the story is reached in Jesus' exclamation of admiration of the petitioner's faith which exceeds the faith of what Jesus has found in Israel. So from the standpoint of form we have both a pronouncement story and miracle story. The dialogue elements are missing in John's version, and it resembles more of a pure form of a miracle story. But even here there is an emphasis on the official's faith. This mixture of forms strongly points to the historicity of the event.

The Matthean and Lucan rendition of this story would seem to have come from Q, but the differences between the two are also striking: Matthew identifies the ill person as a servant who is paralyzed; Luke identifies him as a "slave" but does not specify the disease; Matthew says the centurion himself came to Jesus but Luke an embassy of elders who emphasize his worthiness because of his love for Israel; Luke has a second sending—the man's friends come from the house and say the words about the man's worthiness and his faith in Jesus' ability to just give the command for healing; Luke does not contain a word of Jesus that effects the healing; Matthew inserts the word about the gentiles being included in the kingdom to the exclusion of Israel (8:11–12).

Luke generally seems to always be more faithful to the Q tradition than Matthew. Matthew's tendency also is to shorten the traditions he includes in his Gospel which would seem to support Luke's version as the more original. However, the sending of a second delegation which conveys the centurion's message of his unworthiness seems artificial. Why wouldn't that have been a part of the original message given by the Jewish elders? Luke also is one who likes dualities as effectuating a persuasive witness. So I judge Matthew's version as the more faithful to the Q tradition. Also John's outline agrees more with Matthew's version than with Luke's.

In John, Jesus is not in Capernaum but in Cana; it is an official that makes the request and not a centurion;[651] the ill person is specified as the man's son; John adds the saying about people seeking a sign; the man returning to his house is met by his slaves who report the healing of his son. John agrees with Luke that there was a meeting with the man as he returned home but with different messages in each case. He agrees with Matthew that the man himself initially met Jesus with his request for healing. However, John's version of the story comes from a different stream of the tradition and on the basis of multiple attestation therefore lends credence to the historicity of the event.

The affliction involved varies between the evangelists: in Matthew the person is paralyzed, in Luke he is sick and ready to die which agrees with John who says he has a fever and is near the point of death. Apparently the severity of his affliction prevented him from being brought to Jesus which a paralysis or near death condition would warrant.

There is a clear similarity with the story of the Syrophoenician woman's daughter (Mark 7:24–30; Matt 15:21–28): the healing takes place at a distance, both are gentiles (but not necessarily in John), both

AN OFFICIAL'S SERVANT AT THE POINT OF DEATH

are initially apparently rebuffed (which is only an implication in Matthew and Luke but somewhat more explicit in John), but the suppliants win Jesus over in the end with deferential pleading.[652] Their similarity suggests that what Jesus originally said to the centurion was "Am I supposed to go into your house and heal?" (Matt 8:7), voicing the Jewish avoidance of entering a gentile house and thereby contracting impurity.[653] Supporting this interpretation of the verse is the emphatic use of ἐγὼ ἐλθών (egō elthōn) "Am I to come . . ." making it an indignant question; the centurion's reply matches such a question and expresses an amazing faith in Jesus. If Jesus readily agreed to go with the centurion then the centurion would have said this in his initial contact with Jesus. The similar and parallel story of the contact with the Syrophoenician woman would suggest an original rebuff by Jesus. And John in 4:48 actually reports an initial rebuff by Jesus. Matthew in general conceives of Jesus' ministry as a mission only to Israel (10:6; 15:24). But there are countervailing arguments: immediately preceding this story is the healing of a leper whom Jesus touches and cures although the leper, because of his disease, is not fully included in Israelite society; Jesus' ready assent in 8:7 to come to the centurion's house, although the centurion had not initially asked Jesus to do so, would elicit his amazing confession of faith in vs 8 and so waive the gracious offer of Jesus to enter his house. He's willing to receive less than Jesus offers having faith that Jesus could heal his servant even from a distance and thereby evincing a faith that causes Jesus astonishment.

I've suggested that John 4:48 is Johannine redaction ("unless you see signs and wonders you will not believe"). Matt 8:7 ("I will come and heal him") might also be Matthean redaction,[654] but something must have stood in its place in the tradition. Luke's version simply has the elders of the Jews, who come bringing the centurion's request, heading off any objections by Jesus by emphasizing the centurion's worthiness to have Jesus enter his house. So Luke bypasses any rebuff on Jesus' part, suggesting that perhaps that was never part of the earliest form of the story.[655] In this way Luke's version has the centurion right from the start anticipating Jesus' possible reluctance to enter a gentile house and sends the elders to represent him. Matthew's saying on the gentiles (8:11) is an obvious insertion on his part. Luke has a similar saying in another context (13:29) which therefore means the saying circulated independently. John's reference to signs is also language unique to him (#2 above in the chart) as is his insertion at the end of the story (#7). John's redaction is also indicated in placing Jesus in Cana, further removing him from the site of the miracle and emphasizing Jesus' miraculous powers (a characteristic of his gospel).[656] John's "royal official" is obviously a Jew, so there is no discussion regarding the appropriateness of Jesus coming into his house. In fact, in this Gospel Jesus never comes into contact with a gentile, suggesting that John has redacted the whole story in that direction and made of the petitioner a Jew and eliminating any suggestion he was a gentile.[657] Only when Jesus is "lifted up" (i.e., crucified) will he "draw all people to himself" (John 12:32, cf., 11:52).

I suspect that the original version of the story behind both renditions probably spoke of an official in Capernaum who was a gentile, and John adapted the story to his own theological perspective making the official a Jew. This official would have been part of Herod Antipas's administration which employed both Jewish and gentile military personnel. Q, written in the 50s in the land of Israel, would have been much closer to the event than John. What motivation would either Matthew or Luke have in specifying the man's ethnicity as gentile if that was not how Q identified him? And if the original story was about a man of unspecified ethnicity or even identified as a Jew, why would Q change the original story? It is more likely that John, with his intense theological motivation to emphasize Jesus' avoidance of gentiles during his ministry, would change the story to make of the official a Jew.

All three versions identify the person to be healed in different ways: Luke consistently refers to him as a *slave* (Luke 7:2, 3, 10). However, in vs 10 he refers to him as "my *servant (pais).*" So for Luke *pais* means "servant." John made the person the official's "*son.*" So in vs 49 he refers to him as παιδίον (*paidion*), the diminutive form of *pais*. In vs 51 he refers to him as *pais* which for him means not "servant" but "son." Matthew consistently refers to the ill person with the ambiguous word *pais* (8:5, 8, 13). As indicated it could mean either "son" or "servant." Matthew employs both meanings in his Gospel. It needs to be said that both Matthew and Luke use the word *pais* in the official's request to Jesus "say but the word and my *pais* will be healed" (Matt 8:8, Luke 7:7). So the original tradition probably referred only to the official's *pais*.[658] So Luke took it to mean "servant" and John "son" while Matthew preserved the original wording.

Overall the three reports have enough in common to perceive that they all rest on one incident and tradition about a healing at a distance.[659] Emphasizing their commonality is that each follows the same basic outline of the story as the chart above makes clear. The story also meets the criteria of discontinuity and embarrassment: Jesus is said to be "surprised" emphasizing Jesus' humanity (occurring elsewhere only in Matt 8:10 and Mark 6:6!).[660] The Q version also contains a large number of Semitisms. Both versions are also set in Capernaum where officials of Herod Antipas's administration would be present being on the border of his tetrarchy with his brother's territory. All of these factors point to a historical event in the life of Jesus.[661]

So the original tradition most likely consisted of a gentile official, no doubt part of Herod Antipas's administration, who asked Jesus, while he was in Capernaum, to heal someone who was part of his household. Jesus initially rebuffed him and the man answers that he knows he is not worthy to have Jesus enter his house but he has faith that if Jesus only would say the word that his household member would be healed. Jesus marvels at his faith and tells him to go for the healing has taken place.

SUMMARY AND ANALYSIS

Contemporary Culture's Philosophical and Scientistic Posture

Hume was the great influence on scientific thinking and historiography during and after his time. The regularity of nature and the human experience of that regularity precluded, for him, the occurrence of supernatural events which implied the suspension of natural law. There are no miracles but only exceptional and unusual events. His definition of miracles is 'something that has never been observed" (which begs the question since he assumes what he wants to prove and that no amount of evidence would be enough to confirm the occurrence of a miracle). Miracles furthermore are reported only by "ignorant and barbarous peoples." He was a radical devotee of the enlightenment and a "metaphysical naturalist," that is, one who believes that there is nothing outside the physical universe. In this view all things are interconnected so no events can claim independence from the total event of the universe. All events are caused by something within the material universe so miracles cannot be made the foundation of a "system of religion." Thus he rejects their occurrence on philosophical, historical, and religious ground.

However, science and its discoveries about the microcosmic and macrocosmic universe have led us to see that the universe has a beginning, that it has a design, as do all living things. (The universe cannot be self-creating. To assert that something can cause itself is unscientific since scientific thought demands that every event has an antecedent cause.) The rational conclusion must therefore be there is a designer. Paradoxically, the universe is consequently a miracle because it is quite out of the order of natural occurrences! That the universe is designed to behave in regular ways does not preclude God acting within his creation.

Our present Western culture is permeated with Hume's understanding of the natural world and his anti-supernaturalism so that this materialist spirit finds incredible the occurrence of miracles. So critical historians find them impossible and interpret them in different ways. For historians the agent of miracles is "non-empirical" and they do not have the tools to account for agents beyond the physical universe. This approach and understanding of reality and the truth about it can be called "egocentric epistemological foundationalism" (or EEF).[662]

Historians limit the possibility of human objectivity, which is a self-refuting assertion: that claim itself has to be relative. So it is possible to describe objective facts of history. Criteria developed by various disciplines such as archaeology, forensic medicine, law, literary theory, and psychology all work at developing objectivity. Historical fact can be established when based on trustworthy witnesses and attestation, document analysis, and the coherent connections between data.

A miracle can be said to have occurred when a coincident cluster of natural things happening is highly improbable (the "constellation miracle") or when an event has violated a natural law (the "violation miracle"). One's relationship to miracles and his or her interpretation of it is dependent on one's worldview. The Christian understands that the universe and the human being have been created by God, and therefore humans are capable of rational thought. If this were not so and we are the result of a purposeless, chance evolution, then our minds would not be a reliable guide to truth nor capable of having a true perception of reality. Evil in the world is due to the corruption by sin of the image of God in which we were created so that the disorder of the world and the solution to this disorder is spiritual.

So in naturalistic thinking miracles are *a priori* regarded as impossible and scientific thinking must follow methodological naturalism. In one view, science and theology are at best complementary ways of thinking and focus on different levels of description. A more satisfactory way of describing that relationship is to understand God as constantly sustaining the universe and supporting its order but that he also is involved in new acts of creation, or "miracles." Both God and man have a free will and both produce "libertarian acts." God's actions leave gaps in the fabric of natural causation.

Contemporary Interpretation and the Existence of Contemporary Miracles

What have contemporary interpreters of the Bible and of miracles made of eliminating the possibility of divine action? Theissen perhaps is a good representative of their response and interpretation. Miracles are understood functionally as literary productions and so provide insight into the sociology of the communities which produced them. They function on various levels: as instruction, entertainment, or persuasion. These functions can work to integrate the individual into the community. Or there is conflict within the community, implying the failure of integration. They are therefore a symbolic transformation of reality in which community members can feel at home. By reframing experience reality is mastered.

The ancient world was rife with miracle-working as well as places where healings were sought. The latter, used by both the poor and the elite, functioned to integrate people into society.

Magic and magicians were also ubiquitous drawing on every kind of religious expression, unrelated to community and filled with optimism in the face of what appeared to be a disintegrating world. It was decidedly anti-social because it could be used to inflict harm as well as defend, protect, and acquire power and knowledge, especially of the future. It could be used to summon the power of demons or seek union with the divine. So it attracted marginalized people in their struggle with the elite. Recourse to this occult realm was a sign of the breakdown of social order. There were therefore attempts to criminalize its practice.

Demon possession was rife in the land of Jesus' time due in large part of the Roman occupation of the land and its disrespectful dealings and negative attitude of most of the procurators toward their Jewish subjects. No politically accepted means were ever developed to channel Jewish frustration and vexation and so it erupted in hostile and aggressive ways. And even when those protests were peaceful they were put down with violence.[663] So even though the people were in their own land it felt like still being in exile. So this hostility of Roman occupation leaving no legitimate outlet for the expression of dissatisfaction led to anger and frustration being suppressed and going underground making openings for demonic possession.

Exorcisms as practiced in the Graeco-Roman milieu was no charismatic activity rather it was based on methods and in this way are to be differentiated from the miracle-working tradition in the life of Jesus.

Illnesses were a great economic threat and could lead to destitution. So Theissen and like interpreters understand miracle stories functioning in the early church to assure the ill they would not be forsaken but cared for within the bosom of the community. So these stories are understood as "symbolic actions" relieving distress. The foreign words introduced in the stories he finds to be evidence of ethnic conflict and witness to the superior power of eastern words over western in the face of the subjugation of eastern peoples by western hegemons. Because miracles stories promise salvation and redemption they also have a missionary intention and their mere telling results in conversions (Acts 9:42). The acclamations which round out the stories herald the victory of Israel's God over demons and pagan gods. So they proclaim a new way of life and call on the world to accept this revelation from God.

Jesus' miracle-working was one aspect of the kingdom of God along with his meals, his proclamation of the kingdom, and in his presence. So the miracles functioned within an eschatological horizon, a factor unique in the miracle-working atmosphere of his age. The exorcisms were also a sign of the collapsing of Satan's rule, so now salvation can come to people who are imprisoned by illness and disease. These stories were also nurtured within the community of the church which was embedded in eschatological expectations and so would be understood in terms of those expectations.

Miracles occur as my brief overview of Moreland's study makes evident.[664] He approaches his study heuristically and how miracles are to be defined and differentiated from mere coincidence. Much of the criticism of miracles comes from the philosophical position that there is no world of the spirit and a God who designed the universe and living organisms. Many take such a position admit to a fear of religion and recognition of the existence of God. His approach is not to assert that miracles prove God's existence but rather the reverse. God's reality also leads us to recognize that miracles would not be seldom occurrences but a regular part of human existence. He develops criteria for the reliability of a report of the occurrence of a miracle.

So in my study of the miracles reported in the Gospels I use his criteria to establish their reliability. These accounts report that Jesus is always surrounded by a crowd or when he removes his subjects from the crowd they enthusiastically proclaim their miraculous healing. These reports also evidence critical refinement: they are terse, unadorned, and unembellished. (The stories of the blind man in John 9 and the ill man by the pool of Bethesda in John 5 are exceptions but they dwell not so much on the miracles per se as on the Sabbath law.) The reports include the amazement of those who witness it implying skepticism. Jewish society was negatively disposed toward magic as potentially perverting Jewish faith. So to report them means they were accepted as reality. The Christian community that preserved them would have been bound by the command to accept nothing without two or three witnesses and to tell the truth was fundamental to early Christianity. It was a community committed to openness and its own faith rose and fell on whether the gospel was true or not (Acts 26:26).

The Healing Miracles in the Gospels: A Summary

All the miracles stories attributed to Jesus I have been found to be grounded in history. The fact that the disciples were commissioned to heal and exorcise and performed such deeds (Mark 6:30; Luke 10:20) means they would not have to make up miraculous tales about Jesus effecting miracles of healing.

The recounting of healing Peter's mother-in-law is an example of a report that could have come from Peter for it is easily rendered in the first person and then subsequently passed on in the third person by Mark's community. This narrative reflects a number of features that portray Jesus' understanding of the kingdom: a meal limning the feast of the kingdom and egalitarianism of a close band of disciples inclusive of women. The mother-in-law in her service embodies Jesus' himself as he seats his servants and serves them (Luke 12:37) and even washes their feet (John 13:3–10).

Jesus' healing of lepers emphasizes his working on the margins of society and reaching out to sinners. The cure of "leprosy" embodies Jesus' concern for the healing of society since a leper had to live outside any and every human community. The healed leper could return to be re-integrated with the community. Both stories of the healing of lepers describe them as kneeling or falling on one's face before Jesus indicating they had experienced the numinous in him. These restorative acts portray the kingdom and its inclusion of sinners and its "corrupt" character (depicted in such parables as the "Leaven in a Lump of Dough," Luke 13:20–21) because of its inclusion of "outsiders" and offenders. This is the time of restoration to God's original creation. It reflects the new exodus celebrated in Isa 35. Jesus in this way realizes proleptically the exodus from exile which is how the Israel of Jesus' time interpreted the Roman occupation of its land. So that in spite of the fact they lived in the promised land it was an existence in exile since Rome was the overlord who had usurped God's rightful reign as Israel's king (the emperor even called himself a god!). In Luke 9:31 the word which is translated by the versions with "departure" or "passing" in the Greek reads ἔξοδος, *exodos*, quite a loaded word. The passage occurs in the story of the transfiguration where Jesus is speaking with Moses and Elijah, evoking the exodus from Egypt through the figure of Moses and the eschatological restoration through the figure of Elijah. Implied is that Jesus' passion, death, and resurrection accomplish his universal ransom and the establishing of God's kingdom, the end of Israel's exile, and the world's salvation (Rom 8:23).[665]

The joy expressed in these stories reflect the experience of encountering the kingdom and may have been the impetus for Jesus in creating the story of the man who found a treasure in the field.

Sin and disease were linked in Israel's culture of Jesus' day. In the story of the healing of a paralytic the real focus of the narrative is on Jesus as the "son of man" who has the power to forgive sin and on the presence of the kingdom in his ministry. In forgiving sin Jesus continues the central aspect of the ministry of John. Jesus refers to himself as "son of man" who is declaring forgiveness. The figure of the son of man was also one which would come in the eschatological future. So present and future are coordinated corresponding to the kingdom which in Jesus also had this double aspect.

So a number of themes are woven together in this event: the son of man as presently active who will come in the future, the kingdom both as a present and future reality, the community of the new age living in the light of that coming kingdom, and the subtle presence of the cross in the scribes' sneering, derogatory and judgmental reference to Jesus as "this man." So forgiveness and healing are two sides of the same coin. Jesus as son of man has authority over sin, demons, and diseases. The passive voice in which the declaration of sins occurs implies God's action which is at work in the "beloved son." The healing is not some proof of forgiveness but Jesus presents an argument from the greater to the lesser. In declaring the man healed Jesus is also acting as a high priest.

Forgiveness was especially needed in the divided society of Jesus' day and especially vis-à-vis the Roman overlord. Although the behavior of many a procurator was despicable the central government was tolerant toward Jews and Judaism.[666] So forgiveness was offered by Jesus outside the Temple sacrifices. Forgiveness and healing are intimately connected which the culture would understand since sin and disease were connected.

Although the miracle stories follow in general a form they each portray different human aspects as well as various facets of Jesus' person and actions. The woman with a hemorrhage who surreptitiously sneaks up behind Jesus to touch him in order to be healed and avoid the censure of those she has rendered ritually unclean by physically coming into contact with her in the pressing crowd limns a vivid psychological realism. So too does her falling at his feet, revealing her recognition that she has experienced the presence of the numinous. The disciples' brusque question also falls into this aura of realism. Unique here also is Jesus declaration that she possesses salvation. So the miracle is embedded in a very human situation reflecting historical and psychological reality. Jesus revises the law of purity which held that only impurity was contagious. He brings purity to the woman and to sinners who enter the kingdom and their cleansing leads to repentance,

Jesus encountering again scribal criticism in healing the man with a withered hand (as he had in the cases of the stammering man and the blind man) represents a clash of honest differences of the understanding of God and his will for his people: the scribes insisted that doing as God bids in the Torah is Israel's duty while Jesus insists rather acting according to God's mercy is paramount in this case. Of course, both approaches serve God. (I've noted repeatedly that the Pharisees also insisted that human need and welfare superseded the requirements of Torah. But they also affirmed that one can break the Torah by verbally promoting a disallowed action.) Here again Jesus is acting in terms of the kingdom in restoring the conditions of the original creation by reestablishing God's original intention for his creation. The creation precedes the giving of the law. Healing can't wait for tomorrow demanded by the law—the new creation and the kingdom are here! The restoration of this man's hand

Invading the Realm of Demons, Disease, and Death

takes precedent over Torah. The Sabbath also resonates with God's "rest" after his creation work. So Sabbath and creation's restoration cohere.

The silencing that Jesus demands of those he heals has nothing to do with some so-called "messianic secret." Rather it has to do with Jesus' concern to only reveal his true character as the "beloved son" on his timetable and therefore initiate the fulfilling of his Father's will that he be offered up as a sacrifice. That revelation takes place when he tells his parable of the wicked tenants when he had gone up to Jerusalem. It was also a practical concern and took into account that the procurators and Herod Antipas were apt to violently put down any popular movements even if peaceful.

Jesus' in healing of the stammering man is acting on the basis of Isa 35 and the restoration of creation. It is also wisdom's action.[667] Wisdom was intimately association with creation, so Jesus here is functioning like wisdom.[668]

The healing of a bind man closely parallels the previous story with two striking differences. His healing is effected in steps and Jesus lays his hands on him a second time which reflects the difficulty of the healing. The word "restore" is used here again pointing to the kingdom's restoration of creation.

That a blind man is named in the story of the healing of Bartimaeus emphasizes its historicity and that Mark's community knew of him or his family or perhaps they were even members of Mark's community. In that case the community preserved the story of one of its members. His crying out to Jesus calling him "son of David" connects Jesus with a primitive Christology and the tradition of Solomon as a miracle worker. In this way Jesus is thought of as a miraculous healer like Solomon. There is no word or gesture that heals him, only that his faith had "made him well." Jesus emphasizes again that faith is the required attitude in healing which also underscores that Jesus preserves the independence of the person healed and eschews making people dependent on him as some kind of guru. The recovery of sight by the blind is a sign of the kingdom and the intent of God is to save his people (Isa 35:4–7). These works of Jesus were a graphic call to Israel to give up its occupation with Rome's egregious offenses against Israel and accept the presence of the kingdom which now is already among them in the fellowship of Jesus. Jesus' miracles are pointing to the dawn of the new age and the presence of that new age among the people who submit to it and enter it.

SUMMARY AND ANALYSIS

The story of the crippled woman afflicted for eighteen years suggests demonic possession because she does not ask for healing, indicating the possessing demons does not want to leave his victim. Demons hate humans and by possessing them afflict with sufferings. Again Jesus is in a synagogue to catch the ears of many people at one time with his kingdom proclamation. The synagogue ruler, unfamiliar with the careful and subtle exegesis of the law, as were the Pharisees who would allow the "saving" of people on the Sabbath, criticizes Jesus doing work on the Sabbath. Jesus poses an argument by means of the lesser to the greater as would a Pharisee. If an animal is rescued on the Sabbath why not a human being who has been afflicted not for a few hours but years! The Jubilee is here restoring people which elicits the rejoicing of the bystanders, the only appropriate response when the Jubilee dawns. It is time to celebrate, not grouse about Rome and its shenanigans. The grandeur of the kingdom has broken into the world of time and space.

Curing "leprosy" was part of Jesus' healing ministry. The Samaritan who returns to give thanks to Jesus in the story of the ten lepers recognizes the numinous presence of God in his healing and his "loud" voice reflects again the joy connected with healing and the consequent experiencing the kingdom. Those who do not return to give thanks are like the nation which has not received the kingdom and so abstain from hostility toward Rome.

The story of the man with dropsy is a combination of miracle story and pronouncement story like the two previous stories. These stories can then be designated "controversial miracle stories." Jesus addresses the issue of healing on the Sabbath before anyone criticizes him. So controversy dominates the story. The comparison in Jesus' argument is an equal comparison (*a pari*), an argument he, no doubt, used frequently. Jesus doesn't frivolously flout the law but again emphasizes the presence of the Jubilee which brings with it the restoration of the people. In this incident Jesus is in a house eating on the Sabbath and there is no hostile questioning of his action. Feast and healing come together here which images the Jubilee.

Archaeology has verified the existence of five porticoes at the Pool of Bethesda. That fact along with the occurrence of Semitisms and naming Bethesda as the place of the miracle of healing of the lame man in John 5 all contribute to the historical character of the story. In this case the disease is not specified but since the man lay on a mat and had no one to place him the pool it can be assumed he was crippled in some manner.

Invading the Realm of Demons, Disease, and Death

The healing takes place on the Sabbath but the healing is not criticized for that reason; rather that the man carries his mat, unlawful work on the Sabbath.

The story has several peculiarities: the man does not ask to be healed and even seems ambivalent about it, he does not know the identity of his healer until later, he never thanks him, and Jesus connects his malady as due to sin (vs 14 in contrast to Jesus' pronouncement in John 9:2 where he denies that the blind man's malady is due to sin). These peculiarities give a rather somber flavor to the whole narrative in contrast to the exuberance and joy found in the other miracle stories. (John also places the story within the context of the murderous hostility of Jesus' compatriots, 5:16 and 18.) John's Gospel is hardly devoid of joy and rejoicing because of the presence of Jesus.[669] Why is the usual joy lacking, especially in a story of a lame man of thirty-eight years healed of his disorder? The man's apparent resistance to healing and not giving thanks would point to the widespread resistance to Jesus' proclamation of the kingdom and the nation's refusal to recognize him as the sent one. It reverberates with Jesus' lament over Jerusalem, as representative of the whole of Israel (Luke 13:34–35), which he then leaves to its own devices:[670]

> "O Jerusalem, Jerusalem, killing the prophets and stoning those who are sent to you! How often would I have gathered your children together as a hen gathers her brood under her wings, and you would not! Behold, your house is forsaken."

So this miracle story is a commentary on and a graphic illustration of the lack of response to him. The crippled man embodies the nation as did the Geresene demoniac.[671] The demoniac personifies the nation in its occupation ("possession") by Rome and the crippled man the nation in its refusal of Jesus' invitation to enter the kingdom. In the former story there is a joyful response of the demoniac which, however, is balanced out by the rejection of Jesus by the inhabitants of Gergasa. In the case of the crippled man the people not only reject Jesus but seek to kill him (John 5:1, 16–18), a reaction not balanced by any joy or wonder attached to the healing.[672] In other words the die is cast. Jesus, the beloved son, will fulfill the Father's will and meet his sacrificial death.

Again a reference in the healing of the man born blind to a prominent feature of Jerusalem, namely the pool Siloam, indicates the story came from the early Christian community and witnesses to its historicity, although it has extensive additions added to it by John. The unusual making of a clay with his saliva to anoint the man's eyes is a detail also undergirding its historicity. The clay alludes to the first creation when God formed man "from the dust of the ground" (Gen 2:7) after a mist watered the ground. So Jesus creates a sign that interprets his understanding of the kingdom which brings healing. The kingdom is the new creation. So Jesus calls the people to become a new creation and "to see" (i.e., understand) that the way forward for the nation was embracing and entering the peaceable kingdom of God and participate in the new creation (cf., 2 Cor 5:17). The washing in the pool of Siloam resonates with the Noachic flood which also brought about a new creation. The washing can also be an allusion to baptism which Jesus practiced through his disciples (John 4:2), signifying entering the kingdom and the new creation. So Jesus used multiple symbolic actions to display the meaning of the kingdom and thereby attract people to it. But the event and its meaning falls on blind eyes and deaf ears as the people and the Pharisees resist Jesus (see 9:27). Pharisees would definitely have been a part of the human landscape of Jerusalem. The man's questioners find it hard to accept that he has been healed and even more emphatically insist they will have nothing to do with Jesus (and by implication with the kingdom) but will remain devoted to "Moses" and the law—the precise zeal and dedication that will lead the nation to destruction.[673]

This double action also fulfills the requirement of two witnesses (Deut 17:6, 19:15). So Jesus carefully plotted the course of this healing to provide a Torah-true witness to the people and its leadership that the man was indeed healed of his blindness.[674] His two parents also provide such a double witness (vs 20) as well as the man himself (vss 11, 15). So there was a triple double witness to the veracity of the healing. This leads to the final witness of the healed blind man which summarizes for John what the miracle witnesses about Jesus:

> The man answered, "Why, this is a marvel! You do not know where he comes from, and yet he opened my eyes. We know that God does not listen to sinners, but if any one is a worshiper of God and does his will, God listens to him. Never since the world began has it been heard that any one opened the eyes of a man born blind. If this man were not from God, he could do nothing." (John 9:30–33)

He clinches his argument with "God does not listen to sinners" (vs 31). In this way the man also witnesses to his faith in Jesus apart from the miracle.

The healing at a distance of an official's servant has John's rendition of the healing of the official's servant has a double attestation appearing both in Q (although the Lucan and Matthean versions are quite different from one another) and in John. We meet here again a mixture of forms: it is a miracle story but contains elements of a pronouncement story. There are a multiplicity of variants between the three versions of the story. Common to all three is the healing at a distance. Jesus initially rebuffs the request. Matthew has been found to be more faithful to the original tradition (Q) and John is in closer agreement with Matthew than with Luke. The story was apparently that of a gentile officer in the service of Herod Antipas's court who appeals to Jesus in Capernaum to heal someone in his household. Jesus initially rebuffs the man but he counters that with the confession that he is indeed unworthy to have Jesus come under his roof and that Jesus, in terms of his healing power, is like himself in his ability to command obedience from his underlings. Jesus then, marveling at this robust faith, tells him to return to his home that the healing has taken place. I have suggested that this encounter of Jesus with the faith of a gentile along with that of the Syrophoenician woman contributed to the development of his understanding that the kingdom was open to the gentile world.

The Historical Context of the Miracles

As all of Jesus' words and activities that I have described in the two previous volumes of this series Jesus' healing activity must be placed within the context of first-century Judaism and its historical situation.[675] Israel's conception of itself included the divine gift of the land (the temple being the chief expression of that consciousness), the Torah, and God's election of the people. It was a time of crisis. The Roman occupation with its paganizing features, such as the erection of pagan temples and the provocative and offensive actions of the procurators, stood in opposition to that tripartite understanding. A pagan government ruled and not God, the rightful king of Israel. So the perception persisted that Israel was still in exile.

SUMMARY AND ANALYSIS

The responses to this crisis of faith gave rise to various movements. The Pharisaic movement thought that this "exile" could be brought to an end by all of Israel living as priests, John the Baptist by baptism and repentance, while the Saducean leadership encouraged living with the status quo, drawing on the long and successful experience of living as a dependent hieratic state under the Persians. The Essenes waited patiently for the signs of God's intervention when the final battle against Israel's enemies would commence and victory would ensue when they joined the fray. They expected a priestly and royal messiah who would lead the nation in this final eschatological battle and rid the nation of Roman occupation when the kingdom of God would be established. Alongside these movements was the recrudescence of the judges of old (called "bandits" in the sources), militaristic messianic movements, and prophetic actions convinced that God would finally intervene and establish his reign.

The Jewish worldview included a plurality within the divine essence. It was thought that Israel was the true Adamic humanity, and as such she was called to act in the role of Adam as the source of peace and order in the world, restore creation, and rid Israel of internal corruption.[676] Judaism exercised a critical function over against herself. So Israel's vocation was to restore the creation. Sacrifice and repentance addressed the issue of sin and forgiveness. Based on the martyrologies of the Maccabean literature and Isaiah 53, it was thought that Israel's sufferings were sacrificial and redemptive. All of this was thought of within historical parameters. The present world had to be renovated. Jewish culture was embedded in the Bible and in the stories of Israel's sufferings and vindication, exile and restoration, of prophets and kings, and in the divine promises assuring of God's ultimate victory.

I have emphasized in my studies that Jesus was embedded in this Jewish context, and his words and actions must be understood in relationship to that environment. My investigation of Jesus' parables and pronouncement stories demonstrated how intimately they were related to his Jewish context of first-century Israel. He was calling Israel to eschew violence, hatred, and opposition to Rome and enter the kingdom, practice hospitality, forgiveness rejoicing in their God of compassion, and to be the light and salt of the earth. Jesus was understood to be a prophet (e.g., Mk 6:4; Luke 7:16).

His miracles resonate with the OT prophets like those of Elijah and Elisha who also performed miracles emphasizing that they were true prophets of Israel's God (1 Kgs 17:24). So healing stories would begin as prophetic stories. They were demonstrations of the present existence of the kingdom of God, his compassionate concern for his people, and the down payment and assurance of the certain breaking in of the fullness of the kingdom. But the miracles were also ambiguous. They could elicit the suspicion that Jesus was practicing magic, an activity forbidden by Torah. In this way there were those who thought of him as a false prophet and working in conjunction with Satan to mislead the people. It is for that reason that Jesus often sought to hinder spreading the news of his miracles. But he could not stop that activity, either because of his personal compassion for people and because they were a vital property of the kingdom, the kingdom demanded such as a sign of the restoration. The similarity of Jesus' ministry with Elijah and Elisha suggests he saw the present circumstances of Israel and its penchant for revolution against Rome as an idolatry, subverting faith in God and the rule and reign of his kingdom which Jesus brought about by his proclamation, teaching, table fellowship, and healings. The end of exile was near and a new historical existence was coming into being. So he summoned people to celebrate and enact the restoration.

The presence of the kingdom in Jesus' activities meant the founding of a community, the faithful remnant which remained loyal to Israel's God in opposition to paganism as well as to Jewish authorities and those who would turn Israel from her vocation to be and work for the restoration of the world. Animosity toward Rome and dreaming of ridding Israel of its occupation only subverted Israel's true vocation. So Jesus as prophet drew on the rich tradition of Israel which told the stories over and over again of suffering and vindication.

This all would necessarily lead to conflict regarding the nature of the kingdom and would lead to the charge that Jesus was leading the people astray. The issue was not law and anti-nomianism but eschatology and politics. The Pharisees emphasized living according to Torah. So they worked at interpreting the Torah and the oral law in such a way they could be observed in the contemporary environment. Jesus saw these boundary markers as the problem. For him it was the time in the presence of the kingdom to relativize the temple, purity laws, the Sabbath laws, and circumcision. Because these practices were symbols that defined Israel in light of Deut 13 he was judged as a perverter of Israel and disloyal to Israel's God (John 7:12). To join therefore in the new community of the kingdom was to court judgment and death. Jesus replaced these traditional symbols with his own and was reordering Israel's

SUMMARY AND ANALYSIS

symbolic universe. So God was reconstituting Israel around Jesus as the restored Israel. In this way Israel was finally home and no longer exiled. Israel, however, had turned inward when her vocation was instead to be the light of the world. Jesus was not struggling against Israel but for her. The real enemy was to be found within and not externalized in Rome.

The way of the kingdom was a new way of being. Victory was to be achieved not by violence but the radical ethic of non-retaliation and taking up one's cross. Restoration will come by suffering and tribulation, followed by ultimate vindication. So the kingdom meant the Lord's return to Zion, the reconstitution of God's people, the defeat of Satan, and the return from exile. Jesus was bringing Israel's story to its divine consummation. In this, Jesus functions as the rightful king-messiah. As the true messiah he takes upon himself suffering, death, and judgment.[677] God is acting redemptively through suffering, the way of peace, love, and the cross. So Jesus conquers not militarily but by exorcisms, controversies, healings. But his ultimate victory will be his death and therewith he takes on the nation's exile and the nation's fate. Israel's real enemy was Satan leading the people to think of defeating the world with the world's methods. Jesus enacted symbolically the Lord's return and his victory. He takes on the task which God had reserved for himself. Just like the Gerasene demoniac who embodied the Roman occupation of Israel so those whom Jesus healed embodied the nation and in restoring them to health he enacted the restoration of the Israel. So Jesus himself in his suffering and death bore the guilt of the nation and took on himself its suffering and so stood in the breach.

CHAPTER 4

The Miracles of Jesus
Raising the Dead

Your dead shall live, their bodies shall rise.
O dwellers in the dust, awake and sing for joy!

Since raising the dead is so extraordinary I have relegated the stories of Jesus accomplishing such miracles to this separate chapter. These actions are perhaps even more suspect than the other miracles ascribed to Jesus because they appear even more implausible to a world that is embedded in a scientific (or perhaps more accurately, scientistic) mode of thinking and because there is no known way to bring a person back from the dead.[678]

The three raisings that appear in the gospels are:

1. Raising Jairus's Daughter: Mark 5:21–24, 35–43; Matt 9:18–19, 23–26.; Luke 8:40–42, 49–56.
2. Raising of a Dead Man at Nain: Luke 7:11–17.
3. Raising of Lazarus: John 11:1–44.

THE RAISING OF JAIRUS'S DAUGHTER: MARK 5:21–24, 35–43; MATT 9:18–19, 23–26; LUKE 8:40–42, 49–56.[679]

There are a number of characteristics in the story as presented by Mark that point to a historical report:[680] the vivid portrayal of Jairus's[681] emotional appeal connected with his anxiety about his daughter being in danger of dying; the messengers who come to report that the girl had died so that Jesus need not be bothered by showing up at Jairus's house; the mockery of the mourners when Jesus insists she is only sleeping; and the command of Jesus preserved in the original Aramaic.[682]

Matthew and Luke both record and understand that Mark's report meant that the girl had truly died, eliminating any ambiguity that some commentators think that Jesus' insistence that she was only sleeping, and meaning she was not actually dead. Luke emphasizes her actual death by saying the girl's spirit returned (8:55). That Jesus actually meant not sleeping but the "sleep" of death seems to be underscored by telling the mourners they need not lament. So on the basis of the Marcan text alone, some commentators assert that it is uncertain if the text really meant a raising from the dead actually took place.[683] However, how could Jesus know, after having been told that the little girl was dead, that she in reality had not died? So he must mean that when he says she was but sleeping, she slept the sleep of the dead. Matthew and Luke also understand that the child had actually died. So I conclude that Jesus did raise her from death.

The place of this occurrence is not certain only that Jesus and his disciples were somewhere on the north shore of the Sea of Galilee.[684] The synagogue leader (ἀρχισυνάγωγος, *archisynagōgos*, "primate of the synagogue"[685]) prostrates himself before Jesus which emphasizes his extreme anxiety as well as his respect for Jesus.[686] Apparently Jesus' fame as a healer was known to him. So his public display of humility portrays his belief that a divine power resides in Jesus that can heal and restore life (vs 23). He refers to his child in the diminutive as "my little daughter" a term of affection which indicates how fondly this distressed father regarded his child. The story does not record a verbal answer of Jesus but rather an assenting action: "he went off with him . . ." (vs 24).

While Jesus was still speaking to the woman whom he had cured of a hemorrhage (see chapter 3, #4 above) messengers arrive from the house of the father reporting to the father that his daughter had died (the verb ἀποθάνω, *apothanō* is in the aorist tense meaning "is dead").[687] So they question whether Jesus should still be bothered by coming to the synagogue primate's house. They refer to him as "teacher," implying that death is beyond his power to do anything further.[688] Who would expect the dead to be raised? This news and the question corroborate that the girl had indeed died. The word translated by the English versions as "overheard" (παρακούω, *parakouō*) is better translated by "ignoring" (as in the RSV).[689] That meaning underscores Jesus' words which follow. We can well imagine how crestfallen the father would have been at the news, and Jesus responds with heartening words to the dejected man who (apparently) has lost his beloved daughter: "fear not, only have faith."

At this point, as Jesus, his disciples, and the crowd are walking together, he separates himself and the three disciples, Peter, James, and John, as they enter the house of the primate.[690] He is greeted by a "commotion and loud weeping and wailing" (NAS, NJB, NRS). The scene is not due to professional mourners—after all, the girl had just died, so members of the family and perhaps some neighbors are referred to. The scene again witnesses to the actual death of the girl as does the mocking laughter (καταγελάω, *katagelaō*, "laugh at, ridicule")[691] when Jesus asserts that she is only "sleeping." To present Jesus as the object of derision is entirely unique to this story and evokes the criterion of embarrassment.[692] In the LXX the word used by Jesus (καθεύδω, *katheudō* "sleep") is used of the sleep of death.[693] But here it is opposed to death. Jesus means that she has indeed died, but it is to be compared with a sleep from which he will now awaken her. Like sleep her death at this point is not permanent. So in the presence of Jesus, not only are demons exorcized, and the ill made well, but even death must yield![694] With this expression Jesus stands in these circumstances as in the place of God.[695] So as Jesus establishes the kingdom death becomes mere "sleeping." Taylor aptly observes that the word describes death as God sees it from which a person can be awakened.[696] Jesus asserts, as God's agent then, he has power even over death (see Luke 7:22).

So after he puts the crowd outside (some degree of force is implied and the emphatic "Jesus himself," which enforces the idea that force was involved)[697]—whose lamentations represent faithlessness—he, together with his three disciples and the mother and father, enter the room where the dead girl lay, with the confidence that he will restore her to life. Taking her hand Jesus says *"talitha koum"* (a transliteration of the Aramaic טליתא קומ). *"Koum"* is the masculine imperative "arise," but a number of manuscripts read the feminine *"koumi"* (*"koum"* is the obvious original). It could be that using the masculine form was popular usage at the time of Jesus or that Galileans dropped the pronouncing of the final "i." The use of foreign words and phrases are a standard usage in the miracle stories of the Hellenistic world. But that is not Mark's intent here because he cites Aramaic in other than healing stories (3:17, 7:11, 14:36, 15:22,

34).[698] The girl "immediately" gets up and walks. Her age is mentioned to explain that ability (i.e., she was not an immobile infant).[699] The amazement of the bystanders is emphasized again pointing to the actual death of the child. The repetition of the verb literally "being astonished with a great bewilderment" is Semitic, another reflection of the antiquity of the tradition.[700] Their reaction corresponds to encountering a theophany or an epiphany.[701]

Jesus then commands them not to make the incident known and to give the daughter something to eat. It is difficult to see how the command for silence could be fulfilled because the whole village would come to know of the miracle and then the news of it would be spread abroad. In fact Matthew has in place of this command for silence that the report was spread throughout the countryside (9:26). This command is not some part of a "messianic secret" motif, as I've already explained. It is Jesus' way of insuring that he will be the one to reveal his identity in his own time and the place of his choosing.[702] However, it could well be that this is the one place in the story that Mark has textually intervened since it does not really make sense and does not fit comfortably into the context of the situation as the narrative describes it. To have the girl fed reflects Jesus' compassion for her.

On the basis of the text alone it can be said that Jesus brought Jairus's daughter back to life. All the points made in the analysis above make of the story a historical event: the antiquity of the tradition, the reference to the petitioner's name, and his status within the synagogue administration, the Semitic background, the preservation of the original Aramaic, the element of embarrassment, and the witness that the girl had actually died. Of course, one's worldview is involved in making a decision of historicity. If one's point of view is "metaphysical naturalism," then any miracle is, by definition, excluded as possible.[703] But the very existence of the universe and living creatures points to a designer who is active within the material universe, making miracles not only possible but inevitable.

The coming restoration of the kingdom is already present, already active. The ridiculing response of the crowd is also a sign of Israel's response to Jesus and the coming kingdom. The astonishment reflects the human response to the numinous but would appear not to lead to faith and repentance or to a joyful response to the presence of the kingdom, an attitude that would avert the death of the nation that was inevitable if Israel continued on its present path of taking into her own hands the end of exile promised by the kingdom by opposing Rome. The restoration of life to Jairus's daughter is then the proleptic presence of the kingdom which overcomes death. It is a call to trust in the God of Israel and his creative power whose reality can be taken more seriously than the reality of death.[704] God is the God of life (Mark 12:27!). Nothing is impossible with God. The whole of the OT is a witness to this God who brings life from death creating an existence that is in fellowship with himself. The miracle here includes the creation of faith which believes that God can triumph over death. In this way the miracle points away from itself to us who hear the story and are challenged to trust that God can (and will!) raise the dead.

RAISING OF A DEAD MAN AT NAIN: LUKE 7:11-17.

It is remarkable that each of the three narratives that report Jesus raising the dead are basically recorded only by one evangelist. This is also true of the story of the raising of Jairus's daughter since both Matthew and Luke had received the report from Mark. That each one has only one witness to raising the dead does not bring into question their historicity. That has to be decided on the basis of an examination of each story. So their single attestation would seem to even substantiate their historicity. Since there are only three that paucity points to the tendency not to multiply their number artificially with the object of increasing Jesus' stature and claim to divinity. Rather the tendency seems to have been in the opposite direction: to report only what was actually known and remembered, although it appears to have been a regular part of Jesus' miraculous activity (Luke 11:22; Matt 11:5). Though extraordinary, the raising from the dead in Jesus' environment might not have been any more amazing than cleansing a leper.[705]

The similarity to the OT story of Elijah raising the dead son of the widow in Zarephath (1 Kgs 17:17-24) is impressive: Elijah like Jesus meets a widow at the gate of the town; he raises her son from death and like Jesus "gives him to his mother" (1 Kgs 17:23; Luke 7:15). However, the dissimilarities also stand out: the widow in the Elijah story is a non-Israelite; Jesus raises the man in Nain by a word, whereas Elijah goes through a rather elaborate procedure in raising the widow's son; Nain is a town in Israel while Zarephath is a gentile town; in Jesus' case there are people present when the raising takes place; Elijah and Elisha both know the women and their sons for some time; there is no long background to the story of the widow at Nain tracing the history of the son from health, to sickness, and death; the widow in Luke's story takes no initiative with Jesus, so there is no petition, no act of faith; there is no accompanying acclamation regarding the miracle as in the Elijah and Elisha stories. There is also a similarity to the story of Elisha raising the son of a woman in Shunem located in the lower Galilee not far from Nain (2 Kgs 4:8–37). However, he initially fails to raise the boy by sending his servant Gehazi to lay his staff on him. He then comes personally and goes through a similar procedure as Elijah and raises the boy. The similarities with this story are obvious as are the dissimilarities.[706]

The city of Nain obviously had a wall since a gate to the city is mentioned. In fact, archaeology verifies there was a wall there which is now in ruins. The city was located on the north slope of the hill of Moreh about ten miles as the crow flies from Nazareth and about a day's journey from Capernaum. These realities also undergird the historicity of the narrative. Jerome says there was a church there but he never visited it.[707] Egeria,[708] the fourth century pilgrim, visited the church which was built on the site of the widow's house whose son was resurrected by Jesus. She also visited the tomb at the burial site, still in use today, where her son was to be buried. It's about a ten minute walk from the city.[709] So the story is set in an actual place suggesting that the story is a historical report. It also has a Semitic substratum.[710]

All the English versions refer to a "dead *man*" in vs 12. Luther, however, correctly translates "and there one bore out a dead [person]" ("*da trug man einen Toten heraus*"). The text nowhere identifies the dead one as "a man" at this point. That must wait for vs 14 where Jesus refers to the dead person as a "young man" (νεανίσκος, *neaniskos*, "a youth").[711] The fact that the dead person is described as an "only son" makes the death even more poignant. The woman was a widow so this son would be the only support for her in her widowhood and as legal representative in Israel's patriarchal society. Without him she would end up destitute and devoid of protection. The verb "carried out" (Gk, ἐκκομίζω, *ekkomidzō*, "to carry out [for burial]") occurs only here in the NT pointing to Luke reproducing ancient tradition.

The "large crowd" (the adjective "large," ἱκανός, *hikanos* is used frequently by Luke and was perhaps a colloquial expression) accompanying her would have consisted of professional mourners and musicians with flutes and cymbals.[712] The mother would walk before the bier. The terrible circumstances into which this widow had been cast because of the loss of her son is intuited by Jesus (the father was not walking beside her) and so it was natural that he would have compassion for her because of the dire situation into which she now found herself. So, again in the face of death, Jesus seeks to solace this woman with the words "cease weeping" (the verb is in the present tense meaning the action is ongoing). Luke characterizes Jesus with the appellative "Lord" (κυριός, *kyrios*). This title is used frequently by Luke to designate Jesus so he is telling the story in his way and means here that Jesus, the bringer of life, is accosting grief and death.[713]

Jesus touches the bier indicating that the bearers should halt. Contact with the dead brought with it ritual defilement. But in the case of Jesus he brings holiness, forgiveness, and life. Jesus avoids words at this point because of the solemnity of the occasion. So he addresses the dead man emphatically by saying "*to you*, I say arise!" Death gives way and the man "sits up" (ἀνακαθίζω, *anakathidzō*). The young man could not have been in a trance or coma. Jewish custom demanded the preparation of a body for burial (washing and placing the body in a shroud). Then there are those who sit with the body until the burial takes place. (See Acts 9:37–40 for these practices.) If the person were breathing that would obviously be noticed. Jesus' compassion envelops the whole scene and continues as he "gives the young man to his mother" (cf., 1 Kgs 17:23): death destroys relationships, Jesus restores them.[714] The widow has him back, the son she so desperately needs.

It is not difficult to imagine what the reaction of the crowd might be when the young man sat up[715] in his bier. But instead of some kind of raucous joy it is said "fear seized them" and led them to praise God. The immediate thought is to give thanks to God for the wonder of this miracle which restored the widow's son to her. In this they say God is present by means of the person of Jesus who they, in terms of their own history and culture, designate "a great prophet" (emphasis on "a"). It does not say "the" which would refer to the expected prophet according to Moses' prophecy in Deut 18:15. Given Luke's Christology for whom Jesus is Messiah, Lord, and Son of God this is remarkable. He has to be accurately reproducing the tradition which he has received.[716] After so many years of lacking a prophet in Israel (the Pharisees had judged that prophecy had ceased and the study of the Torah took its place as a way of discerning God's will and purpose for his people) it seemed now indeed a prophet had arisen and the voice of God could once more be heard in Israel![717] The phrase "God has visited his people" occurs relatively infrequently in the Bible and elsewhere in the NT only in Luke 1:68 which points to its historical nature. The people who witness this raising from the dead express their sense of having experienced the numinous presence of God. This word of God's visitation through Jesus then spreads everywhere (vs.17).[718] The reference to "the whole of Judea" probably means to refer to all of Jewish territory including the Galilee.[719]

All of the evidence points to Luke reproducing a story that was handed down to him from among Jewish Christians in the land of Israel which faithfully recorded an actual event in the life of Jesus. Eusebius quotes a certain Quadratus's treatise to Hadrian defending Christianity:

> "But the words of our Saviour were always present, for they were true, those who were cured, those who rose from the dead, who not merely appeared as cured and risen, but were constantly present, not only while the Saviour was living, but even for some time after he had gone, so that some of them survived even till our own time."[720]

RAISING OF LAZARUS: JOHN 11:1–44.[721]

This is the greatest "sign" that John records in his Gospel and unlike the other "signs" which are jumping off points for theological reflection.[722] However, the typical Johaninne reflection, instead of occurring external to the sign, here it occurs within the confines of the story itself.[723] Jesus is presented as giving little disquisitions as the story develops each on a typical Johannine leitmotif: light and darkness, God's glory, resurrection, and the union between himself and God. In this way it is the crowning incident and the interpretive nexus of the whole set of miracles or "signs" that John includes in his Gospel. So it seems fairly easy to distinguish redaction from tradition.

However, given this shape of the present story, suffused as it is with Johannine redaction, commentators have diverged from one another in discerning the original tradition as it was handed down to John. Meier has a concise list of eight commentators and the verses they considered to have been in the tradition that John received in constructing his version of the miracle.[724] The only verses all eight have in common which they consider as original to the tradition are 1, 3, 6b, 17, 34, and 44, which would seem to pare down the tradition to the extreme. However, as difficult as it seems to be to find agreement on the reconstruction of the

Invading the Realm of Demons, Disease, and Death

exact wording of the tradition, it is possible to discern at least some likely elements of the tradition by excluding those verses that reflect John's intervention into the tradition.

Meier lists four reasonable criteria for discerning John's intervention in the story.[725] Using those criteria I judge the following to be insertions of John into the story: vs 2—John's identification of Mary as the one who anointed Jesus (John 12:1–8); vss 4–5a which are replete with Johannine imagery.[726] Jesus performed miracles and healings out of compassion and as manifestations of the kingdom of God. God's glorification by miracles is Johannine language but could be John's equivalent way of expressing the synoptic understanding that they are manifestations of the kingdom; vs 6 does not accord with Jesus' behavior; vs 8 refers back to John 8:59 and 10:31. When someone sought his help he always responded immediately; the fact that he finds Lazarus dead when he arrives in Bethany accords with the fact that the travel time from the Galilee could well have taken several days (It's about 120 miles as the crow flies from Capernaum to Bethany so it might well have taken three or four days to arrive there); vss 9–11a also reflect Johannine imagery (see John 9:41, 12:35); the little "catechetical" dialogue in vss 22–27 is also a Johannine interpolation.[727] Vs 18 would seem superfluous in the context of the earliest community which would know the geography of the Holy Land. But it could have been added early in the development of the text.[728] Vss 40 and 42 also contain Johannine language, theology, and concepts.

Even though the occurrence of the proper names of people involved in the miracle stories are rare they are hardly unknown. There is Jairus the petitioner (Mark 5:22) and Bartimaeus the healed blind man (Mark 10:46). The naming of the little family of brother and sisters points to the historicity of the story and the fact they were dear to Jesus and probably members of the primitive Christian community.[729] The fact that the place where the miracle occurs is specified, though somewhat distinctive (the locus of the Bartimaeus healing is also named, Mark 10:46–52) it too points to the historicity of this report.[730]

So the original tradition may have looked something like this:[731]

> Now a certain man was ill, Lazarus of Bethany, the village of Mary and her sister Martha. 3 So the sisters sent to him, saying, 'Lord, he whom you love is ill.' 5 Now Jesus loved Martha and her sister and Lazarus. 7 Then after this he said to the disciples, 'Let us go into Judea again.' 17 Now when Jesus came, he found that Lazarus had already been in the tomb four days. [18 Bethany

was near Jerusalem, about two miles off,] 19 Many of the Jews had come to Martha and Mary to console them concerning their brother. 20 When Martha heard that Jesus was coming, she went and met him, while Mary sat in the house.[732] 21 Martha said to Jesus, 'Lord, if you had been here, my brother would not have died.' 28 When she had said this, she went and called her sister Mary, saying quietly, 'The Teacher is here and is calling for you.' 29 And when she heard it, she rose quickly and went to him. 30 Now Jesus had not yet come to the village, but was still in the place where Martha had met him. 31 When the Jews [the people] who were with her in the house, consoling her, saw Mary rise quickly and go out, they followed her, supposing that she was going to the tomb to weep there. 32 Then Mary, when she came where Jesus was and saw him, fell at his feet, saying to him, 'Lord, if you had been here, my brother would not have died.' 33 When Jesus saw her weeping, and the Jews [the people] who came with her also weeping,[733] he was deeply moved in spirit [fiercely indignant] and troubled [distressed];[734] 34 and he said, 'Where have you laid him?' They said to him, 'Lord, come and see.' 35 Jesus wept. 36 So the Jews [the people] said, 'See how he loved him!' 37 But some of them said, 'Could not he who opened the eyes of the blind man have kept this man from dying?' 38 Then Jesus, deeply moved [fiercely indignant within himself] again, came to the tomb; it was a cave, and a stone lay upon it. 39 Jesus said, 'Take away the stone.' Martha, the sister of the dead man, said to him, 'Lord, by this time there will be an odor, for he has been dead four days.' 41 So they took away the stone. And Jesus lifted up his eyes and said, 'Father, I thank you that you have heard me.' 43 When he had said this, he cried with a loud voice, 'Lazarus, come out.' 44 The dead man came out, his hands and feet bound with bandages, and his face wrapped with a cloth. Jesus said to them, 'Unbind him, and let him go.' 45 Many of the Jews [the people] therefore, who had come with Mary and had seen what he did, believed in him; 46 but some of them went to the Pharisees and told them what Jesus had done.[735]

Even eliminating the obvious interpolations of John, what is left is still a lengthy story which is so different from the terse three-part structure of the miracle stories found in the synoptic gospels:[736] 1. The presentation of the need and the plea for help; 2. the miracle occurs with a word or action; 3. the reaction of those present and/or a conclusion. Elements 2 and 3 are basically contained in vss 43–44. The first element has grown into the large and even complicated story preceding the miracle in parts 1-5 in the outline and structure delineated below. It is in this part in which John has intervened so heavily. But even after the removal of his hand this section remains long and detailed. This may be due to the fact that these sisters and their brother were members of the primitive Christian community and so the details of his being raised from the dead would be precisely remembered and oft repeated. It had to have been a very comforting and encouraging story for the community.

As the story stands with the additions excised it presents a connected and consistent narrative. However, even with the elimination of the obvious Johannine insertions, the language still is redolent with his language such as referring to the people as "the Jews." The references to "the Jews" in the story probably read "the people" in the tradition which John received.[737] The reference of the people to Jesus' ability to "open the eyes of the blind [man]" in vs 37 John has added the singular referring back to the healing of the blind man in chapter 9 rather than to the blind in general as in 10:21. In this way by changing the plural to singular he embeds the story in the immediate context of his gospel. Vss 9–10 are also obvious insertions, referring as they do to the "law of the hour" i.e., Jesus' "hour" comes from the divine δεῖ (*dei*, "must"), the time of his sacrificial death on the cross (cf., 9:4).[738] Martha's mild censure of Jesus in vs 21 (repeated later by Mary and the gathered people vss 32 and 37) was a part of the original tradition. Jesus' profound emotions are understandable because of his deep love for the three members of this little family (vs. 5). He apparently had a long and endearing relationship with them (cf., Luke 10:38-42, John 12:1-8).

The word "believe" in vs 45 is probably redactional since it is part of the Johannine vocabulary. Some other word for the reaction of the people probably stood in its place in the tradition. Miracle stories always refer to the reaction of the bystanders.[739]

The structure of the Johannine account is arranged in a chiasm:

1. Introduction: Lazarus's illness/Jesus' delay (vss 1–6)

2. Jesus and the dialogue with the disciples: he goes to Bethany to wake Lazarus from the sleep of death (vss 7–16)

3. In Bethany: Jesus encounters Martha and Mary both of whom exclaim that if Jesus had been there Lazarus would not have died as do the people who had gathered to comfort the sisters. Jesus joins with the sisters and the crowd in weeping (vss 17–37)

4. Jesus arrives at the grave site (vss 38)

3′. Jesus' second encounter with Martha (vss 39-40)

2′. The stone at the door of the cave is removed. Jesus' prayer and the raising of Lazarus (vss 41-44)

1′. Two reactions to the raising (vss 45-46)

Elements 1 and 7 involve two components each; 2 and 6 have to do with raising Lazarus; 3 and 5 concern Martha and Mary; element 4 is the central constituent in the story. The surprising result of this analysis is that the raising does not occupy the central component of the story but rather Jesus' arrival at the tomb. The central position emphasizes Jesus confrontation with the reality of death. Preceding and following this element are the people who surround Jesus with their consternation, perplexity, and sorrow. Jesus does not stand above all of that but rather participates in it with his own emotional reaction. Vs 33 in particular emphasizes the intensity of this reaction: ἐνεβριμήσατο τῷ πνεύματι καὶ ἐτάραξεν ἑαυτὸν (enebrimēsato tō pneumati kai etaraksen heauton). Most of the English translations render the phrase with "he groaned (or was greatly moved, greatly distressed or disturbed), in the spirit and troubled." We have encountered the word ἐμβριμάομαι (embrimaomai) in other miracle stories (Matt 9:30; Mark 1:43). This "groaning" contains an element of coercion arising from displeasure, anger, indignation, and antagonism. It can also mean even rebuke, reprimand, reproach, chide, inveigh against. So it expresses "indignant displeasure" usually with the dative of the person toward whom it is felt.[740] It occurs only once in the LXX at Lam 2:6 (cf., Mark 14:5) where it is rendered by most translations with "fierce (or burning) indignation."[741] Luther understood and accepted the meaning of the word and translated more acurately, "ergrimmte er im Geist und betrübte sich selbst" ("he was furious in the spirit and so was distressed within himself"), coordinating the two parts of the sentence. The translations tone down and soften the meaning of the verb perhaps because otherwise it is hard to understand and their reluctance to characterize Jesus with such seemingly strong negative emotions. The second verb ταράσσω (tarassō) means "disturbed" or "troubled," emphasizing that the word in the preceding phrase should be translated with its usual meaning. I translate the word with "indignation."[742]

Why would Jesus react in this way? Bultmann interprets Jesus reaction in vs 33 as anger over the faithlessness which is expressed in the lamenting people.[743] But then Jesus himself weeps (vs 35), negating this interpretation. My understanding of this difficult verse is that Jesus, the bringer of the gift of the kingdom which stands opposed to death, and that he himself arrived too late to bring health to Lazarus elicited this response of indignation and his being "troubled." So then Jesus could also participate in the sorrow being expressed in the customary lamentation attendant on the death of a loved one in Jewish society as well as being troubled that he had arrived so late. This reaction speaks volumes then about Jesus' own humanity and his identification with human need and experience and his own deeply felt regret that he had arrived so late on the scene. It also emphasizes that not all who die are raised to life only to die again and that in our own encounters with death Jesus is present and participates in our sorrow (cf., 1 Thess 4:13: we sorrow but not like those who "have no hope").

Jesus expresses the same emotion in vs 38 after the people, like Mary and Martha, recognize that Jesus could have healed Lazarus reminding Jesus that unfortunately he had arrived too late to accomplish a healing. This time however, his indignation, his strong displeasure, was not "in the spirit" but "in himself" (which perhaps defines what "in the spirit" in vs 33 means). Both of these reported reactions of Jesus follow the exclamation that had he been present he could have healed Lazarus and preserved him from death. The verse again reports Jesus' strong displeasure with himself. It is therefore not surprising that Jesus "wept" (vs 35, different from the professional mourning that was involved by the visitors). His weeping, his sorrow, was made all the more intense because of his having arrived late. The bystanders recognize the depth of his sorrow which sprang from the love in which Jesus held his friend Lazarus.

Jesus gives thanks to his Father for having been heard. This prayer is reminiscent of Jesus and his thanksgiving prayers.[744] Reflected here is Jesus' intimate connection with God. So both Father and beloved son are at work in what follows. This intimacy between him and his Father will now reveal that God is also at work in Jesus in raising Lazarus. The dialogue between Father and the beloved Son is on-going. This revelation will bring about belief as well as opposition. The verb "heard" is in the aorist tense and means that his prayer had occurred in the past perhaps while Jesus had made his way to Bethany. However, the use of the past or even future tense by the OT prophets expressed the certainty of a message spoken in the present.[745]

Jesus commands then that Lazarus "come out" of the tomb. He hears his voice (see John 5:25) and in spite of his being bound with burial cloths he comes forth, a sure witness that he was truly dead.[746]

Commentators have sought to find the roots of this narrative in the parable of Lazarus and the rich man.[747] In both parable and miracle story a person named "Lazarus" appears. The parable is divided into two parts. The first part describes a poor man Lazarus who dies. In the second part of the parable the rich man begs Abraham to send Lazarus to his five brothers to warn them of their fate and to keep them from sharing in the torment of their dead brother.[748] Abraham rebuffs him by reminding him that they have the Scriptures ("Moses and the prophets") to warn them. The rich man persists and says if only someone would rise from the dead then his brothers would listen and repent. But Abraham answers that if they won't listen to Scriptures neither will they be convinced if someone rises from the dead. This is precisely what happens in the case of the miracle story: Lazarus rises from the dead but some will still not believe and plot to kill Jesus (vss 46–57) and Lazarus (12:9–11). A third similarity is the fact that Lazarus never speaks in either parable or miracle story but is only spoken of by others.

However, the differences between miracle and parable are also striking. The Lazarus of the parable has no family, is destitute, suffers with sores that the dogs lick, and apparently suffered with evil his whole life. The Lazarus of the miracle story comes from a well-to-do family who owns a house, a tomb, and one of its members—Mary—can pour a year's wages of ointment on Jesus (12:1–8). There is also no antithesis to Lazarus as is the rich man to the Lazarus of the parable. The parable also takes place in the world of the spirit, whereas the miracle story takes place entirely within historical realities. The immediate reaction to the miracle is that "many" do believe in contradistinction to the assertion of Abraham in the parable that a resurrection would not convince the brothers of the rich man to believe. So the only real connection between the parable and miracle is the name and the brief reference to rising from the dead in the parable.[749] So Meier concludes, "... explaining the Johannine story of Lazarus by way of the Lucan parable is a classic case of explaining the obscure by the more obscure."[750] So I would explain the resonances between the two by suggesting that Jesus may have invented the parable on the basis of his experience with the raising of Lazarus and the negative response that issued from it.

The tradition as I have reconstructed it above may have been even shorter[751] but the various characteristics of the story that I have mentioned pointing to a historical event witness to this raising from the dead as a deed accomplished by Jesus which he himself asserted as part of his ministry (Matt 11:5; Luke 7:22) and as a witness to the presence of the kingdom of God.

SUMMARY AND CONCLUSION

A common element characteristic of the miracles of Jesus raising people from the dead is that women play a prominent part in all of them: it is Jairus's beloved daughter who is raised, a bereft widow's son, and Mary's and Martha's brother. This characteristic in fact runs through all the scriptural accounts of raising the dead: Elijah raising the son of a widow, Elisha raising the son of a woman who had originally seemed to be barren, and Peter raising Tabitha, a beloved member of the community of Christians in Joppa. Then Heb 11:35 summarizing the faithful of the past refers to women who "received their dead raised to life again." Women were limited to the domestic sphere and not considered to be full members of society and not responsible for its direction.[752] So they were considerably more subject to the vicissitudes of life. Particularly a widow. A woman had to be under the authority of a man, whether a father, husband, or grown male offspring. Women were the focus of Jesus' raising to life their beloved dead as a sign of his own resurrection to the joy of his own mother, Mary who was told by Simeon that "a sword will pierce through your own soul" (Luke 2:35)[753] a reference, of course, to his crucifixion.

Remarkable in these three miracles is the specificity of place or of the people involved. Jairus is named as the father of his dead daughter, Nain (the existence of whose walls are verified by archaeology) the place of the widow who lost her son, and Bethany as the place where Lazarus was buried[754] along with his named sisters. This specificity points to the historical nature of these reports.

In each case the evidence is given which point to an actual death of the person involved and not some kind of swoon or coma: Jairus is told not to bother Jesus any further when the messengers come to inform him of his daughter's death and the mocking laughter directed at Jesus by the mourners when he insists she is only "asleep;" the dead young man in Nain is being taken to the burial grounds; and Lazarus has been in the tomb for four days and may already be giving off the odor of decomposition.

In the Jairus and the widow of Nain stories the Semitic background and language are evidence, pointing to old tradition. That Jesus appears in the Lazarus story as so thoroughly human in his emotional reactions to the lateness of his arrival and in his mourning over the death of his friend also evinces the antiquity of that tradition.

Apparently these three reports exhaust the number of instances of Jesus bringing people back to life. Their very paucity, and that the earliest community obviously did not artificially multiply such stories, also speaks to their actuality and historical reality. The Jairus and widow of Nain stories also bear little evidence of redaction whereas the story of Lazarus does. In that case, however, John's reflections stand out and rather than alter the story in any way they only reflect the underlying reality of what Jesus meant by them. They point to his resurrection, to his intimate relationship with the Father, and to giving comfort to his own mother when she would have to experience that sorrow and "sword piercing her heart" as he had to suffer his excruciating death.

These miracles of raising the dead bring to the fore primarily the person of Jesus, the one who emptied himself of divinity. He acts in these events then as only a human being comparable to Elijah and Elisha who could also awaken the dead. The will of Jesus, like theirs, was aligned with God's will. So they could be called "men of God" while he was declared the "beloved son" who was so intimately aligned with God that he was, unlike them, free of sin. This alignment then enabled God to work directly through him so that, as we have observed, people sensed in his mighty works God's numinous presence. These life-restoring miracles witness to the kingdom and that it was not just a state of mind but had an actual existence in the world. Jesus called together a community of people who heeded the call of the kingdom, joined in it, lived according to its precepts and the ethic of forgiveness, constituting a counterculture that eschewed the hostilities, the competition and rivalry, the accepted "norms" of the society—especially that of limited good, honor and shame, patriarchy and purity, and the violence advocated and perpetrated by the various anti-Roman ideologies and movements.[755] Rome did not need to be opposed because the kingdom was meant for the gentiles too and to join with Israel and sit at table together at the feast of the kingdom (Matt 8:11; Luke 13:29). So the kingdom was "flesh and blood," not just some skeletal, vague "spirituality." It held the people together in a robust renewal of life and faith. It was not just a vague soupçon of sanctity but true renewal that meant the revolution of personal faith and the way life was lived in the world.

Jesus did not reject Judaism to found some kind of new religion. Rather, he was bringing Judaism to its eschatological fulfillment. The nation was to be the light of the world (Matt 5:14) and the salt of earth (Matt 5:13).[756] But he warns the people that they can lose their "saltiness" so they have to let their light shine like a "city set on a hill" which can hardly be hid. Their light consists on letting the world see its "good works" (Matt 5:16). The kingdom showed the way to make this happen.

Jesus' miracles of raising the dead are the realization of the kingdom. They point to the new life of the kingdom as opposed to the dead end that the nation was tending toward in its opposition to Rome and seeking by its own methods to realize Israel's independence and in that way trying to insure the reign of God rather than the hegemony of Rome. So Jesus was facing a culture of death. The kingdom was resisting faithlessness and lovelessness. These raisings to life were meant to say Rome looks like death in its hostilities toward the nation perpetrated by the procurators. But the new life of these raisings were guarantees of the new life that awaited the nation if it would but enter the kingdom. The kingdom was a culture of new life, forgiveness, and a rock-solid hope all of which fostered courage in the face of Roman antagonisms and aggressions.[757] So Jesus was bidding through these raisings to take courage for death was undone and with joy join the resistance that works and will save the nation.

The kingdom is already active and present among them in Jesus' activity of bringing sight to the blind, making the lame walk, cleansing lepers, restoring hearing to the deaf, raising the dead, bringing good news to the poor, and creating blessedness for those who accept him and take no offense at him (Matt 11:4–6). To find this kingdom is to turn from the policies of revanchism and live in the kingdom and its morality of sharing, giving as one has received, forgiveness, and hospitality. Here the nation will find joy and build on a rock and not the sand of revolt which will lead to the rain storm and flood of Roman retaliation bringing about the collapse of the house of Israel (Matt 7:24–28).[758]

CHAPTER 5

The Miracles
The Theophanies

For there is nothing hid, except to be made manifest;
nor is anything secret, except to come to light.

These last series of miracles attributed to Jesus are usually called "nature miracles." That nomenclature does not seem apropos to all the stories assigned to this class of miracles. Why not include the raisings of the dead? Why would the transfiguration be included in this category, or a coin in a fish's mouth? In the following review of theophanies in Scripture it will be clear that these stories (except for one) are really "theophanies."

The miracles that fall into this category are:

1. Stilling of a Storm: Mark 4:35–41; Matt 8:23–27; Luke 8:22–25.
2. Jesus Walks on Water: Mark 6:45–52; Matt 14:22–33; John 6:16–21.
3. Feeding of the Five Thousand: Mark 6:32–44; Matt 14:13–21; Luke 9:10–17. Feeding of the Four Thousand: Mark 8:1–10; Matt 15:32–39.
4. Cursing of a Fig Tree: Mark 11:12–14, 20–26; Matt 21:18–22.
5. Catching a Shoal of Fish: Luke 5:1–11; John 21:1–14.
6. Water Changed into Wine: John 2:1–11.
7. A Coin in a Fish's Mouth: Matt 17:24–27.

8. A Transfiguration: Mark 9:2–8; Matt 17:1–9; Luke 9:28–36.

THEOPHANY IN THE OT

A "theophany" is a manifestation of God in the world, a divine self-disclosure. For Israel God's reality was different from the material world and universe and not limited by it in time and space (see Ps 139). Yet in a theophany God reveals himself within a particular space and time. For example he can be revealed in a thunderstorm (Ps 18:7–15); he can manifest himself on a mountain (Exod 33:23). The manifestation on a mountain is particularly prominent. The mountain with its peak reaching up to the heavens and whose roots go down to the underworld produces a sense of awe, particularly when its peak is enshrouded in clouds. So the mountain becomes easily thought of as a natural a place of divine manifestation and a cosmic center. So as a connection between the heavens, the earth, and the underworld, it becomes a site for theophany and a sacred place. Sanctuaries were constructed on mountains to realize contact with the divine. Thus it was also a favorable site for human habitation and cities grew up around them. In this way, mountain, sanctuary, and city would come to represent the cosmos, and the mountain became the center of society.[759]

In contradistinction to the pagan cultures surrounding them, Israelite monotheism combined into the one God all the various functions which were distributed among pagan gods. YHWH is divine warrior manifested in the thunderstorm, ruler of the universe, and revealer of his divine will in laws, decrees, and as judge of the nations. Sinai and Mount Zion are the important places in Israel's story where God appears and from which he marches forth to fight for Israel in their battles with the nations.[760] Sinai is the quintessential place of God's revelation in giving the Torah. God is manifest in the thunderstorm there and is recognized as Israel's divine warrior. Elijah traveled back there (called Horeb in this narrative) where he experienced divine revelation reminiscent of Moses. This story shows that Sinai continued to be regarded as the site of theophany down into the time of the monarchy. But Mount Zion superseded the importance of Sinai after its capture by David and God's presence was understood to dwell there (Ps 11:4, 46:5; Isa 6:1–13). Apocalyptic foresaw the day when the theophany of God would be a daily reality.[761] The divine warrior would appear to fight the nations and permanently remove them as a menace to Israel's security (Isa 66:15–23; Ezek 38–39; Joel 31–21; Zech 9), and God would finally be enthroned over an eternal kingdom of peace and prosperity.[762]

It was from the temple, built on Mount Zion, that God ruled over the world and history. From there he communicated the divine will and where he was enthroned on the praises of Israel. Sacrifices were presented to him and from there his blessing went out over the whole land.

Other places of theophanies occur at water sources, such as a spring, a well, a river, or at a sacred tree.[763] Like the mountain the tree's roots reached into the underworld and its branches into heaven and thus unites the underworld, the earth, and the heavens above like a mountain. But theophanies could also occur in a wide variety of places such as at the ark, a mobile artifact.

A theophany can assume various forms such as the thunderstorm which in its power as well as its benevolent aspect of providing rain produced a sense of the holy, the *mysterium tremendum*. The thunderstorm was the paramount form of the theophany in ancient Israel with its dual aspect of threat and beneficence. These divine encounters often elicit terror (Gen 28:17) and fear of death (Gen 32:30). The cherubim represent the storm in iconographic form: the body of the lion representing the roar of the storm and the eagle wings the winds of the storm.[764]

Another form a theophany can take is that of the human body: God can be described as having ears, a nose, a mouth, hands and feet. God is represented as marching into battle (Hab 3:12–13), riding a chariot (Ps 18:10), shooting arrows and hurling spears (Hab 3:9), as speaking (Exod 19:3), having human emotions such as anger and compassion (Exod 15:7), and having a face (Ps 27:7–9). As the divine warrior he appears as the commander of a heavenly host waging war against spiritual forces. He also appears as king who reigns over the universe with a divine council of heavenly attendants and ministers.[765]

In the Hellenistic-Roman world of Jesus' day divine interventions, the self-disclosure of the gods and the imposition of their wills was part and parcel of the way the world and the world of the spirit were conceived. Note how quickly Paul and Barnabas are thought to be the incarnation of the gods Zeus and Hermes (Acts 14:11–13). Examples of divine manifestations by the gods abound in the literature.[766] Paul's encounter with the risen Christ has a similar content of these story but are extensively different in form. So in form they resemble more the theophanies of the OT.

Invading the Realm of Demons, Disease, and Death

THE THEOPHANIES IN THE PERSON AND LIFE OF JESUS

Stilling of a Storm: Mark 4:35–41; Matt 8:23–27; Luke 8:22–25.

There are traits in the story that point to an eyewitness: the reference to the time, that Jesus is taken "as he was" into the boat (vs 36), the reference to "other boats" and the cushion on which Jesus slept, and the implied accusation of the disciples asking if Jesus cared about their perilous situation (vs 38).[767] Bultmann finds that the phrases "on that day" (vs 35) and "as he was" (vs 36 related as it is to 4:1) are part of Mark's redaction.[768] The second phrase could mean "they took him along since he was in the boat [already]."[769] The detail that "other boats were with them" (vs 36) seems like an unnecessary detail so it points to an actual reminiscence (both Luke and Matt omit the phrase). They are not mentioned again so they must have been scattered during the storm.

All of a sudden a storm (Gk., λαῖλαψ, *lailaps*, "sudden storm, squall") sweeps down on the lake, a frequent and normal occurrence.[770] The "waves" beat against the boat coming over the sides. Jesus is in the stern of the boat asleep on a cushion. This detail, integral to the story, again points to an eyewitness report. The disciples' apprehensive and fretful question is softened by Matt and Luke: Matt has "Lord, save, we perish" and Luke, "master, master we perish." "The disciples are sure that death stares them in the face, and they resent the fact that Jesus is asleep, seemingly oblivious to their plight."[771] That Jesus is sleeping may have something to do with the lateness of the day (vs 35) and it cannot help but witness to Jesus faith resting securely in the Father's care and protection.[772] The disciples' question, though somewhat of a rebuke, also is phrased with the negative οὐ (*ou*, no, or not) which expects a positive response. Of course he cares for his disciples. Their question is a complaint that he seems withdrawn from their plight, but at the same time they have faith he is able to do something. The disciples have witnessed him perform miracles so somehow they have an inchoate trust that he can do something in this threatening situation. They call him "master" but they don't really allow him to be their "master."

Jesus wakes and he "rebukes" wind and commands the sea to be still. This rebuke is like that of Jesus addressing the demons as he exorcized them (Mark 1:25, 9:25). So Jesus confronts the storm as a hostile force, almost personal, that seeks to destroy those who are in the boat.

This is not a primitive animism⁷⁷³ but a force used by the demoniac to attack and crush Jesus who had entered the house of the "strong man" and plundered it (Mark 3:27).⁷⁷⁴ The storm is "exorcized" and a "great calm" (γαλήνη μεγάλη, *galēnē megalē*) ensues. The miraculous calming is emphasized by the calming also of the water which one would expect to continue to be turbulent for some time after the end of the wind storm. So in this miracle Jesus proleptically portrays the eschaton and the overcoming of all evil and the establishment of the liberty of the new creation.

Before the disciples can react Jesus, with a rebuking question, asks them why they are so cowardly and don't yet seem to have faith. The questioning rebuke matches the disciples' own rude, complaining question. If they were not cowardly and lacking faith they could have responded something like the father with the demon-possessed son when the father petitions Jesus, "'... if you can do anything, have pity on us and help us.' And Jesus said to him, 'If you can! All things are possible to him who believes.' Immediately the father of the child cried out and said, 'I believe; help my unbelief!'" (Mark 10:22-24). Here the disciples speak not from faith but with cowardice and lack of faith, so they deserve to be branded as such.⁷⁷⁵ So he is rebuking them for not having faith in God not faith in the power of Jesus to control the forces of nature."⁷⁷⁶ Therefore Jesus calls them to have faith and free them from their cowardly fear.⁷⁷⁷

Implied here is that Jesus' own faith in his Father was absolute so that through him, the Father's agent who knew God had control of the tempest (Ps 106:9; 107:29), could act through him as in the story of the Jewish boy through whose prayer God acted.⁷⁷⁸ In this way Jesus was the agent of a Theophany which witnessed to God's action as the storm subsides.⁷⁷⁹ Their anxiety comes from lack of faith in God's care for them (Luke 12:7) which then leads to δειλός (vs 40 *deilos*, "coward, timid").⁷⁸⁰ When Jesus asked the disciples "if they still do not have faith," he is rebuking them for not having faith in God "not faith in the power of Jesus to control the forces of nature."⁷⁸¹ Implied here is that Jesus' own faith in his Father was absolute so that through him, the Father's agent who knew God had control of the tempest (Ps 106:9; 107:29; Job 9:8),⁷⁸² could act through him as in the story of the Jewish boy through whose prayer God acted. Their anxiety comes from lack of faith in God's care for them (Luke 12:7) which then leads to cowardice.

Jesus' "not yet" looks back at the experiences of his disciples with him and what he has accomplished with his teaching and miracles which should have, by now, produced faith. Simultaneously, it looks forward to when the disciples will have faith.

Finally, the report of the reaction of the disciples is described with typical Semitic phraseology, "they feared a great fear." They are unable to describe Jesus' identity but recognize his miracles and that "even the wind and the sea obey him." They can't quite come to say they have encountered the numinous though their emotional reaction witnessed to it. They have witnessed a theophany.[783]

The story reads as a straightforward report on an incident in the life of people of the first century and would be judged on those grounds as something that actually happened in the lives of those persons who make up the subject of the story. Only be focusing on the occurrence described would the story be subject to questioning its historicity. Can someone actually control and change the weather by fiat?

There are commentators who categorize the story as a "sea rescue" or as an "epiphany" (i.e., the manifestation of the divine).[784] That it is not primarily a sea rescue is heard in the response of the disciples who do not give thanks for being "rescued" but question the nature of Jesus and the mystery of this person who calmed the sea and the wind. So strictly speaking it is not a sea rescue. Although, according to Meier's definition the deity manifested is not initially present Jesus is revealed and manifested in a different way by his action in stilling the storm. In a sense he is not initially present in the way that he is revealed by the end of the story. Somewhat of a parallel to this story is Gideon's encounter with a theophany (Judg 6:11–24). The LORD appears to Gideon as the angel of the LORD and commissions Gideon to save Israel from the oppression of the Midianites. Even though the LORD is present throughout the whole encounter Gideon does not recognize the LORD until he consumes Gideon's offering of a meal by fire from a rock. This miracle is the event that reveals the identity of Gideon's visitor. Our story is plainly a theophany like the Gideon story.

Emphasizing the theophanic character of the story is the psalmic references to God as the stiller of the storm (Ps 66:7; 89:9; 107:29).[785] The disciples could hardly not have had these references in mind as they questioned who this is with them calming the storm and the sea. They had to be nonplussed and as faithful Jews could only resist the obvious implication that the divine One was with them in the person of Jesus.

Meier enumerates the similarities between the story and the story of Jonah in Jon 1: the prophet and crew are threatened by a great storm of wind; the prophet is asleep in the hold of the ship; the captain urges the prophet to do something so they do not all perish; the prophet gives the command to throw him into the sea and the storm immediately abates. The crew then "feared a great fear." But the Gospel story is a reversal of the Jonah story: Jesus is the prophet who is totally obedient to God; an angry God does not have to be appeased, but Jesus himself stills the storm with two words; Jesus himself appears in the role of God who tames the chaotic sea.

The historicity of the story is compromised, according to Meier, by the pervasive presence of OT motifs, phraseology which serves to present Jesus as exercising divine behavior and incorporating divine characteristics within himself.[786] So he finds in the story a "narrative high Christology." The Marcan redaction that he perceives in the story has adapted it to the idea of the messianic secret and the "obtuseness of the disciples" in their failure to understand who Jesus really is. Furthermore, the rescue of the disciples is congruent with and fits the miracle tradition of the early church which recounts how disciples were often saved."[787] So the story is impressed with the experiences of the post-Easter church and its theology.[788] He concludes that the story is "a product of early Christian theology."

The denial of Peter and the abandonment of Jesus by the disciples at the time of his arrest suggests that traditions about the disciples and their lack of comprehending of Jesus' true nature as the beloved son of God would appear in other traditions which included them in their telling. That further suggests that Mark derived his understanding of the obtuseness of the disciples not from his imagination or his theology (à la messianic secrecy scheme) but from the tradition itself. Secondly, Meier's concept of the tradition as Mark received it renders it but a bare bones outline of some kind of event in a storm which is hardly imaginable as a story that the Christian community would have nurtured. Thirdly, Meier's theory (although admittedly his careful and detailed analysis raises weighty issues) assumes that only the church had a theology and not Jesus or the disciples. As I have shown in my previous book investigating Jesus' baptism,[789] that event was a great revelation to him as he was designated God's "beloved son." That designation carried with it a whole realm of associations including his sacrificial death as well as an intimate personal relationship as God's agent and God as his Father who has called him to found his kingdom and save the people from certain destruction.[790] That status was an empowerment to establish the kingdom by word (he taught "not as the scribes") and mighty acts which are chronicled in the miracle stories.

The calming of the storm is not merely an ad hoc occurrence and spur-of-the-moment mighty work of Jesus. The restoration of Israel, which he was bringing about in the proclamation and presence of the kingdom, also meant the restoration of creation. This restoration meant that God in his kingdom is once again king of Israel and of all creation renewed.[791]

Finally, how are we to imagine the origin of the story if it is a "product of early Christian theology"? Someone in the Christian community, reflecting on how to present Jesus as Son of God, thought up showing him like God as master of wind and wave by saving the disciples from a storm and so made up the story of the stilling of the storm perhaps based on the story of the walking on the water (Mark 6:45–52)? Such a theory seems fantastical in a community dedicated to the "truth of the gospel." Even Meier has to admit that his theory is not "absolutely certain."[792]

So I conclude we have before us an actual incident in the life of Jesus and his disciples.[793] The disciples' response to the miracle makes clear that this was not a "rescue" like those recorded in the book of Acts but a theophany, a numinous encounter like Gideon had. But their own theology held them back from being able to recognize Jesus' identity as the "beloved son" of God. (Perhaps a "messiah," Mark 8:29, but then not a suffering one, Mark 8:32.) The "not yet" of vs 40 could be a Marcan interpolation but it could well have been part of the tradition because it aligns with other traditions depicting the disciples as not grasping Jesus' nature as the "beloved son." In that case it would be an accurate rendition of what Jesus actually said to his disciples.[794]

Jesus Walks on Water: Mark 6:45–52; Matt 14:22–33; John 6:16–21.

Matthew has added the reference to Peter walking on the water to the story. (This insertion reveals Matthew's style and vocabulary.)[795] Luke omits the story altogether.[796] But we do have two independent witnesses in Mark and John (Matt obviously being dependent on Mark). The attachment of the walking on the sea with the feeding of the five thousand both in Mark and John suggest a primitive connection between the two stories going back to the earliest Christian community.[797] The geographical realities are not especially clear. It seem that Jesus has gone to the eastern shores of the Sea of Galilee to a "deserted (or more accurately "desert") place" (Mark 6:31, cf., John 6:1). The western shore of the lake is hardly "deserted" or a "desert." The "desert" (ἔρημος, erēmos, desert) lies to the east and south of the Holy Land i.e., across from the Galilee which would place them some distance from Bethsaida which is implied by the notice that Jesus and his disciples had arrived there by boat (Mark 6:32).

However, John too, like Mark, connects the walking on the sea to the place where the multiplication of loaves had taken place. But John and Mark each connect the two miracles in their own unique way. Their passage by boat does not preclude the ability of crowds to arrive before them at the "desert place" since they came from "all the cities" (both near and far Mark 6:33). We can imagine as the crowd followed they would pick up others along the way.[798]

The chronological references are another matter. In Mark 6:35 "the late hour" implies that the time was almost at sunset. Mark 6:47 says evening had arrived, i.e., the sun had set. These references make it difficult to fit in all the circumstances described: the feeding, the time of Jesus at prayer, and the disciples arriving in their boat in the middle of the sea as the sun set (Mark 6:47). We can conclude that although the two stories of feeding and walking on the sea were already combined in the tradition, the combination is a second stage in their transmission. I conclude that the two did not originally occur together in Jesus' ministry.[799] Jesus' dismissing the crowd in Mark 6:46 is Marcan redaction integrating the story of the walking closer to the feeding. This dismissal of the crowd does not appear in John 6:15 but rather Jesus hides himself from them for they wanted to make him king by force.

The point of the story in Mark is that Jesus wished "to pass them by" (6:48, παρερχόμαι, parerchomai, "pass by") as he walked on the sea.[800] This same verb in the past tense is used in Job 9:11 just after vs 8 where God is described as "treading the waves of the sea." The verb is also used in the LXX of Exod 33:19, 22, and 34:6 where God "passes before Moses" an obvious theophany. So the "passing by" of Jesus means he wills to be close to his disciples and display his transcendent majesty, his divine identity.[801] So the story is not meant to be one of rescue.[802]

So Jesus' "wish" was to demonstrate his dominion over the unruly waters and the natural forces of wind and waves and in this way reveal his divine power and dignity (Ps 77:19; Job 9:8).[803] The language in the LXX of the Job passage parallels that in John 6:19 describing God "walking on the sea" which is an image that conveys God's boundless mastery over

Invading the Realm of Demons, Disease, and Death

the chaotic waters and so over all the forces of the creation. Humans do not have this power.[804] When God speaks to Job "out of the whirlwind" in Job 38 it is a theophany: God "shut up the deep" and set limits to its extent (38:8–11). No human was present at the creation and able to walk "in the recesses of the deep." A similar image occurs in Hab 3:15 and Isa 51:9–10, using mythological language of "cutting Rahab in pieces" and "piercing the dragon," which describes the act of saving Israel by making a path through the sea. This saving act is transferred to Wisdom in Prov 8:29, Sir 24:5–6, and Wisd 10:17–18. The Johannine and Marcan stories with their references to the reaction of the disciples indicate Jesus was obviously not walking on the shore as some commentators would maintain. That would hardly elicit any fear. Rather Jesus is presented as possessing the power of YHWH who made his way "through the sea" whose "footprints were not seen" (Ps 77:19). So clearly Jesus wanted to evoke these OT passages and reveal himself in a theophany as to his true identity which his resurrection clearly proclaimed.[805]

The time reference ("fourth watch" vs 48) points to the historical character of the story.[806] The disciples, when they see him "shout out" (Mark 6:49, implying fright[807]) which in the following verse is further identified as terror (ταράσσω, *tarassō*, stir up, shake, unsettle, throw into confusion, and in the passive, as here, troubled, frightened, terrified[808]). In John 6:20 they are described as "being afraid." Mark explains their reaction as due to their thinking that they are seeing a ghost (φάντασμα, *phantasma*, an "appearance" hence a ghost or spirit Mark 6:49).[809] Why would they interpret an appearance of Jesus in that way? This reaction suggests that the story is a post-resurrection appearance of Jesus which Mark has retrojected back into Jesus' earthly ministry (no doubt because he received it in combination with the feeding story). Jesus reassures them by saying to them "Take heart, it is I. Be not afraid." On one level Jesus is saying, "I am the Jesus you know so you don't have to be afraid." On another level, however, because the phrase "it is I" literally reads "I am" (ἐγώ εἰμι, *egō eimi*), he is invoking God's own self-identification as the "I am" (Exod 3:14). Jesus makes the startling asseveration of his divinity. So in this "I am" the story reaches its climax after the central event of his walking on the sea. The "I am" conveys two meanings: Jesus identifies who he is on two levels: he is Jesus the crucified and risen one, the one with whom they lived and shared his ministry; and the "I am" resonating with the divine name, he is "the image of the invisible God, the first-born of all creation" (Col 1:15). Isaiah 43:1–13 connects

THE MIRACLES

the Lord's self-identification as the "I am" with being Israel's savior. So God as the "I am" includes his self-revelation as the one, true God beside whom there is no other, the Creator, and the Redeemer.[810] So they have no reason to be afraid.

The implication here is that in his resurrection Jesus revealed his divinity, that is, he was no longer "emptied" of his divinity as during his pre-resurrection, earthly ministry but was now "highly exalted" (Phil 2:9). His divinity is now revealed and clearly seen and experienced.[811] He is the incarnate Son of God, one with the Father. The "I am" is with his people.

Jesus is then described as climbing into the boat and the wind ceasing. The disciples' reaction is again portrayed. They are "amazed" (ἐξίστημι, *existēmi*, "astonish, amaze," and even "be out of one's mind, mad" see Mark 3:21, 2 Cor 5:13). The vss 51b-2 are Marcan redaction. Mark introduces and underscores the disciples' obtuseness which anchors the story in the pre-resurrection life of Jesus and Mark's theme of the disciples not grasping the meaning of the multiplication of the loaves (cf., Mark 8:13–21). So for Mark even the revelation of his divine nature does not penetrate the disciples' dullness of heart. (Cf., the story in John 6:20–21 where they immediately take Jesus into the boat and reach the land.[812]

So the story in its original setting of the post-resurrection life of Jesus is a theophany: Jesus reveals his divine nature before his disciples.[813] He walks before them as God did in the garden before Adam and Eve (Gen 3:8). So the theophany also witnesses to the restoration of the creation. The eschaton, by Jesus' resurrection, has invaded the present world order and the kingdom reconstitutes the creation and the people who enter it are themselves a new creation (2 Cor 5:17).[814]

Meier finds John's version of the story to be the more primitive: the narrative is shorter and lacks the usual Johannine symbolism and theological commentary.[815] He finds John's possible interference in the story in the reference to darkness (vs 17), to Jesus as not already having come to them (vs 17), and the secondary miracle of immediately reaching the land when Jesus gets into the boat (vs 21).[816] His walking on the water is also never called or mentioned as one of John's "signs." He finds that the miracle actually interrupts the flow of John's text where the emphasis is on the miracle of the loaves and Jesus' disquisition on himself as the bread of life. So why did he retain it in his gospel? Perhaps because it witnesses to a high Christology which is a major emphasis in his gospel.

Invading the Realm of Demons, Disease, and Death

Narratively it also gets Jesus back to Capernaum where the rest of the chapter takes place. For these reasons then John preserved the relatively primitive form of the text.[817]

Bethsaida (Mark 6:45) is probably the original reading since Capernaum (John 6:17) was where John wanted Jesus to end up (the villages are less than three miles apart on the north shore of the sea of Galilee). Another contradiction is the motivation for the disciples leaving Jesus and crossing the lake on their own. In Mark Jesus "compels" (ἀναγκάζω, *anankadzō*, compel, restrain, Luther translates "*treiben*," force or impel) the disciples to get into the boat and go before him" while in John they simply go "down to the lake" of themselves, get into a boat and leave for Capernaum. The parenthetical remark by John ("Jesus had not yet come to them") is the hand of John at work. He makes such remarks elsewhere in his Gospel (12:33; 18:14).[818]

Both Mark and John refer to the strong wind which arose and in Mark how it made it difficult for the disciples to make any headway. But the wind has not placed them in any particular danger. Both evangelists refer to the fear the disciples feel when Jesus appears walking on the water. But now the two evangelists go their separate ways: In Mark the problem the disciples are having making headway is overcome when Jesus steps into the boat. The wind dies down. He concludes the story with his own redaction that emphasizes the disciples' lack of understanding in spite of what they have heard and seen. In John the story quickly comes to a conclusion: Jesus gets into the boat and the boat reaches—"immediately"—their destination. A second miracle.

This little analysis suggests the contents and flow of the original tradition: It had to be in the form of a miracle story whose narration falls into three parts: 1. The circumstances in which the miracle occurs are described; 2. The word or action of Jesus that effected the miracle follows; and finally 3. The reactions of those who witnessed the miracle are then noted.[819]

The structure of the narrative in both gospels is as follows (Mark's structure is given first). They both exhibit a chiastic structure.

a. Jesus sends the disciples and the crowds away

b. Jesus goes into the mountain to pray

c. Evening falls and the separation between disciples and Jesus is pointed out

d. Jesus is able to observe the disciples' difficulty in rowing their boat against the wind
  e. Jesus goes to them walking on the water
  d'. The disciples see him and thinking he's a phantom cry out
  c'. Jesus speaks to them reassuring them that indeed it is he and they are not to be afraid
  b'. Jesus climbs into the boat and the wind dies down
  a'. The disciples are amazed and beside themselves

The central element is Jesus' walking on the water indicating that this element is the focus of the narrative. a-a' emphasize the separation between Jesus and the disciples; b-b' are antithetical describing separation and reunion between Jesus and the disciples; in c-c' the separation between Jesus and the disciples is explicitly noted and Jesus seeks to ally their fears; d-d' describe the disciples physical and spiritual difficulty. The story is told from Jesus' standpoint.

John's version in the following analysis can be seen to be the shorter of the two:

  a. Jesus retreats to a mountain to avoid the people forcing kingship on him
  b. At evening the disciples go down to the lake, get into a boat, and head to Capernaum
  c. A great wind arises on the lake creating billows on the lake
  d. When they were some miles off they see Jesus walking on the water and coming near to them in their boat and they are afraid
  c'. Jesus speaks to them reassuring them that it is he and they are not to be afraid
  b'. They bring him into the boat
  a'. They immediately reach Capernaum

Again the central element is Jesus walking on the water after indicating how far the disciples were on their trip and their reaction to seeing Jesus walking on the water. In giving the distance that the disciples have rowed underscores the feat of Jesus in walking that same distance but on the water! a-a' Jesus and the disciples go in opposite directions but are joined in reaching Capernaum; b-b' the boat is the common theme in which

Jesus and the disciples rejoin one another; c-c' Jesus reassures them in the face of the wind storm and his unexpected appearance. Again the corresponding elements of the story on each side of the central element match but not quite as closely as in the Marcan rendition. So the Johannine version exhibits less refinement and development and is therefore the more primitive version of the story which supports Meier's insight (see above). The complexity of the narrative is emphasized because the corresponding elements on each side of the central element do not parallel one another in the same way as in Mark indicating what we have is a historical report that is fashioned to emphasize Jesus walking on the water. To be noted is the more succinct form of John's story and that it is told from the standpoint of the disciples (who would have been the source of the story).

Mark's version hints at a second miracle, the immediate end of the wind storm while John's version has an additional miracle added to Mark's two: the boat immediately arrives at Capernaum after Jesus enters the boat. Both Mark and John tether the story with that of the feeding of the five thousand. They disagree on the destination of the trip on the lake, Capernaum or Bethsaida? The motivation for the lake trip of the disciples varies in these versions. Mark also emphasizes the separation between Jesus and the disciples throughout his telling. So Mark sets up a bipolar antithesis between the disciples and Jesus. They are harassed at sea while Jesus is alone in the calm of prayer on the land. In the central element of each rendition both Mark and John agree: Jesus came to the disciples walking on the water and reassures them with the same words. Also in both stories Jesus and the disciples are reunited, the disciples' difficulty resolved.

Thus the basic content of the original story is quite clear: the disciples get into a boat to travel on the sea of Galilee, probably to Bethsaida, meet a distressful situation of a strong wind that is against them while Jesus has stayed behind on the land. Jesus then comes to them walking on the water and assures the frenzied disciples that "I am [with you], don't be afraid." Jesus and the disciples are reunited and they then reach their destination. We have here a theophany: Jesus shows his true essence as the incarnate God of the fathers. The hurried departure, reference to Bethsaida, the disciples constrained by a strong wind, and their fearful cry at seeing, what they think is a ghost points to the historicity of the narrative.[820]

Merely on the level of the transmission of the Jesus tradition the double attestation of this story points to its historicity. Meier denies its historicity on the grounds that the miracle does not cohere with the other miracle stories that have to do with helping others and were part of Jesus' kingdom proclamation. Secondly, he notes that in this story "the elements of epiphany (i.e., what I call theophany) and of OT allusions" become central to the narrative rather than an aspect of the story.[821] He notes, however, that the Johannine version conforms to post-resurrection appearances of Jesus particularly John 21:1-14: it is situated by the Sea of Galilee, the disciples are "bereft of Jesus and are experiencing a difficulty," and Jesus reassures them of his identity and stills their fears. Mark's version fits this pattern and particularly that of Luke 24:36-49 (but without a commissioning): the disciples "supposed they had seen a spirit" (πνεῦμα, *pneuma* 24:37).

Meier's observation that the miracle does not cohere with the other miracles is exactly right and points to its post-resurrection provenance. The miracles of healing and exorcisms were part of Jesus' proclamation of the kingdom and signs of the kingdom's presence. The walk on the water has its focus on Jesus, his identity, and his person: he is God incarnate. His resurrection initiates the mission to the world the center of which is Jesus himself. The proclaimer of the kingdom now becomes the one proclaimed.

Feeding of the Five Thousand: Mark 6:32-44. Matt 14:13-21. Luke 9:10-17. John 6:1-15.

Feeding of the Four Thousand: Mark 8:1-10. Matt 15:32-39.[822]

The prelude to the feeding story, in Mark 6:32-34, has been thought to be a Marcan redactional attachment and a stage setting for the miracle which follows.[823] These verses indeed provide the setting and help interpret how the miracle is to be understood: Jesus is the shepherd of Israel pasturing his people. They are made to lie down in "green pastures" (vs 39 echoing Ps 23:2) where he feeds them and "restores" their life (Ps 23:3, cf., Mark 8:3). John's version is also prefaced with a sailing over the Sea of Galilee (6:1-2) with a crowd following him and the notice that there was abundant grass in the place (6:10). And of course, John emphatically emphasizes Jesus as the "Good Shepherd" (10:1-21). Mark 14:27 also demonstrates that Jesus thought of himself as shepherd of his people Israel (cf., Rev 7:17). The designation is messianic.[824] So it is quite possible that this little prelude was long a part of the passage on the feeding.[825]

The actual multiplication of the bread and fish is never explicitly reported and the reader must infer that result from the fact that all are fed and from the number of crumbs gathered after the feeding. The event, unlike other miracle stories, is told in all four gospels and twice more in Mark and Matthew in a variant form. The feeding of the five thousand in John bears similarities with the Marcan account with its reference to the number of people fed and the presence of five loaves and two fish. John also shares similarities with Luke and Matthew: the reference to healing the sick and to the crumbs that are "left over."[826] Meier finds that the minor agreements between Matthew and Luke over against Mark do not constitute a sufficient reason to conclude that there was a Q version of the story.[827] He asks two apposite questions that must be answered on the basis of the version of the story that occurs in the four gospels: 1. Is John's version dependent on Mark? 2. Do the two renditions in Mark represent two versions circulating in the tradition or has Mark created one on the basis of the other?[828]

Most commentators hold John to be literarily independent of the Synoptic gospels. Brown's chart mentioned in the note finds a mixture of similarities and differences between John and the synoptic version which point to his independence. Most striking is that Mark's reference to a "desert place" does not appear in John's version which reference would have well-served John in his bread of life discourse (John 6:22–59) during which his opponents refer to God having given manna to Israel *in the desert* (6:31, cf., 6:49).[829]

The two feeding stories in Mark share a striking resemblance in content and structure. One would not expect the disciples in the second story to show no anticipation that Jesus would perform once again a multiplication of loaves and fish after having experienced just that under similar circumstances. It is not due to the disciples' obtuseness since Jesus makes no mention of such lack of insight. Later when Jesus does rebuke them (Mark 8:15–21) it is not because they don't remember but their lack of understanding the deeper meaning of the miracles. The fact that the Johannine version shares elements with both of Mark's feeding stories suggest one early, but variable, form of the story in the oral tradition.[830]

There are also seven words in the story of the feeding of the four thousand that occur only in this passage in Mark.[831] These hapaxlegomena in Mark suggest that he derived the story from the tradition and did

THE MIRACLES

not create the second story on the basis of the first. That it was a traditional story is supported by the fact that the Johannine version draws on it as well as the story of the feeding the five thousand.[832] However, there are more parallels between the Johannine story and Mark 6.[833] The question then presents itself: are the two stories both traditional but alternative versions of a miraculous feeding or do they witness to and report on two different events in Jesus' ministry?

There are redactional elements in all three versions of the story. In John the notice that Jesus already knew what he was going to do, that Jesus himself distributes the bread and fish to the crowd (in the Marcan versions the disciples do), and that perhaps the mention of Passover all look like John's intervention into the story. Meier suggests that the elements of the stories that conform to the usual form of miracle stories (I list them above in the exposition of the walking on the water) would be close to the archaic form of the story:[834] the circumstances, the action of Jesus, and the response of the crowd.

Circumstances: In this story the miracle occurs on the shore of the Sea of Galilee (but not in the second feeding of Mark 8). John does not emphasize the lake as Mark does who reports many crossings made by Jesus consequently it could have been part of the original telling. The reference to a "desolate" place occurs only in Mark's two stories. Such a motif would have served John's telling in the discourses of chapter 6 (see vss 31-3, 49). (It is possible that it was originally part of the tradition available to John but somehow got dropped during its transmission.) A large crowd is present (crowds are not usually emphasized by John); the dialogue between Jesus and the disciples concerning the size of the crowd and the impossibility of feeding such a large group (only Mark's second telling refers to the dire need of the crowd and that if dismissed they would "faint on the way"); in Mark's two versions it is the disciples who have the loaves and fish in John it is a "young lad;" only Mark's first version and John refer to the grass in the place (perhaps an allusion to Ps 23:2 emphasizing Jesus as the Good Shepherd). That connection with Ps 23 is supported by Mark 6:34 immediately preceding the story of the feeding where Jesus refers to the crowd as sheep "without a shepherd." So Mark could have added the reference to the grass and John too because he mentions that it was Passover (vs 6:4).

In having the crowd gather in groups and recline in the grass emphasizes that the feeding was a feast limning the messianic feast of the kingdom (cf., Exod 18:25).[835] The crowd is brought into a community overcoming the fractures and competition within Jewish society.[836] The kingdom of God becomes manifest and the crowd is brought together as the eschatological people of God.[837]

Action: Jesus effects the miracle after giving thanks and breaking the bread and fish for distribution (in Mark's two versions the disciples distribute the pieces and in John it is Jesus himself. (John's tendency is to emphasize Jesus and relegate the disciples to the background). Jesus is recapitulating the main meal of the day within the family which consisted of bread and fish. Bread was the main ingredient which was not cut but broken before it was distributed. So Jesus acts as housefather of the large crowd. In this way he creates a table fellowship of all those present.[838]

Response: the crumbs left over are collected, twelve baskets worth, stressing the reality of the miracle (the number twelve for the baskets suggest the twelve tribes so that in this way the crowd represents all Israel; so Jesus, as God did in providing manna for the twelve tribes in the wilderness, does the same for contemporary Israel.[839] John also adds that the crowd wanted to make him king as a result of the miracle which hints at divinity, since God is Israel's true king, and therefore his kingdom's presence in the multiplication of the loaves.[840] This earthly table becomes an image for the heavenly, eschatological messianic banquet. So the good Shepherd does not let his people be in want but even in the wilderness provides for them (Ps 23).[841] In this way he brings about the eschatological fulfillment, the end-time salvation, of the exodus from Egypt.

So the originating tradition would have referred to the lake side, the large crowd, the reference to the impossibility of feeding such a large group, the disciples who are in possession of the food and who ultimately distribute it, Jesus giving thanks and breaking the bread and fish, and the twelve baskets of crumbs that are gathered. The expression of incredulity on the part of the disciples that Jesus would think that he and they could feed such a crowd (Mark 6:37; 8:4; John 6:7) serves as an anticipatory reaction to the actual feeding miracle. Of course, the tone of this astonishment on the part of the disciples is also a kind of reproof of Jesus.[842]

In the first feeding Jesus "blesses" (εὐλογέω, *eulogeō*) the bread and fish whereas in the second he "gives thanks" (εὐχαριστέω, *eucharisteō*). The words are interchangeable. The Jewish prayer at meals began with a blessing or thanksgiving: "Blessed are you, O Lord, our God, king of the universe who makes bread grow from the earth" with hands outstretched and the lifting of the eyes to heaven (cf., Luke 1:68). Similar wording occurs in Mark 14:22 which does not imply that Mark is making a connection with the institution of the Eucharist. Jesus is merely following Jewish practice and custom in each case. The verb describing Jesus handing the bread over to the disciples to distribute it to the people is in the imperfect tense (ἐδίδου, *edidou*) suggesting the continuous action of Jesus. Perhaps this word describes the miracle itself as Jesus continues to break the loaves. One of Jesus' intention was surely to image in the feeding the eschatological banquet and Messianic feast of the Kingdom of God.[843] That the people are satisfied (χορτάζω, *chortadzō*, "feed to the full, satisfy with food") which emphasizes the miracle that Jesus has effected as does the observation that "twelve baskets full of broken pieces and of the fish" were gathered (Mark 6:43): more than what existed before the feeding! The phrase suggests translation Greek[844] indicating the antiquity of the story.

There are parallels galore with the feeding stories in the OT, in the Rabbinic literature, and in the Graeco-Roman world of the time.[845] On the other hand precise parallels to the gospel accounts are not to be found in the environment of Jesus' day.[846] Closest to the gospel versions is the Elisha miracle in 2 Kgs 4:42–44. Meier notes the parallels and differences:[847] Elisha orders barley loaves along with some other fare to be distributed among the people and his servant objects that it's hardly enough; the prophet insists his command be obeyed; all are fed and there's some left over. By following this OT story the gospel stories proclaim that one who is greater than Elisha is now present: in the gospel stories the food at hand is greatly decreased to but five loaves and two fishes but the number fed is not a mere one hundred but four or five thousand! The differences in the Elisha story, however, are just as striking: a geographical setting is missing; no crowd is described, there is no great hunger attributed to the hundred; Jesus commands the people to recline on the grass; Jesus performs the rites observed by a Jewish father at the beginning of a meal; the disciples do not resist Jesus' command; the leftovers are not precisely measured. The structure of the Elisha story is that of prophecy and fulfillment not, as in the gospel story, of a mighty work, a theophany.[848]

The story is multiply attested: in the two forms of the story we have in Mark and in the gospel of John. The story also coheres with Jesus' understanding of the kingdom of God as a banquet and with his practice of open commensality. That latter practice is confirmed by the inclusion of "sinners" in his table fellowship and the criticism it engendered (Mark 2:15–17; Mark 14:25; Matt 8:11–12; 11:18–19; Luke 19:1–10). This practice is also confirmed by the criterion of embarrassment because it conflicted with the church's practice of excluding abject sinners from its midst (e.g., 1 Cor 5:1–5).

So what actually happened? Meier lists all the rationalistic explanations to the miracle some hyper-imaginative (e.g., Jesus had food supplies hidden in a cave from which the disciples passed him portions so that he could distribute them to the crowd).[849] All seem to agree there was some event behind the narrative "some especially memorable communal meal of bread and fish, a meal with eschatological overtones celebrated by Jesus and his disciples with a large crowd by the Sea of Galilee."[850] But verification of a miracle is, for Meier, beyond the capability of a (modern) historian.

It needs to be noted that if we had three independent sources for an event that did not defy our modern prejudicial scientism the historian would affirm the historicity of such an event. We know miracles happen (chapter 1). Now, if God can create a universe out of nothing it seem a small thing to affirm he could multiply bread and fish. If there were some rationalistic explanation to the miracle it certainly would have been reported that way.[851] Taylor remarks that because the narrative "has not yet attained the rounded form of a Miracle-story proper it stands nearer the testimony of eyewitnesses. Mark knows the circumstances in which the event happened . . . and is able to tell the story with the detail furnished by a living tradition."[852]

The story does not have a sacramental aspect to it[853] but there is an inescapable resonance with the feeding of Israel in the wilderness. So it does bear a transcendental quality. Jesus was recapitulating that foundational experience of Israel (cf., Exod 15; Num 11; Ps 78:17–25). Jesus was not only fulfilling the Scriptures (cf., Psa 132:15–18) but was reconstituting Israel, showing that God even now desires to feed his people, relieve them of anxiety, and proclaim that God and his kingdom was among them in spite of the Roman occupation so they could give up their desire for revolutionary answers to their occupation and consequent animosity toward their Roman overlord. God himself, as in the Exodus, would lead his people once again out of the "exile" into the promised land of emancipation from Rome so they needed to put their full trust in him. The ancient exodus from Egypt finds its eschatological fulfillment as Jesus feeds the people in the wilderness. God is in control of history and will bring about their liberation if they but put their trust in him.

The feeding is a foretaste of the Messianic banquet (Isa 25:6–8; 55:1–7) at which the Messiah will preside and a down payment on his intention of ending their present exile.⁸⁵⁴ 1 Enoch 62:9–16 could well be a commentary on Jesus message to his people by way of the feeding:

> "On that day, all the kings, the governors and high officials, and those who rule the earth shall fall down before him on their faces, and worship and raise their hopes in the Son of Man; they shall beg and plead for mercy at his feet. But the Lord of the Spirits himself will cause them to be frantic, so they shall rush and depart from this presence. Their faces shall be filled with shame, and their countenances shall be crowned with darkness. So he will deliver them to the angels for punishments in order that vengeance shall be executed in them-oppressors of his children and his elect ones. They shall rejoice over (the kings, the governors, the high officials, and the landlords) because the wrath of the Lord of the Spirits shall rest upon them and his swords (shall obtain from them a sacrifice. The righteous and the elect ones shall be saved on that day; and from henceforth they shall never see the faces of the sinners and the oppressors. The Lord of the Spirits will abide over them; they shall eat and rest and rise with that Son of Man forever and ever. The righteous and elect ones shall rise from the earth and shall cease being of downcast face. They shall wear the garments of glory."⁸⁵⁵

God will not leave his people to perish in the desert of their political occupation.⁸⁵⁶ So they could eschew taking their liberation into their own hands by fomenting violence against Rome but rather "seek the welfare of the city where I have sent you into exile, and pray to the LORD on its behalf, for in its welfare you will find your welfare" (Jer 29:7). Jesus in feeding them in this way exhibits a vivid assurance that God has their physical welfare in mind as well as their longing for an end to their "exile" and that they are on the way to entering the promised land of liberation.

Cursing of a Fig Tree: Mark 11:12–14, 20–26. Matt 21:18–22.⁸⁵⁷

Cursing was a divine prerogative. It was forbidden to humans especially the cursing of one's parents (Exod 21:17, such a cursing would also directly violate the fourth commandment), as well as the handicapped (Lev 19:14), and the king (Exod 21:17).⁸⁵⁸ In fact, they were crimes punishable by death. Unless YHWH stood behind a curse it could have no effect. He could turn a curse back on its originator or turn it into a blessing. God's word is effective and a curse would have its effect in its own time.

God's curse was always related to sin and his judgment on sin. Blessing and curse were part of the covenant God made with his people and which they agreed to be faithful to. If they abided by the stipulations of the covenant they would experience blessing and if not they would bring on themselves the result of the curse (Deut 11:26; 28:15). In Holy War the ban (Heb, חרם, *HEREM*) that was demanded by God meant that no spoil or plunder could be taken but their enemies and all they possessed had to be destroyed.[859] Those who broke the ban were under the penalty of death.

My conclusion in my previous exposition of this story is that it was a prophetic action on Jesus' part pronouncing judgement on the nation if did not repent of its militaristic opposition to Rome and the violence attendant on it.[860] The time is ripe and the nation must eschew violence. The dawn of God's kingdom is here in Jesus' words and deeds. But if the nation withholds the expected fruits of repentance it will die. His ministry is the season of opportunity to turn now to the kingdom and avoid the judgment that is impending if the nation continues to pursue the path it is now treading.

The potency of the word pronouncing the curse is clearly demonstrated in Jesus' curse of the fig tree. The fact that it is directed to the fig tree rather than the nation itself is a sign of God's mercy. The actual curse is provisional depending on Israel's response. So Jesus here acts in God's stead as he in effect pronounces God's judgment on the nation. It is a provisional curse and would come into effect only if the nation would not repent. As it was, they did not and the curse of the Roman destruction was visited on the people.

Catching a Shoal of Fish: Luke 5:1–11. John 21:1–14.[861]

Luke places the story early in Jesus' ministry connected with the call of Peter, James, and John whereas in John's gospel the story is a post-resurrection event and appears in the chapter 21, the appendix to John's gospel, written perhaps after the evangelist's death and by one of his disciples. John's version also includes seven disciples. These differences elicit the question as to whether they are two different stories or different versions of the same incident. If it is the same incident which version preserves the original setting of the story?

The differences between the stories are pronounced. In Luke there are two boats. Jesus gets into one of them, Peter's boat, has him push off a little distance from the land, and sitting down he teaches the crowd. When he was finished he told Peter to take his boat out into the deep and let out his nets. Peter objects saying they had caught nothing during the night. But Peter relents, does what Jesus instructed him to do, and catches such a great shoal of fish that the boats were about to sink. Peter falls at Jesus' feet and asks him to leave since he is sinful. Jesus admonishes him not to fear and calls him to be a "catcher of men." So he and the two brothers, James and John, leave everything to follow Jesus.

In John's gospel the event occurs after the resurrection and seven of the disciples are all alone on the lake apparently with only one boat. It is evening and they fish all night but catch nothing. At daybreak Jesus appears unrecognized on the shore and asks them if they have anything to eat. They respond they have nothing. Jesus tells them to cast their net on the right side of the boat. The shoal of fish they catch is so great they can't draw it into the boat. John identifies for Peter the unrecognized figure on the shore as Jesus at which point Peter jumps into the water and swims to him. The other disciples arrive on shore and they see a fire prepared with fish and bread on it. They bring some of the fish (the text identifies the number as 153) and Jesus gives them to eat of the fish and bread.

Though the differences are striking the "grid," of the stories, Meier insists, is the same:[862] Peter is the main actor; the disciples have spent the night fishing; Jesus directs them to cast their net, they do and catch a great shoal of fish that threatens to break the net; it is Peter who then acts (the mention of John recognizing Jesus is probably redactional); the narrative is related in the third person; and the other disciples share in the great catch but never speak. In both versions Jesus calls them to follow him (although in John it occurs after Jesus asks Peter three times if he loved him), there is a similar vocabulary,[863] and Peter is referred to as "Simon Peter." This "grid" appears to support the conclusion that one story underlies both versions.

The general tendency in the Jesus tradition is to retroject post-resurrection stories into the pre-resurrection ministry of Jesus not the reverse. There is no clear example of the latter.[864] Meier presents an extensive argument for the post-resurrection provenance of the story that is quite convincing.[865] As it is, Luke 5:1–11 is a theophany[866] which is one of his arguments in understanding the story as a retrojected post-resurrection story. Peter's recognition of himself as sinful is dependent on the implied story of his denial of Jesus during his trial. John's version then is a narrative of Jesus' appearing "first" to Peter after the resurrection (Luke

24:34; 1 Cor 15:5). Luke adapted the story to the call narrative of Mark 1:16–20 and provides a good psychological explanation as to why the disciples responded so immediately to Jesus' call as described in Mark. In the Lucan version Jesus speaks as the resurrected one when he bids and consoles the disciples to "fear not" (Rev 1:17, Mt 28:10). The narrative of John also has a "strange form." The disciples realize a great catch of fish but the miracle doesn't take place to feed or meet a need. In fact the great shoal is not used to feed the disciples at all and in fact is left behind as they leave the scene (John 21:20). To these observations can be added that Jesus addresses not Andrew, James, and John but Peter alone.[867] The narrative is also replete with Lucan vocabulary.[868]

The evidence points to John's version of the miracle to be closest to the original tradition and which narrates a post-resurrection appearance of Jesus to seven of his disciples. Luke's version was the more derivative having been retrojected back into the public ministry of Jesus and connected with the original call of four of Jesus' disciples.

Water Changed into Wine: John 2:1–11.

The reference to "the third day" does not imply the "third day" of Jesus resurrection. What would that mean in the context of the miracle? The best explanation of the temporal allusions in John and Mark 9:2 suggest that it was part of the tradition in each case which was connected with something in the tradition which was lost in the process of its transmission. Perhaps both Mark and John found the reference meaningful[869]

The following analysis reveals the chiastic structure of the narrative:

a. Jesus mother and his disciples are in attendance at a wedding in Cana (vss 1–2)

b. The wedding runs out of wine which is reported to Jesus by his mother (vss 2–3)

c. Jesus responds by asking why she meddles in something that is his affair (vs 4)[870]

d. The mother tells the servants to do whatever Jesus tells them (vs 5)

e. There were six stone water pots each containing 20 or 30 gallons (vs 6)

f. Jesus tells the servants to fill them up (vs 7)

f'. They fill them to the brim (vs 7)

e′. Jesus tells them to draw some out and take it to the master of the feast (vs 8)

d′. The master tastes the water become wine and calls the bridegroom (vs 9)

c′. The master tells him he has kept the good wine until last (vs 10)

b′. This was Jesus' first sign (vs 11)

a′. His disciples believe in him (vs 11)

The elements f-f' are central to the story and its focus. Therefore it must point to when the water became wine, the central point of the narrative. It also identifies the story as theophanic, revealing Jesus' true nature.[871] The reference is indirect because Jesus doesn't say anything openly over the water. That there are six stone vessels matches the practice in the Galilee of the time because stone vessels could not contract impurity and so could be used for a variety of liquids and still ensure their ritual purity.[872] The reference to these stone vessels speaks powerfully for the historicity of the event reflecting as they do the wide spread practice of their use.

There also is no direct acclamation of Jesus or amazement at the incredible transformation of the water become wine. There is the more or less witness to the miracle by the master of the feast in praising the quality of the wine. But the witness is indirect. He is ignorant of what has occurred. The disciples, however, are led to "believe in him" but it doesn't say how they came to know of the miracle. This is the only miracle too where Jesus' mother is present. The story also has no parallel in the synoptic gospels as does the feeding of the crowd, the walking on water, and the catching of the shoal of fish.[873] So this miracle prominently distinguishes itself as unique in all of the gospel miracle stories. Even within the gospel of John it stands out because it has no discursive material attached to it (The only other miracle story that lacks such material is the healing of the official's son.) The implied parallel to the story is the multiplication of loaves. Because John lacks the narrative of the institution of the Lord's Supper these two miracles stories bear witness to the institution narrative dealing, as they do, with bread and wine. Of course, the discourse connected with the multiplication of the loaves directly reflects its connection with eating of Jesus' body in the Eucharist whereas this water into wine story makes no such connection.

Meier does not accept the theory of the existence of a "signs gospel" that would have included the miracles reproduced by John comprising also the change of water into wine miracle. He bases that on the deft interweaving of the story into the context of John's gospel: "The third day" (2:1) refers back to the enumeration of days preceding the story (1:29, 35, 43). In 1:50–51 Jesus promises Nathanael that he will see "greater things" in fact a theophany with "the angels ascending and descending on the son of man."

Jesus refers to his mother with the unadorned "woman" which usage, though not found in the OT or Greek, occurs throughout John's gospel. He also avoids using her proper name. Some symbolic relationship between the two is implied.[874] Jesus further explains his distancing from his mother in terms of his hour that has as "not yet come." Jesus' "hour" is the hour of his glorification by his death on the cross (7:30; 8:20; 12:23; 27; 13:1; 17:1).[875] All of this comes under the rubric of Jesus, as the second person of the Holy Trinity, is always and everywhere in control of events including his crucifixion.[876] The wine miracle results in an abounding gift pointing to the messianic banquet which transcends the Jewish ritual of purification.[877]

The abundance of the gift is evident in the other miracle stories of John's gospel: Jesus creates the sight of a man *born* blind; he raises a man to life after *four days in the tomb*; a man paralyzed for *thirty-eight* years is healed; Jesus walks on the water but the disciples reach the far shore *instantaneously*. In each case John's gospel intensifies the miracle and the divine power of Jesus is underscored.

Jesus creates an abundance of wine as a sign of the flourishing and the joy accompanying the coming kingdom (Isa 25:6; Jer 31:12; Joel 3:18; Zech 9:17). The kingdom is also depicted as a wedding feast celebrating YHWH and his bride Israel (Isa 54:4–8). In the NT Christ is wedded to his people taking the place of YHWH (Rev 19:9; Eph 5:22–32; John 3:29).[878] So Jesus realizes proleptically the presence of the kingdom in his ministry and the feasting of the redeemed in the age to come.[879] And the "best wine" has been kept "until now" (vs10), that is, the realized eschaton by which John means to say, Jesus' incarnation is the new wine kept until now when his glory is revealed in the signs he performs.[880] Jesus in his open commensality, his miracles of healing, his teaching as not like one of the scribes is calling his people to the messianic banquet and to share in the wine of the new covenant, namely the fruits of salvation in these actions culminating in his sacrificial death. This gift of salvation is lavish, like the quantity of wine. To enter the kingdom is to share in the Spirit that descended on him in his baptism. That the water of Jewish purification is turned into wine also points to the new covenant brought by the presence of the kingdom (Jer 31:31–34) and that this kingdom is open to all the world tearing down the wall of distinction between Jew and Gentile (Eph 2:14).[881] The old covenant has now given way to the new.

Meier points out in terms of the historical nature of the passage that the ἀρχιτρίκλινος (John 2:9 *architriklinos*, "master of the feast") in the Graeco-Roman world was the chief slave who was in charge of managing a banquet. In this passage, however, he appears as more of a friend to the groom in the way he chides him for holding the best wine for the last. So he appears here more like a συμποσίαρχος (*symposiarchos*, "president of a drinking party" (Lat., *magister bibendi* usually the head of a communal meal of some voluntary association or club). He does find a parallel in Sirach 32:1–2 who refers to the position as ἡγούμενον (*hēgoumenon*, "master" or "governor of the feast") similar to the συμποσίαρχος or *arbiter bibendi*. The context makes clear that he is chosen from among the guests. He doesn't think that this position in Sirach describes the *architriklinos* of John 2:9 since such a person is not a guest or the best man. In this story he is related to the groom more on the level of a friend and has taken on some of the aspects of the *arbiter bibendi*. So Meier concludes he doesn't represent a functionary at a wedding in first century Jewish society.[882]

However, given that the feast took place in a small village, the "master of the feast" could well have been a villager and a close friend of the groom. He also doesn't think it reflects Hellenistic influence since it's a small peasant village not influenced by the Hellenistic culture of the day. This latter idea is not cogent since Jesus himself, who came from a small hamlet, knew some Greek.[883]

Meier also does not find historical evidence for the rule of vs 10, and since weddings lasted for seven days from and to which people came and went, it is doubtful that such a fluid attendance would notice a change in the quality of wine. However, this fails to recognize that the master of the feast would be there the whole time and that the feast takes place in a small village so that many of the guests would choose to be there most of the time.

That Jesus and his mother Mary would give commands to the servants might not be peculiar since it appears they were both well known to the family of the groom. Again the size of the place suggests close relationships. He identifies the whole of the story as a creation of John but I

Invading the Realm of Demons, Disease, and Death

would reject Meier's criticism by the fact that the story is an intimate look into village life and is rife with the informality of village relationships.[884]

Along with Meier most commentators understand the story symbolically and theologically to the exclusion of a historical occurrence.[885] To assert that John sat down in writing his gospel and made up a story whole cloth seems highly unlikely and even fantastic. What we are not used to is an intimate look into village life and a somewhat private affair that diverges somewhat from the rest of the gospel tradition which reported on what was public and open about Jesus' activity. Probably the story was passed on by the disciples, after all, it was they who "believed in him" (vs 11). In this way it is similar to the story of the transfiguration, again a very private affair which only the three disciples Peter, James and John were privy to (note that each story is prefaced by a time reference).

My judgment is that the story is historical. (Note that John never reports that Jesus tells parables but his "signs" are like enacted parables that point to the kingdom that is proleptically present already in his mighty works.) The only Johannine feature in this miracle story may be that Jesus refers to "his hour." But the phrase could well have been part of the tradition handed down to John. That does not mean that Jesus did not intend to reveal the intentions of his ministry: the miracle is like, as I said, an enacted parable proclaiming the kingdom of God which message declares God's kingdom as inclusive and no longer restricted to Israel. Here was the new wine celebrating the eschatological feast which Jesus' "hour" is establishing. God's spouse is no longer restricted to Israel but now includes the world as John's reflection in 3:13–21 underscores. The water of Jewish purification has become the invitation to the world to join in the great marriage feast of the now expanded family of God (cf., Mark 3:31–35).[886]

Although in my judgment the miracle was an actual event I think the story is one of the more difficult to affirm along with the multiplication of the loaves and fishes. After all, we are talking about the chemical H_2O, water, having added to it color and alcohol (C_5OH) and other chemicals. The composition of wine consists of about 86% water, 12% ethanol, 1% glycerol, .4% organic acids, 0.1% tannins and phenolics, and 0.5% other compounds. So these chemicals would have to have been created by Jesus' miracle and in just the right proportions to make a "good wine" (John 2:10). It is akin to the creation of the universe, a *creatio ex nihilo*, creation out of nothing. So Jesus is asserting that the coming of God's kingdom is a new creation, something that never existed before.

Along with Paul we could call what God has done in Christ a "mystery ... that the Gentiles should be fellow heirs partakers of his promise in Christ" (Eph 3:3–7), the mystery "which from the beginning of the ages has been hidden in God who created all things" (Eph 3:9). But as one of my colleagues, a scientist, pointed out to me, this miracle is utterly trivial in relationship to raising the dead, especially a man who has been dead four days and is exuding the odor of corruption.

A Coin in a Fish's Mouth: Matt 17:24-27.

This event is not accurately described as a miracle or theophany even less as a "nature miracle." I would characterize it as an occurrence of remarkable intuition or prescience. Meier recognizes its idiosyncratic nature and its Matthean style, vocabulary, and theology.[887]

The following analysis verifies Meier's judgment and reveals the following eccentric structure to the narrative:

a. When they came to Capernaum, the collectors of the half-shekel tax went up to Peter and said, "Does not your teacher pay the tax?"

b. He said, "Yes."

a'. And when he came home, Jesus spoke to him first, saying, "What do you think, Simon? From whom do kings of the earth take toll or tribute? From their sons or from others?"

b'. And when he said, "From others," Jesus said to him, "Then the sons are free."

c. "However, not to give offense to them, go to the sea and cast a hook, and take the first fish that comes up, and when you open its mouth you will find a shekel; take that and give it to them for me and for yourself."

However, not to give offense to them, go to the sea and cast a hook, and take the first fish that comes up, and when you open its mouth you will find a shekel; take that and give it to them for me and for yourself."

The narrative is unbalanced by Jesus' two-part expanded response to Peter's answer. Both parts of the response involve a prescience on Jesus' part: he knows about Peter's encounter with the tax collectors and he foresees what Peter will find when he follows Jesus' command to catch a fish. One could conclude that Jesus' expanded response was added to the initial story of Peter's encounter with tax collectors except that Peter's answer to Jesus' initial question demands a response from Jesus.

Jesus at first asserts that Peter and Jesus are free from paying the half-sheqel temple tax because they are sons of the kingdom and therefore free (cf., John 8:32–36). However, he then arranges to pay it and so quit themselves as loyal Jews and so not give offense.

The payment of this half-sheqel tax in the time of Jesus is well attested.[888] It was to be paid by every male Israelite twenty years of age and over (Exod 30:14–15) whether poor or rich. It was paid in the Tyrian sheqel which meant money changers often had to be involved. The money was collected within a given community and then delivered to the Jerusalem authorities. The tax was used to pay for the daily burned offering and all other sacrifices offered in the name of the people.[889] After the destruction the tax was paid by Jews to the temple of Jupiter Capitolinus.

Jesus' declaration that the "sons are free" and the command to find the money in a fish's mouth is outside the balance formed by what precedes and so becomes the point of this little narrative. The little *mashal*[890] in a' leads to the conclusion in c. However, Jesus is not saying that the "sons of the kingdom" should *not* pay the tax but that they are free of it. He's arguing something like Paul in 1 Cor 8 and 9: though one is free to eat meat sacrificed to idols the Christian can choose not to for the sake of the brother; although the Christian is free from all law he is also chooses to be the servant of all.[891] Jesus is also concerned with not "scandalizing" as is Paul. The concern is not to cause another to fall from faith. In this way one always acts not out of coercion but total freedom, out of voluntary acts of love for others.

A Transfiguration: Mark 9:2–8. Matt 17:1–9. Luke 9:28–36.

The story and the form of the Transfiguration is without an analogous parallel in the gospels.[892] The "after six days" could refer to a time of preparation, the traditional period of time required for self-purification and before closely approaching God (Exod 24:16).[893] The event takes place on a mountain perhaps Tabor or Hermon.[894] The verb "led them up" (ἀναφέρω, *anapherō*) is a word used in the cultus of various gods referring to the bringing up of a sacrificial offering. The verb resonates with Jesus once more being declared to be the "beloved" by the voice of God as in his baptism underscoring his position as the one who would be sacrificed.[895] He is marked for humiliation and exaltation.[896] His designation as the "beloved son" places the cross in the background of his whole ministry (and, it also needs to be said, behind every passage of the gospel tradition!) He accepts the designation shown by his describing himself elsewhere as "son" in absolute terms (Mark 12:6; 13:32; Luke 10:22). His thorough-going obedience reflects Abraham's own. So this event underscores that Jesus is the one who has come to suffer and die.[897]

The dove imagery in the baptismal story recalls the "Spirit of God moving over the face of the water" (Gen 1:2) at the creation and therefore reveals Jesus' baptism as the beginning of the new creation. It is also amounts to Jesus' prophetic call and a profound reordering of his existence. He is now no longer a τέκτων (*tektōn*, "carpenter," Mark 6:3) nor just a prophet but one who speaks directly and with authority for God ("I say to you . . ." Matt 5:22–44). His baptism is multi-valent: in it he identifies with sinful Israel, indeed the sinful world; so he doesn't stand above his people but with them. This new creation resonates in the whole of Jesus' ministry: the descent of the Spirit reflects Isaiah's theology of the new creation (Isa 11:2); he restores the original divine intention for marriage as it was promulgated at the time of the creation (Gen 2:24; Mk10:2–12); his exorcisms and healings were a restoration of creation; his uniting all people, Jews and Gentiles, in the kingdom reverses the confusion at Babel; calming of the sea recalls God bringing order out of chaos in the original creation; the "splitting" of heavens is like the splitting of the Jordan when the people entered the promised land: the kingdom is universal inviting all peoples to enter into and enjoy the new creation.

So Jesus in terms of his humanity stood in an intimate relationship with God. God was his *Abba* (by which Jesus indicates he is a dear son and close to God as a child is dear and close to its father). As God's son he was also the Messiah (the Davidic kings were named as such). This did not make him a mystic but rather like a prophet of old. (He identifies himself as a prophet, Mark 6:4). As a prophet he was not so much concerned with ritual purity as with doing the will of God and so he would not shrink from transgressing social and cultural norms where the kingdom and its ethics would demand it. Jesus, in predicting his passion, reflects Dan 7 where the son of man represents the holy ones of God who suffer under the persecution of the "fourth beast."

The meaning of μεταμορφόω *metamorphoō*, "transform, change form") is more closely and expansively defined by 1 Cor 15:43–54 although the word ἀλλάσω (*allassō*, "change, alter") is used there. Matt and

Invading the Realm of Demons, Disease, and Death

Luke emphasize the radiating face of Jesus. Mark (the originating version of the narrative) emphasizes the unearthly whiteness and luminosity of his clothing.[898] The distinction is important. The radiating and whiteness of his clothing are characteristic of those who partake of heavenly life and its purity (Rev 3:4–5).[899] Because only his clothing was radiating it does not point to his divinity but rather his status as son and partaking in heavenly life. That only his clothing is involved also emphasizes that this is a pre-resurrection event. So Jesus gives the three disciples an actual experience of the kingdom and existence in it. Though his life will be given in the death of sacrifice that is only precursor to the glory of the kingdom and the ultimate goal of his life and death which is his Lordship and the glory of his exaltation when his divinity will be made explicit.[900] The change in Jesus' clothing also resonates with the verb "led them up" and its association with sacrifice identifying Jesus as the messianic priest.[901]

However, Matthew's and Luke's change from radiating clothing to Jesus' body make the transfiguration to mean his resurrected body. Paul speaks of the change that takes place at the resurrection: the new, changed body of the resurrected person is glorious, spiritual, heavenly, bearing the image of Christ, incorruptible, and immortal.[902] This eschatological state also extends to the clothes that were worn (1 Enoch 62:15–60).[903] So Jesus appears to bear the fullness of his resurrection body and glory in Matthew's and Luke's version. His physical body has been transformed into the fullness of the body of the resurrection which Paul has described in 1 Cor 15 (cf., Phil 2:9, "he is highly exalted"), the very same nature into which our bodies will be transformed in the resurrection. The radical difference in this regard between Mark and the other two synoptists also underscores his version as the original and as a pre-resurrection occurrence.

The figures of Moses and Elijah undergird the interpretation of the event as a proleptic experience of the end time since these two figures were expected to appear at the end of time (Deut 18:15, Mal 4:5). Both of these figures were understood in Judaism as having been taken to heaven. Their coming and appearance bound together the past of Israel with the eschatological future.[904] But Jesus is the one people are to listen to and hear. But Jesus is not just one prophet among others. He supersedes all others (Deut 18:18–19). And here again God speaks and points to the one who is now to be regarded exclusively. The cloud is a sign of God's presence testifying that it is God himself who speaks here and whose beloved son Jesus is. That Jesus himself is described as coming on the clouds (Mark 13:26; 14:62) and his people meeting him in the clouds at his coming (1 Thes 4:17) indicates the scene anticipates Jesus' final coming in the glory of the Father.[905]

Peter's desire to erect three tents one for each figure in the scene evokes the feast of Tabernacles which requires the nation to erect tents as a reminder of the wandering in the wilderness after the exodus. During this feast (Heb., "Sukkoth") the whole Temple mount was illuminated during the eight days of the feast and the Hallel was sung every day. Singing, rejoicing, and dancing were, in fact, a marked feature of the feast. All the feasts had an eschatological emphasis but this was true of Tabernacles to an even greater degree. Popular notions connected it with the harvest and the vintage which in turn made the connection with the eschatological "harvest" of the gathering in of the nations in the eschatological feast of Sukkoth.[906] There were water rites accompanying the feast signifying a paradisial stream coming from Jerusalem in the eschaton which would cleanse from sin and fructify the land. It was related to the water streams in the Garden of Eden. Eschatological hopes of the feast were also centered in the house of David. So an original agricultural festival was transformed to include not only the rejoicing in the gifts of nature but also in the hope in what God was doing for his people. It pointed to the day when the true Messiah of the house of David would appear and the coming of YHWH's universal reign. The feast also promoted the most extraordinary freedom in terms of the people's access to the temple and its various courts celebrating the eschatological liberty promised by the feast.

So Peter in his own way interpreted the meaning of the vision before him: Jesus was the royal Messiah who now appears in his eschatological glory limning the eschaton and the coming of the kingdom fulfilling the expectations related to Sukkoth ala Zech 14. The promises of Sukkoth and which Sukkoth celebrated have finally arrived and he would enshrine the Lord's glory in each one as the Lord enshrined his glory in the tabernacle in the wilderness. Since Mark reports that Jesus predicted the destruction and end of the Temple (a change in Jesus' eschatology from that of one centered in Sukkoth to one of his own coming to judge the world[907]) he brought the story of the Transfiguration into line with Jesus' revised eschatology by disparaging Peter's remark judging it to be offhanded and inappropriate and due to his bewilderment and fear.[908] But Mark interpreted its meaning in terms of Jesus' revised eschatology which he presents in chapter 13: the event of his coming at the end time to dwell with his people (Rev 21:1-3). In terms of Jesus' revised eschatology, however, before that takes place there will be tribulation, the heavens and earth must pass away, then Jesus will appear in the glory in which he now, according to Mark, proleptically reveals himself. Peter's interpretation of the event means he is still operating under Jesus' initial construal of the eschaton in terms of Zechariah's prophecy (Zech 14) and John's placing of the "Temple Cleansing" at the beginning of his ministry.

I am in agreement with Caird who is bold enough to suggest that the story reproduces Jesus' own experience of the event.[909] Luke reports that Jesus was at prayer like he is in the Garden of Gethsemane when he takes along these same three disciples with himself, suggesting that he is facing a "trial of his spiritual stamina in which he would be glad of their companionship." He finds a clue to the nature of the trial when Luke identifies the content of the conversation with Moses and Elijah as dealing with his "departure" (Gk, ἔξοδος, lit., "*exodos*," "going out, departure") i.e., his death.[910] That topic would fit in with God's own command "to listen to this beloved son of mine," who will not be spared but sacrificed. The topic also coordinates with Moses' presence who was God's agent of divine deliverance. Here the new deliverer is present who will rescue the whole world by his "exodus."

In verse 7 a cloud is describes as overshadowing "them" (presumably meaning all six people present). The cloud is a symbol of God's presence as he guided Israel in the wilderness. It also, like Moses and Elijah, points to the inbreaking of the eschatological time. The eschatological time has, with the presence of God's only beloved Son the eschatological teacher, arrived. The cloud also makes of the story a theophany.

Two expectations within Judaism of Jesus' day are satisfied by this theophany: the appearance of the end-time prophet like Moses (Deut 18:15) and the return of Elijah at the dawning of the end-time (Mal 4:5). When they appear, the hope of Israel, this glorious end-time, will have entered history. This theophany proclaims this expected one has come who is, however, God's "beloved son," the sacrificial lamb, whom he will offer up, unexpectedly, for the sins of the world.

This analysis points to the story as historical.[911] However, the analysis also suggests that this is not a post-resurrection experience but can only be understood as occurring during Jesus' ministry (cf., Moses' face shining with the divine radiance Exod 24:29–35 and Peter's interpretation of the event as a fulfillment of Zechariah's eschatology).[912] Only post-resurrection does the event point to the divinity of Jesus (cf., v. 10).[913]

SUMMARY AND CONCLUSION

The stilling of the storm is like an exorcism of Jesus: it is a hostile force that can destroy. So he is creating the calm of the new age, restoring creation. The disciples reveal themselves again as faithless as they demonstrate their lack of trust in God, the one who has power over wind and wave. Jesus' calm sleep reveals the deep trust that he had in his Father-God. That trust, in turn, reveals the presence of God in a theophany.

In the walking on the water Jesus reveals divine power directly and so I have judged it as a post-resurrection event. The reaction of the disciples as he appears walking on the water involves thinking he is a returning, avenging ghost which supports the contention that this is a post-resurrection event. Jesus identifying himself with the divine "I am" is further corroboration of that contention. It also identifies him as the crucified and risen one who redeems Israel. The distinctiveness of the story from the other miracle stories also points to its post-resurrection provenance. Here again we encounter a theophany. This time, however, it is the divinity of Jesus which reveals itself, the God who is with us.

The story of the catch of the great shoal of fish is also a post-resurrection event. In John's version of the story Jesus, as in the previous story, is not (or is mis-) recognized. He correctly places it in the time after Jesus' resurrection. In both versions Peter reacts and witnesses to his consciousness of his denial of Jesus at his trial and that he is in the presence of the numinous.

In the feeding story Jesus functions as the shepherd of Israel pasturing his people and as God's agent who provides food for his people in their wanderings. The groups that Jesus has the crowd gathered in suggests the messianic feast of the kingdom. At the same time Jesus is creating the intimacy of table fellowship and kinship in the midst of the fractures within Jewish society. The feedings are part of his practice of "open commensality" and the reconstitution of Israel. It is a powerful demonstration of sharing counteracting the idea of limited good and the anxiety attendant on concerns for sufficient daily food. God is with his people and will not let them perish in the wilderness of their perceived exile. So the people can leave off pursuing revolution. Here we have a mighty invitation to enter the kingdom and avoid the curse which would come upon them if they refused. Jesus graphically pictures this judgment when he curses the fig tree.

Invading the Realm of Demons, Disease, and Death

The abundant water changed to wine limns the messianic banquet and the transcending of Jewish ritual purification. That it takes place at a wedding also prefigures the final joining and marriage of Jesus with his people in the new age. This is the wine of the new covenant, the fruits of ultimate salvation wrought by Jesus sacrificial death. The old covenant now gives way to the new which includes not only Israel but the world. The historicity of the story is supported by the fact that it is an authentic glimpse and intimate peek into village life in Jesus' day and its informal relationships. The story is also a witness to the fact that Jesus would at times choose his actions very carefully in order to concretize his proclamation and the parameters of his mission. The change is a creation from nothing, like the creation of the universe. So God's kingdom is a new creation, something that has had no prior existence, a "mystery which has been hidden in God (Eph 3:9).

Jesus' prescience is at work in the story of the coin in the fish's mouth. The story exemplifies the freedom of the kingdom where its members are set at liberty to choose to take into consideration the needs of others over their own. The kingdom means love and its members are free to do voluntary acts of love on behalf of others.

In the Transfiguration Jesus is once more declared the "beloved son" which resonates with Jesus leading his disciples up the mountain, a verb associated with bringing up of a sacrifice. That it is only his clothing that radiates whiteness portrays his status as son, his messianic priesthood, and the heavenly life of the kingdom. So this is a pre-resurrection event and points to his coming passion. Since Moses and Elijah were expected at the end of days their appearance with Jesus also points to the eschaton. The cloud, a symbol of God's presence, is also an eschatological sign because it accompanies Jesus at his final coming. Peter's desire to erect three tents interprets the event also eschatologically but in terms of the feast of Sukkoth which expected the ingathering of the nations and their subjection to the God of Israel. After the resurrection the community could well look back at this event as a hint of Jesus' divinity.

The theophanies encompass a wide range of purposes. However, the underlying unity is that of revealing Jesus' status as the beloved son who, as God's sacrificial offering, restores creation, reconstitutes Israel, establishes the new covenant, and prepares, via Peter's restoration, for the post-resurrection continuation of his work.

CHAPTER 6

Summary

Blessed be the Lord, the God of Israel,
Who has visited and redeemed his people
raising up a horn of salvation for us
in the house of his servant David.

In chapter one I followed the trajectory of science whose methodology began as a discovery of the mind of God (Newton). So scientific thinking actually had its beginning under the impetus of Christianity and its anthropology: man was created in God's image but was also infected by original sin. So human beings could understand the natural world and how it worked but at the same time because of humanity's fallibility perceptions of the natural order was subject to error and self-deception so had to be constantly corrected. The results of all investigations of the natural world had to be tested and subject to modification and amendment. So the results of scientific inquiry is open ended and has to be capable of integrating new information. Consequently, there is no such thing as "settled science." Early on it was understood that at scientific method's foundation there was a designer.

However, under the influence of LaPlace and Hume science became a denial of the existence of the world of the spirit conceiving of the universe totally in materialistic terms. But then unexpectedly discoveries of materialistic science has led to evidence of the world of the spirit: the universe has a definite beginning some 13.8 billion years ago. Scientific method has become somewhat more humble under the influence of discoveries that have forced it to go beyond a mechanical view of the universe (e.g., that it is like a clock).

Mechanistic determinism utterly breaks down at the atomic level where indeterminacy rules. Heisenberg determined that the "uncertainty principle" constrained human measurements at the atomic level: the position and direction of motion of a particle cannot simultaneously be measured. The principle also means that the observation of a particle changes it so prediction is no longer possible.

The development of non-Euclidian geometries refutes the idea that mathematics gives access to supersensible truths. Mathematics does not have transcendental significance. Physics itself can only deal with aspects of the material world that can be treated quantitatively. So scientific investigations can only give us partial knowledge of reality. There are universal constants such as the electric charge of the electron. If any of these constants were changed the universe as we know it could not exist. So the universe has a design which leads to the possible development of life. So these constants are fine-tuned which make possible the emergence of human beings. This is called the "anthropic principle:" the universe is designed to produce humans. So the universe is not some random, impersonal and mechanistic thing that arbitrarily and erratically produces life and ultimately humans. Rather the universe was designed and finely tuned to produce humans. It's a "put-up job!"

Scientific method has discovered the mathematical structure of the universe but it has hit the wall in discovering the essence of matter. We know the external characteristics of atomic and sub-atomic particles such as their size, mass, and electric charge but not what they are in and of themselves. They are described as probability waves with a freedom of action which cannot be determined beforehand. So there is freedom built into the material universe along with its design.

Furthermore, the Higgs boson was discovered which imparts mass to atomic particles and creates the Higgs field which pervades the universe. If it were to change at any given point in the universe it would spread at the speed of light through-out the universe and bring it to an end. So the universe could end at any time. This possibility corresponds to biblical conception which teaches the universe was created out of nothing, out of the "void," and can fall back into that void at any time and come to an end.

SUMMARY

So scientific discoveries affirm biblical teaching: time is linear, the universe has a beginning, and it can end at any moment of God's choosing.

Darwinism more or less rules the world of biological sciences with its concept of "natural selection," that is, the appearance of various life forms, including humans, as the result of chance mutations. Darwin did not have the knowledge we now have as what it takes to generate the kind of information found in a genome. Nor did he have any idea of the utter complexity of even a single cell. The more the cell is studied the more complex it is found to be. Darwinism, however, does explain small variations in a given species but cannot explain how one species could develop from another. The chance of a mutation being beneficial is one out of 10^{37}! (i.e., it's all but impossible.) There is not enough time since the creation of the universe to produce one useful gene. In other words, the information found in DNA points to a designing intelligence. Just as encoded information in a book, a radio signal, or a computer code when traced back to its source always ends up in arriving at a designing mind not some material process.

Darwinism is no longer just a scientific theory, however, but the foundation for a world view and an ersatz religion for many a person left bereft by a materialist view of the universe and life. That is why challenging it often elicits a strong and irrational reaction.[914] In fact, predictions based on intelligent design are proving to be cogent.

Near death experiences report the encounters people have who have suffered catastrophic events and been close to death or actually dying. The experience includes observing the resuscitation procedures, the meeting with a figure who exudes unconditional love, and a moral sense of judgment on the basis of the law of love and the realization that one is personally responsible for every thought, word, and deed. These experiences coordinate with the investigations summarized above in biology that human beings are not the product of some random material process but rather the result of a the action from a sphere beyond the material universe.

My review of the evidence for demonic possession also witnesses to the existence of the world of the spirit. It is also obvious from these investigations that the world of the spirit is not all light and goodness but is also the home to evil.

I followed all of this evidence pointing to the existence of the world of the spirit. My study of the biblical account of creation revealed a convergence with scientific investigations of the material universe and human experiences. That congruence witnessed to a directing intelligence and designer. The creation account in Genesis 1, of course, is written in terms of its time and place and its religio-cultural milieu. The study discovered that the account is actually a de-mythologizing of the contemporary Babylonian creation myth. The creation is not the result of the struggle of the gods but the one God creating out of nothingness and out of chaos by his word alone. So there is tension between the creative word of God and the attractive power of the "void" (i.e., nothingness") which is a perduring threat of drawing the created order back into itself. So the universe can come to an end which, biblically speaking, will not occur until God allows it (corresponding to the discovery of the Higgs field and its ability to change its potential bringing the universe to an end). In this way theology and scientific knowledge have converged and are in accord with one another.

Sin disturbs this equilibrium because the whole of creation is infected with it and makes the created order to be directed no longer upward but downward. So sin is not merely an infringement of a moral norm but alienation from God resulting in the disordering of creation. So creation is now subject to death and destruction.

In the Babylonian creation myth man is created to be the slave of the gods and to make life easy for them. In the Genesis account the human is created in God's image and is the ruler of creation i.e., has royal prerogatives.

So the truth is one.

Finally, I defined what a miracle is: an event that cannot be explained by the cause and effect relationship between events in the world of space and time. In the ancient world the idea of natural and supernatural did not exist. The material world was understood to be embedded in the world of the spirit. There was an expectant, easy intercourse between the two.

Jesus' miracles were signs of the presence of the kingdom of God so that the coming of the kingdom was in some sense already present and active. Jesus doesn't interpret them as God's intervention. Frequently he mentions the faith of the individual. The language of these reports doesn't use the word "miracle" but "mighty works," "wonders," "marvels," or even "strange" occurrences. He often commands healed persons not to talk about their healing. He did not want to be known as a miracle worker.[915] His miracles are witnesses to and the very presence of the kingdom of God. His exorcisms in particular are invasions of Satan's kingdom and the "plundering his house" (Mark 3:27). The healings also involve forgiveness of sin. Forgiveness and freedom from satanic possession are also a call to believe the good news and to enter the kingdom "Now is the day of salvation" (2 Cor 6:2). Their function in Jesus' ministry also aimed at freeing Israel from the hostility and revolutionary dreams of ending Roman rule in the Holy Land. They were establishing an alternate world: the peaceable reign of God. Israel's real enemy was Satan and his rule. God's reign meant the time of salvation had already impinged on the present where instead of being turned inward with an exclusive focus on itself, Israel finds a foretaste of God's rest in the kingdom (Heb 4:1–10) as Jesus celebrated it in which competition ended, sharing reigned, and the Jubiliee inaugurated.[916]

The ancient world and the world of Jesus also recognized the orderly working of the material world, for example, the regular turn of the seasons and the conditions by which one can predict the weather. There was a distinction between the created order and the Creator. So nature had its own autonomy.

Contemporary scholarship mostly approaches the miracle stories from a materialist point of view. It questions their historicity because they violate, what has now become the entrenched modus operandi in our culture and society, the idea that the universe is a closed nexus of cause and effect. They are understood then as products of the community and not historical reports based only on some vague recollection of Jesus' activity that somehow had healing effects. The focus is on their function within the Christian community where they were nurtured. Locating the stories in this way leads to the determination of their form, what kind of stories they are, so that they can be compared to other stories in the contemporary environment. Connected to this process is a second approach which seeks to determine their social and religio-historical and existential function. However, the massive amount of these stories, their existence in unrelated sources, and their variation in style and tone all tell against the notion based on materialistic suppositions that they are inventions of the early Christian community.

The miracle stories follow usually a common form: a description of the context, the situation in which the miracle occurs; the miracles take place by a word or action of Jesus; and the story concludes by relating the reaction of the observers. However, this form is absent from the so-called "nature miracles' (which I've designated "theophanies" because they are a "manifestation of God" and his self-disclosure). These stories find their counterpart in the OT theophanies.

The miracles also explain why Jesus generated the crowds that followed him as well as the clash with the authorities and groups such as the Pharisees. Jesus' name was also employed by others who were not part of his ministry. Jesus himself describes his ministry in terms of miracles on the basis of Isa 35:5–7 (Matt 11:4–5; Luke 7:22). Qumran also described the messiah in the same terms that Jesus used of himself. However, Jesus' self-consciousness was based on his baptism where God called him his "beloved son" i.e., he is destined as a sacrifice, God's own sacrifice.

In chapter 1 I enumerated the various scientific discoveries that point to a creator and designer of the universe and of life on planet earth along with studies that require the conclusion there is a world of the spirit beyond our material universe. These investigations have also corroborated the occurrences of miracles in our contemporary world. A brief exposition of the creation account in Gen 1 demonstrated, though written in terms of its times, coordinates with modern-day scientific discoveries. The truth is one. With this preliminary investigation, my study prepared for an objective examination of the miracles of Jesus without having any pre-conceived notions regarding their historical veracity and authenticity. What follows is a summary of the results of that research.

To be possessed of a demon meant to be ostracized by the community in Jesus' day because it rendered a person ritually unclean. So Jesus' exorcisms meant not only the healing of an individual but healing of the body politic and the removal of division within Israel.

Jesus was not the only exorcist in his time. But he differed from them. The exorcists of the ancient world recited incantations, invoked the power and authority of a pagan deity, and called upon the deity to effect the exorcism. Exorcisms were also effected by the personal power and charismatic force of the exorcist. Jesus exorcizes by a simple word. Implied was that the power of God was active in and through him (Mark 3:22–27).

I have made extensive references to Richard Gallagher's book. This initial skeptic made scientific inquiry into contemporary claims of demon possession and was driven to the conclusion that such phenomena exist.

Demons are not of major importance in the OT but appear to have emerged in the time of early Judaism when it was perceived that where faith in God wavered these demonic powers entered into and overpowered people. One psychological aspect of demon possession is the internalizing of anger and repressing it within, turning it against oneself.

SUMMARY

Anger was rampant in Jesus' society because of the Roman occupation of the country and its usurpation of God as the rightful king and governor of Israel. Rome, through its procurators and their frequent mismanagement and even purposeful incitement of the people, amplified the rage.[917]

Demonic possession included somatic and psychic injury such as dumbness, lameness, and epilepsy. These maladies are clearly distinguished from demon possession when such possession is not involved. Demons can also mimic actual maladies. For example, the demon possessed boy's symptoms look like epilepsy but that condition is only mimicked by the demon which possesses the boy (Mark 9:14–29). The demon possessed are not judged as morally defective but as victims. Demons torment their victims so they are opposed to God's good will.

Demon possession cannot be reduced to psychological explanations such as a double ego. The behavior and speech of the possessed is always and only that of the demon.

Jesus's exorcisms are not only healing miracles but are part of the struggle between the realm of Satan and God's kingdom. Satan battles to take the word of God out of the heart of the people. Jesus' power in exorcisms was not due to his divinity because he had "emptied" himself of it (Phil 2:7) but due to his absolute trust in his heavenly Father. That trust was expressed in his sense of God as his "Abba" an intimate closeness which grew in him especially after his baptism when God called him his "beloved son." God for him was an almighty love.

Contemporary psychology has discovered the power of trust, especially in situations of a relationship that develops between a healer and a patient.

Jesus' exorcisms are also not merely a matter of casting out the individual demon. They are confrontations between Jesus and the kingdom of God and the whole dominion of Satan ("the ruler of this world" John 12:31). Jesus accomplished his exorcisms not by the use of magical formulae and repetition of them but by a single word. The Geresene demoniac is an exception (Mark 5:8) where Jesus apparently repeated the command that the demon(s) leave the man. But then again the man was possessed by a "legion" of demons. The Geresene demoniac uniquely embodies Israel and its political situation, its occupation and subjugation by Rome. As Jesus' exorcism of the man's "legion" of demons also bears an additional dimension of a dramatic portrayal of how this "exile" of Israel will be overcome: not by human might or power but by God's Spirit (Zech 4:6). The Romans, though they exercise power over land and sea are ultimately accountable and subject to God. So Jesus appears in this story as embodying the power of God, the Divine Warrior who claims sovereignty over the cosmos.[918] But the demons, as embodying Rome, seek to preserve and secure their interests, power, authority, and control over the land. So Jesus, by his exorcism, plunders Satan's kingdom and proleptically brings about the demise of Rome's occupation.

The kingdom of God promises his ultimate victory which then is promulgated by the repeated telling of this narrative and which then brings a comforting message to all those who would hear it and enter the kingdom. With the telling of this story the kingdom is proclaimed and rings out with the good news that God will eventually prevail so there is no need to foment rebellion which only promises devastation. So Israel should focus on the exorcism of its own demons.

I've suggested that the exorcism of the Syro-Phoenician's woman's daughter functioned to affirm that Gentiles also have access to the kingdom. This encounter represents a turning point in Jesus' thinking. In this way the story functions much like the previous one, as a metaphorical inclusion of the Gentiles in the kingdom. However, his ministry to the "sinners" of Israel rather than to the "righteous" (Mark 2:17) already would naturally imply the inclusion of "Gentile sinners."

Jesus asserts that prayer is required to exorcise certain demons in the story of the demonic possessed boy emphasizing that exorcisms are not accomplished by one's own power but by God's power. In this way Rome will not be exorcized by Israel's power (Zech 4:6!) but by God in his own time and way. For now the people must joyfully enter the kingdom and let God take care of Roman occupation. So Jesus laments his "faithless generation" which he has to endure (Mark 9:19).

The story of the exorcism of the dumb demoniac by its emphasis on the crowd's lack of faith and the Pharisees hostile interpretation of Jesus' exorcistic activity summarizes well the response of the nation that is hell-bent on military opposition to Rome courting, as a result, destruction.

Jesus has invaded Satan's realm and was shifting the foundation of Judaism from Torah to kingdom. The kingdom, ala Jeremiah, meant "seeking the welfare" of the political regime under which God had placed them. Josephus gives the gist of his exhortation to his countrymen during the final days of the war expressing the Jeremian advice in political terms:

SUMMARY

> "The Romans ... respected the holy places of their enemies, and until now had kept their hands off them; while those who had been brought up in them–if they were kept safe from injury–would alone enjoy them, were actually bent on destruction ... they knew that the might of Rome was irresistible and that submission to her was no new experience for themselves ... Since they had succumbed and submitted for so long, to try to shake off the yoke was the action of men courting death, not of lovers of freedom ... Fortune indeed, had passed over to them from every side, and God, who moved from nation to nation handing them empire, now rested over Italy. It was an immutable law among animals and men alike that all must submit to the stronger ... that is why their ancestors, far superior to themselves in soul and body and in resources to boot, had yielded to the Romans—a thing they would not have tolerated if they had not known that God was on the Roman side ..."[919]

The nation felt it was in exile even while living in their own land because of the Roman occupation. The kingdom, Jesus proclaimed would set things right in God's own time and in his own way. God's kingdom was already among them revealing God's plan promising he would lead the people out of their exile as he had done in the past. The people had only to accept the kingdom, which Jesus proleptically made present, and practice seeking the welfare of Rome in spite of the procurators frequent insufferable outrages perpetrated against the people.[920] So Jesus was in line with the prophets of old exhorted the people "rend your hearts and not your garments," after all, the prophet continued, their God was "gracious and merciful abounding in steadfast love" (Joel 2:13). This moral demand of the kingdom, required great discipline and, above all, a change of heart!

The pervasive presence of anger and hostility toward the Roman overlord opened the way for demons and their work. The desire to "exorcise" Rome from the Holy Land suppressed faith in God to act in his own time and way. So Jesus' ministry of exorcism was part of his work to rescue and spare the nation of the sure destruction which would come to pass if it did not accept his invitation to enter the kingdom.

Jesus graphically portrays the coming victory of God over the Roman overlord in exorcising the "legion" from the Geresene demoniac. God conquers Rome's hegemony not by force of arms (i.e., a "Holy War"[921]) but by invading Satan's stronghold. He ultimately subdues the evil one by the cross and resurrection of his "beloved son."

Invading the Realm of Demons, Disease, and Death

So in this way the peaceable kingdom will restore Israel and it is already at work by Jesus' proclamation of the kingdom, his open table fellowship, in his miracles of healing, exorcisms, and raising the dead. To follow him and sit at his table is to participate already in the defeat of Rome and the end of exile. This defeat is a harbinger of the new creation promised by the kingdom. New creation means pure joy.

In chapter 3 I initially provide an overview of the various approaches to miracles in our contemporary environment. Referring back to chapter 1 I put the miracles of Jesus into the context of what science has discovered about the universe and the material creation. The universe has a creator and designer and so does not preclude God's interest in and his interaction with his creation. So we can expect "miracles" to take place. Because the material universe was created at a specific point of time we would have to say the universe itself is a miracle. So the scientist can continue to discover the nature of the universe and its laws and the believer can continue to pray (C.S. Lewis).

Criteria for establishing the occurrence of a miracle are (1). An event can only be explained as an act of God; (2). An event occurs as a result of a number of natural things happening but the likelihood of them all in a simultaneous conjunction is unlikely (the "constellation" miracle); (3). An event occurs when a natural law has been infringed (the "violation" miracle).

Without following the evidence that points to a divine creator and designer positing a purely chance development by impersonal forces and purposeless evolution would render it impossible to have confidence that our acquired knowledge of the natural world is reliable. That knowledge would merely be the way our minds have organized our perceptions. So there could be no validity to human reasoning and no true science. Our minds would be no reliable guides to truth.

God as creator and designer implies his constant activity in sustaining his creation and is involved in new acts of creation, i.e., miracles. The laws of nature govern event to event causality but the free acts of persons produce libertarian acts. So God as a free agent can leave scientifically detectable gaps.

The miracle stories of Jesus have, of course, a literary form and a relationship to the needs of the community in which they originated. They functioned in different ways within this context: as instruction, persuasion, catechesis, and even entertainment. The sociology of literature understand the miracle stories as symbolic.[922] What this line of

SUMMARY

interpretation fails to take into account is the community's pre-existent faith in Jesus. The community was called into existence by faith in the crucified and risen One and it would call upon its memory of him and his words and actions as its members encountered the various vicissitudes of existence to meet their existential needs. But they can't be limited to this functionalist understanding which would make these stories mere symbols, products of human subjectivity.

Of course, the ancient world was filled with miracle working and miracle stories. The working in the world of the realm of the spirit was taken for granted. However, the narratives of Jesus' miracle working are essentially different from that of the pagan world: there are no formulas and rituals. Jesus acts in terms of Israel's God: he speaks a word and the miracle is accomplished. Jesus in this way appears in the place of God and as his agent. His miracles witness to a new creation i.e., that are part and parcel of the paradoxical manifestation of the kingdom which is both present and not yet. They proclaim the kingdom as already breaking into time and space. They are also told in a terse and sober manner without a florid embellishment, reminiscent of the creation story in Genesis 1.

The miracles of Jesus take place mostly in the Galilee and there not so much in the villages but in the countryside reflecting where peasant farmers would be found. This location specified by Mark indicate that members of his community came from those locations which undergirds the authenticity of their occurrence.

The little vignette of Jesus healing Peter's mother-in-law and the subsequent meal limn the kingdom and its healing and feasting. The mother-in-law, in her serving, embodies the Lord himself as he seats his servants and serves them (Luke 12:37) and even washes their feet (John 13:3–10).

Jesus' cure of "leprosy" embodies his concern for the healing of society and its divisions since a leper had to live outside any and every human community. The healed leper could return to and be re-integrated with society. More than the other healing miracles of Jesus' the cure of leprosy incorporated the dimension of community pointing to the communal nature of God's coming kingdom and its presence already in Jesus' own ministry.

The Samaritan who returns to give thanks to Jesus in the story of the healing of the ten lepers indicates that this man senses the numinous presence of God in his healing and his "loud" voice reflects again the joy connected with the kingdom in his healing experience. Those who do not return to give thanks are like the nation which has not received the kingdom and its abstention from the rising hostility against Rome.

When Jesus declares the forgiveness of sins to the paralytic he is continuing the central aspect of the ministry of John. In this story Jesus refers to himself as "son of man" who is declaring forgiveness. One aspect of the meaning of this term refers to the future coming eschatological figure. So the future and present are coordinated corresponding to the kingdom which also is characterized by this double aspect. Jesus as son of man had authority over sin just as he does over demons and diseases. The passive in his declaration "your sins have been forgiven" implies God's action which is at work in the "beloved son." Forgiveness was especially needed in the divided society of Jesus' day and especially vis-s-vis the Roman overlord. Although the behavior of many a procurator was despicable, the government was tolerant toward the Jews and Judaism.[923]

So forgiveness was offered by Jesus outside the official Temple sacrifices. Forgiveness and healing are intimately connected since the culture understood that sin and disease were connected. The healing of the paralytic is not a proof that Jesus could forgive sin rather he is reasoning from the lesser to the greater. Jesus appears in this story as a priest whose sacrifice is himself.

Jesus reverses the law of purity which held that only impurity is contagious: he brings purity and ritual cleanness to the woman who had a hemorrhage. In this Jesus brings salvation to the woman beyond her healing. Jesus' intentions were to bring purity to the sinners who enter the kingdom. Their cleansing then leads to repentance. Here again Jesus overcomes the divisions of society and renders the woman capable of entering the fellowship of the worshipping community.

The healing of the man with a withered hand evokes restoration in particular, that of an individual, and the restoration of creation in general. To restore creation reaches back to the original creation of the cosmos by God which preceded the giving of the law. So the restoration of this man's hand takes precedent over Torah. The Sabbath is the commemoration (and celebration!) of God's "rest" after his creation activity. So the Sabbath was intimately connected with creation and by implication creation's restoration. The kingdom included and meant restoration. This story is full of subtleties and deeply reflects the mind and thinking of Jesus.

Jesus in healing the stammering man is acting on the basis of Isa 35 and also, as in the former story, the restoration of creation. It is also wisdom's action. Personified wisdom was intimately connected to creation so Jesus embodies personified wisdom.[924] Jesus' demand for silence regarding his miraculous activity took into account that the procurators and Herod Antipas were apt at putting down violently any popular movement that attracted crowds, even peaceful ones.

The healing of the blind man closely parallels the previous story with two striking differences: the healing was effected in steps and Jesus lays his hands on the blind man a second time reflecting the difficulty of the healing. The word "restore" is used here again pointing to the kingdom's restoration of creation.

Either Bartimaeus, the blind man at Jericho, was a member, or his relatives were members of Mark's community. So Mark's community preserved the story of one of its members. There is no word or gesture that heals him only that his faith had "made him well." Jesus emphasizes again that faith is the required attitude in healing which also underscores that Jesus preserves the independence of the person healed and eschews making people dependent on him as some kind of guru.[925] The recovery of sight to the blind is a sign of the kingdom and the intent of God to save his people (Isa 35:4–7). These works of power by Jesus were a graphic call to Israel to give up its occupation with Rome's egregious offenses against Israel and accept the presence of the kingdom which is now already among them in Jesus' fellowship.

The crippled woman was probably possessed by a demon who afflicted her with her crippled condition. Demons hate humans and by possessing them afflict them with suffering diseases. Again Jesus is in a synagogue to catch the ear of as many people that he can at one time with his kingdom proclamation. The ruler of the synagogue is unfamiliar with the subtleties of Torah interpretation and particularly Pharisaic teaching and its liberal application of the law which would allow the saving of people on the Sabbath. They, like Jesus, would argue from the lesser to the greater: if the saving of an animal is allowed on the Sabbath you can certainly save a human being on the Sabbath. The people rejoice–they sense the presence of the Jubilee: it is time to celebrate not grouse about Rome and its shenanigans. The grandeur of the kingdom is here!

Because the healing of the man with dropsy is a combination of miracle story and pronouncement story it can be, along with those other healing stories that exhibit such a combination, designated a "controversial miracle story." Jesus addresses the issue of healing on the Sabbath again even before anyone criticizes him. So controversy dominates the story. The comparison in Jesus' argument is an equal comparison (*a pari*), an argument he no doubt used frequently.

Archaeology has verified the existence of five porticoes at the Pool of Bethesda. The man Jesus heals there seemed ambivalent about being healed which is a subtle opposition to Jesus. Jesus ignores the ambivalence and healed him. There is no giving thanks nor does the man ask about Jesus' identity and only learns of it later. So there is no celebration and rejoicing but seeming indifference limning the unresponsiveness of the nation in general to Jesus' preaching.

The story of the healing of the man born blind has extensive additions to it added by John. Jesus placing clay on the man's eyes points to the new creation which is effected by the proleptic presence of the kingdom of God in Jesus' ministry. The man's washing in the Pool of Siloam, which brings about the return of his sight, points in the same direction in addition to evoking baptism. Baptism is the entry point into the kingdom, the establishment of God's new creation (2 Cor 5:17). The questioners of the man find it hard to accept that he has been healed and ever more emphatically insist they will have nothing to do with Jesus (and by implication the kingdom) but will remain devoted to "Moses" and the law–the precise zeal and dedication that will lead the nation to its destruction.[926] The once blind man points out the illogic of their rejection of Jesus. How could an abject sinner bring about the curing of blindness.[927] He clinches his argument with "God does not listen to sinners" (vs 31). In this way the man witnesses to his faith in Jesus apart from the miracle. He really does "see."

The healing at a distance of an official's servant is doubly attested. It appears both in John and Q.[928] We meet here again a mixture of forms: a pronouncement story and a miracle story. There are a multiplicity of variants between the three versions. Common to all is the occurrence of a healing at a distance of a member of the official's household. Jesus initially rebuffs the request for healing and the quester answers he knows Jesus' command to heal will be effective just as his commands are obeyed by his servants. Jesus marvels at his faith and tells him to return to his house for the healing has taken place.

I've noted that the authenticity of the stories of the raising of the dead by Jesus are even more suspect by the scientific world view of our present age because it is reasoned that there is no known way to bring back a person from the dead. However, my examination of the three incidents reported by the gospels demonstrated their historicity.

SUMMARY

In the case of the raising of Jairus's daughter the vivid portrayal of his emotional appeal, the report of his daughter's death and its certainty, the mockery of Jesus by the mourners (Jesus appears as an object of derision, an element of embarrassment), the preservation of Jesus' command in the original Aramaic, the lack of any exalted titles for Jesus, the antiquity of the story, and the Semitic background all support the historicity of the report.

That the child had actually died is supported by the wailing of the mourners and their mocking laughter when Jesus insists she is only "sleeping." The kingdom turns death into a mere "sleeping" a divine perspective on death because God can "awaken" a person from death. Jesus had comforted the father who was devastated by the death of his beloved child so faith again was demanded which, he is assured, will cast out fear. When the child appears alive the reaction of the crowd of villagers "being astonished with a great bewilderment" corresponds to encountering the numinous. This "beloved" child evokes Jesus' own death and resurrection as God's own beloved.

The kingdom has to do with life and faith whereas the present course of the nation, not trusting in God and his creative power to bring about Israel's liberation from exile, i.e., bringing life from death, will lead to the nation's ruin.

In the story of the raising of the widow of Nain's son there is no initiative on the part of the widow so there is no petition, no act of faith, nor any acclamation on the part of the crowd. Jesus acts entirely on the basis of his very human compassion and concern for the widow and her future. (He intuited her widowhood by the absence of the father in the funeral entourage.) A woman without a man to provide protection and a livelihood was destined to poverty and even death. Contributing to the historicity of the story is the reference to a gate, implying the town had a wall which archaeology has substantiated, the presence of a hapaxlegomenon (occurring only once), and its Semitic substratum and flavor. There is no raucous joy at the raising of the young man but rather the praise of God which includes celebrating what they perceive as the presence of a prophet in Israel and the resurgence once again of God's word, which seemingly had been silenced for generations. So God's presence, his "visitation," is recognized. This word is used in the Bible to describe God's action in history in judgment of sin or in favor by relieving distress. They had experienced the numinous presence of God. The joy of the kingdom is once more manifest in this story.

Invading the Realm of Demons, Disease, and Death

The kingdom has to do with God's compassion and his salvivic action for his people if they would only enter the kingdom and share in that attitude and behavior. Jesus doesn't wait for repentance but continually works to establish the kingdom in the face of hostility, division, animosity, and rebellious fervor. He is like an island of tranquility, peace, and resting in the love of God and his compassion in the midst of a raging sea.

That same compassion is evident in the story of the raising of Lazarus, Mary's and Martha's brother. Without a male head in the home Mary and Martha would have, like the widow of Nain, been subject to a terrible poverty. The historicity of the story is undergirded by the mention of the three members of this little family who were probably members of the primitive Christian community and the specificity of location. That membership probably also contributed to the length and detail of the tradition that was handed down to John. Jesus' own emotional reaction to the death underscores his close and endearing relationship with the family.

The center of the story is Jesus' arrival at the tomb, that is, he confronts death itself. Surrounding that central element are the people with their dismay, perplexity, and grief which Jesus also shares with them. Jesus never sets himself above the people. Rather in his pursuit of a life of wandering dependence on the people and their hospitality puts himself on an even more abject level than the peasants living, as they do, from hand to mouth. The humanity of Jesus is graphically portrayed in his venting of his emotion of "indignation" (vs 38) which expressed his identification with the loss felt by others by Lazarus in death and his deeply felt regret and displeasure with himself that he himself had arrived so late on the scene (and having been chided by both Mary and Martha because of that late arrival when he could have healed Lazarus and preserved him from death).

Apparently Jesus had been in intense prayer petitioning his Abba to call back Lazarus from death to life. So in this story we meet Jesus in his full humanity and in his intimate and profound relationship with God, his Father, who had named him his "beloved son." He was both conscious of and certain that God had "heard" his prayer so he could with full confidence and authority call out for Lazarus to "come forth" from his tomb.

In this story we are privy to Jesus' own consciousness and grappling with himself as a human being.

SUMMARY

I began chapter 5 with a survey of the meaning of a theophany. A theophany is the occurrence of God's self-disclosure. In the OT that disclosure could be in a thunderstorm. The most important of all divine disclosures is the giving of the law on Mount Sinai and also when he goes with Israel's army to fight their battles against pagan foes as the Divine Warrior. As the Divine Warrior he also wages war against spiritual forces.

My interpretation of the miracles covered in this chapter, usually called "nature miracles," is to describe them more aptly as theophanies. So when Jesus calms the storm on the Sea of Galilee he's embodying a theophany, manifesting the divine because God is depicted as calming the sea (e.g., Ps 106:9). So Jesus is the agent of a theophany pointing to God and he is revealed as his beloved son through whom God is active in establishing his kingdom.

Jesus as agent of a theophany, however, is only revealed to his disciples, not the nation in the stilling of the storm. So it is much more like the private theophany to Gideon who is called by God to rescue the nation from the Midianites. Jesus is called to rescue the nation from itself and the disaster which threatens if it does not turn from its present path of rebellion against Rome and lack of trust and reliance on God to save his people from their internal exile.[929]

We meet Jesus in his humanity again in the stilling of the storm which he is sleeping through, apparently exhausted, in the back of a boat. That exhaustion is emphasized by the disciples and their anxiety about the storm which they fear is life threatening: this is one intensely tempestuous storm indeed! They have an amorphous trust in him that he might be able to do something perhaps at least appreciate the plight in which they find themselves and share their terror.

In the incident of Jesus walking on the water the disciples reacting with terror because they thought Jesus might be a phantom (Gk., φάντασμα, *phantasma*, an appearance, hence a ghost or spirit) clearly suggests that the story was a post-resurrection event retrojected back into the ministry of Jesus. The only other narrative where Jesus is thought of in these terms is his post-resurrection appearance to the disciples described in Luke 24:37 where they think he is a "spirit" (πνεῦμα, *pneuma*, a spirit. The word can also refer to an evil "spirit"). It would only be the period after the death of Jesus that his appearance would be interpreted as a ghost or spirit. In his walking on the water Jesus powerfully reveals his divine nature which was not possible pre-resurrection. The terror of the disciples also points in this direction. They obviously think Jesus is still dead in the tomb. Their faithlessness at the time of Jesus' arrest and their abandonment of him in the moment of his deepest need would lead them further to think he is now appearing as a phantom to accuse and punish them.

On another level the walking on the water evokes OT images of God where his dominion over the forces of chaos is displayed by walking on the "deep" (Ps 77:19). So Jesus' walking on the deep powerfully expresses his divine nature. Underscoring the display of divinity is Jesus' identifying himself as the "I am" (vs 50) evoking God's own self-identification (Exod 3:14). The resurrected, glorified body of Jesus was no longer subject to the constraints of the material cosmos (cf., Luke 24:36–37; John 20:19 where he passes through walls).[930] His wanting to "pass them by" resonates with the reference to God who "passes before Moses" (Exod 34:6 the same word, παρέρχομαι, *parerchomai*, is used by the LXX). So this expression too underscores Jesus' revealing his divinity in a post-resurrection appearance. Jesus meant in this theophany to allay the fears of the disciples and comfort them (vs. 50). It must also have functioned that way in the primitive Christian community of Mark.

The multiple attestation of the story of the multiplication of loaves and that it also appears in a variant form in the feeding of the four thousand point to its historicity. These stories point to Jesus as the good shepherd of Israel, a royal designation, and that he appears as agent to the divine feeding of Israel as God had fed her during the time of the wilderness wanderings. So we encounter in this story another theophany. Jesus proleptically celebrates the feast of the kingdom, the messianic banquet, creating the community of the new age and limning its peace and overcoming the fractures, animosities, and antagonisms of first century Jewish society in the Holy Land.

The cursing of the fig tree is a dramatic evocation of the curse that will come upon Israel if she does not repent and turn from revolutionary violence, enter the kingdom, live according to its ethic and produce its fruit, live at peace waiting patiently for God to act, and bring about the end of her exile as a suffering subject of Rome and its cruel rule that deposed God and his prerogative as Israel's true ruler and king.

The catch of the great shoal of fish is a post-resurrection event and is a manifestation of Jesus' divinity and the power of the resurrection. It portrays the ministry which his disciples are now to undertake—to reap the harvest of people by the proclamation of Jesus and his resurrection bringing his saving power to the nations.

SUMMARY

As in the miracle of the multiplication of loaves, Jesus creates an abundance of good wine whereby he depicts graphically again the joy of the life of the kingdom as a wedding feast and the messianic banquet as opposed to the grief and animosity in his contemporary society. The kingdom is among the people, the old is superseded by the community of the new age. The old rites of purification are transformed into the new wine of the kingdom. The changing of water into wine is like an enacted parable. The wine is a creation *ex nihilo*. The kingdom is God's new creation—something that never existed before except in a preliminary way in Israel's society under her Davidic kings—a mystery hidden by God and now revealed in Jesus the messiah who is the bridegroom of his bride, the new people of God (Eph 3:9) who have entered the covenant of the kingdom which tears down the wall of distinction between Jew and Gentile (Eph 2:14).

The coin in a fish's mouth might be called a teaching miracle: Jesus asserts the essential freedom of the children of the kingdom. So it enacts the ethics of the kingdom. This freedom enables those who possess the kingdom to live as capable of making the concerns and conscience of one's fellow member of the kingdom as primary and not one's own. Because the sons of the kingdom are free they can freely acquiesce to one another and be more concerned with the brother than with one's own desires (1 Cor 9:19–23).

This is true love and true freedom.

That Jesus is once again called "beloved son" in the transfiguration placing the cross at the center of this experience. He is the one not to be spared but sacrificed by his Father The sacrificial motif is also present in the verb "led up" (ἀναφέρω, *anapherō*, Mark 9:2) since it is used in connection with sacrifice. Jesus' clothing "glowing whiter than any fuller could whiten" a garment interprets the cross as John repeatedly refers to it as Jesus' "glory." It is not divine glory but the glory of the new creation.[931]

So Jesus is the messianic priest. The event is a proleptic experience of the end time kingdom shown by the presence of Moses and Elijah, both of whom were expected at the end of days. The cloud also points to the end time when Jesus will come "with the clouds" (Mark 13:26). Peter's desire to erect the tents of Sukkoth interpret the transfiguration as a sign of the eschatological feast when the nations will join Israel in its worship of the one God of Israel.

In these theophanic miracles God is disclosing his presence in his son Jesus with whom he was "well pleased" (Mark 1:11). This disclosure

Invading the Realm of Demons, Disease, and Death

by God demonstrates and puts his stamp of approval on Jesus. Jesus is at the turning point of holy history and of God's dealing with his people and the world. These disclosures reach their apex in the pre-resurrection event of the transfiguration and in the post-resurrection event of Jesus walking on the water. The transfiguration witnesses to the glory of the coming kingdom and the walking on the water God's triumph over the forces of chaos which embody sin and death by the sacrifice of his "beloved son."

Significant is that both of these theophanies occur only before the disciples. So they are not public events.[932] Their public revelation occurs only through the witness of the church as part of the proclaiming of Jesus and the salvation God has wrought by his passion and resurrection. That they occur privately also supports their character as theophanies because theophanies are usually given only to individuals.

The other theophanies fill out the various aspects of what God accomplishes in Jesus' ministry which effects the proleptic presence of the kingdom: the stilling of the storm is a realization of God's protective presence; the feeding of the multitude and catching a shoal of fish reveal Jesus as the good shepherd (Ezk 34:11–31); and the changing of the water into wine the abundance which the sons of the kingdom will enjoy at the messianic banquet.

The opposite is proclaimed by the cursing of the fig tree—again witnessed only by the disciples: God's curse impends over Israel if she will not repent and turn away from violence and animosity and the factions of the divided house that Israel has become and enter the kingdom.

The theophanies all point to Jesus' intention to make obvious to his disciples that God was acting in his ministry and so functioned as an assurance that they were not alone in the world but as they would become witnesses to Jesus' life and resurrection God would be active in and through them.

As I placed my two previous studies of the parables and the pronouncement stories in the context of Jesus' contemporary environment so the miracles must be seen within the same context as these verbal activities of Jesus.

Israel's society was in turmoil and disintegrating. There were factions vying with one another each with its own agenda and answer to the crisis the society faced: living in exile within its own land because of the pagan Roman occupation whose emperor claimed divinity, an idolatrous affront to Israel usurping God's rightful place as the only real king of

SUMMARY

Israel. The Pharisees called the nation to be a "kingdom of priests" by following their understanding of Torah which for them consisted of the dual law, oral and written. The Saducean leadership in Jerusalem was satisfied with their subservient and dependent existence on Rome and so strove to keep the peace at the expense of being servants to the nation. As long as the Temple functioned according to their understanding of the Torah and their emoluments flowed in regularly they were more or less insulated from the vicissitudes of life. The Essenes called Israel to withdraw into its fellowship, follow its understanding of Torah, and wait for the great eschatological battle when Israel would bring in the kingdom of God waging war against and defeating the "sons of darkness" (Jews outside their community and Gentiles).

Israel's society was further riven by the competition between various revolutionary movements which included "bandits," messianic leaders who claimed to be the kings of Israel in the line of David, and prophets.[933] The latter groups were basically non-violent although in some instances when these prophets gathered large crowds many of their followers carried weapons. They were savagely put down by the procurators. The "bandits" took on the role of OT "judges," opposing any kind of kingship espoused by the leaders of the messianic movements, espousing the ancient egalitarian ideals of the tribal federation whose only true leader was God himself.

Adding to the general foment was a new ideology which grew up in the first century: that paying taxes to Caesar meant idolatry. Since taxes supported the state and the state was ruled by emperors who claimed divinity the taxes were seen as supporting such idolatrous claims. (So it was an inflammatory question indeed when Jesus was asked whether these taxes should be paid Mark 12:13–17.[934])

The nation was divided economically between the elites and the peasants who made up 98% of the population tilling the soil of small farms and confined to a subsistence living. Frequently the well-to-do would confiscate their little farms and add them to their large latifundia having foreclosed on loans leaving the peasant working the soil of land as a day laborer that formerly had belonged to him. Many of these men so deprived of their land ended up joining revolutionary groups so that Josephus could write that the country was overrun with "bandits" who stole from the rich and gave to the poor.

Invading the Realm of Demons, Disease, and Death

Much of these revolutionary activities and tensions were exacerbated by the Roman procurators and by their rapacious actions and lack of consciousness and appreciation of Jewish sensitivities and faith.

So the society was saturated and fragmented with competition, the struggle for survival, focus on ridding themselves of Roman hegemony, distinguishing themselves from Gentiles and their paganism, and both internal and external economic exploitation. The society was turned inward in its struggle against Rome, in its competitiveness, in its struggle for existence, in its preservation of its faith and life, and its concern to live as the people of God and to comply with its revealed law, the Torah. It seems that what got lost was its vision to be the "light of the nations." Turmoil may be too mild of a word to characterize first century Israel.

This agrarian society was governed by certain unspoken social values: patriarchy, honor-shame, cultic purity, limited good, corporate personality, and the patron-client relationship. Here I will describe only the idea of limited good for a detailed description of the others refer to my previous study.[935] Limited good referred to both physical goods such as food but also social good such as friendship, status, power, influence and security. The former was especially crucial. If my neighbor has more that means I have less. Everything was deemed to be in short supply. It meant preserving the status quo. Threatening a man's means of livelihood was to invite reprisal.

On the following page is a summary of the various social tensions that beleaguered the people of Israel in the Holy Land of the first century and the responses to them by some of the groups that I have described.[936]

SUMMARY

Responses of Judges, Prophets and Messiahs to the Factors contributing to the Crisis of Jewish Society in the Holy Land

Factors / Responses	Judges / Bandits	Prophets	Messiahs
Economic Inequality drought/famine loss of land marginal existence absent wealthy landowners taxes class distinctions loss of land day laborers	*Answer to the crisis:* redistribution of wealth they act as God's chosen leaders oppose the wealthy promote egalitarianism: the people would be in charge	*Answer to the crisis:* Inaugurate the kingdom by divine intervention establish God's reign of justice and righteousness	*Answer to the crisis:* Inaugurate the kingdom by human action as divine representative initiate a kingdom of justice
Social Tensions Jews vs. Gentiles aristocrats vs. Peasants population density urban vs. rural	egalitarianism social justice armed resistance	re-conquer and re-settle the land: a new "conquest" all of God's people a "kingdom of priests"	re-establish divinely appointed kingship and just rule of a Davidic king
Political Injustice Roman rule: vacillating policies Lack of strong indigenous leadership Hellenistic political ideals vs. Jewish ideals Jewish leadership regarded illegitimate	re-establish theocracy revolution: create conditions for the kingdom of God leadership by charismatic election: the people choose their leader	divine intervention that will remove the oppressive Roman regime leadership by a divinely chosen prophet and prince like Moses and Joshua	Revolution: establish the conditions for the kingdom Re-institute Davidic kingship and the just rule of a divinely anointed king

Invading the Realm of Demons, Disease, and Death

Religious Competition Pharisees, Sadducees, Essenes Variation in Torah observance Apocalypticism vs. Pragmatism Conservative Jerusalem vs. more laxity among peasants	Re-institute the old tribal unity where religious observance is determined by the united tribes	divine intervention will re-establish the law written in the hearts of God's faithful people	Unity will be brought about by the people united under the chosen messianic king
Ecological Divisions Israel: buffer state countryside: radicals the Galilee: agricultural Jerusalem: urban Hellenism in urban centers	sphere of activity: rural a conservative return to the rural ideals of the peasants	Rural phenomenon recalling the exodus and reestablishing the faithfulness of the wandering people of God	Re-uniting the whole land—the united kingdom— under the one sovereign Davidic monarch
Historical Memory Priestly legitimacy secularizing of leadership Roman expansion ideals of theocracy foreign domination debasing of Jewish institutions	Rejection of historical development of kings and hierarchy and secularism: return to the old tribal traditions	A thorough revolution of present circumstances that would replace foreign domination with the establishment of the kingdom of God	A re-conquering of the land as of old by David and subjecting Israel's enemies to the new Messianic king

Jesus spoke in parables because stories are easily remembered and they have an uncanny ability to change the hearts and minds of people. Jesus' parables are bi-focal: the coming kingdom of God and the historical situation of contemporary Israel in the Holy Land. These two foci are coordinated: by entering the kingdom the people would avoid the historical disaster that awaited them as a result of pursuing rebellion against the Roman overlord. His concern was the renewal of his society and calling it back to its roots living peaceably under their King, the God of Israel. That kingdom was already proleptically present in the community of the new age that Jesus was gathering together. It already had a historical presence so it was no pie in the sky. In this sinners were invited, people sat at table with him, they shared their goods, lived in forgiveness of one another, and eschewed violence.[937]

Most of the parables portrayed the kingdom of God, its nature, and how it functioned. The kingdom was a gift and did not involve human striving and accomplishment although, paradoxically, human action was involved. This paradoxical aspect of the kingdom is like the sowing of seed: humans sow the seed by proclaiming the kingdom but God would cause its sprouting and growing. So Jesus was therefore no "quietist" sitting on his hands waiting for God to intervene and save the nation. God's kingdom required action on the part of human beings: there's sowing the word, hunting for the lost, casting a fishnet, working in a vineyard, harvesting, investing the "talents" you are given, building, and preparing, The parables are verbs! So Jesus stood between the quietists and the revolutionary activists.

Another paradox of the kingdom was that it was not only holy and divine but involved corruption as in the leaven that leavens a lump of dough.[938] Corrupt members of society are included. The kingdom was like coming unexpectedly upon a massive treasure hidden in a field totally altering one's perspective and filling the one whom it finds with an overwhelming joy. One's response to being found by the kingdom (that passive points to God at work) is open ended. Each individual has to determine how to respond (cf., the parables of the Treasure in a Field, the Pearl of Great Price).[939]

These portrayals of the kingdom are then both warning and promise: they warn against pursuing violence and promise the unutterable joy of being surrounded with the Father's loving arms (the parable of the Prodigal Son[940]). The time is short. The nation will be sifted between those who accept the kingdom's invitation and those who reject its grace. So the kingdom is not based on a strict justice but unalloyed divine favor. It is based on God's generosity not on who deserves what (the parable of the Unjust Steward[941]). So the time is critical. The kingdom can break in at any time and accepting its invitation is crucial before it's too late. But merely listening to Jesus and even being well-disposed toward him is no ticket into the kingdom but rather doing the will of God (Mark 3:35). One has to accept him as the one sent by God who does his will by living out the ethics of the kingdom. However, Jesus points toward a proper response. He exhorts his hearers to "lay up treasure in heaven." One of the ways of doing that is to let your neighbor in on the joy of living in the kingdom.

The kingdom reverses roles: the master will serve the slave, enemies are prayed for, forgiveness of gigantic debts thrives, insiders become outsiders and outsiders insiders. The obedient and disobedient are reversed too. The one who has accepted Jesus' invitation and sits at his table but who doesn't quite fit the norms of society is the one who obeys God while those who think of themselves as righteous but who reject the invitation and who even malign Jesus for his fellowship with sinners is disobedient. The Founder of the feast of the kingdom does not take out revenge on those who do not accept his invitation to sit at table with him but stoops and includes those who are dishonorable, the poor, the outcasts, and the sinners. And he's like a father who suffers dishonor in order to win the sinner's acceptance of his forgiving, motherly love and affection that looks like indulgence.[942] The kingdom is not defined by legalities but by a Father-God who lays down his honor to win the sinner's acceptance of his love. The old structures of forgiveness following repentance is reversed. First one is embraced by the kingdom and its divine love and from that inclusion repentance ensues.

The kingdom swings wide its embrace because it includes also Gentiles. It is open to the pagan world and its decadence.[943] In the parable of the Unjust Steward the kingdom emerges from an oppressive debt system which is undermined by fraud not by violence.[944] So God is at work in unexpected places, circumstances, and persons. This parable reveals that the God of Israel is active in the wider world and the kingdom does not need to be taken by force of arms. So Jesus presents the nation with a choice of accepting the kingdom's invitation and putting this new life into practice. The fullness of the kingdom is impending and will break into the world in its own time. It can arrive at any moment like the deluge which broke upon the world in Noah's time. The parable of the Great Assize reveals how the world will be judged: on the basis of how it has treated God's people.[945] So the kingdom, contrary to the revolutionary spirit of the time, could not be brought about by human achievement and force of arms. Jesus' proclamation of the kingdom sabotages the prevailing idea that rebellion will bring in the kingdom. Jesus in his own way was like Jeremiah of old who advised the nation not only to tolerate the overlord but to pray for his welfare (Jer 29:7, cf., Rom 13:1–7).

SUMMARY

In the kingdom no one is a victim and without power. A woman, the lowest member of society up against the massive patriarchy, with her pestering voice can subvert the unjust powers of the world.[946]

The hospitality practiced by the villagers Jesus elevates to a central feature of the kingdom and as a national healing balm. Even if it is practiced with impure motives, as in the parable of the Neighbor Who Comes at Midnight, the kingdom will grow.[947] In the parable of the Pharisee and the Tax Collector Jesus spurns the judging of others but rather to be aware of the sins that skulk about in one's own heart bringing to consciousness that one stands in need of God's mercy no less than even an abject sinner.[948] In that way in the kingdom each member lives in the love and forgiveness that has been showered on oneself. To practice God's own forgiving love is to shun animosity and revanchism. In this way even the heart of Israel's enemies might be changed. If not, the great joy and the forgiveness one finds in the kingdom will liberate one from the anxiety connected with Roman rule, exploitation by the wealthy, and the daily concern for food and clothing. Forgiveness then is central to the kingdom. One need not sacrifice animals in the Temple to obtain it. It is available in the kingdom. The God of Israel is personal and relates to each individual. So the poor who rely on God like Lazarus in the parable will recline on "Abraham's bosom" in the kingdom while the uncaring rich are consigned to everlasting separation from the feast of the kingdom.[949]

This little overview of how Jesus conceived the kingdom in terms of the parables he told reveals that he was not just focused on "spiritual" realities but was concerned with the historical situation of his people and that they escape from the trajectory of disaster toward which their present attitudes and actions tended. It was not some kind of political program but directed toward the individual but with the goal of bringing the whole nation into subjection to the kingdom. He was remaking the society from the ground up. Nor was his teaching a kind of utopianism. But the ethics of the kingdom built on the very essence of Judaism and her God and his character. He was firmly rooted in the OT Scriptures and the prophets and on the inherent rebellion of Judaism against the world's status quo.

Anomalies in the narratives of Jesus' birth witness to a transcendent aspect to his person and being. Immanently he was known to be of Davidic descent. These two features mean that Jesus cannot be understood apart from God and that he was to effect Israel's restoration. So Jesus thought of himself as one with God and at one with his people.

He subjected himself to both God and man. Although Jesus possessed no divine power (Phil 2:7) he was conscious of being in a unique filial relationship with God evidenced by his claiming authority to forgive sins, his power over demons, and having an exclusive knowledge of God (Matt 11:27). So he grew up knowing his birth was surrounded by unusual circumstances and that his name was divinely revealed (Heb., יהושע, "Yehoshua," "Joshua" "savior," Gk., Ἰησοῦς, Yēsous, "Jesus").

The priest John, at the waters of the Jordan, proclaimed that the end of exile was near but that now the new Joshua must come, the "mightier one," and guide the nation out of exile into the new promised land. Jesus' own baptism meant that he understood that he himself had to enter the kingdom that he would proclaim is near. As he was baptized the Spirit came upon him confirming his filial connection to his Father-God by designating him the "beloved son" i.e., the "first born" who belongs to God by sacrifice, a sacrifice that atones for sin and by whose merit God will resurrect the dead.

He immediately then is "thrown out" into the wilderness recapitulating Israel's own desert wanderings where he reverses her faithlessness with his faithfulness to God relying on his word and enacts a new exodus into the kingdom that he proclaims.

Jesus uses the self-designation "son of man" for himself. Sometimes it is only an illeism but most frequently as a title with the association of transcendence representing both the faithful of Israel and Israel's defender. The title also is associated with the messiah who is judge of the world and works for justice and the vindication of Israel. In Jesus' usage the son of man is spoken of as the coming one, as the presently acting one, and the one who would suffer and be raised from death. As "son of man" Jesus embodies the kingdom, and it is through him and his ministry of proclamation, open commensality, and miracle working that the kingdom has its historical expression. So Jesus filled the rather neutral terminology "son of man" with his own content.

Jesus might have been a disciple of John at least until John's death. He shared some characteristics of John's ministry: preaching repentance and baptism, the call to "bear fruit," and the fire of judgment. But unlike John, Jesus was itinerant, ate and drank with sinners, sent his disciples out as envoys, and in contrast to John's asceticism the life of the kingdom was filled with joy, merriment, eating and drinking, and exuberance.

In Jesus' personal encounter with his contemporaries we find the same basic message which he proclaimed in his parables.[950] Here again

SUMMARY

he is not focused on just divine, heavenly realities but the historical circumstances of the nation and its people. He intentionally chose an itinerant ministry which eschewed a permanent home and made him dependent on the peasantry and their hospitality. In this way he chose to live more abjectly than even the peasant underscoring his teaching to live without anxiety for life's necessities and depend on God. So his life and words were totally congruent. He took upon himself the peasant's poverty, struggles, and longing for justice. He pushed for the solidarity of the people and called for them to be mutually supportive so that all were to be givers and receivers.

Jesus refused to be identified with the judges of old who functioned also martially. Rather he emphasized reconciliation, forgiveness, and acquiring "treasure in heaven." The kingdom is not established by revolutionary violence but by hospitality. In it one did not seek honor and security but to render service and not by acquiring wealth but by the sharing of goods. When Jesus refuses to be called "good" he witnesses to his divine "emptying" (Mark 10:18). God is the center of the kingdom! In contrast to Israel's culture which identified wealth with God's blessing and exemplary piety Jesus turns that popular notion on its head and asserts that the rich cannot enter the kingdom. They hardly met the kingdom's requirements.

Jesus proclaimed no apocalyptic scenarios but only that the kingdom was at the door and when it arrived in full force he would return to judge the nations. So he is the lord of the Sabbath, forgives sin, and binds Satan. So in him there is something greater now present than even Solomon (Luke 11:31). Even at that he does not aggrandize himself but identifies with the people and their sins. He only asserts precedence in the sense that God is at work through him and that he was "son" because his whole person, thought, word, and deed were defined by his relationship with God, a relationship that any human could enter. So his call to the people was to enter into this relationship and fully realize their sonship (Hos 11:1).

Jesus didn't quite meet John's expectations: John thought more in terms of a militaristic "mightier one" who would end injustices and purge the world of sinners not of one who sat at table with them. Jesus understood his ministry in terms of Isaiah's "servant" (Isa 42:1–3) who restores wholeness and liberates. Jesus was establishing the peaceable kingdom that overthrows the oppressor by an inward revolution of the people's heart that would erupt in radical love, forgiveness, serving others, and the sharing of goods. He rejected the social norm of limited good and the stringent zero sum reckoning of the patron-client relationship. Jesus didn't confine himself to a certain space like John and the Jordan River. He moved out into the every day world of his people seeking the lost and bringing the kingdom to them.

So between John and Jesus there is a great turning in the eschatological program: John ends the first period of Israel's holy history and he ushers in the new period, the dawning of the eschatological time of salvation. The restoration of Israel and the end of exile are already happening as people respond to the invitation to enter the kingdom.

Following the usual scholarship I divided the pronouncement stories into biographical and controversy and scholastic dialogues which I now will survey.

It was no doubt early on in his ministry that Jesus established the inner circle of twelve disciples, the number twelve constituting the leadership of the new age and corresponding to the twelve tribes of Israel. Reconstituting Israel would then fulfill the mission to be the "light to the nations." That meant they joined Jesus in his itinerant ministry and leaving everything else behind. Following him took precedence over all other social obligations. Also early on his ministry, following John's chronology, Jesus "cleansed" the Temple, meaning he prepared it for its eschatological function of being a house of prayer for all nations and where the nations would join Israel in the worship of the one God of Israel when the day of the Lord arrived. He was following the eschatological expectations of Zech 14. His actions also resonated with Zech 3 where the priest Joshua (i.e., "Jesus") is named as the one who will rule God's house and "have charge of his courts." So Jesus' action was more priestly than prophetic.

Jesus does not countenance "insiders" and "outsiders" among those who follow him. The kingdom is broad and capacious in its range. The kingdom then appears in, under, and among various surprising venues, people, and circumstances and even demands the love of enemies and those who persecute Israel. That love was expressed when Jesus rebuked James and John for wanting to call down fire on the Samaritans who would not accept Jesus' message. But this was not something new for it was at the heart of Judaism which called for the love of God and neighbor and constantly emphasized his mercy. So Jesus pointedly extended this love ethic even to tax collectors who were thought of as traitors because they supported Rome. To love them would be tantamount to participating in their infidelity. In this Jesus was urging the uprooting of bitterness and the healing of the nation of its disunity. Israel was to be one as God is one. So this love meant to separate one's behavior from the person. Rome was the ultimate enemy both politically as the hated occupier and religiously as idolaters. The love of this enemy meant Rome had to be seen as individuals, concrete persons, with whom one could have a relationship.[951] Of course, this extension of the love ethic would be seen as traitorous and as a participant in Rome's idolatry.

So there had to be a radical assault on the idea of "enemy" which demanded a multiplicity of contacts that are not of a formal, socially defined nature. Rome had provided for such a reordering by exempting Jews from military service, protecting the sanctity of the Temple, and recognizing the Torah as a sort of a constitution for Israel. Jesus in his open commensality challenged the Jewish prohibition of even entering a Gentile house and so encouraged the practice of hospitality even toward the Roman. That hospitality could be based on Israel's own Scriptures. Genesis witnesses to the shared humanity of both Jew and Gentile. All of mankind has a common origin in Adam and Noah. The story of the healing of a Gentile official's household member in whom Jesus finds a faith he had not experienced among his own people suggests the rapprochement that is possible between Jew and Gentile. Jesus was saying in effect that the man had found the kingdom and would that all his countrymen could! So Jesus did not just propose a theoretical idea of love of the outsider. The kingdom demanded a concrete acting out of love and overcoming hate and fear. Love is a discipline cultivating actions and attitudes which provided the foundation for love. This transformation of Israel by love will save her from the disaster that is sure to come if she continues on her present course.

Love is possible, however, only between mutually free people so Jesus proclaimed in his eschatological message the arrival of the Jubilee. The Jubilee, every seventh Sabbath of years, i.e., every fifty years, the ground was to lie fallow, debts were to be remitted, bonded servants to be set free, and property remanded to its original owner. But there is no evidence that the Jubilee was ever practiced. It remained a theoretical concept. The exodus was a divine redemption of the people whom God had bought for himself. So the exodus was a model of the Jubilee and its redemption theology. God's people were to be slaves to no one nor to one another. Resident aliens also had a safeguarded relationship of dependency on Israel.

Invading the Realm of Demons, Disease, and Death

So the Jubilee had to do with liberty and restoration. It preserved the equality and independence of the individual Israelite as well as the relationship with her God. The LORD had given them the land so no one could lose the land that was apportioned to the individual. The Jubilee in this way conserved the socioeconomic foundation of the people's covenant relationship with God and the unity of God, land, and people. From Lev 25:13–17 it is clear that the sale of land was really only a sale of use. The purchaser was only buying a number of harvests until the Jubilee when the land was to be returned to the original owner.

Prophetic thinking eschatologized the Jubilee. For example, in Isa 61 the Servant of the Lord is to proclaim liberty and announce the year of the Lord's favor, i.e., the Jubilee. God's people, and indeed the whole creation and the world, is to be set at liberty (cf., Rom 8:19–23). Jesus, in his visit to Nazareth according to Luke 4:16–30, presents his ministry as the inauguration of the Jubilee. By also characterizing his proclamation of the kingdom as an announcing the release of captives Jesus is claiming a royal prerogative. He also calls for release from debts in his prayer (Matt 6:12) and in the parable of the Unforgiving Servant (Matt 18:23–35). So in the kingdom, according to Jesus, God wipes away all debts. The demand is directed particularly to the wealthy who lent to the peasant who was frequently forced to borrow because of a poor growing season to help tide them over when a better yield from his land could be realized. This often led to the loss of the land and the various revolutionary groups could exploit these circumstances to recruit a man and his sons into their membership. Worse yet, the family could be imprisoned until the debt was paid. So a Jubilee of debt forgiveness would solve much of the social crisis into which Israel had sunk. The corollary to debt forgiveness was simply not to charge interest at all (Matt 19:21; Luke 6:34–36; 12:33; 14:13). This demands an unsullied trust in God which will be rewarded in the kingdom (Mark 10:28–30).[952]

Jesus' exorcisms can also be seen under the rubric of the Jubilee for they are a liberation from enslavement to a demon. Jesus enacts the Jubilee in the case of the Geresene demoniac: Rome is metaphorically driven out and the land released from oppression.

The open commensality that Jesus practiced as he ate in intimate fellowship with the marginalized, sinners, and outliers created community. For such people it must have seemed like a liberation from their despised status and being included within God's people, no longer in

SUMMARY

exile. Perhaps in such circumstances Jesus declared that the "kingdom of God is in your midst" (Luke 17:21).

The kingdom demanded a re-ordering of one's priorities and an alteration of one of Israel's most fundamental values: family had to take second place. To be discipled to Jesus and the kingdom required total self-surrender and emancipation from all other social obligations. However, in this way the disciple, in giving away all that one had the poverty of others was relieved, and at the same time making oneself dependent on others for hospitality practiced, in a radical way, the Jubilee. The Jubilee meant practicing mercy so ritual purity was not a great concern. Mercy is divine and imparts a purity that avoidance of ritual impurity could not convey. So Jesus' conflict with the Pharisees was not observance of the Torah but rather the focus on external behavior to the exclusion of the inner disposition. Interiority and the purity of intention were of ultimate importance to him.

Living this life of poverty was like the requirements of the men who fought Israel's battles: they had to maintain their camp as if they were serving as priests in the Temple (Deut 23:9-14). So Jesus seems to have thought of his ministry into which he invited his disciples as involved in a kind of military campaign. The battle was not against a tangible foe but satanic forces as they possessed individuals and the nation.[953] In the battles of Israel's Holy Wars combatants had to be unencumbered (Deut 20:5-8). Jesus required the same of his disciples (Mark 6:7-9; Matt 10:9-10; Luke 9:3). So this was no facile flaunting of Israel's social norms. But they were still stigmatized: they were itinerant, left off familial obligations, renounced social connections, and made themselves dependent on village hospitality.

So Jesus founded a new family of kinsmen among those who would hear the word of God and keep it (Mark 3:35). In this family God is Father of all (eschewing patriarchy), and both those settled followers in the villages and those who accompanied Jesus in his itinerant ministry, were brothers and sisters. It was not blood relationship and being a descendant of Abraham that counted in this new Israel. So the Jewish values of loyalty, care, and mutual love that characterized the family were transferred to this new community of the kingdom.

In this new family of the kingdom, because of their humility, children and the physically and morally defective were models for receiving the kingdom resulting in upending the priority and honor that accrued to the male elders in Israel's society. The kingdom is not something earned but it is pure gift which means trusting God above everything else and relying fully on him as children do with their parents. Zacchaeus, the tax collector, is an example of this child-like trust in God. The joy he finds in entering the kingdom is reflected in his resolution to make restitution far above what the Torah required (Luke 19:1–10). So Jesus turns the social pyramid upside down.

Jesus was not forming a sect like the Essenes who believed only their members were God's true Israel. His ministry and his appeal was to the whole nation like the prophets of old. He also promoted the validity of the Torah although the kingdom and its requirements had priority. So when Jesus heals on the Sabbath it is in the light of the presence of the kingdom and its Jubilean restoration of Israel. The time of salvation is here so healing cannot wait. No one would put new wine into old wineskins (Mark 2:22). A Pharasaic principle was that human life and its preservation superseded the requirements of Torah. Besides, the Sabbath meant "rest" and a reprieve from the bondage of labor, a foretaste of the feast to come. So the Torah remains in force until the kingdom is fully established (Matt 5:17–20). The kingdom is an invasion of the realm of disease which placed a person outside the community because it rendered a person ritually unclean. So healings were embodying God's mercy and they bring joy to the person who is delivered from disease and affliction.

Jesus was not against paying taxes either to the Roman state nor the Jewish commonwealth (Mark 12:13–17; Matt 17:24–27). In fact for him one had to go beyond the faithful payment of tithes and taxes and show the mercy of the Jubilee by giving alms generously and forgiving debts and so exceed the righteousness of the scribes and Pharisees (Matt 5:20). He was calling Israel back to its deepest roots to be children of their merciful and compassionate God. The Jubilee was here and as the essence of the kingdom its practice was to be a permanent state of affairs.

When untoward events happened to people Jesus rejected the thinking that the people involved were being punished for some sins they committed. In fact he used such events in a prophetic manner to warn the nation, which was becoming inured to violence, to turn about and repent lest it be destroyed.

The Torah for Jesus was summed up in the love commandment to love God and neighbor, the neighbor being anyone with whom a Jew would come into contact. So his understanding of Torah was subsumed under the demands and character of the kingdom. The Torah had to be interpreted in a new way: God's mercy and compassion were primary. He altered the way Israel was to look at the world and her life in the world. He was inaugurating the new covenant of Jeremiah (Jer 31:31). The ordinances, Temple, Jerusalem, and even the state itself were not central or essential because in the kingdom people will do what is right, living in and immersed in the grace, mercy, and forgiveness of God (Ezek 36:24-28; Joel 2:28-29). Obedience is interiorized and so obedience naturally follows. Jesus, however, was not critical of Torah as such but rather the nation's exclusive absorption with it and neglecting her cosmic mission to be a light to the nations. This inner attitude is vividly portrayed in what I have interpreted as a parable of Jesus: the Widow's Mite.[954] Again Jesus turns the tables on the hearer's expectation: that the rich man who deposited a large amount in the treasury would be praised. But it is the poor widow who, comparatively speaking, deposited much more because it was her "whole life" witnessing to her total dependence on God and trust in him to provide. So she is the one who has the treasure of the kingdom.

So merely fulfilling this law of love did not constitute inclusion in the kingdom. The kingdom demanded the self-giving of the whole person, denying the self, and taking up one's cross and following Jesus (Mark 12:32; 8:34-38). So Jesus embodied in himself the kingdom. The love commandment renders superfluous the Temple sacrifices (Mark 11:17). The giving of one's whole life is what Jesus would do on the cross as God's beloved son. His love for the Father and his people leads him to give his life for the nation (Mark 10:45) and sparing the nation the end-time messianic woes.

The story of Jesus' visit to Mary and Martha portray both the positive and negative responses to himself that he encountered among his people: Mary sits at his feet in repose, embodying the eschatological Sabbath rest, eager to learn from him while Martha is resentfully critical of both (Luke 10:38-42). The word of God takes precedence over eating (Matt 4:3). Hearing Jesus brings one into the kingdom. Because the nation will not hear it is doomed.

In Jesus' teaching on the indissoluble character of marriage he explicates another facet of the kingdom (Mark 10:1-12). The kingdom restores the original created order established by God. It takes precedence over the Torah which came later. So the kingdom restores the primordial, pristine creation of God at the beginning of the cosmos. Here Jesus speaks as the one greater than Moses. Marriage rests on God's own character. God himself limns the indissolubility of marriage: he is the faithful husband of his wife Israel and will never abandon her.

Jesus goes up to Jerusalem for his final hour. He came to the realization that the nation as a whole would not accept the kingdom and its way. So here he would assume the messianic woes of the end-time and be Israel's "ransom" from the threatening judgment of the coming kingdom and so accomplish the end of exile and Israel's redemption. When he arrived at the top of the Mount of Olives and viewing the whole of the city which lay before him and the beauty of the holy Temple he broke down and wept as he reflected on the future doom of the Holy City and the nation. By refusing the kingdom Israel had chosen the way of destruction. He had called on the people to enter the joy of the kingdom, follow the way of peace and passive resistance, pray for their overlord, live in forgiveness with one another, and share their bounty eliminating much of the anxiety that plagued them. So the judgment that will come upon his people causes him great sorrow. To dramatize the threat of destruction Jesus, in a prophetic action, curses the fig tree (Mark 11:12–14) which "withers to the root."

While in Jerusalem Jesus faces opposition which presages his coming passion. He is confronted by Pharisees who ask the loaded question asking if paying taxes to the Roman government was "lawful." Whether he answered yes or no whichever answer he gave would either make him guilty of treason or enrage the populace. The conflict was between God and anti-God, Tiberias, the Roman emperor who claimed divinity. Jesus' response "render to God what is his" and to the emperor "what is his" asserts the sovereignty of God over all worldly orders. It will be in the cross that God exercises his sovereignty over the world.

He is confronted also by Sadducees who deny the resurrection of the dead. In this the antithesis is between God and not-God. Their denial rejects God's fundamental character as the life-giver who ultimately will be victorious over death and restore life by the resurrection of the dead.

As Jesus bears his cross to the place of execution he is greeted by weeping women whom he advises to "weep for themselves" because of the coming catastrophe and then adding that if the Romans inflict the cross on Jesus the "green tree" what will they do to Israel, "the dry tree"? Then Simon of Cyrene is impressed into service and forced to carry Jesus' cross so he bears the wood of the cross while Jesus bears the cross of Israel's condemnation in his heart.

SUMMARY

For the wealthy Jesus' proclamation of the kingdom meant not to hoard but to share their wealth. He affirmed the people's experience of still being in exile in their own land but the liberation was not to hope in some kind of *Deus ex-machina* of an intervention by God but the creation of the community of the new age in which one is already at home with Israel's Father-God. There was, however, a military aspect to Jesus' behavior. He and his disciples were like men mustered into a holy war but not as aggressors against Rome but as the invaders of Satan's kingdom, binding him, and plundering his house.

Jesus refocused the anger and aggression that had captured the heart of the people against Rome and redirected it against Satan and his kingdom and engendering love, and love for even one's enemies. The kingdom was like a net and the net was God's love and forgiveness which was to be cast far and wide to include both brother Jew and Roman stranger. Sublimating aggressive anger in this way also allayed fear.

With the promise of love and forgiveness within the kingdom went also, however, a threat of judgment. To follow one's own prescriptions promoting the way of violence for alleviating Israel's crisis will assuredly result in suffering the horrors of Roman retribution.

Like John, Jesus emphasized that not blood relation, being a descendant of Abraham, won a person's place in the kingdom but rather hearing and doing God's will. The kingdom is not a static reality but dynamic and has to do both with one's inner attitude and external behavior. The marks of the kingdom Jesus outlines in his reading before the congregation in Nazareth's synagogue: initiating and celebrating the Jubilee, forgiving debts, concern for the poor, and living in forgiveness. This enacts the "year of the Lord's favor."

Jesus was not an ascetic withdrawing from the fray of everyday life like the Essenes. Nor was he waiting for an apocalyptic divine intervention. He was intricately woven into the fabric of the daily life and struggles of the people as he journeyed from village to village. Dependent on village hospitality he also brought priceless gifts: he healed diseases, drove out vexing spirits, and created fellowship at table. He was like a mobile Temple bringing the forgiveness of sins and incorporating people into the kingdom. He also lived in the repose of total reliance on God and his loving care. Anxiety about the needs of life were swallowed up in that repose. This beneficence of God was universal. In this he is integrating the character of wisdom into his self-understanding. Wisdom is not merely a teacher or provider of guidance or an instructor in the way of salvation. But he like Dame Wisdom is the summoning "I." "Whoso finds me," says Dame Wisdom, "finds life" (Prov 8:35). Jesus bids his people to find life in and through him as he invites them to enter the kingdom of God. Like wisdom he invites people to sit with him at table and reveals to them the hidden knowledge of God (Matt 11:27; Prov 8:14–36). His healing, exorcisms, using parables and aphorisms instead of using the prophetic "Thus says the Lord," the gathering of disciples, and his infrequent appeal to the Torah but rather the created order, and claiming that something greater than Solomon was present in him and his activity all point to his association with wisdom.[955]

In my first book of this series, *What Was the World of Jesus?* I described three models that developed in Israel from her beginning as a nation. These forms of Israel's political existence served as paradigms for any future renewal: prophet-king (messiah), priest, and judge.[956] As I indicated above Jesus explicitly eschewed the role of judge. He, however, does identify himself as a prophet (Mark 6:4) and was so identified by others.[957] When he "cleansed" the Temple he claimed priestly authority to take charge of the temple precincts. Jesus' chosen title for himself was "son of man" which included his identification with the suffering servant of Isaiah and the royal messiah. As son of man he embodied the nation. He also was inaugurating the Jubilee. As the agent of the kingdom of God he was identifying himself with the fullness of Israel's past and the expectations of God's saving help in the future. So Jesus recapitulated Israel's history and existence by filling the roles of prophet, priest, and king. In addition, he embodied the important figure of personified wisdom whose outlook and activities characterize his own. Above all, however, he was the beloved son who would be "given" out of God's love for the nation and the world (John 3:16). His miracle activity of driving out demons, healing, and raising the dead undergird his making the kingdom present and its presence as actual. He's showing there is a better way than violent rebellion. God is truly present with his people and is calling them through Jesus to enjoy that presence and its restorative power. God desires an abundant life for his people and it is available in his servant and beloved son Jesus. It is something like the Deuteronomic cry to choose life (Deut 30:15–20):

> See, I have set before you this day life and good, death and evil. If you obey the commandments of the LORD your God which I command you this day, by loving the LORD your God, by walking in his ways, and by keeping his commandments and

his statutes and his ordinances, then you shall live and multiply, and the LORD your God will bless you in the land which you are entering to take possession of it. But if your heart turns away, and you will not hear, but are drawn away to worship other gods and serve them, I declare to you this day, that you shall perish; you shall not live long in the land which you are going over the Jordan to enter and possess. I call heaven and earth to witness against you this day, that I have set before you life and death, blessing and curse; therefore choose life, that you and your descendants may live, loving the LORD your God, obeying his voice, and cleaving to him; for that means life to you and length of days, that you may dwell in the land which the LORD swore to your fathers, to Abraham, to Isaac, and to Jacob, to give them.

However, Jesus was not calling the nation to greater Torah observance but to obedience to the new "Torah" of the kingdom of God and its ethics of love, forgiveness, and the sharing of goods. The nation at this point was worshipping the god of revanchism, violence, and rebellion. So the warning of Deuteronomy remains the same: blessing and curse are set before Israel in Jesus' call to enter the kingdom. "Obey his voice . . . for that means life . . . and length of days, that you may dwell in the land which the Lord swore . . . to give [you]." The nation did not listen, and its doom was sealed in the devastating war with Rome some forty years later.

Epilogue
Retrospect and Prospect

The Jesus of history was not some divine man who had divine powers and so was capable of producing miracles. Phil 2:7 reveals the nature of his historical existence. He had "emptied" himself of divinity and so had no powers beyond that of any other mortal. His miracles were not some kind of proof of the working of his divine nature. The fact that the ancient prophets of Israel were able to perform miracles, including raising people from the dead, supports the total humanity of Jesus.

I began the second book by investigating the birth, baptism, and temptation narratives which revealed he was, however, conscious of an intimate filial relationship with God. He was designated God's "beloved son" both at his baptism and at the transfiguration event and experience. This designation is charged with deep biblical associations. The beloved son Isaac and other "beloved sons' of the patriarchs underwent symbolical deaths and resurrections. So this designation meant he was destined for sacrifice and that he would take upon himself Israel's travail as the suffering servant (Isa 53). It also made him God's messianic king.[958]

In the two books previous to this study on Jesus' parables and the pronouncement stories it became clear that Jesus was not propounding some universal truth like messages dropped from heaven but that his words were directly related to the historical situation in first century Israel in the Holy Land. He was seeking a spiritual and behavioral revolution of his people. He saw clearly that their present disposition toward hostilities and revolution against Rome would end in destruction. The stories that he told in his parables resonated with Israel's history which was a story telling culture (see the OT!). But his parables were also subversive especially because they asserted that the kingdom of God included corruption i.e., included sinners. To associate corruption with the Holy One of Israel was highly provocative and opened up criticism making of him a perverter of Israel's faith.

In my investigation of Jesus' parables I did not make Jesus somehow superior to other story tellers of Israel and in this way denigrate other Jews and early Judaism. But like any other Jewish teacher he had his uniqueness. He, like any prophet of the past, presented both God's promise and judgment on the culture and people of his day. His criticism was directed at specific aspects of Jewish society: the almost universal hatred of Rome, its exclusive focus on Torah observance (especially by the Pharisees), and neglect of Israel's calling to be a light to the nations.[959] He was not opposing people but ideologies. Jesus did not, nor do I assert that he did, reject his people, Israel.[960] Rather he was striving for its renewal and its salvation and to spare it from certain catastrophe.[961]

The examination of the pronouncement stories we find Jesus offering the alternative of God's kingdom to the popular seeking of God's kingdom by revolution against Rome. The kingdom is both present and coming in its fullness in the future. These pronouncements were challenging indeed. He upended Judaism's values by welcoming marginalized people, sinners and Gentiles, into this topsy-turvy kingdom; by claiming the right to forgive sins; by inverting social relationships claiming the apparently God-blessed rich were rejected and adults were to become like children; by the audacious demand to pray for the hated Roman enemy; by the claim that God's kingdom allowed the Torah to be broken for the sake of healing people on the Sabbath; by judging divorce and remarriage as constituting adultery. It was little wonder that Jesus could be accused of having a demon.

The kingdom also meant the Jubilee had dawned. Now debts should be forgiven and the sharing of ones goods should abound. Even peasants could act with the noblesse oblige of the wealthy because they had an infinite treasure in heaven and so could consider themselves rich. It meant too, that one could live as if the exile were over and therefore enjoy the freedom of acquiescing to the conscience of the "weaker" brother or sister, include even the Romans, and thereby live in and create a community of love.

Jesus and his disciples were like an army arrayed against, not the Romans, but spiritual, demonic forces that had invaded the world. So this was a new kind of Holy War that totally destroyed the enemy. As warriors in this invading army they left family and friends, village and community, work and its responsibilities behind and entrusted themselves to the support of village hospitality. This was a new family that absconded with the Jewish values that accrued to the family: loyalty, mutual support, protection but whose only patriarch was God himself.

The miracles were the invitation to enter the kingdom as they historicized God's compassion and mercy as had the exodus so many years before. So the miracles are the way of the new exodus from the slavery of the nation's bondage to its conviction they are still in exile because of Rome's occupation. The exorcisms paved the way to that entrance, the healings and raisings from the dead actualized the new life of the kingdom, and the theophanies were the witness that God was truly with Jesus, set his stamp of approval on him, and that he was present with those who joined him in these meals that were a foretaste of the messianic banquet of the kingdom. So the presence of the kingdom was concretized in the open commensality that Jesus practiced: here was celebrated forgiveness, acceptance, and being enfolded within the kingdom. Here the incapacitating hostility toward Rome ended, the anxieties attended on living with the idea of limited good was overpowered, and the divisions that plagued the society was replaced with mercy toward one's fellow member of Israel. In the fellowship of the kingdom the individual was transformed by joy.

In the next volume of this series on the Jesus of history I will examine all the individual sayings of Jesus that are scattered all over the Gospels. (An example of these sayings occur in what is called the Sermon on the Mount in Matthew 5–7 where the evangelist has collected many of them.) They will, like the parables, the sayings included in the pronouncement stories, and the miracles, be set within the historical situation within which Jesus was active and as he endeavored to bring renewal to his beloved nation so as to avoid the doom which threatened if the nation continued on its present path. I have already alluded to several of these saying through this and my previous studies such as "turn the other cheek" and "go the extra mile" and have seen how they fit so intimately within Jesus' time and place. So be ready for further discovery of the liveliness of the contents of the gospels.

Endnotes

1. The major contributors to the study of the "historical Jesus" in the nineteenth century pursued the removal of miracles from theology. For example D. F. Strauss' *Life of Jesus* postulated they were myths which arose out of the common consciousness of the earliest Christian community. Bultmann followed up on this interpretation but asserted that myth could not be separated from the NT and so the only alternative was to demythologize the gospels by interpreting them for twentieth century Christians. Other twentieth century interpreters simply ignored the miracles or relegated them to insignificance focusing on Jesus and his message. Academics and theologians of a liberal persuasion continue to maintain a vigorous skepticism about the miraculous. This attitude is built, of course, on the conviction of a "closed universe" and a materialistic understanding of life. Only the world of matter exists and there is nothing "beyond it" i.e., there is no "world of the spirit." As the following discussion makes clear, the investigations of scientists are now revealing this is no longer tenable in face of hard evidence.

2. A literary type determines the form of a particular text. For example a news report differs from a fairy tale in its style and content. The Gospels contain various forms such as miracle stories, pronouncement stories, canticles, sayings, narratives, and parables. For the form critics the earliest church produced these units and their form was determined by the use to which they were put within the life of the community. So, according to them, the individual units of traditions we find in the Gospels developed out of the life of the church. The Germans called this the "*Sitz im Leben*" i.e., the situation in the life of the church. So Bultmann, *History*, 4 asserts, "The proper understanding of form criticism rests upon the judgment that the literature in which the life of a given community . . . has taken shape, springs out of quite definite conditions and wants of life from which grows up a quite definite style and quite specific forms and categories." So each form will have its own life situation, that is, reflect the influences at work in the life of the community. There is a weakness within the form critical supposition that the community was the creator of the tradition and shaped it all in terms of the various needs of the community. The shaping needs to be reversed. Jesus' teaching and actions shaped the life and the outlook of the community from the beginning. Of course, this is not to say that there was no recall of the various words and deeds of Jesus, such as the miracles stories, later in the life of the community. So I would make the generation of the traditions we find in the Gospels more complex and nuanced than the form critics allow. For the work of the form critics see Bultmann, *History*, Dibelius, *From Tradition to Gospel*. See especially, McKnight, *What is Form Criticism?* for a wonderful summary of the whole enterprise and a seven page annotated bibliography that covers the field

from its beginnings up to the year 1967.

3. See Pritchard, *Ancient Near East*, 2:26. Of course, there the resemblance ends. The creation account in Gen 1 could not be more dissimilar and distinctive from these myths so it is a total misnomer to characterize it as myth. For example in the "Babylonian Theogony" the gods are paired and by incest and murder one divine pair succeeds another. They are true myths, i.e., the stories and adventures of gods. Gen 1 is not a story of a god but the narrative of God's action in creating the universe which accords with the scientific findings that the universe had a beginning and it was fine tuned to create life demonstrating that a designing mind stands behind the universe.

4. In fact, Newton developed a number of compelling arguments for "natural theology," that is for the reality of God based on examination of complex systems in the material universe. See Meyer, *God Hypothesis*, 50.

5. Meyer, *God Hypothesis*, 20–22. He asks why did scientific thinking arise in Europe and not elsewhere. The material necessities for the rise of scientific thinking existed all over the world: well-developed societies which allowed the time to think about the world, simple technology, a system of writing, and mathematical notation. So why in Europe? He references the historians Ian Barbour, Peter Hodgson, Herbert Butterfield, and Joseph Needham who identify Judeo-Christianity as the crucial element which provided the intellectual presuppositions underlying its rise.

6. Meyer, *God Hypothesis*, 59. His description appeared in his *A Treatise of Celestial Mechanics* in 1798.

7. Meyer, *God Hypothesis*, 51, who also sees the events of the Thirty Years' War as influencing this turn of thought. This devastating conflict between Catholics and Protestants with their opposing claims of the sources of religious authority and the attendant exhaustion it engendered left people open to, and interest in, the search for new ways of thinking. So an Enlightenment philosopher like David Hume (1711–76), in rejecting the reality of God, denied the possibility of miracles, particularly because they violate the laws of the natural world.

8. Sullivan, *Limitations of Science*, 133–35. Sullivan summarizes the results of this thinking in a quotation from Bertrand Russell, p. 133: "That man is the product of causes which had no provision of the end they were achieving; that his origin, his growth, his hopes and fears, his lives and beliefs, are but the outcome of accidental collocations of atoms; that no fire, no heroism, no intensity of thought and feeling, can preserve an individual life beyond the grave; that all the labours of the ages, all the devotion, all the inspiration, all the noon-day brightness of human genius, are destined to extinction in the vast death of the solar system, and that the whole temple of Man's achievement must inevitably be buried beneath the debris of a universe in ruin—all these things, if not quite beyond dispute, are yet so nearly certain, that no philosophy which rejects them can hope to stand." Quoted from Sullivan, *Science and Religion*, 216. This depressing, disheartening, and shattering assessment of human existence makes Jesus' miracles invading the realm of death even more impressively poignant.

9. Meyer, *God Hypothesis*, 13–49, in his first two chapters covers the development of scientific thinking and how the early investigators like Boyle, Kepler, and Newton understood their work as revealing the intelligibility of the universe and therefore the mind of its designer. It was the two nineteenth century historians John Draper and Andrew White who came up with the idea that science and biblical faith were at war with one another.

10. Wisdom of Solomon 13:1–9 expresses the outlook and attitude of the materialist perfectly: "For all men who were ignorant of God were foolish by nature; and they were unable from the good things that are seen to know him who exists, nor did they recognize the craftsman while paying heed to his works; but they supposed that either

fire or wind or swift air, or the circle of the stars, or turbulent water, or the luminaries of heaven were the gods that rule the world. If through delight in the beauty of these things men assumed them to be gods, let them know how much better than these is their Lord, for the author of beauty created them. And if men were amazed at their power and working, let them perceive from them how much more powerful is he who formed them. For from the greatness and beauty of created things comes a corresponding perception of their Creator. Yet these men are little to be blamed, for perhaps they go astray while seeking God and desiring to find him. For as they live among his works they keep searching, and they trust in what they see, because the things that are seen are beautiful. Yet again, not even they are to be excused; for if they had the power to know so much that they could investigate the world, how did they fail to find sooner the Lord of these things?"

11. Sullivan, *Limitations of Science*, 138.

12. James Clerk Maxwell (born June 13, 1831 in Edinburgh, Scotland) was a physicist best known for his formulation of electromagnetic theory.

13. Sullivan, *Limitations of Science*, 139.

14. Sullivan, *Limitations of Science*, 141, where he refers to Arthur Eddington's "The Domain of Physical Science."

15. Sullivan, *Limitations of Science*, 142.

16. Sullivan, *Limitations of Science*, 143, referring to Jeans, *Mysterious Universe*.

17. Sullivan, *Limitations of Science*, 144.

18. Sullivan, *Limitations of Science*, 145. For Eddington both the external universe and our minds are homogeneous in nature. The material world is "mind stuff."

19. Sullivan, *Limitations of Science*, 147.

20. Sullivan, *Limitations of Science*, 148.

21. Sullivan, *Limitations of Science*, 151–52.

22. Sullivan, *Limitations of Science*, 153.

23. Sullivan, *Limitations of Science*, 157–58.

24. I'm including here his wave equation by way of illustrating the abstractness of concepts that now describe the strange world of atomic and sub-atomic physics:

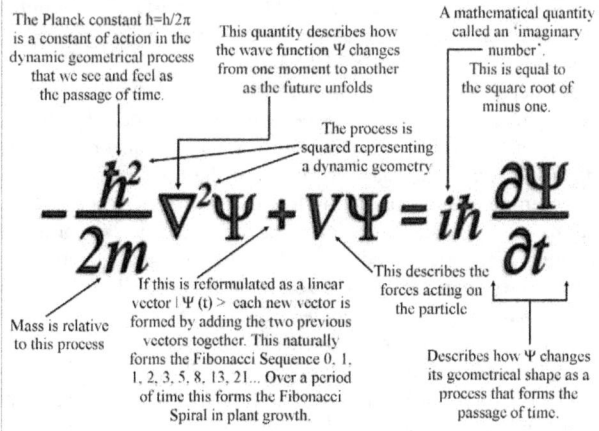

The Schrödinger equation is a linear partial differential equation that describes the evolution of a quantum state in a similar way to Newton's laws (the second law in particular, that force equals mass times acceleration, F=ma) in classical mechanics. However, the Schrödinger equation is a wave equation for the wave function of the particle in question, and so the use of the equation to predict the future state of a system is sometimes called "wave mechanics." The equation itself derives from the conservation of energy and is built around an operator called the Hamiltonian ("h"). H is the Hamiltonian operator, which corresponds to the sum of the potential energy and kinetic energy (total energy) of the quantum system. The Hamiltonian is a fairly long expression itself. You can refer to the article in Wikipedia on the Hamiltonian.

25. Sullivan, *Limitations of Science*, 160.

26. Sullivan, *Limitations of Science*, 162. In this regard Sullivan underscores, for the layman, an unexpected aspect of the scientific endeavor. He finds an aesthetic motive in scientific work and in the satisfaction a scientist derives from his work. It is like that of an artist. He detects the language of artistry in the writings of science. There are frequent reference to "elegance" and "beauty." So nature itself is seen as possessing a harmony and simplicity that is beautiful. So for the great men of science, science is an art and he himself an artist and the results of research are a work of art because it is "a faint and imperfect copy ... of the supreme work of art which is nature itself" (162–67). He also observes that there are moral values in science the chief of which is a disinterested passion for truth—a most "unpopular virtue" he says. Of course, scientific success is not possible on any other grounds and its success is measured by its truthfulness. A scientist who misrepresented observations or deliberately concocts arguments in order to reach pre-determined conclusion would be stultifying himself as a scientist. Without truth science is meaningless. He notes too that the reaction to most scientific facts is indifference but where a scientific theory impinges on the philosophic or religious interests people are then no longer indifferent (172–75).

27. If you could count one molecule a second, as I pointed out to my grandson, it would take over 300 trillion years to count them all.

28. Sullivan *Limitations of Science*, 182–83. The uncertainty principle is expressed in the mathematical formula $\Delta x > h/4\pi m \Delta v$. Δx is a fundamental physical constant characteristic of the mathematical formulations of quantum mechanics, which describes the behavior of particles and waves on the atomic scale, including the particle aspect of light. The German physicist Max Planck introduced the constant in 1900 in his accurate formulation of the distribution of the radiation emitted by a blackbody, or perfect absorber of radiant energy. The significance of Planck's constant is that radiation, such as light, is emitted, transmitted, and absorbed in discrete energy packets, or quanta, determined by the frequency of the radiation and the value of Planck's constant. The energy E of each quantum, or each photon, equals Planck's constant h times the radiation frequency symbolized by the Greek letter *nu* (ν), or simply $E = h\nu$. A modified form of Planck's constant called h-bar ($\hbar$), or the reduced Planck's constant, in which $\hbar$ equals h divided by 2π, is the quantization of angular momentum. For example, the angular momentum of an electron bound to an atomic nucleus is quantized and can only be a multiple of h-bar. The dimension of Planck's constant is the product of energy multiplied by time, a quantity called action. Planck's constant is often defined, therefore, as the elementary quantum of action. Its value in meter-kilogram-second units is defined as exactly $6.62607015 \times 10^{-34}$ joule second.

29. Sullivan, *Limitations of Science*, 183–84.

30. Sullivan, *Limitations of Science*, 175–77.

31. Sullivan, *Limitations of Science*, 184–88. I will discuss biology and the theories of evolution in more detail below.

32. These are 20 of the 48 constants listed at https://en.wikipedia.org/wiki/List_of_physical_constants.

ENDNOTES

TABLE I An abbreviated list of the CODATA recommended values of the fundamental constants of physics and chemistry based on the 2014 adjustment.

Quantity	Symbol	Numerical value	Unit	Relative std. uncert. u_r
speed of light in vacuum	c, c_0	299 792 458	m s^{-1}	exact
magnetic constant	μ_0	$4\pi \times 10^{-7}$	N A^{-2}	
		$= 12.566\,370\,614... \times 10^{-7}$	N A^{-2}	exact
electric constant $1/\mu_0 c^2$	ϵ_0	$8.854\,187\,817... \times 10^{-12}$	F m^{-1}	exact
Newtonian constant of gravitation	G	$6.674\,08(31) \times 10^{-11}$	m^3 kg^{-1} s^{-2}	4.7×10^{-5}
Planck constant	h	$6.626\,070\,040(81) \times 10^{-34}$	J s	1.2×10^{-8}
$h/2\pi$	$\hbar$	$1.054\,571\,800(13) \times 10^{-34}$	J s	1.2×10^{-8}
elementary charge	e	$1.602\,176\,6208(98) \times 10^{-19}$	C	6.1×10^{-9}
magnetic flux quantum $h/2e$	Φ_0	$2.067\,833\,831(13) \times 10^{-15}$	Wb	6.1×10^{-9}
conductance quantum $2e^2/h$	G_0	$7.748\,091\,7310(18) \times 10^{-5}$	S	2.3×10^{-10}
electron mass	m_e	$9.109\,383\,56(11) \times 10^{-31}$	kg	1.2×10^{-8}
proton mass	m_p	$1.672\,621\,898(21) \times 10^{-27}$	kg	1.2×10^{-8}
proton-electron mass ratio	m_p/m_e	$1836.152\,673\,89(17)$		9.5×10^{-11}
fine-structure constant $e^2/4\pi\epsilon_0 \hbar c$	α	$7.297\,352\,5664(17) \times 10^{-3}$		2.3×10^{-10}
inverse fine-structure constant	α^{-1}	$137.035\,999\,139(31)$		2.3×10^{-10}
Rydberg constant $\alpha^2 m_e c/2h$	R_∞	$10\,973\,731.568\,508(65)$	m^{-1}	5.9×10^{-12}
Avogadro constant	N_A, L	$6.022\,140\,857(74) \times 10^{23}$	mol^{-1}	1.2×10^{-8}
Faraday constant $N_A e$	F	$96\,485.332\,89(59)$	C mol^{-1}	6.2×10^{-9}
molar gas constant	R	$8.314\,4598(48)$	J mol^{-1} K^{-1}	5.7×10^{-7}
Boltzmann constant R/N_A	k	$1.380\,648\,52(79) \times 10^{-23}$	J K^{-1}	5.7×10^{-7}
Stefan-Boltzmann constant $(\pi^2/60)k^4/\hbar^3 c^2$	σ	$5.670\,367(13) \times 10^{-8}$	W m^{-2} K^{-4}	2.3×10^{-6}
Non-SI units accepted for use with the SI				
electron volt (e/C) J	eV	$1.602\,176\,6208(98) \times 10^{-19}$	J	6.1×10^{-9}
(unified) atomic mass unit $\frac{1}{12}m(^{12}C)$	u	$1.660\,539\,040(20) \times 10^{-27}$	kg	1.2×10^{-8}

33. To alter even slightly, say the value of the force of gravity or the electromagnetic force, would derail the whole process of the development of the universe. For example, altering of a given number, you would end up with the wrong kind of stars or no stars at all completely eliminating the possibility of life. Glynn, *God: The Evidence*, 28. Fred Hoyle initiated the research on how the atomic reactions in stars produced the various chemical elements. He was initially an atheist but during the 1950's in discovering the "fine tuning" of the universe (see the table in the note above) and that these numerical properties fell within very small ranges by which alone complex forms of life can exist his atheism was totally shaken. Added to that are the "contingent" properties of the universe, that is, those constants whose alteration would not affect the fundamental laws of physics are also delicately balanced to allow for the possibility of life. So we live in a "Goldilocks universe" in which the fundamental forces of physics and the universe's contingent properties have just the right strengths and values to make life possible. At an even more fundamental level the quarks, which make up protons and neutrons, must have precise values "exquisitely tuned" allowing for the production of elements like carbon, an essential element for a "life-friendly universe." Furthermore, the gravitational constant G has to be of a certain value in order for stars to be hot enough to produce the fusion reactions which enable the production of elements such as carbon. Also, if G were weaker it would prevent stars developing into supernovae and ejecting these elements which are necessary for life in the universe. However, if G were greater stars would be too hot and only the heavier elements would be produced and nucleosynthesis would take place to quickly reducing the production of elements needed for the formation of planets. Stars would not last long enough to form solar systems capable of supporting life. See Meyer, *God Hypothesis*, 130–32, 136–38.

34. The principle was first enunciated by Brandon Carter at a conference in 1973 in Poland celebrating the 500th anniversary of Copernicus' birth. The principle, in effect,

turned the Copernican revolution on its head which had placed not the earth and its human inhabitants at the center of creation but because the earth revolved around the sun making the sun the new center. This revolution was interpreted as dethroning humankind from its privileged central place in the universe. Now, Carter asserted, the universe revealed itself to be expressly designed for the emergence of human beings. Glynn, *God: The Evidence*, 22–23.

35. Glynn, *God: The Evidence*, 23. See also Meyer, *God Hypothesis*, 146, for the striking quotation from Charles Townes.

36. Glynn, *God: The Evidence*, 31 quoting Fred Hoyle. Hoyle was one of the great astronomers of the twentieth century and a prolific writer. He coined the term "Big Bang" as a derisive name for the emergence of the universe at a definite time in the past.

37. Glynn, *God: The Evidence*, 31

38. Meyer, *God Hypothesis*, 147.

39. Meyer, *God Hypothesis*, 148–49.

40. Meyer, *God Hypothesis*, 151. He mentions other factors that are finely tuned: (1) The expansion rate of the universe. If it were faster galaxies couldn't be formed; if slower it would have collapsed. (2) The density of the universe one billionth of a second after the big bang would have to had the precise value of 10^{24} kilograms/cubic meter. If it had been just one kilogram less galaxies would never have developed. That is one part out of 10^{24}! (3) The cosmological constant had to be one part in 10^{90}. Without this latter fine tuning there would have been no life in the universe. (4) The masses of the fundamental particles. "These requirements for the existence of life, again defying our ability to describe their extreme improbability, have seemed to many physicists to require *some* explanation." (153).

41. Charles Lyell's study *Principles of Geology* showed how natural forces could account for the present shape of the landscape rather than a creator God and, of course, *The Origin of Species* seemed to put the final nail in God's coffin.

42. Glynn, *God: The Evidence*, 43 and 179 n. 53 refers to a prediction based on this anthropic principle that was verified experimentally. He concludes, "The final defense against the anthropic principle has come increasingly in the form of scientific myth making, the concocting of ever more spectacular constructs that might in some way escape the more obvious implication of the cosmic coincidences-namely that the cosmos is the product of an intelligent creator." (50). I would suggest that Occam's Razor should come into play here: the simplest solution is the correct one.

43. Other peculiar quantum phenomenon are known as "entanglement" and "tunneling." In an article in *New York Times*, July 22, 1997 Malcome W. Browne described these phenomena. The following is excerpted from this article. Entangled particles are identical entities that share common origins and properties, and remain in instantaneous touch with each other, no matter how wide the spatial gap between them. In an experiment in Geneva, Switzerland two photons of light nearly seven miles apart responded simultaneously to a stimulus applied to just one of them. The twin-photon experiment by Dr. Nicolas Gisin of the University of Geneva and his colleagues was the most spectacular demonstration yet of the mysterious long-range connections that exist between quantum events, connections created from nothing at all, which in theory can reach instantaneously from one end of the universe to the other. In essence, Dr. Gisin sent pairs of photons in opposite directions to villages north and south of Geneva along optical fibers of the kind used to transmit telephone calls. Reaching the ends of these fibers, the two photons were forced to make random choices between alternative, equally possible pathways. Since there was no way for the photons to communicate with each other, classical physics (i.e., Newtonian physics) would predict that their independent choices would bear no relationship to each other. But when the paths of

the two photons were properly adjusted and the results compared, the independent decisions by the paired photons always matched, even though there was *no physical way* for them to communicate with each other. "Tunneling" is the bizarre ability of particles to sometimes penetrate impenetrable barriers. "Tunneling" is based on the fact that quantum theory is statistical in nature and deals with probabilities rather than specific predictions; there is no way to know in advance when a single radioactive atom will decay, for example. The probabilistic nature of quantum events means that if a stream of particles encounters an obstacle, most of the particles will be stopped in their tracks but a few, conveyed by probability alone, will magically appear on the other side of the barrier. The experimenters found "that a barrier placed in the path of a tunneling particle does not slow it down. In fact, particles detected on the other side of the barrier have made the trip in less time than it would take the particle to traverse an equal distance without a barrier– in other words, the tunneling speed apparently greatly exceeds the speed of light. Moreover, if you increase the thickness of the barrier the tunneling speed increases.

44. Christian Doppler discovered in 1848 that the motion of an object affects the waves coming from it. So, for example, when a train approaches you with its whistle sounding the tone rises and as it draws away the waves expand and the tone deepens. The motion toward you causes the frequency of the sound waves to contract and as it moves away they expand creating the difference in tone. The same is true of light. In 1912 Vesto Slipher documented that the light emitted from distant galaxies shift toward the red end of the spectrum indicating, that their wave lengths had been stretched. They were moving away from the earth. Then in the 1920's Edwin Hubble determined that the more distant galaxies were receding at a greater velocity than those that were nearer. Meyer, *God Hypothesis*, 83–93.

45. Needless to say, that was not an easy fact for many a scientist to accept. Even Eddington said he found the metaphysical implication troubling and that the idea of a beginning was "repugnant" to him. It has also been shown that the mass of the universe is slightly less than the critical density that would cause it to recollapse. The expansion is actually accelerating due to so-called "dark energy." Meyer, *God Hypothesis*, 94, 96, 105.

46. See Schilling, *Elephant in the Universe*. This theory of dark matter was first proposed by Jacobus Kapteyn, a Dutch astronomer, in 1922. He is noted for his discovery of galactic rotation.

47. Schilling, *Elephant in the Universe*, 319–20.

48. What if this so-called "dark matter" is the unseen presence of God himself shaping and guiding the universe and its development? In that case it might always remain undetectable except for the detectable effects which scientists observe. Of course, this is pure speculation.

49. Meyer, *God Hypothesis*, 110, quoting Robert Jastrow of the Goddard Space Institute describes the experience of the results of scientific research. The scientist, he wrote, "has scaled the mountains of ignorance; he is about to conquer the highest peak; as he pulls himself over the final rock, he is greeted by a band of theologians who have been sitting there for centuries."

50. See Mack, *End of Everything*, 129–56.

51. See below where I discuss the nature of the biblical account of creation.

52. Cf., Glynn, *God: The Evidence*, 166. "The knowledge of the Spirit is prior to the knowledge of reason. Where reason follows Spirit, the results are good; where it rejects or parts ways with the Spirit, the results are invariably disastrous, whether one speaks of the political, societal, or personal spheres. Reason rediscovers and reconstructs in slow, cumbersome, linear, and partial fashion what Spirit already knows. There is nothing morally or socially admirable about the post-Enlightenment world that does not go

back to values that were given to humankind whole in a priori form in the New Testament. Jesus already 'knew' what modern humanity has only painstakingly discovered after two thousand years, and has yet to fully learn." In this regard see also Barr, *Modern Physics and Ancient Faith*. He demonstrates that what is really at war with religion is not science itself, but a philosophy of science, namely, scientific materialism. He argues that the great discoveries of modern physics are more compatible with the central teachings of Christianity and Judaism about God, the cosmos, and the human soul than with the atheistic viewpoint of scientific materialism.

53. Emerson, *Selected Essays*.

54. The video can be found on You Tube. David Berlinsky is an author and senior fellow of the Discovery Institute's Center for Science and Culture; David Gelernter is an author and professor of Computer Science at Yale University and senior fellow of Jewish thought at the Shalem Center; Steven Meyer is an author and founded the Center for Science and Culture of the Discovery Institute and former professor at Whitworth College.

55. See Meyer's chapter "The Cambrian and Other Information Explosions" in *God Hypothesis*, 189–213. There he discusses the mathematical probabilities and chances of the production of specialized proteins that would make possible the building of new organs, tissue, and cell types, i.e., the development of new plant and animal organisms. Such effective and functional "mutations" developing on their own are all but impossible. Even a relatively short protein of 150 amino acids represents one sequence among 10^{195} possible combinations! (That's 1 followed by 195 zeros! To put that in perspective there are only 10^{65} atoms in the universe.) The chances of hitting on just the right combination is astronomically miniscule. So the Darwinian theory which propounded that "natural selection" explained the development of complex biological organisms can only account for "the survival of the fittest, but not the arrival of the fittest" (196). There is not enough time in the 13 billion year history of the universe to hit on the right, beneficial, and functional combinations that would produce a new organism. The information imbedded in these amino acid sequences is like information embedded in written language. The generation of functional information is associated with conscious activity that conveys meaning (e.g., a computer programming language). Matter and symbols arranged with a goal in mind is the product of a rational agent. There is a designer.

56. You can google "genetic code" to get an idea of the complexity of the code that genes contain.

57. "*Giving Up Darwin*." And so the other references to Gelernter's article.

58. Meyer, *God Hypothesis*, 15–16 refers to a conference in 1985 where the biophysicist, Dean Kenyon, announced he had repudiated his previous understanding of the evolutionary origin of life which asserted how a living cell might have "self-organized" from a "pre-biotic soup." Experiments had shown that "simple chemicals do not arrange themselves into complex information-bearing molecules" and move in the direction of producing life unless "biochemists actively and intelligently guide the process"! Meyer later met with one of Kenyon's colleagues, Charles Thaxton, who also affirmed that the information found in DNA "pointed to the past activity of a designing intelligence."

59. Meyer, *God Hypothesis*, 181 observes that even Richard Dawkins, an atheist and well-known and published critic of creationism and intelligent design, publically acknowledged that the information embedded in DNA might represent the signature of "some kind of designer." But not a divine one! He proposes that perhaps some alien civilization that evolved somewhere else in the universe may have designed then seeded the first life on earth! You'd think such an intelligent person would realize he's

only pushing the same question back a step. Who created those alien life forms? Such a preposterous suggestion only reveals how a person can make of their denials a (false) religion (i.e., an irrational belief system) that depends on a blind faith. Meyer, 265–66 in his evaluation of this suggestion writes ". . . asserting that life arose somewhere else out in the cosmos does not explain how the information necessary to build the first life, let alone intelligent life, could have arisen. It merely pushes the explanatory challenge farther back in time and out into space. Indeed, positing another form of preexisting life only presupposes the existence of the very thing that all theories of the origin of life must explain and have yet to explain—the origin of functional biological information."

60. These two masters were earlier contemporaries of Jesus. See Roemer, *What was the World of Jesus?*, 480–81.

61. Meyer, *God Hypothesis*, 290–91 refers to the work of the Dutch structural biologist Peter Tompa and the American biophysicist George Rose who have demonstrated mathematically that even having all the requisite parts of a cell will not insure they will self-organize into a living system. There are $10^{79,000,000,000}$ different possibilities of combining the proteins even in a simple single-cell yeast! The different combinations of combining all the proteins including the DNA and RNA molecules, ribosomes, lipids, and glycolipid molecules grows even exponentially larger exceeding the number of elementary particles in the Universe (10^{80}) and even the number of events since the big bang (10^{139})! So only intelligent design can account for the development of life since evolutionary models cannot account for the information necessary to produce the first cell. Secondly, only an intelligent agent can generate the kind of information present in the biomacromolecules necessary for life.

62. A similar explosion of mammals occurred in the aftermath of the mass extinction that ended the age of dinosaurs when a large asteroid struck 66 million years ago in what is now the Gulf of Mexico. Roughly three-quarters of all species went extinct in the aftermath. Hundreds of fossils found in Colorado offer a snapshot of how life rebounded. The discovery includes the exceptionally preserved remains of at least 16 mammal species, as well as many turtles, crocodilians, and plants that lived within the first million years after the global devastation. To the frustration of many paleontologists, however, life in the period immediately following the extinction event has been very poorly documented in the fossil record—until now. Described in the journal *Science*, the new fossil bonanza is already revealing some key details about how life made a comeback. That includes new insight into the stunning growth spurt mammals experienced in the first 300,000 years after the catastrophe. Laboratory examination of these fossils made exquisitely clear that mammals grew a lot larger in the first million years after the mass extinction. The biggest mammals that escaped the global die-off weighed no more than a pound. But just 100,000 years later, the largest species among their descendants were about 13 pounds, as heavy as a modern raccoon. And another 200,000 years later, "the largest mammals had again tripled in weight, to about 45 pounds," according to the paleontologist Tyler Lyson. That's about as heavy as an American beaver, and much heavier than any pre-extinction mammals. About 400,000 years later, another growth spurt gave rise to even larger mammals weighing over a hundred pounds, or about as much as a pronghorn. Their arrival occurs with the appearance of fossils from the first representatives of the bean family, including the leaves and protein-rich seed pods sought by many herbivores. "We were surprised how well everything lines up," Lyson said. Important to note here is the correlation between simultaneously occurring events of body size, floral diversity, and climate warming.

63. It seem that human beings cannot exist without some kind of belief system that mimics religious commitment. Whereas true religion is always open to questions, challenges, and working through to the fundamental truths of faith such as Christianity

ENDNOTES

did by means of the development of its formal creeds achieved by the struggles of the councils of Nicene, Constantinople, Ephesus and Chalcedon.

64. Moody, *Life After Life*.

65. See Glynn, *God: The Evidence*, 99–137. I'm following him in the ensuing discussion.

66. Kübler-Ross, *On Children and Death*, quoted by Glynn, *God: The Evidence*, 117.

67. Quoted by Glynn, *God: The Evidence*, 118. He also mentions another investigator Melvin Morse, reporting on an eleven-year-old boy who was resuscitated from a heart attack and who had observed it from above in the emergency room. The report was found to be accurate in every feature. He quotes Morse: "An eleven-year-old cannot describe an emergency room resuscitation with any great accuracy no matter how much television he watches" (119).

68. Glynn, *God: The Evidence* 119–20.

69. Glynn, *God: The Evidence*, 121. Glynn then deals with the chief materialist explanations of these experiences: 1. anoxia (oxygen starvation): However, that produces not clarity but confusion 2. hallucinations or dreams: However, subjects do not report them in that way. Hallucinations are usually a distortion of reality and accompanied by anxiety. Contrariwise, subjects report a sense of serenity and peace. They also have a life-transforming effect. 3. Birth Tunnel memory: However, the eyesight of babies is too poor to observe the birth canal. 4. Endorphins: However, theses opiates do not induce the state of NDE's. 5. Hypercarbia (elevated levels of carbon dioxide): In experiments with psychiatric patients such a state seemed to produce similar out of the body experiences and a profound sense of security. However, not all people reported such experiences and no hospital would permit such elevated carbon dioxide levels in their patients. Sabom also reported that in one case the patient actually had elevated oxygen levels. 6. right-temporal lobe involvement: This area of the brain is involved with emotion and the sense of certainty of experience. Persons with damage to this area can also have a distorted sense of time. When stimulating this area electromagnetically a quarter of such trials produced an out of the body like experience and the sense of another presence. However, these experiences are transient and in NDEs also include language, body image, a narrative line, and even smells all of which are known to involve others parts of the brain.

70. Glynn, *God: The Evidence*, 130.

71. Glynn, *God: The Evidence*, 135–36 references Plato's experiences and the otherworldly journeys described in the Egyptian Book of the Dead and the Tibetan Book of the Dead. Note, although Glynn does not provide his book with a bibliography, he references a plethora of studies in the notes to his chapter on NDEs. He doesn't mention the number of encounters with the world of the spirit in the Bible, while not NDEs, they take place while a person is conscious, such as the encounters that Moses, Isaiah, Micaiah ben Imlah, and Saul of Tarsus all had.

72. Glynn, *God: The Evidence*, 137.

73. Gallagher, *Demonic Foes*. He graduated from Princeton University and was trained as a resident in psychiatry at Yale University School of Medicine. He is one of the foremost experts in the world on diabolic attacks.

74. Having worked in a psychiatric hospital for sixteen years I often encountered patients who thought they were diabolically possessed. But it was always obvious to me that such was not the case since they did not, for example, utter vile blasphemies, speak in languages they had never learned, or possessed and exhibited extraordinary strength. Psychoses often involves hearing voices which is not to be equated with possession even though those voices can demand that the person commit crimes such as murder.

75. Gallagher lays out his scientific approach in his introduction distinguishing himself from pop-culture which propounds wild theories about the paranormal and exaggerates claims of demonic attacks. Gallagher, *Demonic Foes*, 1–15.

76. Gallagher, *Demonic Foes*, 8.

77. Gallagher, *Demonic Foes*, 11.

78. Here I would prefer the word "transcendent." "Supernatural" is not a biblical word or concept. The world of the Bible sees no bifurcation of "natural" and "supernatural." The created order is embedded in the world of the spirit and there is a continuous interplay between the two. For example, Israel understood that God was present in the Temple because it was his "footstool" (1 Chr 28:2; Ps 99:5; 132:7; Is 66:10) implying that God's presence extended through the realm of the spirit and the material universe so that his presence united the two realms. So there was no question of a constant and continuing communication between the transcendent and the material world. That the world of the spirit would interact with our world and impinge upon it was taken for granted.

79. It was recovered by English archaeologist Austin Henry Layard in 1849 in fragmentary form in the ruined Library of Ashurbanipal in Nineveh (present day Mosul in Iraq). See Roemer, *What was the World of Jesus?*, 605–6 where I summarize the Babylonian creation myth. For the text see Pritchard, *Ancient Near East*, 1:31–39. This mythic epic had its origin most probably in the early second millennium B.C. and was recited annually at the Babylonian New Year's Festival. In other words, the Jewish exiles were enveloped in the Babylonian culture and religion and their erudite and scholarly priests would be highly cognizant of the details of their religio-cultural surroundings.

80. McCurley, *Genesis*, 9.

81. The epic was recited and ritually dramatized annually at the Babylonian New Year Festival by which, it was believed, the orderly universe and its persistence was insured for the coming year. One finds similar themes, for example, in the Viking and Nordic mythology. In it the universe also begins with a crime scene: three gods ramble along a deserted beach and mold the world out of the body of a murdered giant and create the first humans Ash and Elm from driftwood. See Price, *Children of Ash and Elm*. Such myth-making seems to be endemic to ancient pagan cultures.

82. The phrase is used in Jer 4:23 to describe the land because of God's judgment.

83. In this regard compare the Memphite Creation Theology which portrays Ptah as creating by "heart and tongue" i.e., by thought and word. Toward the close of the account it states that "so Ptah was satisfied" (or "rested"). See Pritchard, *Ancient Near East* 1:1–2. The text is from the 8th century B.C. but its roots extend back to the 2nd millennium.

84. Dahl, *Resurrection of the Body*, 59–73.

85. See Roemer, *World of Jesus*, 462–63.

86. See Roemer, *World of Jesus*, 462–63 on the "Hebrew totality concept." God called the world out of chaos and formlessness and holds it unceasingly over the abyss. Chaos is the great enemy of the created order.

87. "Sin" is not just the trespassing of some moral norm. At its profoundest depth it is alienation from God resulting in rebellion and the disordering of the creation.

88. Rapidly" is a relative term, of course. The process is rapid but even then, because of the size of the universe, will take, as it is estimated, 10^{100} years. This depletion is due to the second law of thermodynamics called entropy. Entropy means devolving into greater and greater disorganization i.e., chaos.

89. Von Rad, *Theology*, 148. Theologically, God deals with this disturbed relationship between him and creation by means of covenants. The covenant creates Shalom (translated with the rather inadequate word "peace") which means the restoration of

wholeness and harmony, a state of communion between two parties, and securing a state of intactness, orderliness, and righteousness. See von Rad, *Theology*, 130, 138–39 who understands soteriology lying at the basis of the creation stories. Creation itself is part of the saving work of YHWH culminating in the call of Abraham and the election of Israel. Ps 19:1–4, quoted in the title of this chapter, is in harmony with the creation account declaring that the created order points to its designer and originator.

90. Indeed the word for moon does not appear until Gen 37:9 in the Joseph story as part of his dream and the word for sun not until Gen 15:12 in the Abraham story where it is only marking the time of day.

91. Pritchard, *Ancient Near East*, 1:36.

92. The English "good" does not quite catch the broader and deeper meaning of the word. In Hebrew the word includes the meanings "joyous, glad, pleasing, desirable, suitable, lovely, kind." The LXX catches the meaning better by translating the word with טוב ("good, beautiful, pleasant, free from defects, fine" and even "morally good").

93. McCurley, *Genesis*, 15.

94. Meyer, *God Hypothesis*, 502, n 19 in this regard affirms that he doesn't think a "bright line of demarcation between science and metaphysics can be drawn."

95. Meier, *Marginal Jew*, 2:513–15. See Francis J. Beckwith, "History & Miracles," in Geivett and Habermas, *In Defense of Miracles*, 289, n 2 provides a little bibliography of scholarship which describes the arguments against the historicity of miracles and which assert, much like Meier, "that history as a discipline is not equipped to handle the task" (87).

96. In this regard see Kemp, *War That Never Was*, who debunks the idea that there was always two distinct and warring camps, religion and science. That construal is belied by the fact that all the early scientific investigators were themselves people of faith. This conflict theses he traces back to the late nineteenth century by two influential books in particular: John William Draper's *History of the Conflict between Religion and Science* (1874) and Andrew Dickson White's *History of the Warfare of Science with Theology in Christendom* (1896). Kemp recognizes that there was conflict over heliocentrism in the seventeenth century and over the age of the earth and evolution today. There are scientists today, such as Stephen Jay Gould, an atheist, who understands science and religion as "non-overlapping magisteria." However, Christianity makes claims about the physical universe especially in the teaching of the bodily resurrection of Jesus. Then there are those scientists who take "ontological naturalism" as foundational to science which avers that the world of the spirit does not exist or if it does has no causal impact on the natural world. For them to admit even one miracle is to disrupt the regular, repeatable nexus of a material cause and effect universe. But such a position, Kemp observes would demand that it could not be admissible that scientists could make mistakes. Science does not require the impossibility of miracles anymore that it requires the impossibility of fraud and blunders in the scientific endeavor. Christian theology teaches that miracles are clearly recognizable and infrequent and rare enough to elicit wonder. Kemp shows that the relationship between Christian theology and science has been a complex relationship and far more multifaceted than the warfare protagonists have asserted. There have been multi-sided debates whose participants have held more highly nuanced positions than is usually recognized.

97. Of course, within the scientific endeavor there are unresolved tensions. There are contradictory theories and various results from a multiplicity of experiments. But no one would say there is a war between science and science! The same can be said of theology. For example the church had to wrestle with the doctrine of God as it became more complex with the revelation of Christ and the work of the Spirit. These tensions drove theology forward as the Christological controversies led to the understanding of

God as a Trinity. See Pelikan, *Melody of Theology*.

98. David Hume (1711–1776) played a major role in excluding the possibility of the occurrence of miracles. I will focus on his arguments in chapter 3.

99. See Malinowski, "Magic, Science and Religion," 19–84. (The edition I'm referring to here is a reprint of the original book published in 1925.)

100. Meyer, *God Hypothesis*, 240.

101. Meyer in his book *God Hypothesis* does not merely present the scientific facts pointing to a designer but also engages fully with the arguments of those who reject the "God hypothesis" and delineates their flaws both logically and scientifically: those who assert that the universe could emerge from nothing (368–87); the "many world" idea (390–93); the idea that every imaginable mathematical structure has a physical expression, i.e., mathematics produces universes (394–99); the false allegation that finding a designer is the old idea of the "god of the gaps" explanation (409–30); and the idea that the "laws of nature" produced the universe (431–33). Finally Meyer engages with Hume's skepticism regarding the uniformity of nature who argued that the universe's uniformity is induced only from a limited number of observations and this inductive reasoning is circular: justifying inductive reasoning assumes that the principle of nature's uniformity (440–41). However, those who argue in this way *live* as though they believed in that uniformity. Furthermore, if God exists and is a God of order then there is good reason to trust in the design of the human mind and the reliability of its built in assumptions about the world. Those very assumptions lead to the development of science and the scientific method. This "propositional argument" for the existence of God does not prove his existence but it "suggests that positing God's existence allowed one to live consistently–such that one's stated philosophy would match one's implicit beliefs as expressed in action (442). So only those who believe in God have a belief system that matches the way they think and act on a daily basis. Such belief is also more hospitable to science than a God-denying naturalism. So a belief in a benevolent God enables the "belief in the reliability of the human mind and in the truth of the assumptions we make about the world that makes knowledge possible" (447). The alternative of living in a godless universe is to "eat, drink, and be merry for tomorrow we die" (449. Cf., 1 Cor 15:32 and the philosophy of that "practical atheist" in the parable of the Rich Fool, Luke 12:16–20. See Roemer, *Who in the World was Jesus*, 165–68). See also Ortland, *Why God Makes Sense*, who revisits the classical cosmological, teleological, moral, Christological arguments for God's existence. Theism, he asserts, explains the elegance of Mathematics, the beauty of music, and the value of love.

102. Meyer, *God Hypothesis*, 222 quoting Richard Dawkins. The religious fervor of materialist scientists was evident in 2004 when Stephen Meyer presented a paper to be published in the Smithsonian's journal *Proceedings of the Biological Society of Washington* titled "The Origin of Biological Information and the Higher Taxonomic Categories" in which he presented evidence of intelligent design. The piece was peered reviewed and Meyer made suggested changes. The editor, Richard Sternberg, was forced out of his position after an avalanche of criticism followed the publishing of the article accusing him of being "religious." So here we have all the trapping of an irrational belief system (i.e., a false religion): Heretics are branded, certain ideas are banished, invective and stigma are invoked, and circular reasoning is followed: critics of intelligent design argued that the idea was unscientific and should not have been put forward in a peer-reviewed journal. So when it was, they argued, it shouldn't have been because it was unscientific. Dr. Gelernter in the discussion summarized above also noted how colleagues at Yale responded with similar irrational responses rather than engage in a scientific discussion. These attitudes and reactions smack more of religious fanaticism than a scientific mindset that is open to new facts, new ideas, and

new hypotheses. This hostility toward evidence is engendered apparently because it threatens their (false) "religion." The Bible calls this "original sin" and documents how it leads to idolatry. In this case the idol is human autonomy. If one lives with the belief in a universe of "pitiless indifference" and no sense of accountability to a transcendent reality how can a humane world be constructed where human life is guided by moral principles that values life and the care of the world and its environment? I suspect that the materialist who adopts some kind of morality is only drawing on the moral sense that is embedded in our humanity by God and explicated by our Judeo-Christian heritage and human law. The materialists know that if they were to be truly consistent with their "religious" belief in materialism there would be no morality but mere "blind, pitiless indifference" toward others and the world. I suspect too, that their adoption of some kind of morality serves the purpose of avoiding having their views and their "religion" thoroughly rejected.

103. The materialist's moral consistency with the "pitiless indifference" of the universe shows itself, however, in the way they treat scientists who argue even scientifically for a designer of the universe. See examples of this immorality in the preceding note.

104. In this discussion of miracles John Meier's second volume of *A Marginal Jew*, 509–1038, in which he has exhaustively engaged with the idea of miracle both ancient and modern and with the interpretation of the miracle stories in the Gospels is indispensable reading. I will constantly refer to this work. He gives a representative and fulsome list of works that have dealt with the miracles, n.4, 522–24.

105. Cf., here Meier's definition in *Marginal Jew*, 512–15 and the others he lists in n. 5, 525.

106. See Twelftree, "Miracles of Jesus," 118. In terms of the Judaism of Jesus' day he maintains that the kingdom of God meant God's action in the world, so "it would not be surprising that even the sayings of Jesus require us to look primarily to the miracles as the tangible expression of the ruling power of God in his ministry." He finds support for this contention explicitly in the saying in Luke 11:20. "But if by the finger of God I cast out demons, then the kingdom of God has come among you."

107. Meier, *Marginal Jew*, 513 and nn. 14 and 15, 527 on the other hand, sees as the essence of miracle as a special act of God. But what do you do with Jesus' declaration "Your faith has made you well" (Mark 5:34 cf., Mark 2:5; 10:52)? Here Jesus is attributing only implicitly the miracle of healing to God working through the faith of the person involved. Of course, this healing faith is in the person of Jesus in whom one has faith to accomplish the healing. See Roemer, *Beloved Son as Tantalizing Teacher* on the healing of an official's household member Matt 8:5–13, Luke 7:1–10, and John 4:46–53. Evidently, Jesus was prescinding from the premises of the Graeco-Roman world where reference to a deity was intrinsic to miracles. Jesus then was in effect saying he is in himself the ultimate source of the healing (cf., Mark 5:30) an extraordinary assertion in the context of the ancient world!

108. Von Rad, *Theology*, 144. Night is the survival of the darkness of the chaos which is, by the order of creation, kept within bounds.

109. Cf. also Mark 4:28 where Jesus recognizes this order and the creation's autonomy.

110. In Luke 12:54–56 Jesus refers again to this recognition of the creation as working in orderly ways when his contemporaries were able to predict the weather.

111. Theissen, *Miracle Stories*, 21. This discussion is based on the first chapter of this book "Introduction: Task and Method" which can be read for a detailed survey of the history of interpretation of miracle stories.

112. Theissen, *Miracle Stories*, 31.

113. Alan Richardson, *Miracle Stories of the Gospels*.

114. Theissen, *Miracle Stories*, 33.

115. Theissen, *Miracle Stories*, 35–39. The "holy" he explains is what stands out from everything that is profane, has the power to impose obligation, is experienced as an "Other" and the historical phenomenon by which the "Other" is encountered is not the object of worship but the divine which is revealed by means of it. It is further characterized by ambivalence for it both attracts and repulses.

116. Theissen, *Miracle Stories*, 39 observes that in Christianity a radical transformation of the "holy" occurred. The "holy" is no longer attached to the impressive works of the Greek gods nor in the idea of a divine command but in the cross "a folly to Greeks and a scandal to Jews" (1 Cor 1:23).

117. For example, Theissen, *Miracle Stories*, lists and describes thirty-three motifs in these stories (47–80), six themes (81–118), four variations of these motifs, (125–173), how the stories were changed as they were transmitted over time, (174–195), the various ways the stories are incorporated into the Gospels, (196–211), and the compositional principle used by each evangelist as he incorporated them into his narrative (211–228).

118. Which seems to me a rather insipid understanding compared to how miracles functioned in the ministry of Jesus creating the reality of the new age of the kingdom he proclaimed when God would reign supreme and the "red in tooth and claw" (the phrase comes from Alfred Lord Tennyson's poem *In Memoriam*) of the present creation no longer obtained but rather peace and harmony (Is 11:6)!

119. Hume, *Enquiry Concerning Human Understanding*, 59. https://www.earlymoderntexts.com/assets/pdfs /hume1748.pdf. Hume does not discuss the evidence for miracles but simply juxtaposes the possible miracles over against the person who witnesses to it.

120. Meier, *Marginal Jew*, 2:512–13.

121. To engage in a little speculation, what if miracles are the acceleration of "natural" processes by a mechanism not yet understood? Biblical faith proclaims God as the Creator and the universe as his creation which he upholds and keeps it from falling back into chaos (see above and Roemer, *World of Jesus*, 604–10). Humans are creatures who have certain powers and abilities but who cannot, for example, restore sight to the blind. Only God is able to do that. Thus a miracle is not something a person can effect so it points to God's power and activity (Meier, *Marginal Jew*, 2:513–14). But Meier says such a judgment cannot be made by a historian and such statements are theological. That bifurcation of science and theology is at the root of modern world views and sensibilities despite the evidence I've assembled above. Of course, the Bible knows of no such bifurcation. So when Meier says that even in the face of evidence that there is "no reasonable or adequate cause of any human activity or physical force" in an event a historian goes beyond his capacity as historian to affirm that God has or has not directly acted in the event he is actually describing the modern inability to have a unified understanding of the world.

122. Jesus himself is called the "power of God" in 1 Cor 1:24, i.e., the incarnation of his power.

123. And this greatest of all miracles is attested by hundreds of witnesses, 1 Cor 15:5–6.

124. Meier, *Marginal Jew*, 2:617. See his little summary of the commentators who give short shrift to the miracles in n 4, 632–33.

125. Meier, *Marginal Jew*, 2:619. He notes that 40% of Mark is devoted to miracle stories, n 12, 636.

126. For a description of these various sources see Roemer, *Who in the World was Jesus*, 65–72.

127. For John the great exorcism is the casting of Satan out of the world by Jesus' death on the cross (John 12:21).

128. Josephus, *Ant.*18.3.3.

129. See Roemer, *Beloved Son as Tantalizing Teacher.*

130. E.g., see Mark 3:22-30 the Dispute About Exorcism, Mark 9:38-41 the Rival Exorcist, (Roemer, *Beloved Son as Tantalizing Teacher*), Jesus' mandate to his disciples to exorcise (Mark 3:14-15; 6:7-12), and references to his own activity (Luke 4:14-21; 7:18-35).

131. "In short, multiple sources intertwine with multiple forms to give abundant testimony that the historical Jesus performed deeds deemed by himself and others to be miracles... hardly any other type of Gospel material enjoys greater multiple attestation than do Jesus' miracles." Meier, *Marginal Jew*, 2:622.

132. That miracles characterized the early church's activity also corroborate a continuity with Jesus and his activity.

133. Eve, "Meier, Miracle and Multiple Attestation," however, questions the independence of the sources that Meier claims to underlie his criterion of multiple attestation (28). He argues that (1) the occurrence of something in a number of sources may only indicate that it was popular or useful; (2) multiple attestation only shows that what is attested is earlier than the sources in which it appears; and (3) if that older, common source had survived the available sources might no longer appear to be independent. The criterion he says assumes "that the traditions about Jesus' deeds and words progressed down totally separate paths without influencing each other from the moment of his death . . ." (31). But he has to admit that Q might indeed be an independent source from Mark (36). He also questions the independence of Luke's special material (L) expressing the possibility of its origin due to Luke's own composition. (For a discussion of these sources see Roemer, *Who in the World Was Jesus?*, 65-72.) In this he finds some agreement with Meier in that Meier has asserted that the parables unique to Luke are his composition (Meier, *Marginal Jew*, 5:209-10. (I find that judgment to be utterly fantastic. See the exposition of these Lucan parables in Roemer, *Who in the World Was Jesus?*) He also questions the independence of John from the synoptic gospels noting the verbal similarities, for example, between John and Mark in the story of the anointing (John 12:1-8; Mark 14:3-9) although he finds John's narrative of the feeding of the 5000 independent of the synoptic versions, 38-40. Finally he questions the authenticity of Josephus' reference to Jesus and his wonder-working activity (*Ant* 18,63-64) suggesting it was a Eusebian forgery (41). He, however, concludes that Mark and John "look secure" to be independent sources. But to him M and Josephus look "dubious" and L and Q are "somewhere in between" (42). So for him "the criterion of multiple attestation does not have the probative force" that Meier assumes (43). He observes, and this is his most trenchant argument questioning the use of multiple attestation to establish authenticity, that Meier establishes the authenticity of the Jesus' miracles on the basis of a detailed examination of each miracle story and thereby vitiates the need to appeal to multiple attestation. He writes, "Logically all multiple attestation can show is that material must be older than the sources in which it is independently attested, but if the sources first have to be scrutinized on other grounds to show that they are the bearers of older independent traditions, there seem to be little work left for the criterion of multiple attestation to perform" (44). Although I think the various sources are independent I also agree that each narrative needs to be independently investigated. Multiple attestation does, however, at least indicate that this activity of Jesus was not some foreign importation into the tradition about him.

134. E.g., in the gospel of Mark 200 of 425 verses "deal directly or indirectly with miracles." Meier, *Marginal Jew*, 2:619-30. On sources for the gospels and the criterion

of multiple attestation see Roemer, *Who in the World Was Jesus?*, 65–72, 73–74. In the excursus, pages 576–616, Meier lays to rest the arguments that finds outright parallels between Jesus and the Greek Apollonius of Tyana, the Jewish traditions about Honi and Hanina ben Dosa, that identify the miracle stories in the Gospels as an *"aretology"* (a supposed genre that contains a cycle of miracles). Meier finds that the word occurs infrequently in ancient literature and its meaning is not univocal and labeling Jesus a "divine man" (θεῖος ἀνήρ, *theios anēr*) is an appellation which cannot lay claim to express a clear and coherent concept. However, he nuances his trenchant investigation by denying that he wishes to "minimize the importance of pagan and Jewish parallels in the study of the Gospel miracles . . . but to stress . . . [that] we must take into account differences as well as similarities." (600–601).

135. E.g., see the Question of John the Baptist, the Dispute about Exorcism, and the Rival Exorcist in Roemer, *Beloved Son as Tantalizing Teacher*.

136. See Roemer, *What was the World of Jesus?*, 235–36.

137. Meier, *Marginal Jew*, 2:874–77. He finds Theissen's category of "gift miracle" helpful in that it fits the feeding miracles and the Cana wine miracle but only those two. So he concludes that the so-called "nature miracles" are *sui generis* each constituting its own category.

138. The word is from the combination of the Greek, θεός (*Theos*, "God") and φαίνω (*phainō*, "shine forth, appear, show oneself").

139. Hiebert, "Theophany in the OT," 505a. In this subsequent discussion I am following Hiebert's article.

140. Jeremias, "Theophany in the OT," 896b.

141. See Roemer, *What was the World of Jesus?*, 13–16 on the "holy war."

142. Here one may think of the Greek Mount Olympus the home of the Greek gods and the Canaanite assembly of the gods sitting on the sacred mountain.

143. Hiebert, "Theophany in the OT," 508b.

144. Hiebert, "Theophany in the OT," 510b–511a.

145. See Jer 46:18, Hos 5:1, Ps 89, Jud 4:6, 12, Deut 27, Josh 8:30–35.

146. See Ps 18, 29, 97, 144. Indeed, theophanies are associated with the Temple and Mount Zion: Ezek 1:10, Amos 1:2, Mic 1:2–4, Zeph 1, Is 6:1–13.

147. Hiebert, "Theophany in the OT," 509a who also suggests that the storm imagery may also be reflected in the pillars of cloud and fire which accompanied Israel in the desert as well as in the priestly writer's use of the term "glory" which describes God's presence (Exod 40:34–38) and by Ezekiel description of his theophanic experience (chapter 1).

148. Hiebert, "Theophany in the OT," 510b.

149. See Roemer, *Beloved Son as Tantalizing Teacher* for the exposition of this pericope.

150. See Meier, *Marginal Jew*, 2:880–84 for a thorough evaluation of the story. He concludes it is basically a Matthean construction which "has no claim to go back to the time of Jesus."

151. Twelftree, "Miracles of Jesus," 105. So he questions E. P. Sanders thesis that the action in the Temple was the interpretive key to understanding Jesus and Ernst Fuchs's thesis that it was Jesus' association with sinners. I'm following this article in what follows.

152. Twelftree, "Miracles of Jesus," 109.

153. Twelftree, *Jesus the Exorcist*, 139 cites Origin in *Contra Celsum*, the magical papyri, and the prohibition by the Rabbis to use Jesus' name in healing (e.g., jAbodah Zarah 27b). See also Mark 9:38, Acts 19:13, Luke 10:17.

154. Twelftree, "Miracles of Jesus," 116.

ENDNOTES

155. The text referred to is 4Q521, "A Messianic Apocalypse." It reads in part, ". . . [the hea]vens and the earth will listen to His Messiah . . .for the Lord will consider the pious and call the righteous by name. Over the poor His spirit will hover and will renew the faithful with His power. And He will glorify the pious on the throne of the eternal Kingdom. He who liberates the captives, restores sight to the blind, straightens the b[ent] . . ." See Vermes, *Dead Sea Scrolls*, 391–92. Twelftree, "Miracles of Jesus," 116–17."

156. Contra Twelftree, "Miracles of Jesus," 117. But he sees the possibility that Jesus appealed to his baptismal experience as the source of his authority in Mark 11:27-33 (122). See Roemer, *Beloved Son as Tantalizing Teacher*. The eschatological endowment with the Spirit was not in the performance of miracles as Twelftree insists (124) but in his baptism from which his proclamation and his miracle work proceeded.

157. Cf., Luke 11:20 "But if by the finger of God I cast out demons then the kingdom of God has come upon you." See Roemer, *Beloved Son as Tantalizing Teacher*, 112–14 and the discussion there and where I write, "So Jesus places his exorcistic activity in the framework of the Kingdom of God which, though it lies in the future, is present already in his driving demons out of people. So Jesus sees the world as enemy occupied territory–which it was politically. But that political occupation was nothing compared to its tyrannical occupation by Satan who keeps it in the power of his clutches that no human can shatter. In Jesus the kingdom of God invades this enemy occupied territory. So Jesus' final statement about it and against it is a judgment: if you don't stand with him you are siding with the evil one (Luke 11:23). So quite appropriately Luke follows up this apothegm with the parable of the Returning Demons (11:24-26)." Twelftree, "Miracles of Jesus," 118.

158. See Meier, *Marginal Jew*, 2:617–18.

159. Cf., Acts 3:6, 4:30, and 9:34 where the name of Jesus is invoked in connection with healings.

160. As in the divine liturgy the congregation stands as the Gospel book is brought into the midst of the congregation where the Gospel reading for the day is announced and read: the manifestation of Christ is recognized as his words and actions are once more made present among the people.

161. Acts 3:1–10, 5:12, 6:6 (summary reports), 9:36–42, 19:12.

162. I'm following here the enumeration in Meier, *Marginal Jew*, 2:633–34, n 6 except that I have added the "Transfiguration" to the category of "theophany." He also notes that the two feeding stories may actually be describing the same event and one is a variant of the other. The evangelists' redaction may also move a story from one category to another. For example, Luke makes the healing of Peter's mother-in-law into an exorcism. He also observes (618) that there are other passages that could be added to the list: the seven demons Jesus cast out of Mary Magdalene (Luke 8:2) which is unnarrated; Jesus confers on the disciples the power to exorcise and heal (Mark 6:7; Matt 10:1); the disciples perform miracles or sometimes fail to (Luke 9:6; 10:17–20; Mark 3:15; 9:18, 28, 38); Jesus himself has extraordinary knowledge of events (John 1:48; Mark 2:8; 14:12–16). Jesus also talks about his miraculous activity describing its significance. There are notices of Jesus escaping from threatening opponents which remain unexplained (Luke 4:29–30; John 7:44; 8:20) and so might seem "miraculous."

163. Grundmann, *Markus*, 44 might be an example of this when he remarks that in the ancient world "illnesses which evoked difficult to explain extraordinary alterations [in people] were attributed to demons. Such interpretation is connected with the observation of the so-called splitting of the consciousness of the possessed person. Healthy consciousness loses its unity. What then speaks out of the ill person next to the real ego is an imaginary ego which partially wins full control." (My translation.) I would suggest that Jesus and the people of his day were adept at recognizing the difference between

demon possession mimicking disease and real diseases.

164. See the little profile of this history and an overview of contemporary commentators in Twelftree, *Jesus the Exorcist*, 4–10 who also presents a succinct critique of all of these approaches. He differentiates his own approach from all the other studies by making the historical Jesus the aim of his investigation of exorcistic activity. He wants to discover how his contemporaries saw Jesus, how he understood his own exorcistic activity, and the significance he gave to it. (11)

165. It was thought that demons could also possess physical locations but such situations do not appear in the ministry of Jesus.

166. See Schürer, *History of the Jewish People 2*, 29–80.

167. See Roemer, *What was the World of Jesus?*, 45–51 for the history of Alexander's conquest and the three Hellenistic empires that resulted after his death.

168. Jaffee, *Early Judaism*, 34.

169. Jaffee, *Early Judaism*, 37. See also Roemer, *World of Jesus*, 45–62 which describes the Hellenization process and its effects on the Jews and how it led to the Maccabean revolt which effected political independence for about one hundred years.

170. Israel always understood herself as a theocracy but under different governmental forms. From the time of the conquest of the land in the 13th century B.C. through the time of life under the Persian Empire Israel developed three forms of acceptable political ideals: the charismatic direction under the judges with its amphictyonic organization, a royal structure founded by Saul and David, and a politically dependent hieratic state under the rule of priests during Persian hegemony. See Roemer, *World of Jesus*, 1–13.

171. Jaffee, *Early Judaism*, 40.

172. See Roemer, *World of Jesus*, 95–108. Perhaps the height of this Hellenization was reached when Alexander Jannaeus crucified eight hundred rebels and had the throats of their wives and children slit before them as they hung on their crosses. (103)

173. Life under Persia was comfortably compatible as Persian religion was monotheistic and the government did not interfere in the religious practice and politics as long as the taxes were paid. Persia in fact supported and promoted the various religions of the ethnic groups over which it ruled which promoted a cross-cultural and cross-theological fertilization between Judaism and Persian theology. See Roemer, *World of Jesus*, 450–53.

174. See Roemer, *World of Jesus*, 516–31. Cf., Jaffee, *Early Judaism*, 14–15.

175. The Jewish philosopher Philo, a slightly older contemporary of Jesus (c. 20 B.C. to c. A.D. 50), who lived in Alexandria represents the quintessential effort on the part of the Jews to relate to the wider Graeco-Roman world. He worked at combining Torah and Greek philosophy into one system and so presented Judaism as more ancient and so philosophically respectable. The Greek translation of the Bible, the so-called Septuagint, was also an Alexandrian accomplishment which made the Bible accessible to the whole Roman world as well as to Jews who had lost the ability to speak and understand Hebrew/Aramaic.

176. Wright, *Victory of God*, 195.

177. The only reference to "evil spirits" occurs only in Acts is 19:12–13.

178. See the parable of the returning demons in Roemer, *Who in the World Was Jesus?*, 347–50. The Roman occupation was like being possessed by demons.

179. Malina and Rohrbaugh, *Social Science Commentary*, 234.

180. In the following discussion I'm following Twelftree, *Jesus the Exorcist*, 22–47 in his chapter 3 on "Exorcism and Exorcists."

181. Twelftree, *Jesus the Exorcist*, 43.

182. Twelftree, *Jesus the Exorcist*, 43–44.

ENDNOTES

183. Such as 1 Enoch, Tobit, Jubilees, Philo of Alexandria, Pseudo-Philo, the magical papyri, and Lucian of Samosata, the Testament of Solomon, and some of the writings from the NT apocrypha. These are suggested by Twelftree, *Jesus the Exorcist*, 16–17. I would not include Philostratus's *Apollonius of Tyana*. He was a later contemporary of Jesus who was a peripatetic neo-Pythagorean sage (died c. A.D. 98). It is my judgment that Philostratus has one eye on the Gospels as he constructed this history of Apollonius over a century after his death and wrote his story mirroring the Gospels to make a kind of counter-claim for Apollonius. The factors rendering it difficult to affirm the historicity of much of this writing is catalogued by Twelftree, *Jesus the Exorcist*, 24 n5.

184. Twelftree, *Jesus the Exorcist*, 28–29. He refers to two Cynics Menippus who lived in Gadara (c. 50 B.C.) and Meleager in Tyre (born c. 140 B.C.).

185. Twelftree, *Jesus the Exorcist*, 29 quotes Seneca's saying that "good does not spring from evil, any more than figs grow from olive trees" (cf., Matt 7:16).

186. Luther translates with "beschwören" "adjure, entreat, implore, exorcise." The word also functions in the sense of "gaining power over a spirit by magic" as well as "banish, expel, put under the ban, excommunicate, exorcise." See *Duden: Stilwörterbuch*, 120.

187. See also 1 Kgs 22:16//2 Chr 10:15, Dan 6:13, 1 Sam 14:27. The Gerasene demoniac in Mark 5:7 seeks to keep Jesus from exorcising the "legion" of demons within him indicated by the following sentence which says Jesus was telling the demons to leave the tortured man.

188. Josephus, *Ant*, 8,2,5 referred to by Twelftree, *Jesus the Exorcist*, 36. Josephus recounts the story as evidence of Solomon's divine gift of knowledge. So he was a successful exorcist because of God's favor. Consequently, Solomon's ability was based on his standing with God.

189. Twelftree, *Jesus the Exorcist*, 41 where he refers to 11QapPs^a, the Greek Magical Papyri, and Josephus, *Ant*. 8.2.5 and the story of Sceva's sons (Acts 19:14).

190. Twelftree, *Jesus the Exorcist*, 42.

191. See e.g., Roemer, *Who in the World Was Jesus?* and the parable of the Mustard Seed, 134–37; Leaven in a Lump, 198–201; and the Unjust Steward, 247–59.

192. Roemer, *Tantalizing Teacher*, 140–41.

193. Vermes, *Dead Sea Scrolls*, 310. The song reads in part "To David. O[n words of incanta]tion. [Cry out al]l the time in the name of the Lor[d] toward heave[n when] Beli[al] comes to you. [And sa]y to him: . . .. Your face is a face of [nothin]g and your horns are horns of dr[eams]."

194. See Roemer, *Tantalizing Teacher*, 112–14.

195. Twelftree, *Jesus the Exorcist*, 40.

196. The Greek Magical Papyri (PGM) is the name given by scholars to a body of papyri from Graeco-Roman Egypt, written mostly in Greek (but also in Old Coptic and Demotic) containing a number of magical spells, formulae, hymns, and rituals. The materials in the papyri date from the 100s B.C. through the fifth century A.D. The manuscripts came to light through the antiquities trade from the early 18th century onward. The texts were published in a series, and individual texts are referenced using the abbreviation PGM plus the volume and item number. Each volume contains a number of spells and rituals. Further discoveries of similar texts from elsewhere have been allocated PGM numbers for convenience. See Schürer, *History* 3, 342–79 for an introduction to the full range of magical texts and practice.

197. Twelftree, *Jesus the Exorcist*, 39.

198. Twelftree, *Jesus the Exorcist*, 49–50 refers to Qumran, Josephus, Philo and Pseudo-Philo's Book of *Biblical Antiquities*. He writes, ". . . people were afraid of the air being filled with unseen beings." (Cf., Eph 2:2.)

199. Twelftree, *Jesus the Exorcist*, 20.

200. However, some text describe the use of diagrams, amulets, and other objects. See Twelftree, *Jesus the Exorcist*, 51.

201. See section A-4.

202. Gallagher, *Demonic Foes*, 5–6.

203. Gallagher, *Demonic Foes*, 166. He presents a brief, informative history of demon possession and how it was dealt with in the ancient near east, 166–75. See Erika Bourguignon, *Possession*.

204. Gallagher, *Demonic Foes*, 8.

205. Gallagher, *Demonic Foes*, 22–70.

206. Gallagher, *Demonic Foes*, 79.

207. Gallagher, *Demonic Foes*, 84 refers to one victim he met who spoke perfect Bulgarian although she had never been exposed to that language. A priest who knew Bulgarian confirmed the language.

208. Gallagher, *Demonic Foes*, 80–82. It goes without saying that people suffering from mental illnesses do not exhibit these paranormal traits.

209. Gallagher, *Demonic Foes*, 85 (emphasis his).

210. Gallagher, *Demonic Foes*, 91.

211. Gallagher, *Demonic Foes*, 95. So this oppressive activity of evil spirits may lie behind the false prophets and other misguided people in history who have led many astray with their false notions. Gallagher gives the example of an oppressed man whose message was that Satan was having a "constructive" dialogue with God and that Satan had decided to reconcile with God. He was supposed to bring this message to the world (100). The deception trying to be perpetrated here is obvious.

212. Gallagher, *Demonic Foes*, 103–29 emphasizes the need for discernment in diagnosing demon possession or oppression as he reports on people who imagine or delude themselves into thinking they are in need of an exorcism. They prefer to believe their complex problems can be easily solved by a magic cure or "deliverance." He recounts one such story in detail and closes the story with the observation such persons are "befuddled," have only a modicum of self-awareness but are "just trying to imitate the features of what they imagine possession to be like" (111–12). He underscores again the need for discernment and that doctors and health professionals who are not familiar with or even believe in the demonic can be of indispensable service by ensuring that medical pathology is not able to explain the observed phenomena being exhibited by a person afflicted with a demonic attack and by ruling out conditions that only mimic the diabolical (112). Concerning the latter he reports that demons tend to imitate medical conditions in order to disguise their presence (113). They create further confusion by adding less dramatic symptoms such as pain and trembling. However, they cannot accurately imitate medical or psychiatric conditions. To make an accurate diagnosis then requires the definition of a constellation of symptoms (114). He notes the obvious, that psychotic symptoms are relieved by medication but not demonic possession. People with borderline personality disorder are also prone to think of themselves as possessed. Such persons are psychologically fragile, subject to feelings of rage and destructiveness, and prone to think of themselves as evil to the core. Many of them express the feeling that they have a monster living within them which easily can lead to thinking of themselves as possessed (119). Gallagher describes other personality disorders such as obsessive individuals, the histrionic, and dissociative. Exacerbating this tendency to claim to be possessed is the cultural environment where people in power are prone to assume that everyday problems are caused by evil spirits (123). He goes on to mention other syndromes that can be misidentified with demon possession: Tourette's syndrome which is characterized by odd physical tics; epileptic seizures; and psychogenic

behaviors. In all of this the author demonstrates his scientific approach and discernment and that he is not apt to accept uncritically every claim of demon possession.

213. Gallagher, *Demonic Foes*, 129.

214. Gallagher, *Demonic Foes*, 142–44. In chapter 7, 131–49 he gives the reader a flavor of how these exorcistic sessions proceed. See also189–98, 201–208 for detailed descriptions of possession and exorcism. He also deals with the phenomenon of false memories often engendered by misguided therapists, 211–30.

215. Gallagher, *Demonic Foes*, 182–87.

216. Gallagher, *Demonic Foes*, 236–37.

217. Gallagher, *Demonic Foes*, 238.

218. Gallagher, *Demonic Foes*, 241–47.

219. See Mark 3:22–30, Matt 12:22–37, and Luke 11:14–23 and Roemer, *Beloved Son*, 112–14.

220. Schmid, *Markus*, 43–46. I emphasize that the following is a summary and not a word for word translation except where I introduce quotation marks.

221. Saul was probably under demonic attack in his irrational pursuit to kill David. See 1 Sam 19 and subsequent chapters.

222. See Roemer *World of Jesus*, 450–53 on Zoroastrianism.

223. Grundmann, *Markus*, 44.

224. Grundmann, *Markus*, 44.This is not to say that Rome was some kind of innocent bystander. It had responsibility for driving the people toward revolt and the ensuing devastation. For Rome's mismanagement and even purposeful misbehavior that enraged the people see the summary in Roemer, *World of Jesus*, 374–85.

225. See Matt 4:24, Mark 1:34, 3:1–11, 6:13, Luke 7:21, 13:32.

226. Schmid, *Markus*, 46. My translation.

227. Schmid, *Markus*, 47 observes that John, although he never records an instance of Jesus' exorcisms, nevertheless witnesses to this activity found in the synoptic Gospels. Satan seeks the ruin of people (John 8:44) and is God's opponent as the "ruler of this world" (John 12:31; 14:30; 16:11) the reality of which is expressed in Mark 1:24. In the cross Satan apparently has prevailed but paradoxically it is really his ultimate defeat (cf., Heb 2:14).

228. Haenchen, *Weg Jesus*, 198–204. Here again I emphasize I am not providing a word for word translation but summarizing Haenchen except where I introduce quotation marks.

229. In this *"kenosis"* (Gk., κενός "emptying") of the divine nature) Phil 2:7 intensifies and further defines this "emptying" as taking the "form of a slave." A "slave" is totally dependent on a master and acts in accordance with the master's will. It is this total dependence on God that provides the power which Jesus exercised. That dependence is made explicit in Mk14:36 when Jesus, though wishing otherwise, submits himself to his Father's will.

230. Haenchen, *Weg Jesus*, 200.

231. Meier, *Marginal Jew*, 2:661 participates in this same spirit of the times. Although, unlike Haenchen, he leaves to conjecture as to how the "charismatic personality" of Jesus could have had a positive impact on people who are demon possessed. He concludes that to regard Jesus' exorcisms as miracles "goes beyond what any scholar can say on purely historical grounds." He, of course, was unaware of the reality of possession, especially of its contemporary occurrence and Gallagher's scientific investigation of its reality would not be available for 26 years after he wrote.

232. Barry Blackburn, *Theios Aner and the Marcan Miracle Traditions* is a thorough-going critique of Theodore Weeden's *Mark-Traditions in Conflict* who proposed that the miracle stories in Mark present Jesus via the mediation of Hellenistic Judaism

under the influence of a *theios aner* concept. The sources admit of no such standard for these ancient miracle workers so there was no such fixed type whose representatives shared a set of invariable characteristics. Haenchen, *Weg Jesu*, 202 too assumes that the miracle stories developed under this so-called *theios aner* concept. He finds, for instance, that the man with a "withered hand" (Mark 3:1–5) was not emaciated but the man was suffering under a convulsive condition by which he was unable to open his clenched fist, a psychosomatic condition. The condition could well have hindered blood circulation and caused the hand to "wither." So when Jesus says "stretch out your hand" his command breaks the internal constraint and allows him to open his hand. Similarly in the story of the calming of the storm where Jesus, he asserts, is portrayed an as exorcist and magician: originally, says Haenchen, Jesus merely broke the fear of the disciples who perceived of the storm as death threatening. So Jesus' trust in God brings about a change in their perception. The power of the storm was broken. Under the influence of a time of "miracle mania" it soon became a story in which the storm ceased and was "turned into superstition instead of a witness to Jesus' trust and power." So Haenchen ultimately falls back into a rationalism that has no consciousness of the realm of the spirit.

233. Bultmann, *History*, 209, n 1. Haenchen, *Weg Jesu*, 87 however, asserts that Jesus doesn't exorcize the demon out of sympathy for the possessed man but to prevent the demon from revealing his true nature. However, he apparently has already done so. In any case "holy one of God' is not, as I show, a particularly revealing epithet but simply refers to an agent of God.

234. Bultmann, *History*, 210.

235. Taylor, *Gospel According to St. Mark*, 171.

236. Taylor, *Gospel According to St. Mark*, 171 and cf., above where Gallagher describes these very characteristics in the exorcisms he recounts with one exception: he emphasizes that to effect the exorcism multiple encounters are required and so it is often a long, drawn out process. So it is expected that the bystanders in this account react with surprise that with a single word Jesus is able to effect the exorcism supporting Taylor's analysis that Mark is recording an eye-witness description of the event and that "we have a piece of very original tradition, not derived from ideas, but fixed in respect of time and place and accredited through personal reminiscence."

237. See Roemer, *World of Jesus*, 566–74 on the synagogue, its liturgy, furnishing, and administration and 528–31 on Capernaum. Luke also places the scene in the synagogue at Capernaum. He generally follows Mark's text but adds that the possessed man had the unclean spirit "of a demon" and cried out with a loud voice. Luke substitutes ῥίπτω (rhiptō "throw, shake, toss") for Mark's "convulsing." He adds that it did not injure him.

238. Waetjen, *Reordering of Power*, 82 suggests that the connection of the exorcism with the synagogue implies that "the synagogue as a socio-religious institution is insinuated to be . . . a subversive reality which in its own way fosters necessity, bondage, destruction of individual sovereignty, and living death. Having established itself in society, like so many other institutions, it is resistant to the teaching of a new moral order which the rule of God inaugurates in which human beings will begin to recover the essential attributes of being divinely human." It, however, would be difficult to corroborate such an interpretation on the basis of any direct evidence in the NT. It was an institution that fostered the handing down of Israel's faith by scriptural exposition, Israel's cultural traditions, and social solidarity. See Roemer, *World of Jesus*, 566–74. However, it could be resistant to Jesus' re-ordering of power by his kingdom proclamation. See e.g., Luke 4:16–30 and 13:14.

239. See Mark 3:27, 1:39, 6:2.

240. Acts is replete with the example of Paul following the same strategy throughout the empire on his missionary journeys.

241. There are various readings for the phrase "he entered the synagogue and taught." Metzger, Textual Commentary, 74–75 prefers to adopt this reading supported by the weight of the evidence of manuscripts including Vaticanus and Bezae. Taylor, *Mark*, 172, however, prefers the reading "he taught in the synagogue" eliminating "he entered."

242. A scribe would cite a tradition that he had taken over from his teacher and so would not speak in his own name but would say something like, "Rabbi X has said that Rabbi Y has said . . . ."

243. E.g., Is 43:1, Jer 2:5, Ez 2:4, Amos 1:3, Obed 1:1, Mic 2:3, Hag 1:2, Zech 1:4.

244. See Roemer, *Beloved Son*, 18–27.

245. Haenchen, *Der Weg Jesu*, 86.

246. Grundmann, *Markus*, 42 observes that "scribal tradition differentiated the teaching out of the mouth of another and the teaching out of the mouth of the Almighty (Pesikta 126a). So Jesus effects the teaching "out of the mouth of the Almighty." (My translation.)

247. See above on the Gallagher's description of the syndrome related to demon possession.

248. Taylor, *Mark*, 174a.

249. Grundmann, *Markus*, 42.

250. Theissen, *Miracle Stories*, 255–56. See the story of Pilate who introduced, even against Roman policy, the military standards into Jerusalem which depicted Roman gods and which were worshipped by the legions in Roemer *World of Jesus*, 235.

251. See Taylor, *Mark*, 177–78. The Hebrew NT translates הנצרי (HNZRY) and the Aramaic נצריא (NZRYA). Acts 24:5 is the only place where the word "Nazarenes" is used for the followers of Jesus and not for a designation of Jesus himself.

252. See Roemer, *Beloved Son*, 112–14.

253. Grundmann, *Markus*, 43 who references Ps 106:116 where Aaron is so designated.

254. Grundmann, *Markus*, 43 who cites Test Levi 18:2, 12 "And then the Lord will raise up a new priest . . . And Beliar shall be bound by him and he shall grant to his children the authority to trample on wicked spirits." See Heb 9:11–15.

255. Many commentators, e.g., Kingsbury, *Conflict*, 39, think that Jesus wants to suppress the demon's recognition of himself by exorcising it. I think this is reading into the story the idea of the so-called "messianic secret" in Mark. The exorcism rather should be seen as part and parcel of his kingdom proclamation and his "coming to call sinners" (Mark 2:17 and to "seek and save the lost," Luke 19:10). Cf., Grundmann, *Markus*, 43: "The unclean spirit sees his ruin before himself so he turns to defensive magic . . . and by the naming of Jesus brings him under his authority and renders him powerless." (My translation.)

256. See above. Only Luther translates it as an assertion.

257. Schmidt, *Markus*, 49 translates the Gk word ἐπιτιμάω (epitimaō, "command, order, scold, warn, rebuke") with "yelled" in order to express the intensity of the encounter between Jesus and the demoniac. However, such an understanding of the verb is not apropos. When the evangelists refer to a loud shout, they use the expression φωνὴ μεγάλη (phōnē megalē, "great sound," see e.g., Mark 5:7, 15:34, Luke 4:33, 8:28).

258. Twelftree, *Jesus the Exorcist*, 69. Its original meaning was "to bind."

259. A number of manuscripts add that the demon left the possessed man "with a loud cry." Cf., Mark 5:7 and Jesus' own final cry, Mark 15:37.

260. See Roemer, *Beloved Son*, 59–61.

261. Taylor, *Mark*, 176a. This characteristic is true of all the exorcism narratives and

distinguishes these gospel narratives from Jewish and Greek stories.

262. Taylor, *Mark*, 176b.

263. Luke uses the synonym ἦχος (ēchos, "sound, rumor") for Mark's ἀκοή (akoē).

264. See Roemer, *World of Jesus*, 516–31 on the Galilee. The Galilee encompassed about 1600 square miles.

265. Also "Gergustenes" in one manuscript, Feerianus, 4th-5th century.

266. Matt reads "the region of the Gadarenes" which is attested by the great uncials Sinaiticus, Vaticanus, Ephraemi, Koridethi and the Syriac versions. The alternative reading attested by the old versions of "Gerasenes" was no doubt an emendation on the basis of Mark and Luke.

267. Metzger, *Textual Commentary*, 23.

268. Origin also liked the name because it meant "dwelling of those that have driven away" which etymology corresponds with the behavior of the inhabitants of the district who urged Jesus to leave (Mark 5:17). Metzger, *Textual Commentary*, 23–4. See here especially Horsley, "Typographical Captivity," who maintains that we are to understand that orality was the dominant purveyor of the gospel tradition and that even the gospels were originally an oral phenomenon. So the diverse names that the manuscripts contain were variations in the oral tradition. In ancient culture orality was the preferred means of communication of even long stories and was highly esteemed and trusted. It was the "living voice" not the "dead letter" of what was written.

269. McRay, "Gerasenes," 991a-b who also notes that Eusebius located the event here and that a lavish church was built there but no evidence of such an edifice is to be found at Gerasa.

270. See Haenchen, *Weg Jesu*, 190–203 has a long discussion on exorcism and the belief in demons in the ancient world. He does not deny the reality of illnesses and the interpretation as demon possession but basically understands it as psychogenetic and Jesus' ability to heal such people as due to his full dependence and trust in God which, because of the ill person's trust in Jesus, he is able to heal them. So for him demon possession is the reflection that the ancient world saw evil behind illnesses as well as behind natural phenomena when it adversely affected human beings. He further avers, *203–204*, that the original encounter cannot be reconstructed but then goes on to maintain that in actuality the historical nucleus could have been the story of a man who was deeply mentally ill. What our age understands as mental trauma, schizophrenia, or depression the ancient world saw as the working of demons. So the belief in miracles of the NT tradition was conditioned by its time just as the belief in the impending end of the world. "We don't have," quoting Lessing, "the miracles themselves but only reports about them." (Of course, that can be said of every report about events of the past!) He finds that understanding the miracles as the breaking of natural law has done the greatest harm to their interpretation. He makes the astounding assertion that the ancient world knew nothing of "natural law"! (But see Luke 12:54–55, Mark 4:28, and Gen 1:11–12.) He tries to avoid the accusation of a lack of faith and falling into modern skepticism by complaining that the "stubborn clinging to a 'biblical world view' has not stemmed the exit of a growing circle of people from Christianity." As I've demonstrated modern scientific investigation has affirmed the existence of demons and even that the universe could end at any time by a shifting of the Higgs boson field (see above, chapter 1). The exorcism of Mark 5 describes exactly the effect of demon possession which has been corroborated over and over again in contemporary manifestations of this phenomenon.

271. Martin Dibelius, *From Tradition to Gospel*. However, there are many parallels in the sources of the transfer of demons to various objects such as water in a container, to other people, and to animals. Twelftree, *Jesus the Exorcist*, 75.

272. Schmid, *Markus*, 108. Haenchen, *Weg Jesu*, 190-1 notices some of the, what he calls, "clumsiness" in the structure of the narrative: the twice repeated coming of the possessed man to Jesus (vss 2 and 6), that the possessed man lived both in the tombs and on the mountains (vss 3 and 5), and the different words used for tombs (vss 2, 3, and 5 μνημεῖον, mnēmeion, and μνῆμα, mnēma). These words, it should be noted, can also mean "monument." These apparent anomalies, however, can be evidence of the story teller's art: Jesus gets out of the boat and is met by a possessed man whose possession by evil spirits is then described. Continuing the scene in vs 6 he takes up again the encounter with Jesus using an aorist participle which then should be translated "After he saw Jesus from afar . . ." The two different words for tombs might be translated "tombs and monuments." It would be easy to imagine that a pagan grave yard would contain monuments and sculptural images perhaps of the deceased who was buried there. So what we have here is not "clumsiness" but the story teller's art. We need to recall that all the elements of the gospels were initially and primarily oral.

273. Matthew reduces Mark's story from twenty verses to seven, a third of the original. He makes of the possessed man two men (the Matthean penchant for doubling). Haenchen, *Weg Jesu*,197, suggests that perhaps Mt knew of the story of two highwaymen who dominated the passage from the coast to the city and combined it with the story of Mark's demoniac. However, I think the simpler explanation is closer to the truth: Matt has shortened Mark's narrative and doubled the number of the possessed. (These are traits visible all over Matthew's gospel.) Mark's fulsome description of the man's incredible strength is reduced to simply that the two were "so fierce that no one could pass that way." He then picks up the story with the demons' question, "Why do you meddle with us" (8:29). He eliminates the dialogue between Jesus and the demoniac which elicited the name of the demons continuing with the request of the demons to be sent into the pigs which Jesus then allows followed by their immediate running over the cliff into the lake. The herders are then described as going off and reporting "in the city" what had occurred upon which everyone there came out to Jesus and asked him to leave their territory. So he eliminates Mark's longer report of how they find the demoniac in his right mind and how afraid they were. Matthew also does not include the final dialogue between Jesus and the formerly possessed man who wanted to accompany Jesus but is told to remain and report what had happened to him. So Matthew's rendition of the story focuses on what could be called the expulsion of Jesus from Gentile territory and underscoring Matthew's version of the sending of the twelve commanding them not to go to the Gentiles (10:5). So the story as told by Matthew is redolent of Matthean redaction and theological concerns.

274. Luke has not dealt so severely with the tradition as Matthew. He adds a further explanatory locator to "the region of the Gerasenes" as being "opposite the Galilee." He also identifies the demoniac as being one of the citizens of the city. He smooths out Mark's presentation by placing the description of the effect of the demons on the man (Mark 5:3-5) after he shouts "Why do you meddle with us?" He then follows Mark closely except for some alterations in wording (e.g., he changes Mark's "sea" to "lake," vs. 33 and eliminates Mark's parenthetical remark that there were about 2000 swine). He adds that the townspeople found him after the exorcism "at the feet of Jesus" (i.e., in the gesture of a disciple). At the end of the story Mark reads that the man proclaimed what Jesus had done for him in the "Decapolis" while Luke confines the proclamation to just the one city.

275. See above on Gallagher's description of the syndrome related to genuine possession.

276. See Roemer, *Tantalizing Teacher*, "Jesus' Baptism," 19-27.

277. The appellation occurs most frequently in the psalms and in Daniel chapters

4–7 in the context of Nebuchadnezzar's peroration, Daniel speaking to the Babylonian court, and in the interpretation of Daniel's dream which is related to world history and Israel's place within it. The designation in this way has a certain universal and Gentile flavor to it.

278. The word is used frequently in the Jesus tradition for the place of "outer darkness" and the "furnace of fire" where there is "weeping and gnashing of teeth" (Matt 8:12; 13:42; Luke 13:28). Gehenna was the town dump south of Jerusalem where a perpetual fire smoldered and so the name was used as a metaphor for the place of eternal punishment (Matt 5:22, 18:9, Mark 9:43, James 3:6 where the versions translate "hell," and especially Rev 20:10 ". . . the devil who had deceived them was thrown into the lake of fire and sulphur where the beast and the false prophet were, and they will be tormented day and night for ever and ever.")

279. The desert was thought of as the home of demons cf., Is 13:21, Luke 11:24, Bar 4:35. Schmid, *Markus*, 110.

280. Haenchen, *Weg Jesu*, 192 who says the verse really belongs before vs 7 but in that case there is another difficulty: that would assert that the demon did not obey Jesus' word of exorcism which would bring into question Jesus' superior power. So he judges the verse to be a later insertion based on vs 7. Its existence also, he says, obscures the sense of the story.

281. Cf., also the story of Jesus' healing of the boy whom the disciples could not heal by casting out the demon that made him unable to speak.

282. Haenchen, *Weg Jesu*, 197 finds these "novelistic" traits due to the development of the narrative in the oral tradition much like that of the healing of the speechless boy in Mark 9:14–27. I would say that these well-developed stories witness to the story teller's art and that Mark's community was made up of a variety of individuals some of whom were gifted story tellers and others who were less so but repeated their remembrances in the simplest of forms. The former could well have included learned scribal elements whose work can also be found in the narrative complex of Mark 11:1–10, 15–17, 27–33 (the original shape of these verses in the tradition). Haenchen construes the original form of the story as Jesus exorcising a demon which went into a herd of swine proving they had actually left their original host.

283. Schmid, *Markus*, 109. See Gen 14–19, Isa 14:14, Dan 3:6, Acts 16:17.

284. Haenchen, *Weg Jesu*, 197 suggests that 5:16 might have been added making the herd of swine secondary to the story.

285. Schmid, *Markus*, 110.

286. See Roemer, *World of Jesus*, 611 on the Decapolis.

287. Carter, "Cross-Gendered Romans and Mark's Jesus," 145.

288. The boar probably symbolizes ferocity and lethal attack. It was used in the arena to attack human victims. Carter, "Cross-Gendered Romans and Mark's Jesus," 153. It is precisely this part of the story that Schmid, *Markus*, 108 finds that all endeavors come to ruin which make possession a mere mental illness.

289. Cf., Zech 4:6, Then he said to me, 'This is the word of the LORD to Zerubbabel: "Not by might, nor by power, but by my Spirit, says the LORD of hosts."'

290. Twelftree, *Jesus the Exorcist*, 63 who refers to 2 Sam 19:16–23b where Shimei asks David to pardon him for having cursed him. Abishai counsels David to kill him. David answers "What have I to do with you?" suggesting David is not to be interfered with in having mercy on Shimei. Cf., 1 Kgs 17:18 and Judg 11:12.

291. See also Rev 9:5, 14:11, 18:7, 11, 15, 20:10.

292. By using this loaded word Mark seems to add eschatological overtones to the story relating it to the birth pains of the Christian mission. In Revelation 12:2 it says of the woman who represents the Church, a type of the Blessed Virgin, "she was with child

and she cried out in her pangs (βασανιζομένη, basanidzomenē) of birth, in anguish for delivery."

293. Psalm 89:9 "Thou dost rule the raging of the sea; when its waves rise, thou stillest them."

294. Carter, "Cross-Gendered Romans and Mark's Jesus," 146.

295. Rome's procurement of beasts for use in the arena proclaimed Rome's control and subjugation of the natural world. Carter, "Cross-Gendered Romans and Mark's Jesus," 148.

296. Carter, "Cross-Gendered Romans and Mark's Jesus," 153.

297. Haenchen, *Weg Jesu*, 195–96.

298. Cf., Ps 28:7–8, 33:16–17, 39, 61:3, 74:13, 105:4, 147:10.

299. I have dealt with this story already in my previous book, *Who in the World Was Jesus?*, 365–67 where I interpreted this encounter with a Gentile woman as the "well spring" of Jesus' developing thought concerning the inclusion of Gentiles in the kingdom and his universalizing parables.

300. As does Bultmann, History, 38. Taylor, *Mark*, 347.

301. Schmid, *Markus*, 142.

302. Matthew has turned Mark's pronouncement story into a genuine exorcism narrative by adding vss 15:22–24 which throws the weight of the story to the woman and her incessant pleading that Jesus exorcise the demon from her daughter which "grievously (Gk., κακῶς, kakōs, evilly, badly) torments her." The disciples ask him to send her away because of her importunity (much like the judge annoyed by the woman's pestering in the parable of the Unrighteous Judge (Luke 18:1–8, see Roemer, *Who in the World Was Jesus?*, 316–23). Jesus then tells the woman that he was sent only "for the lost sheep of the house of Israel" (which has been enunciated previously in Matt 10:6 as Jesus commissions the twelve to go out and proclaim the kingdom and heal; this restriction does not appear in the parallel accounts in Mark 6:7–13 or Luke 9:1–6 nor in the sending of the seventy Luke 10:1–12). It could be that both Mark and Luke eliminated the restriction, Mark because the "vineyard" (i.e., God's chosen) has been "given to others" (Mark 12:9) and Luke because of his interest in the universal mission to the Gentiles. But even for Matthew, this restriction applies only to Jesus' ministry whereas the disciples after the resurrection are told to go to all the nations (Matt 28:19). This pericope, as well as the story of the healing of an official's household member (Matt 8:5–13; Luke 7:1–10; John 4:46–53, see Roemer, *Tantalizing Teacher*, 98–100), suggest that Jesus did indeed restrict his ministry to Israel but because of these encounters with Gentiles in these two stories he broadened his understanding of the kingdom. That broadened understanding is reflected in his parables (see e.g., Roemer, *Who in the World Was Jesus?* and my exposition of the Unjust Steward 247–59, the Good Samaritan 303–6, and the Great Assize 350–56).

303. Taylor, *Mark*, 347.

304. The intervening material of chapter 7 is partially of Marcan provenance and construction. See Roemer, *Tantalizing Teacher*, 117–20.

305. Taylor, *Mark*, 60.

306. See Matt 14:23, Mark 6:46, 14:35, Luke 5:116, 6:121, 9:28, and in 18:1 where he exhorts his hearers to pray. In Matt 6:6 he poignantly exhorts his hearers to retire privately away from the busy world to pray.

307. Mark seeks to present a Gentile ministry of Jesus to show that the good news of Jesus was also meant for Gentiles but he presents no preaching to Gentiles and cannot because there was no such tradition. Nineham, *Mark*, 197.

308. Mark's sources probably comprised some collections of connected narratives e.g., 1:21–39 which verses include the exorcism in the synagogue of Capernaum,

healing of Peter's mother-in-law (the house was close by the synagogue), the healing of many who are brought to Peter's house that evening, Jesus' going to a deserted place to pray the following morning, and his subsequent preaching and exorcisms in the Galilee.

309. Taylor, *Mark*, 349b–50a points out that designating the woman as a Syrophoenician distinguishes her from a Libyphoenician i.e., Carthaginian and that Matthew, however, calls her a "Cannanite" which might imply Jesus was still in the Galilee and had withdrawn only in the direction of Tyre and Sidon.

310. Josephus, *War*, 3, 2, 1.

311. The territory associated with Tyre stretched as far as Lake Huleh and that of Sidon all the way to Damascus. The area between the Galilee and Caesarea Philippi had once been part of Israel and still in Jesus' day was inhabited by the descendants of the northern tribes.

312. See Meier, *Marginal Jew*, 2:659–61 who finds the word "first" so loaded with Christian missionary theology that the story must be the creation of the earliest church. He refers to Paul in Rom 1:16, "first to the Jews" and to the programmatic book of Acts. Paul in his mission always went first to the synagogue and then turned to the Gentile population in the places where he worked.

313. That the word "first" appears in 14 others places in Mark also suggests the phrase comes from the Marcan hand. See Schweizer, *Mark*, 152 and Nineham, *Mark*, 201. This judgment is strengthened by the fact that the phrase does not appear in Matthew's version of the story.

314. Although, Schmid, *Markus*, 142 rightly observes that the word used is the diminutive of dog (κυνάριον, *kynarion*) which designates not the feral and despised street dogs but the house dogs which live with people in their houses. But that still does not mitigate very much the pejorative branding of the woman as the outsider and less than equal to God's elect people! Also there is no corresponding diminutive form in Aramaic. Nineham, *Mark*, 201. Roth, *Hebrew Gospel*, 44–45 provides an interesting parallel to the story from 2 Kgs 13:7–15. Ben-Hadad, king of Damascus, sends his servant Hazael to meet Elisha to inquire about the king's illness and Elisha predicts the atrocities that Hazael will inflict on Israel when he becomes king to which Hazael replies, "What is your servant, who is but a dog, that he should do this great thing?" So Hazael, the non-Israelite, subordinates himself to Elisha and allows himself to be directed by Israel's God and "is assured of divine intervention even before Israel . . . is vouchsafed the overthrow of apostasy and the full establishment of the LORD's rule, and who is portrayed as a notable proselyte."

315. Schmid, *Markus*, 143.

316. Although Codex Bezae (5th-6th century) excludes the verse making it a "western non-interpolation" (the phrase was coined by Fenton Hort, a 19th century Irish text critic). This codex is everywhere expansive of the text of the NT (making many "interpolations" into the text) so when it excludes text (a "non-interpolation") it has a serious claim to originality. For example, Codex Bezae's text of the book of Acts is nearly one-tenth longer than the so-called Alexandrian text type, the basis of all English translations, although it does not contain 22;29b–28:31, the last six chapters of Acts. For a discussion of the text of Acts see Metzger, *Textual Commentary*, 259–72.

317. Taylor, *Mark*, 350b.

318. Ps 22:28, Dan 7:14, 27. Cf., Matt 8:11. See especially Ps 9:5–8: "Thou hast rebuked the nations, thou hast destroyed the wicked; thou hast blotted out their name for ever and ever . . . the LORD sits enthroned forever, he has established his throne for judgment; and he judges the world with righteousness, he judges the peoples with equity."

ENDNOTES

319. So Jesus had been accused of disobedience and his answer to that accusation is in his parable of the two sons. See Roemer, *Who in the World Was Jesus?* 207–209.

320. It was not a Jewish house because the woman would not have then been allowed entrance.

321. Roemer, *Who in the World Was Jesus?* 365–67. See also the exposition of the parables of the Mustard Seed (134–37), Treasure in a Field (148–51), Leaven in a Lump (198–201), A Neighbor Comes at Midnight (230–340), and Unjust Steward (247–59).

322. Cf., Matt 11:12 and Roemer, *Tantalizing Teacher*, 136–38.

323. Taylor, *Mark*, 348. Which is precisely my understanding of Jesus' person. The second person of the Holy Trinity "emptied himself" of all divinity and was subject as a true human person to life in the world. His miraculous activities were not due to his divine nature of which he had emptied himself, but his very human dependence on and trust in God as his Abba. See Roemer, *Who in the World Was Jesus?*, 76–78 and *Tantalizing Teacher*, 4–56.

324. Taylor, *Mark*, 351b who refers to Ex 21:18 where "recovering" is implied.

325. Judaism was open to the inclusion of Gentiles who sought to share in Israel's faith and life. They were called "proselytes" (the word literally meant "one who has come to [Judaism or to God]"). They were circumcised and lived a kosher life. But in the first century, as previously, there was no organized effort to bring Gentiles into Judaism. The initiative lay entirely with the seeker. However, there was the expectation that the nations would join with Israel in their devotion to Israel's God (Is 2:2–4; 60:1–3; Zech 14:16–21). But note, there is no explicit command to initiate an outreach to the nations. Their inclusion was an eschatological occurrence. In this regard see the exposition of the temple cleansing (Mark 11:15–17) in Roemer, *Tantalizing Teacher*, 89–98. Jesus initially conceived of the coming kingdom as fulfilling the eschatological hopes of Zech 14 which included the streaming of the Gentiles into Jerusalem to participate in the Temple worship honoring the God of Israel. So universalism was implicit in his proclamation of the kingdom but without a specific mission to the Gentile world. Consequently, he did not pursue such a mission. But his perception changed and he later predicted the destruction of the Temple (Mark 13) and "the giving of the vineyard to others" (Mark 12:9). See the temple cleansing exposition referred to above. So initially Jesus limited his mission to the Jewish nation with the expectation that at the eschaton the nations would join together with Israel and share her faith (see Is 19:19–25; Mic 4:1–2; Zech 8:20–22). The church, after Jesus' death and resurrection, came to understand that she was living in the eschaton (1 Cor 10:11) so that the gospel had to be shared with the nations.

326. So Jesus had been accused of disobedience and his answer to that accusation is in his parable of the two sons. See Roemer, *Who in the World Was Jesus?*, 207–9.

327. This theme is emphasized over and over again in Jesus' parables. See in particular the parable of the Prodigal Son in Roemer, *Who in the World Was Jesus?*, 241–47.

328. See the parable of the rich man and Lazarus, Roemer, *Who in the World Was Jesus?*, 306–15. The "crumbs" are the pieces of bread that are used to cleanse ones fingers and then thrown under the tables which the household dogs then lap up.

329. In the story of the healing of an official's household member (Matt 8:5–13; Luke 7:7:1–10) Jesus responds with amazement to the expression of absolute faith in Jesus to heal saying that he had never encountered such a faith in Israel.

330. Taylor, *Mark*, 395–96. The omission by Matt and Luke are typical of these two evangelists in dealing with Mark's gospel.

331. The singular is supported by the great uncials Alexandrinus (5th century), Ephraemi (5th century), Bezae, Cyprius (9th-11th century), Purpuraeus (6th century), Koridethian (9th century) and family 1 (12th-15th century), family 13 (11th-5th century),

("the other") Vaticanus (028, 10th century), Monacensis (10th century), Empress Theodora's Codex (miniscule, 9th century) and other later manuscripts. The text, however, is supported by Sinaiticus and Vaticanus and other early witnesses.

332. *History*, 211. Cf., also Haenchen, *Weg Jesu*, 318, n.1 who finds two combined traditions: the first story (vss 14–20) presents "the master and his apprentices" and the second describes "the paradox of an unbelieving faith" (vss 21–27) while vss 28–29 are a redactional appendix. He also finds the reference to scribes in vs 14 to be redactional because they then disappear from the scene.

333. Taylor, *Mark*, 396.

334. Grundmann, *Markus*, 189 cites Lohmeyer who also finds that the structure of the passage is not a mixture of two stories but a clear enhancement of an artful popular narrative.

335. *pace* Taylor, *Mark*, 397b who says it is a case "of hysteria or epilepsy."

336. Taylor, *Mark*, 398a finds it "strange" that Mark, "a non-medical writer" (apparently he's thinking of Luke as a physician) pays such great attention to the boy. Mark does not have such graphic descriptions of the afflictions demons wreak upon their victims in his other three reports of demon possession (see above). This perhaps points to the highly traditional nature of this passage.

337. Taylor, *Mark*, 398b. A gnostic could make that kind of interpretation. Jesus is portrayed, however, much more in the likeness of Moses who came down from the mountain and whose countenance glowed with the glory of God except that Jesus is not described as exhibiting that feature (Exod 34:29–30). Also see Deut 32:5, Num 14:27, and Is 65:2 for the complaints of God and the prophets over the people. Grundmann, *Markus*, 190 might imply such a gnostic understanding when he writes that the saying, ". . . shows Jesus as the faithful one who suffers under the faithlessness of the people, above all that of his disciples who likewise are part of the faithless generation. Jesus as the faithful one is foreign to this generation. In an almost Johannine-like manner this complaint of Jesus portrays him as the one who comes from another world and returns to another world and who must for a certain time sojourn with humanity as a stranger . . . this incongruity based in faith is the significance of this word. But he cannot leave this generation so he has to tolerate it in its unbelief just as God . . . bore with and tolerated his people. So he reveals himself as the servant of the Lord who bears with the people in order to save them." (Translation mine.)

338. Taylor, *Mark*, 398a.

339. An impressive number of manuscript witnesses add that the father "cried out *with tears*" which hardly seems out of place with the impassioned plea of this father who cares so deeply for his son and the suffering he experiences with the torturing of this evil demon.

340. Taylor, *Mark*, 400b Such an attack would have perhaps been directed toward binding the boy (as it was tried in the case of the Gerasene demoniac) or perhaps even to execute the boy to prevent the contagion of his ritual unclean condition which could infect the whole community to say nothing of blighting the community's honor and reputation.

341. Unique also is Jesus' answer to the disciples question in verses 28–29 that "this kind [of unclean spirit] can only be exorcized by prayer." These verses are also unique since there are no other examples where Jesus particularly stressed prayer in connection with exorcisms. Prayer, however, is an important theme for Mark. Jesus himself is a man of prayer in Mark (1:35; 6:46; 14:32–9). He exhorts to prayer (13:18; 14:38). Other references to prayer in Mark occur in chapter 11: the temple as a house of prayer, and a faith that trusts what one asks for in prayer will be so (11:24). Mark suggests that Jesus

then prayed as he voluminously charged the demon to leave the boy.

342. As does Meier, *Marginal Jew*, 2:656 who observes that it is the only narrative of an exorcism in Q and that indeed narratives are rare in Q.

343. Twelftree, *Jesus the Exorcist*, 98–104.

344. But a demoniac that is both blind and dumb is unique in the Gospels.

345. Twelftree, *Jesus the Exorcist*, 102. Cf., Matt 7:28, 9:8, 15:31, 21:14.

346. In fact Codex Bezae, along with a few other witnesses, eliminate the verse, another example of a "western non-interpolation." But the reference back to this verse in Matt 10:26 assures that the accusation was an authentic part of this pericope.

347. See Roemer, *Tantalizing Teacher*, 112–14. The healing is not merely a miracle story because the dumb man functions also in a symbolic way for the evangelist: to open the mouths of his readers and challenge them to witness for Jesus. (This is not unusual for the evangelists. For example, Blind Bartimaeus in Mark 10:46–52 limns the man who could not see but now sees and follows Jesus on the way to the cross as opposed to those who see but do not go the way of the cross.) Chapters 8–9 in Matthew are set off from the surrounding materials by being preceded by the Sermon on the Mount (chapter 5–7) and followed by the calling of the twelve, sending them out on their mission, a description of their mission, how they are to conduct themselves, and what to expect from their mission activity. So these chapters form a kind of counterpoint to the Sermon on the Mount which is a basic "Torah" for Matthew's community and so of great importance ecclesiologically. However, these chapters are not simply a collection of some wonderful deeds of Jesus but are a witness to who he is. So they are also Christological and missiological. See also Meier, *Marginal Jew*, 2:657 for a brief discussion of these two chapter in Matthew. The crowds up to this point in Matthew's gospel have been taught, have witnessed his deeds, and have had the chance to hear his proclamation of the kingdom. The weight of this final story in the section set off in chapters 8 and 9 of Matthew is thus in the two-fold reaction of the crowds and the Pharisees. The crowd's reaction is, however, ambivalent. It acknowledges his mighty acts but falls short of a confession of faith. The Pharisees are contrasted with the crowd by their rejection. The disciples are in the background and it is only in chapter 14 where Peter utters his unequivocal confession of Jesus. The Pharisees' answer becomes full blown in 12:24. That rejection anticipates the passion and rejection by both leaders and people.

348. See Twelftree, *Jesus the Exorcist*, 98–103.

349. See Twelftree, *Jesus the Exorcist*, 103.

350. Isaiah 29:18, 35:6, 42:7, 16, 18–20, 43:8. See Twelftree, *Jesus the Exorcist*, 101–2. Matthew is fond of citing Jesus' activity as the fulfillment of OT expectations. The only place where receiving of sight by the blind and the restoration of speech occur together is in Is 35:5. Matthew also has references to the blind more frequently than either Mark or Luke. Fenton, *Matthew*, 145 also judges it as a Matthean creation because the evangelist wanted to round out the number of healings to 10, include a fulfillment of Is 35:5, and to prepare for the coming teaching section emphasizing that the disciples are to be witnesses with the gift of speaking (10:7, 19).

351. Mark 3:22–27. See Roemer, *Tantalizing Teacher*, 112–14.

352. See Roemer, *Tantalizing Teacher*, 89–98.

353. Ackroyd, *Exile and Restoration*, 189–90.

354. Ackroyd, *Exile and Restoration*, 173.

355. It appears to me that John's placing the "Temple cleansing" early on in Jesus' ministry is the more likely chronology. See Roemer, *Tantalizing Teacher*, 89–98. The historical Zechariah's prophecies in chapters 1–8 emphasize "a complete change of fortune over against present conditions." Ackroyd, *Exile and Restoration*, 175. So they

ENDNOTES

provide a powerful backdrop to Jesus' sense of his mission.

356. See Roemer, *World of Jesus*, 13-16 on "Holy War." One could say that historically the subjection of Rome to the God of Israel came with the Edict of Milan in 313 when Christianity was given legal status (as were all religions) within the empire and freedom from persecution.

357. In each case it has to do with a person's plea on behalf of a beloved other. See Roemer, *Tantalizing Teacher*, 98-100.

358. See Roemer, *World of Jesus*, 13-16.

359. See Ackroyd, *Exile and Restoration*, 118-21 who presents a little taxonomy of scholars who question dividing up the book of Isaiah into three different prophets.

360. Clifford, "Isaiah 40-66," 572a.

361. Which Ackroyd, *Exile and Restoration*, 124 coordinates with the release of Jehoiachin from prison by the Babylonians.

362. Ackroyd, *Exile and Restoration*, 125. He references Ps 89 as witness to this connection between the messianic king and the people.

363. Ackroyd, *Exile and Restoration*, 127.

364. Ackroyd, *Exile and Restoration*, 135.

365. Clifford, "Isaiah 40-66," 572b-73a.

366. See Roemer, *Tantalizing Teacher*, 136-38.

367. See Roemer, *Who in the World Was Jesus?* and the parables of the Sower (125-30), Treasure in a Field (148-51), the Lost Sheep (154-57), the Lost Coin (239-41), the Prodigal Son (241-47), and the Pearl of Great Price (294-96). Cf., others passages such as Matt 25:21-3, Luke 2:10, 6:23, 10:17, 15:7.

368. For the Jubilee see Roemer, *Tantalizing Teacher*, 191-206.

369. Caird, *Luke*, 154-55.

370. See Roemer, *Tantalizing Teacher*, 136-38 on the controversy dialogue "The Question of John the Baptist" where Jesus reflects on the place of John in the span of holy history.

371. Although only John 3:22 refers to this activity of Jesus. Could it be that this activity was suppressed by the other evangelists because it might imply that Jesus was inferior to John? The passage following this verse is a long discourse of John emphasizing his secondary status to Jesus. It looks like an apology for Jesus baptizing. That the church continued to baptize underscores that Jesus also did. In 4:2 John moderates Jesus' baptizing by noting parenthetically that it actually was his disciples that did the baptizing.

372. See the parable of The Great Feast, Roemer, *Who in the World Was Jesus?*, 209-12. Jesus' experience is limned in the parable: the elites did not respond to his invitation but the outcasts and sinners did.

373. The eruption of the volcano and destruction of Pompeii in A.D. 79 was viewed by many Jews of the times as punishment for the destruction of Jerusalem and the Temple nine years earlier.

374. See Roemer, *Who in the World Was Jesus?*, and the parables of the Lord Sheep (154-57), the Lost Coin (239-41), Treasure in a Field (148-51), and the Prodigal Son (241-47). Cf., Is 42:11. 48:20, 49:13, 51:3, 11, 52:8.

375. See Roemer, *Who in the World Was Jesus?*, 207-9, parable of the Two Sons.

376. I have dealt with the following stories in which miracles occur as pronouncement stories and interpreted them as such in Roemer, *Tantalizing Teacher*: 98-100, the healing of the centurion's servant (Matt 8:5-13. Luke 7:1-10. John 4:56-54); 111-12, a crippled woman (Luke 13:10-17); 109-10, a man with a withered hand (Mark 3:1-6; Matt 12:9-14; Luke 6:6-11); 142-44, the cursing of a fig tree (Mark 11:12-14; 20-21; Matt 21:18-19); 114-15, a paralytic (Mark 2:1-12; Matt 9:1-8; Luke 517-26); 110-11,

a man with dropsy (Luke 17:1–6); and 81–82, ten lepers (Luke 17:11–19).

377. Grivet and Huberman, *In Defense of Miracles*, 9. In the following discussion I am following the various contributors to this volume of studies. On pages 321–28 these authors include a large bibliography of studies dedicated to the topic and I refer the reader to this catalogue for further study.

378. Cf., Thomas Jefferson's version of the gospels from which he eliminated all reference to anything that he regarded as "supernatural."

379. Bultmann took this criticism in a positive direction and understood the transcendent language of the NT was not to be discarded but interpreted in terms of its existential significance i.e., living an authentic existence as the basis for the modern person's decision making. See his *Jesus Christ and Mythology*.

380. As the Germans say, "Wie es eigentlich gewesen ist." ("How it actually was.")

381. Here I am following Geivett's and Habermas' taxonomy in the "Introduction" in their study *In Defense of Miracles*, 16–18. The rest of this book is organized to deal with each of these approaches.

382. I have referred briefly to this 18th century philosopher in chapter 1. Here I wish, on the basis of Hume's essay reproduced in Geivett and Habermas, *In Defense of Miracles*, 29–57, to present in more detail Hume's argument against miracles. Hume's essay was first published in 1748.

383. Geivett and Habermas, *In Defense of Miracles*, 33.

384. See Flew's essay "Neo-Humean Arguments About the Miraculous" in Geivett and Habermas, *In Defense of Miracles*, 49.

385. Geivett and Habermas, *In Defense of Miracles*, 42–43. So Hume has three bases for rejecting miracles: philosophical, historical, and religious.

386. There are two types of naturalists: the "physicalists" who posit that everything that exists can be reduced to physical or material objects and other naturalists who reject that everything can be reduced to material objects but who deny divine intervention into the material order. See Ronald H. Nash, "Miracles & Conceptual Systems," 293, n5 in Geivett and Habermas, *In Defense of Miracles*.

387. Nash, "Miracles & Conceptual Systems," 120 who is quoting from Lewis, *Miracles*, 6–7.

388. See above in chapter one the discussion of the Heisenberg uncertainty principle.

389. Purtill, "Defining Miracles" in Geivett and Habermas, *In Defense of Miracles*, 65.

390. Purtill, "Defining Miracles" in Geivett and Habermas, *In Defense of Miracles*, 70.

391. This is Purtill's definition in his essay "Defining Miracles" in Geivett and Habermas, *In Defense of Miracles*, 62–63. See Purtill's explication of this definition 63–64.

392. Purtill in his essay "Defining Miracles" citing C. S. Lewis in Geivett and Habermas, *In Defense of Miracles*, 71.

393. Norman L. Geisler, "Miracles and the Modern Mind," in Geivett and Habermas, *In Defense of Miracles*, 79.

394. Geisler, "Miracles and the Modern Mind," 84.

395. Beckwith, "History & Miracles," in Geivett and Habermas, *In Defense of Miracles*, 87.

396. Criteria developed in various disciplines such as archaeology, forensic medicine, law, literary theory, and psychology are also employed to establish that a miracle has taken place. Beckwith, "History & Miracles," 95–97 and n24.

397. See, for example, Moreland, *Simple Guide* who gives abundant and personal evidence not only for the occurrence of miracles but even for their common and everyday occurrence. I will refer more in detail to this study below.

398. Winfried Corduan, "Recognizing a Miracle," in Geivett and Habermas, *In Defense of Miracles*, 104–5 describes these two types. He notes too that just because

someone is skeptical of miracles happening because of their world view does not negate that a miraculous occurrence has happened no more than an untrained person cannot diagnose a disease. Nor are those who believe in the possibility of miracles obligated to try to convince skeptics especially if the skeptic is unwilling to even entertain the possibility (107). In this regard Corduan reflects on the evidential value of miracles. Do they compel belief in God? He notes that in "pre-scientific times" miracles were not understood as ground for belief in God (Of course, in those times there was no question of the existence of the world of the spirit.), although they were used in Christian apologetics (cf., John 20:31).

399. Winfried Corduan, "Recognizing a Miracle," 108–9.

400. Ronald H. Nash, "Miracles & Conceptual Systems," 116 in Geivett and Habermas, *In Defense of Miracles*.

401. See chapter 1 on how finely tuned the universe is which is asserted also by Scripture, cf., Gen 1:21–5, Mark 4:27–8, Luke 12:54–56.

402. Nash, "Miracles & Conceptual Systems," 125 quoting Lewis, *Miracles*, 14.

403. Nash, "Miracles & Conceptual Systems," 127.

404. Moreland, "Science, Agency Theology & the God-of-the-Gaps," in Geivett and Habermas, *In Defense of Miracles*, 133.

405. Moreland, "Science, Agency Theology & the God-of-the-Gaps," in Geivett and Habermas, *In Defense of Miracles*, 295 n3.

406. Moreland, "Science, Agency Theology & the God-of-the-Gaps," in Geivett and Habermas, *In Defense of Miracles*, 141.

407. Moreland, "Science, Agency Theology & the God-of-the-Gaps," in Geivett and Habermas, *In Defense of Miracles*, 143, emphasis his. So Moreland says such actions do indeed violate the first law of the conservation of energy which means the person "is capable of genuine creativity and novelty." (144).

408. Theissen, *Miracle Stories*, 2. I am following Theissen in the following description of the work of form critics and linguistic studies. In this study the author examines the form of the miracles stories and how that form both constrained the narrator of these stories as well as the possibilities the form offered for their further development. He then also examines how these stories function in relationship to social conditions, the development of the Christian communities, and the self-consciousness of their members.

409. Theissen, *Miracle Stories*, 47–72 lists 33 motifs whereas he observes (8 n.11) that Bultmann, *History*, 218–26 lists 22. For the compositional structure of motifs see 73–74 and their variations

410. Theissen, *Miracle Stories*, 85–112 lists 6 themes: exorcisms, healings, epiphanies, rescue miracles, gift miracles, and rule miracles. He lists the types of characters: companion, crowd, opponent, disciples (43).

411. Theissen, *Miracle Stories*, 26–27.

412. Theissen, *Miracle Stories*, 28–29.

413. Theissen, *Miracle Stories*, 29–30.

414 Theissen, *Miracle Stories*, 33 points out we are constantly transforming reality as proved by our dreams which are full of symbols. Symbol making is a "fundamental process" of the mind.

415. Theissen, *Miracle Stories*, 34–35. The quotation from Bultmann is from his article "New Testament and Mythology" in Bartsch, *Kerygma and Myth*.

416. Theissen, *Miracle Stories*, 234.

417. Theissen, *Miracle Stories*, 238.

418. Slave holders often dumped their disabled slaves on the island of Aesculapius to rid themselves of having to care for them. Claudius ordered that all who were left

there were set free and did not have to return to their previous masters. Asclepius was a hero and god of medicine in ancient Greek religion and mythology. The rod of Asclepius, a snake-entwined staff, (similar to the caduceus) remains a symbol of medicine today. Those physicians and attendants who served this god were known as the Therapeutae of Asclepius. The most ancient and the most prominent asclepeion (or healing temple) according to the geographer of the 1st century BC, Strabo, was situated in Trikala. The 1st century AD Pool of Bethesda, described in the John 5:2 was found by archaeologists in 1964 to be part of an asclepeion. One of the most famous temples of Asclepius was at Epidaurus in north-eastern Peloponnese, dated to the fourth century BC. Another famous asclepeion was built approximately a century later on the island of Kos where Hippocrates, the legendary "father of medicine," may have begun his career. Other asclepieia were situated in Gortys (in Arcadia) and Pergamum in Asia. From the fifth century BC onwards, the cult of Asclepius grew very popular and pilgrims flocked to his healing temples (Asclepieia) to be cured of their ills. Ritual purification would be followed by offerings or sacrifices to the god (according to the financial means of the pilgrim), and the supplicant would then spend the night in the holiest part of the sanctuary- the abaton (or adyton). Any dreams or visions would be reported to a priest who would prescribe the appropriate therapy by a process of interpretation. Some healing temples also used sacred dogs to lick the wounds of sick petitioners. In honor of Asclepius, a particular type of non-venomous snake was often used in healing rituals, and these snakes— the "Aesculapian Snakes"— slithered around freely on the floor in dormitories where the sick and injured slept. These snakes were introduced at the founding of each new temple of Asclepius throughout the classical world.

419. Theissen, *Miracle Stories*, 238.

420. The Greek Magical Papyri (Latin: *Papyri Graecae Magicae*, abbreviated PGM) is the name given by scholars to a body of papyri from Graeco-Roman Egypt, written mostly in ancient Greek (but also in Old Coptic, Demotic), which contain a number of magical spells, formulae, hymns, and rituals. The materials in the papyri date from the first century BC to the fifth century AD. The manuscripts came to light through the antiquities trade, beginning in the eighteenth century onward. These texts were published in a series, and individual texts are referenced using the abbreviation PGM plus the volume and item number. Each volume contains a number of spells and rituals. Further discoveries of similar texts from elsewhere have been allocated PGM numbers for convenience.

421. Theissen, *Miracle Stories*, 239.

422. Theissen, *Miracle Stories*, 240.

423. Theissen, *Miracle Stories*, 241.

424. See the description of the prophetic movements in the first century in the Holy Land in Roemer, *World of Jesus*, 407–27. So the charismatic miracle worker rejects magic (cf., Acts 19:19) and along with his followers distinguish themselves from magicians. Jesus too was accused of being a magician in league with Satan (Mark 3:22). Theissen, *Miracle Stories*, 243 references Origin, *Contra Celsus* I.28 where Origin reports that Jesus was explicitly accused of being a magician.

425. See Mark 1:40, 5:1, 25, 6:34, 7:24, 31, 8:1, 9:14. I've noted before that the capital of the Galilee, Sepphoris, is never even mentioned in the gospels.

426. Theissen, *Miracle Stories*, 246–49. The reports of the spread of Jesus' fame gives the impression that they were told in particular localities.

427. Theissen, *Miracle Stories*, 249.

428. See the history of the procurators and the analysis for the causes of the war with Rome in Roemer, *World of Jesus*, 228–56, 374–84. Theissen, *Miracle Stories*, 250 suggests that "possession" was understood as involving demons because the society

expressed its problems in "mythical language," that the symptoms exhibited by such persons was socially learned, and that even the presence of exorcists induced the frequency! He again is reflecting his rejection of the existence of the world of the spirit to say nothing of his apparent ignorance of the history of demon possession and the work of exorcists throughout the whole history of the church, its presence within all human cultures, and in spite of his knowledge of the first hand reports of demon possession in contemporary Ethiopia.

429. Theissen, *Miracle Stories*, 251.
430. Theissen, *Miracle Stories*, 251.
431. See note 299.
432. See above, chapter 2 and Theissen, *Miracle Stories*, 255.
433. Theissen, *Miracle Stories*, 256 and so "a cult of exorcism would be an act of liberation transposed into the mythical realm." He further denies that exorcisms had any political intent. On the contrary, as I've demonstrated in chapter 2, the exorcisms of Jesus were meant to liberate Israel from its violent hatred of the Romans and its concomitant anger and so save the nation from total destruction. See also the exposition of the parable of the "returning demons" in Roemer, *Who in the World Was Jesus?*, 347–50.
434. Theissen, *Miracle Stories*, 257–59 says not miracles but a belief in miracles functioned in this way. He cites the examples of Apollonius who revived Pythagoreanism, the miracle-promising prophets in Israel in the first century and their appeal to Moses and Joshua, and Jesus who is thought of as Elijah redivivus. Of course Jews would interpret any conspicuous phenomena in biblical terms especially because the Scriptures themselves promised the return of a "prophet like Moses" (Deut 18:15) and the return of Elijah (Mal 4:5). See Roemer, *World of Jesus*, 407–17 for a description of these prophetic movements.
435. Theissen, *Miracle Stories*, 261–63. He refers to the story of Peter's raising of Tabitha (Act 9:36–43). Peter performs the miracle but it is others who spread the word "throughout all Joppa."
436. Theissen, *Miracle Stories*, 265–76.
437. Theissen, *Miracle Stories*, 274 who likes to characterize this belief as "irrationality." It hardly seems to be that since such a belief would not persist if in fact miracles were not occurring. He refers to Lucian of Samosata (125–180 A.D.) who mocked belief in miracles. He was a thorough going satirist and his dialogue "Lover of Lies" made fun of people who believed in the supernatural at all. His work is a precursor of contemporary science fiction and contains the oldest known version of "The Sorcerer's Apprentice."
438. The Christian communities understood that also to be true for them (1 Cor 10:11).
439. See Mark 2:12, John 9:32, 15:24. However, it doesn't seem that Theissen's claim in *Miracle Stories*, 277 that these references really bear the weight of trying to contrast Jesus' healings with the contemporary environment. Their very paucity tells against him. It would also be somewhat anomalous if there were no reaction to Jesus' miracle working activity by those who witnessed them. Theissen, however, seems to contradict himself as he goes on to document the uniqueness of Jesus' combination of eschatology and miracles (278). The miracles are signs of the eschatological in-breaking of the kingdom of God.
440 Theissen, *Miracle Stories*, 287–91 who notes that some have interpreted the dynamic of the miracle stories as coming from unconscious forces within people and human desires. Freud's reductionistic interpretation, for example, reduced them to an expression of the infantile, narcissistic libido which attributes to itself an omnipotence

over the external world. Theissen's ideas don't seem too far removed from Freud's.

441. Theissen, *Miracle Stories*, 291–98 then enumerates the various exegetical strategies to deny or minimizing his interpretation and the obvious importance of miracles in the Gospels. The history of religions school insists they are less miraculous or magical than other miracle stories in the ancient world and sometimes assimilate to them or contrast with them. To which Theissen responds that the argument is prompted by "apologetic opportunism" (293). Redaction criticism seeks to reduce the importance of Jesus' miracles and that Mark and John intended to warn their readers against the belief in miracles to which Theissen justifiably asks whether the evangelists included so many miracles only to warn their readers against them (294). And if the so-called secrecy motif in Mark and John reduces the importance of miracles it would also relativize Jesus' divine sonship since the divine sonship underlies the idea of this secrecy motif. Attempts at an allegorical interpretation fail also, as in the story of the calming of the storm Mark 4:35–41: the boat is not the church and the story rather emphasizes that the disciples in the presence of Jesus have nothing to fear. Nor can the rejection of signs in Mark 8:11–12 be interpreted as a strict rejection of signs. The refusal of a sign is a punishment for unbelief. John's criticism of miracles (20:29) is leveled against connecting seeing with believing and so is not a criticism of miracles but a skepticism which refuses to believe what it has not seen (297). The Beelzebub controversy (Mark 3:22–27) is often considered as evidence that miracles should not be the basis for faith. It is so that they lack the power to create faith because they are ambivalent and one can see either God or Satan at work in them (297). However, one cannot question that superhuman, numinous powers are at work and a stance toward them must be taken. Another tendency to minimize the importance of miracles is based on confusing historical criticism and interpretation (298). This underplaying wants to interpret them in terms of their "historical kernel" which is understood as some natural occurrence. However, the whole intention of miracles stories is the proclamation of the end of the natural, historical system of the world. So this approach reveals "only their origin and not their meaning." Finally, there is the "interiorizing" approach which asserts the miracle is not the point of these stories but to an interior attitude such as opening eyes (i.e., "understanding") to the wonders of creation. But why then is creation itself changed in the miracles? John 5:17 regards them as a continuation of creation and Jesus' works are greater than the Father's (5:20). They are unnecessary if the world is not in distress. Miracles do not belong to creation but redemption and have to do with forgiveness of sin and Jesus' work of redemption.

442. Theissen, *Miracle Stories*, 299–300. He describes miracle stories phenomenologically as something beyond ordinary experience, in conflict with healing cults, divination and physicians; Jesus appears as the victor over disease revealing divine power; they are also ambivalent because the fascination they provoke includes an element of fear and repulsion (301–2).

443. Moreland, *Simple Guide*.

444. Moreland, *Simple Guide*, 27.

445. Moreland, *Simple Guide*, 32–33 gives the example of a hand you are dealt in bridge is unpredictable but not special. If you were dealt a perfect bridge hand that would be special and unique and you could surmise the dealer was cheating. The chances of getting such a hand by a random deal is on the order of about one in six hundred billion! (If you dealt one hand of cards once a minute it would take over a million years to have the chance of being dealt such a hand.)

446. Moreland, *Simple Guide*, 33.

447. Moreland, *Simple Guide*, 38–39 quotes the philosopher Thomas Nagel to that effect. This philosopher admits to a fear of religion and religion's God. Moreland

observes "... the desire to live in state of being free of any divine authority underwrites much of their rejection of a divine father figure. For these people, their fundamental problem with God is not a lack of 'extraordinary' evidence that he exists; it is their habitual approach to life, the urge to let autonomous desire control them, and such an approach necessitates using their mind to make the world safe for their lifestyle by killing that father figure."

448. Moreland, *Simple Guide*, 41. He refers to Craig Keener, *Miracles: The Credibility of the New Testament Accounts*, 2 vols, Grand Rapids: Baker, 2011 which documents the massive outbreak of miracles in the last fifty years.

449. Moreland, *Simple Guide*, 70–71. I have paraphrased his six points.

450. Moreland, *Simple Guide*, 73–87.

451. Moreland, *Simple Guide*, 123–24.

452. These healings he reports in his chapter 6, *Simple Guide*, 121–46. He then proceeds in subsequent chapters to deal with various issues surrounding the miraculous: the history of healing within the church, why people are not healed, growing in faith, how to pray for the sick, hearing the voice of God extra-biblically, angels and demons, and near death experiences. All-in-all this book is a thoroughly researched and, because of his scientific way of proceeding and rationally dealing with obvious issues which miracles evoke, is a convincing witness to the reality of the divine working in our world.

453. This organization is dedicated to supporting Israel and the Jewish people partly to change the image of Christianity among Jews by providing all kinds of support. The organization has founded a museum in Jerusalem to help alter that perception as well as providing real social and medical support especially for the surviving victims of the Holocaust. The description of this event is excerpted from an article in the August 2022 issue of his magazine *foz*, 12. Again, the report satisfies Moreland's criteria of authenticity.

454. See Isaiah 3:1–5, Acts 13:6, Deut 18:10–11, Lev 19:26, 31, 20:6, 27. Exod 22:18, 2 Kings 21:6, Is 57:3, Mal 3:5. But cf., particularly the story of Saul consulting a medium to conjure up the spirit of Samuel in order to inquire about the success of his facing the Philistine in battle. This conjuring is not criticized in context but see Is 8:19. These references indicate that these practices were customary in ancient Israel and came under suspicion because they could lead Israel astray and to the adoption of other pagan practices subverting Israel's exclusive loyalty to YHWH. These prohibitions would have become normative in first century Judaism when Torah was fundamental to its life. Cf., mSanhedrin 7,7 "... the soothsayer (such as he that speaks with the mouth), these are [to be put to death] by stoning, and he that inquires of them transgresses against a warning." And 7,11 "the sorcerer-he that performs some act is culpable..." Danby, *Mishnah*, 393. The paucity of references to magic in the Mishnah indicates its rarity in early Judaism.

455. 2 Cor 13:1, 1 Tim 5:19, Heb 10:28, Deut 17:6, 19:15.

456. Cf., Schmid, *Markus*, 52. "The miracles according to the Gospels and the tradition of the New Testament are such an essential component of the public activity of Jesus that it is impossible to explain them away in their totality as the creation of the primitive church and under the influence of Jewish or Hellenistic miracle stories. There could not have been a tradition of Jesus without miracles. 'We know Jesus as a miracle worker or we don't know him at all.' It is not by chance that the Gospels report miracles only done by Jesus and not by John the Baptist. Also the great Rabbis of Palestinian Judaism at the time of Jesus are not honored as miracle workers. The older Rabbinic literature (the Mishnah) narrates as special blessing the answer to prayer ... [Jesus'] teaching activity and his miracles form an inseparable unity according to the entire

Gospel tradition." (Translation mine.)

457. See the pictorial reconstruction of first century Capernaum by Leen Ritmeyer in Roemer, *World of Jesus*, 586 along with two of my photographs of the ruins. The photo of Peter's house has had a structure built over it to preserve the ruins beneath it from the weather. Archaeology has verified the ruins of this structure were indeed Peter's residence. The house is one of the oldest structures identified as a house-church. Because Peter is said to have come from Bethsaida (John 1:44) he must have moved to Capernaum. And though Peter is reported to have said "we have left all" (Mark 10:28) that has to be modified by the fact that he seems to have maintained a residence in Capernaum.

458. Taylor, *Mark*, 178. Indeed, several important witnesses read the singular "leaving the synagogue he went..." a reading which Taylor prefers. He, like Haenchen, *Weg Jesu*, 89, says it's probable that the story goes back to Peter himself which he told in the first person: "So immediately, as we left the synagogue, we went into my and Andreas' house, with James and John. And my mother-in-law lay ill with a fever..." to which Grundmann, *Markus*, 45 concurs: "This report may reflect the personal remembrance of Simon [Peter]... the narrative is straightforward; any particular tendency is lacking. Also no praise of the helper is narrated." (My translation.)

459. Is 45:7. Cf., the "evil" or "distressing" spirit that invaded Saul which is said to have come from the LORD, 1 Sam 16:14.

460. Nineham, *Mark*, 80. Cf., Luke 8:24 where Luke uses the same word "command" (ἐπετίμησεν, epetimēsen) to calm the wind and the sea.

461. Nineham, *Mark*, 81.

462. Schweizer, *Good News*, 53. See Mark 15:41, Luke 8:3, John 12:2. Grundmann, *Markus*, 47 cites b.Qid 70a, "One is not to allow oneself to be served by a woman."

463. Grundmann, *Markus*, 46.

464. Luke is following the descriptive terms used by physicians which referred to fever either as "great" or "small." Taylor, *Mark*, 179b.

465. The word is used to translate the Hebrew צרעת (tsra'ath) and the Greek λέπρα (*lepra*). Scholarship generally agrees that the Hebrew word does not refer to leprosy nor include it and that the Greek word also refers to a number of different skin diseases. צרעת describes different discrete lesions on human skin as well as on fabrics and the walls of houses. Torah describes these conditions as rendering one ritually impure because they are connected with death and death is opposed to the immortal God. See Wright and Jones, "Leprosy," 277b, 281a.

466. See Lev 13:1–46 and 14 for the law of leprosy, how it is identified, and how and when the leper can be cleansed and declared free of the disease. The Mishnah devotes a whole Tractate to Leprosy ("Negaim"). See Danby, *Mishnah*, 676–97.

467. Nineham, *Mark*, 86.

468. See Roemer, *Beloved Son*, 136–38.

469. Nineham, *Mark*, 86 notes the other difficulties in the passages: "kneeling" in vs 40 is not included by codex Vaticanus, which would stress the "emotional urgency" of the leper; the words "for a testimony to them" ("against them"?) in vs 44 leads the interpreter to ask to whom and about what. Would Jesus have meant as a witness to himself and his healing power and therefore the truth of his kingdom proclamation to the priestly leadership in Jerusalem? This command does follow Jesus' instructions to present the customary sacrifice (Lev 14:10–32). Nineham solves these anomalies by proposing that the present form of the story is a conflation of two different versions of the story. See note below.

470. Taylor, *Mark*, 188–89 labors over the meaning of the word ἐμβριμάομαι (embrimaomai) and finds that what it means in context is a "[s]trong feeling which 'boils

over' and finds expression." He rejects the suggestions of some commentators "give a stern injunction" as not sufficiently attested but likes the suggestion that the word implies "the inarticulate sounds which escape men when they are physically overwhelmed by a great wave of emotion." Arendt, *Greek Lexicon*, 254a translates the expression with "be deeply moved."

471. Grundmann, *Markus*, 50.

472. Nineham, *Mark*, 86-7. He also suggests that in vs 45 the pronoun "he" could easily refer to Jesus rather than the leper.

473. Taylor, *Mark*, 186. The command to silence appears rarely in the 14 miracle stories I cover in this chapter. In the chart below I show the number of each of these stories in each gospel and the number of times the command to silence appears in them. The one time it appears in Luke and Matthew they are following Mark 1:40-45 the story of the healing of the leper. So only three of the fourteen miracle stories have a command to silence. In Mark 8:26, however, there is only an implied command for silence because Jesus commands the blind man not to enter the village. The commands to the demons for silence are meant to prevent the demons from further confounding the situation and to gain power over the demon.

Mark	Matthew	Luke	John
8	7	10	3
3	1	1	0

474. So the command has nothing to do with a so-called messianic secret. See note below.

475. Grundmann, *Markus*, 52.

476. Nineham, *Mark*, 86. His suggestion that Jesus himself did the proclaiming which inhibited his ability to enter settled areas doesn't seem likely. Why would Jesus engage in something that inhibited his movement? Grundmann, *Markus*, 50 also finds two versions: The verses 40, 41, 42 are common to both; version A consists of vss 41 (reading with Codex Bezae "with anger") 43, 44a, and 45; version B consists of vss 41 (reading "having compassion"), 42, and 44b. He gives preference to version A.

477. According to Wrede, *Messianic Secret*, the early church had to come to terms with its recollection of Jesus' non-messianic ministry (but it was, as I have so abundantly made clear in my studies!) and yet understood him as Messiah after his resurrection. How was this apparent anomaly to be explained? Wrede came up with his theory of the "messianic secret:" Jesus wanted to keep his identity secret and tried to keep others from revealing his true nature and so commanded silence and Mark portrayed Jesus as keeping the disciples from a full understanding of himself. However, the gospel tradition held Jesus to be Messiah. And though Jesus is portrayed as commanding silence he allows the miracles to be proclaimed abroad. Furthermore, most of the miracle stories have no commanding word to keep silent. And many of the commands to keep silent are directed at demons and is part of the defensive language of exorcism. (See note 473 above.)

478. German, "*anherrschend*." Haenchen, *Weg Jesu*, 95.

479. See Roemer, *Tantalizing Teacher*, 18-27.

480. For a brief overview of the scholarship related to his theory see Tuckett, "Messianic Secret."

481. This theory of parables is the Marcan hand at work. Jesus meant for his parables to clarify the meaning of the kingdom, get people to think, and change their

attitudes. See my exposition of the parables in *Who in the World Was Jesus*.

482. See Roemer, *Who in the World Was Jesus?*, 137–46.

483. I owe this insight to the docent at the Bible Museum in Washington, D.C., where there is a mockup of a first century Jewish village. Taylor, *Mark*, 194a mentions the conjecture that "and when they had broken through" (ἐξορύσσω, *eksoryssō*) in vs 4b was a mistranslation of the Aramaic "bring [him to the roof]." The suggestion has much to say for it since, if as I suggest, it was the straw covered roof of a court yard.

484. Or "mat" which was used by the poor. During the day it was rolled up to make room in a one-room house of the poor. When such people traveled they would roll needed items up inside the mat so it became a kind of knapsack. Malina, *Social Science Commentary*, 187.

485. In Luke 13:1–5 Jesus breaks the connection between sin and untoward events. So in the present passage Jesus is asserting power over two separate realities, that of sin and disease. The man could well have been suffering both physically and spiritually because he himself made the connection between the two. Grundmann, *Markus*, 59 refers to the third century A.D. Rabbi Alexandrai who transmitted the tradition based on Ps 103:3 ("who forgives all your iniquity, who heals all your diseases") that "the sick cannot rise up until his sins have been forgiven."

486. See Exod 34:6–7, Is 43:25, 44:22. The penalty for blaspheming was stoning (Lev 24:15–6).

487. There were two forms of blasphemy in the scribal tradition: cursing the name of God and "stretching one's hand against God" i.e., assuming God's prerogative." Grundmann, *Markus*, 57.

488. The "Similitudes" of Enoch are chapters 37–71 of 1 Enoch. They are "parables" and deal with the coming judgment of the righteous and wicked. This part of 1 Enoch was written in the first century B.C. 2 Esdras, part of the Apocrypha, is an apocalypse and was written in the late first century A.D.

489. For a detailed discussion and investigation of the term see Roemer, *Tantalizing Teacher*, 61–66. The "son of man" imagery in Dan 7 is derived from Is 11:42, 49, 52–3, and Ps 2.

490. See Roemer, *Tantalizing Teacher*, 242–43, notes 300 and 301.

491. This phenomenon occurs rarely in modern speech but was a frequent locution in the biblical world. Jesus speaks illeistically for pedagogical reasons. By presenting himself from an objective perspective he portrays his unique authority and his status as the beloved son (of God). See Roemer, *Tantalizing Teacher*, 243–44, n 303 and Elledge, *Use of the Third Person*.

492. In keeping with his understanding of himself as son of man who has the power to forgive sins Jesus gives this power to declare forgiveness to his disciples and to all those who enter the kingdom, Matt 16:19, 18:18, John 20:23. This multiple attestation of being able to declare the forgiveness of sins was initiated by Jesus and continued by the church. See also the story of the woman taken in adultery, Roemer, *Tantalizing Teacher*, 100–3 and the parable of the two debtors Luke 7:41–42, 48 in Roemer, *Who in the World Was Jesus?*, 299–303. Forgiveness is central to Jesus' ministry and the church's life and existence: Matt 6:12–15, Mark 11:25, Luke 6:37, 11:4, 17:3–4, 2 Cor 2:7, Col 3:13, 1 John 1:9.

493. Taylor, *Mark*, 198a.

494. Cf., 1 John 2:1, 12, 14 and 1 Cor 4:15. Grundmann, *Markus*, 57.

495. Grundmann, *Markus*, 56.

496. Taylor, *Mark*, 201.

497. To reiterate, forgiveness lay at the very heart of Jesus' ministry, see Roemer *Tantalizing Teacher*, 115.

498. Taylor, *Mark*, 195a-b suggests that the man may have had a hysterical form of paralysis discovered by contemporary psychology and Jesus' declaration of forgiveness was "curative in intention."

499. See Roemer, *What Was the World of Jesus?*, 471 on scribes and scribal activity.

500. Arendt, *Lexicon*, 185a.

501. Nineham, *Mark*, 91 construing the story to mean that Jesus is employing supernatural knowledge concludes that this part of the story is "artificial" so that Mark is reproducing Jewish reactions to the later Christian claim that sins could be forgiven in the name of Jesus. Such torturous interpretations result from insisting the text claims divinity for Jesus when a perfect natural interpretation is sufficient. Taylor, *Mark*, 195b agrees. The phrase "in his spirit" means Jesus' own spirit (Mark 8:12).

502. Grundmann, *Markus*, 56. "The proclamation of the kingdom of God by Jesus included the moment of debt forgiveness."

503. Grundmann, *Markus*, 58.

504. Nineham, *Mark*, 91-92 suggests that that the section on forgiveness of sins, 5b-10, because of its "artificiality" (see note above) and its contradiction by Luke 13:1-5 was added to the original form of the story, 5:1-5a, 11-12. But he has no idea how this story then originated and how it got added to its present location. This difficulty suggests that the simplest explanation is that it faithfully reproduces historical reality. In this connection Taylor, *Mark*, 201 remarks, "The truth is that there is no complete analogy known to us in history, and this fact is enough in itself to show that the narrative is historical, and not simply the precipitate of a believing community." See also Haechen, *Weg Jesu*, 103-6 who claims that Jesus' actual motivation was always sympathy for the ill person so in this instance Jesus is made to appear as "heartless." He also finds that the scribes' reaction does not appear at the end of the story as confirmatory of this position. He supposes that the Marcan community, on the basis of its own practice of forgiving sins, ascribed this power to Jesus who showed he had that power by his miracles of healing. So he claims that "whether this insertion of vss 5b-10 without reflection accrued to the story in the course of the tradition process or was consciously inserted is ultimately unimportant." This assertion does not quite meet Taylor's argument for its historicity.

505. Grundmann, *Markus*, 59.

506. Pace Meier, *Marginal Jew*, 2:709. Mark does interpolate one story within another such as the cursing of the fig tree enclosing the temple cleansing (Mark 11:12-21). This "sandwiching" obviously is the work of Mark's hand which interprets the temple cleansing as a proleptic symbolic destruction. Matthew recombines the two parts of the story and Luke eliminates it altogether. However, Nineham, *Mark*, 157 finds that the style of this story differs from the rest of the passage so he finds it to be another Marcan interpolation. However, the uniqueness of the woman's ailment required a different style and vocabulary. Neither Matthew nor Luke avoid the so-called "magic" but repeat the woman's conviction that she will be healed by touching Jesus' garment. Moreland, *Experience Miracles*, 122-23 tells a similar story of his own healing. The parallels with the Gospel story is obvious. He had come down with viral laryngitis which the doctor said there was nothing to be done and that he just had to wait seven to ten days for it naturally to clear up. However, he had some serious obligations to teach a class at the university, a full day of lecturing (he had hit the limit on canceled classes), and a three hour presentation at a local church on the day after. He was loathed to cancel but he saw no other possibility. He was leaving church Sunday evening and anxious to get home to carry out this distasteful task when two of his elders accosted him and said they couldn't let him go before praying for him. The story continues: "One elder laid hands on my shoulders and the other placed his hand on my lower throat area and started

praying. To be honest, I wasn't listening to a word they said. I had already left the church emotionally, and I wanted to get home to call my secretary. But then something happened. As the two men prayed gently for me, I began to feel heat pour into my throat and chest area from the elder's hand. *After no longer than two or three minutes of prayer I was completely and irreversibly healed!* (His emphasis.) I started talking to the elders normally with no pain, no additional effort, and no trace that anything had been wrong. I never had to make that call to my secretary. The laryngitis never returned."

507. Taylor, *Mark*, 289.

508. Luke 8:46 turns it into an observation of Jesus himself! See also Matt 14:36, Acts 5:15, and 19:12. So there was a tradition that healings were effected by mere contact with something belonging to the healer. Meier, *Marginal Jew*, 2:709 claims the flowing of power from Jesus is a "magical conception." This is a fantastic claim in a Jewish context. The practice of magic is prohibited by the Torah (Deut 19:9–12; Lev 19:26, 31; 20:27; Exod 22:18). And it could hardly be so that such conceptions would be cultivated within early Christian communities!

509. They had a practical aspect to them: they were to be a reminder to remember the commandments and do them (Num 15:39). Matthew added the word to this story probably to underscore Jesus' Torah piety. But Mark 6:56 also mentions that he did wear these fringes. That he wore the *tsitsith* would resonate with Jesus' saying that he had come "not to destroy the Law or the prophets . . . but to fulfill" (Matt 5:17).

510. Meier, *Marginal Jew*, 2:756, n 142.

511. Schmidt, *Gospel of Mark*, 75 translates the "flow of blood" as a "vaginal flow" which is, no doubt, a good assumption in the case of a woman with a hemorrhage. See Nineham, *Mark*, 157 who calls it a "uterine hemorrhage."

512. In the ancient world healing had to do with restoring a person to a "valued state of being" rather than to (modern) functionality. So healers were focused on illness rather than disease, that is, on a disrespected state of being in which social connections are disrupted and meaning is lost. So the ill were forbidden to function in the cultus (Lev 21:16–24). Little attention was given to impersonal cause-effect relationships and so the focus was not on bio-medical aspects of disease but rather on socially imbedded symptoms. Physicians talked about illnesses rather than treating them. If they failed it could mean death. Physicians are not mentioned often in the NT (see Mark 2:17; Luke 4:23; 8:43; Col 4:14). Folk healers were more willing to risk failed treatment. Jesus appears as such. He is the spirit-filled prophet who conquers the demonic and a variety of illnesses and restores people to society. But the acceptance of the healer is essential to healing (Mark 6:5–6). So the healer also had to be in solidarity with society's belief system. Malina, *Social Science Commentary*, 210–11.

513. In this Jesus reverses the prevailing understanding of clean and unclean. According to the prevailing understanding of Torah only the latter can be transmitted. See Danby, *Mishnah*, Appendix IV, 800–4 and the Tractate, *Kelim* ("articles of utility") 604–49.

514. Schmid, *Markus*, 113. Meier, *Marginal Jew*, 2:709 insists the flow of power from Jesus is "a magical conception." It seems to me to be just the opposite: there is no unmediated healing here but rather a means by which the woman is healed. Her touching Jesus' garment is paralleled by the request in vs 23 to Jesus to come to Jairus's house and "lay his hand" on his daughter so that "she might be cured and live." That Jesus was the source and means of conveying the power of God does not imply magic.

515. See Ps 55:5, 1 Cor 2:3, 2 Cor 7:15, Eph 6:5, Phil 2:12, Jdt 15:2, 4 Esd 15:33, and 4 Macc 4:10. Each of the situations described in these passages is related in some way to the numinous.

516. Some important witnesses (Washingtonius 4th-5th century, family 13, and

some of the Sahidic version manuscripts) read αἰτία (aitia, "cause, reason, circumstances, case") for "truth," in vs 33.

517. Taylor, *Mark*, 293a.

518. ἰάομαι (*iaomai*, "heal") occurs in Matt 8:8, Luke 6:18, 7:7, Heb 12:13, Jam 5:16; θεραποίω (*therapoiō*, "heal") in Luke 5:15, 8:43, 13:14; and ὑγιὴς γενέσθαι (*hygiēs genesthai*, "be made whole") in John 5:6.

519. The phrase can literally be translated with the more ambiguous "the things concerning Jesus" i.e., his saving work (cf., Luke 24:19, 27).

520. Souter, *Pocket Lexicon*, 254.

521. Nineham, *Mark*, 165, who notes that diseases were often thought of as "scourges" i.e., punishment for sin (114). The concept is embodied in the word μάστιξ (mastiks, vs 29) which can refer either to a physical lash or scourge which meaning is then carried over to designate severe pain or suffering.

522. All of these details in this paragraph point to Jewish reality and the kingdom of God as Jesus conceived it. It refutes Meier, *Marginal Jew*, 2:709-10 who insists Mark's literary hand is at work here reproducing the magical stories of his world. See Schmid, *Markus*, 113 who also mentions that later legend gave her the name Veronica who then later, as Jesus bore his cross, wiped his face upon which was then imprinted an image of his countenance (Acts of Pilate 7. See Schneemelcher (ed), *New Testament Apocrypha* I, 457). He also references Eusebius, *Ecclesiastical History*, 18 where the historian, talking about Caesarea Phillipi, writes, "For they say that she who had an issue of blood, and who, as we learn from the sacred Gospels, found at the hands of our Saviour relief from her affliction, came from this place, and that her house was pointed out in the city, and that marvelous memorials of the good deed, which the Saviour wrought upon her, still remained. For [they said] that there stood on a lofty stone at the gates of her house a brazen figure in relief of a woman, bending on her knee and stretching forth her hands like a suppliant, while opposite to this there was another of the same material, an upright figure of a man, clothed in comely fashion in a double cloak and stretching out his hand to the woman; at his feet on the monument itself a strange species of herb was growing, which climbed up to the border of the double cloak of brass, and acted as an antidote to all kinds of diseases. The statue, they said, bore the likeness of Jesus. And it was in existence even to our day, so that we saw it with our own eyes when we stayed in the city."

523. Taylor, *Mark*, 220.

524. Luke 6:1-11 develops the tradition and retrojects Mark's reference to Pharisees in vs 6 back into the story. Vs 6 is actually a Marcan interpolation and prepares for the passion narrative. Note too, that Pharisees and Herodians nowhere appear in the trial stories.

525. Vs 6 is pure Marcan redaction fitting the story within the Marcan narrative especially with the final chapters of his gospel which recounts Jesus passion and death. It is important to note that the Pharisees do not appear at all at the trial scenes accentuating that this vs comes from his hand. The Pharisees were also adverse to capital punishment. Cohen, *Everyman's Talmud*, 317 observes that ". . . there was great reluctance [on the part of the Pharisees] to resort to capital punishment and every endeavor was made to avoid it." He then cites mMakkoth 1,10: "A Sanhedrin which executed a person once in seven years was called destructive. R. Eleazar b. Azariah said, Once in seventy years. R. Tarphon and R. Akiba said, If we were members of a Sanhedrin, never would a person be put to death. R. Simeon b. Gamaliel said, In that case they would multiply shedders of blood in Israel!"

526. For this synagogal office see Roemer *World of Jesus*, 571-72.

527. Matthew supplements the story with Jesus referring to the saving of animals which was allowed on the Sabbath. A man is worth more than a sheep!

528. The breaking of the Sabbath law was serious indeed. See Exod 31:14-15 which specifies the death penalty for those who break the Sabbath. Of course Jesus would go to a synagogue on a Sabbath in order to encounter more people. So it would be difficult to avoid healing on the Sabbath.

529. Indeed, even between the two Pharisaic schools of Hillel and Shammai there were differences. The Essenes were much stricter in their interpretation and would have been closer to the school of Shammai. Then there were the people themselves, the differences between Judeans and Galileans. The latter being perhaps the loosest observers of Torah than all the others. The Sadducees were the most conservative and stuck exclusively to the words of Torah and interpreted them in the most literalist (and some would say, wooden) of ways.

530. Meier, *Marginal Jew*, 2:682.

531. For example, see the tithing principles in Deut 14:22-29.

532. In this paragraph I'm following Haenchen, *Weg Jesu*, 128-29.

533. Haenchen, *Weg Jesu*, 129. (My translation.)

534. Grundmann, *Markus*, 73.

535. Meier, *Marginal Jew*, 2:683.

536. Danby, *Mishnah*, 120.

537. All of Meier's objections simply lose their force in the light of the actual conditions on the ground, i.e., Jesus' actual historical context.

538. Taylor, *Mark*, 223b. It's a biblical phrase and occurs frequently in the Torah particularly for Pharaoh whose heart is hardened against Israel, e.g., Exod 4:21, 7:3, 13-4, 8:15, Deut 15:7. It is a phrase used by Jesus in other contexts, cf., Matt 19:8, Mark 10:5.

539. See Roemer, *World of Jesus*, 559.

540. Taylor, *Mark*, 221a.

541. Bultmann, *Tradition*, 213.

542. Taylor, *Mark*, 354a. So most of the English versions read "an impediment in his speech." Grundmann, *Markus*, 156 also interprets the man as a stammerer (Ger, "*lallen*").

543. Taylor, *Mark*, 354b. Suetonius, Twelve Caesars, X,7, "As he sat on the Tribunal, two labourers, one blind, the other lame, approached together, begging to be healed. Apparently the god Serapis had promised them in a dream that if Vespasian would consent to spit in the blind man's eyes, and touch the lame man's leg with his heel both would be made well. Vespasian had so little faith in his curative powers that he showed great reluctance in doing what he was asked; but his friends persuaded him to try them, in the presence of a large audience, too—and the charm worked." Saliva was widely believed to have healing properties in the ancient world. For example, the classical writers Celsus, Galen, and Pliny all mention its medicinal properties—especially the saliva of distinguished persons such as Vespasian! So it is perhaps not surprising that the Jews of the first century seem to have had a tradition that the saliva of a legitimate, firstborn heir could have healing properties against infirmities such as blindness (Talmud, Bava Batra 126b).

544. The use of saliva was thought of as a medicament particularly for eye diseases in the ancient world. Schmid, *Markus*, 144.

545. See section B4 above.

546. Taylor, *Mark*, 354b. Contra Haenchen, Weg Jesu, 277.

547. Taylor, *Mark*, 355a. Jesus' word and the use of saliva were adopted by the early Christian Baptismal liturgy. Schmid, *Markus*, 145.

548. See Witherington, *Jesus Quest* who interprets Jesus and his ministry in terms of

wisdom. See my summary of his work in Roemer, *Who in the World Was Jesus?*, 15–17.

549. This was no imaginary fear. There are ample examples of even peaceful protests by crowds of people who gathered with leaders that were violently put down by the Roman procurators. Fearing a popular movement gathering around Jesus would therefore be a source of anxiety to the Jewish leadership. See the history of these movements in Roemer, *World of Jesus*, 391–437.

550. See Roemer, *Tantalizing Teacher*, 18–27.

551. Haenchen, *Weg Jesu*, 291.

552. A similar instance is also Jesus' visit to his hometown where he was, according to Mark, "not able to do any miracles there except to heal a few sick people . . ." due to their rejection of him (Mark 6:5).

553. Taylor, *Mark*, 369–70. The "realism [of the story] shows it to be anything but a product of invention."

554. Taylor, *Mark*, 372.

555. A difficult reading since his home was probably in the village. Codex Bezae reads the more understandable, "say nothing to anyone in the village" (meaning "Bethsaida," vs 22). We would expect this manuscript to correct what it saw as an error. The former being the more difficult reading is no doubt the original (Metzger, *Textual Commentary*, 99.) Taylor, *Mark*, 372a–73 then supposes it is Mark's editorial comment promoting the so-called "Messianic secret" motif.

556. The text of vs 26 exhibits a number of variants which, however, do not change the basic thrust and meaning of the passage. Bezae reads, "Go off to your house and tell no one in the village." Codex Coridethi, family 13 and a number of uncials read, "Go off to your house and if you enter the village do not tell anyone." Alexandrinus, Ephraemi and other uncials read, "Do not enter the village nor tell anyone in the village." The text of Nestle is supported by Sinaiticus, Vaticanus and family 1.

557. Matt 9:27–31 is perhaps a doublet of this story.

558. Taylor, *Mark*, 446.

559. See Roemer, *Tantalizing Teacher*, 107.

560. Taylor, *Mark*, 447.

561. Josephus recounts the story of an Eleazar effecting exorcisms in the presence of Vespasian with the use of roots prescribed by Solomon (*Ant.* 8,2,5). The tradition of Solomon as an exorcist can also be found in the *Testament of Solomon* (perhaps from the third century A.D. but reflecting traditions from the first century.)

562. See Roemer, *World of Jesus*, 424–25 and the Psalms of Solomon 17:21–44 quoted there. This psalm is the only instance in the time before Jesus that "son of David" is used to designate the Messiah whereas in Rabbinic times it is the usual designation for this figure. Schmid, *Markus*, 204. In the time of Jesus revolutionary fervor was in the air running the gamut from advocating armed resistance to a quietism that waited patiently for God to intervene and bring in the messianic age. The hopes for a Davidic Messiah perhaps lay somewhere in the center of this scale in which God would raise up the Messiah who would drive out the Gentile occupier (see the canticle, the Benedictus, Luke 1:69). Combined with this hope was also the restoration expressed in the Isaianic prophecies in which diseases would be eliminated. Bartimaeus, by identifying Jesus as the "son of David," was reflecting this hope by seeing in Jesus' and the miracles he performed the dawn of this new messianic age. See Matt 11:4–5, Luke 4:16–19, 7:18–22.

563. A good case can be made for the other references to David in relationship to Jesus were Marcan constructions. See 2:25, and 11:10. Noticeable here in the present story is that Bartimaeus changes his address to Jesus from "son of David" to "Rabboni" (vs. 51). So Mark rejects the idea that Jesus is "son of David" because he does not want to associate Jesus with the martial traits linked with David. See note above.

ENDNOTES

564. Meier, *Marginal Jew*, 2:737, n 47, 48 observes that "Son of David" in the OT usually refers to Solomon (1 Chron 29:22, 2 Chron 1:1, 13:6, 30:26, 35:3). Furthermore he notes even more tellingly that "a petitioner in the *Testament of Solomon* 20:1 cries out to Solomon, 'King Solomon, son of David, have mercy on me.'"

565. Meier, *Marginal Jew*, 2:690 sees this as a primitive Jewish Christology and not a Christian theology. So this is how some first century Jews in the Holy Land looked upon Jesus the miracle worker and teacher of wisdom who was believed to be of Davidic descent. "From the vantage point of their own needs, these Jews afflicted with illnesses pictured him not so much as a reigning king upon a throne ala David as rather a miraculous healer ala Solomon. In my view, then, this extremely primitive 'Jewish Christology,' which was not developed further by the early Christian tradition of the first generation, most probably goes back to the time of Jesus himself. The sole clear example preserved for us is the story of Bartimaeus."

566. The Roman "Triumph" was a civil ceremony and religious rite of ancient Rome, held publicly to celebrate and sanctify the success of a military commander who had led Roman forces to victory in the service of the state or, in some historical traditions, one who had successfully completed a foreign war. On the day of his triumph, the general wore a crown of laurel and an all-purple, gold-embroidered triumphal toga picta ("painted toga"), regalia that identified him as near-divine or near-kingly. In some accounts, his face was painted red, perhaps in imitation of Rome's highest and most powerful god, Jupiter. The general rode in a four-horse chariot through the streets of Rome in unarmed procession with his army, captives, and the spoils of his war. At Jupiter's temple on the Capitoline Hill, he offered sacrifice and the tokens of his victory to the god Jupiter. The Maccabee Jonathan conducted something of a triumphal procession in 143 B.C. through the Holy Land confirming and projecting his independence from Seleucia. See Roemer, *World of Jesus*, 75.

567. Grundmann, *Markus*, 222 says the demand of the crowd for silence has nothing to do with the "messianic secret" motif but rather "has its basis in [the desire] that the stillness of the solemn pilgrim procession toward Jerusalem should not be disturbed by the noisy beggar" (translation mine).

568. Sitting at this spot outside Jericho (so-called Roman Jericho which lay about a mile south-southwest from OT Jericho and contained a palace of Herod the Great) on the road leading up into Jerusalem, some 20 miles away, was a perfect place to beg because of all the pilgrims who would be passing that way. Outside of the bustle of the town he would command more attention. Also Passover was a popular time of giving alms to the poor.

569. The title occurs in the NT only here and in John 20:16. In the Targums it is used for addressing men and God. Grundmann, *Markus*, 222. "The Sifra (Lev. 19:32) posits that the obligation to honor the elderly also applies to all Torah scholars, even if they never taught you anything. Quite surprisingly, no subsequent Medieval or early modern source repeats that obligation. The *Shulchan Arukh* (*Yoreh De'ah* 243:6, 244:1) follows the unanimous precedent and states that one's only obligation to respect Torah scholars consists of rising when they enter one's vicinity and refraining from insulting them. The *Birkei Yosef* (*Yoreh De'ah* 244:6) notes that the Sifra's extensive list of mandatory respectful practices was disputed and concludes that the law requires nothing more than rising and refraining from insulting." See https://www.torahmusings.com/2012/05/who-can-be-called-rabbi/.

570. *contra* Bultmann, *Tradition*, 213, Grundmann, *Markus*, 221.

571. Meier, *Marginal Jew*, 2:690.

572. Meier, *Marginal Jew*, 2:684.

573. See the discussion in chapter 2 above on the healing of a demoniac boy (Mark

9:14–29. Matt 17:14–21. Luke 8:37–42.). See also Luke 11:14, Mark 9:17, 25.

574. See chapter 3 Roemer, *Tantalizing Teacher*, 109. I deal with this healing story as a controversy dialogue there, 111–12.

575. The word in English is pure Greek and a transliteration (ὑποκριτής) and means an actor, or one who play acts. The German word is particularly graphic: "*Scheinheilige*," one who [only] appears to be holy.

576. Plummer, *Luke*, 343.

577. Cf., Plummer, *Luke*, 341and his generalizing comments on vss 10–17.

578. Although I have dealt with this miracle story in Roemer, *Tantalizing Teacher*, 136–38 as a pronouncement story I want to deal with it here again as a miracle story and because it is only one of two accounts of the cleansing of a leper (the other being Mark 1:40–45, see #2 above) in the Gospels. That I'm including and discussing it again in this study reflects the complex character of this story. Is it "miracle story" or "pronouncement story"? And what kind of pronouncement story? Is it "biographical" or does it imply elements of a controversy? All of this leads to disagreement about its origin and the theological point of the story. The gamut of interpretation runs from supposing it is a Lucan creation to seeing it as a precipitate of a process that goes back to the historical Jesus. See Meier, *Marginal Jew*, 2:701–2. Meier himself participates in what I would call calumny of Luke as a historian. He insists, for instance, all the parables unique to Luke are this evangelist's creation. (Meier, Marginal Jew, 5:196–209) and see my interpretation of the Lucan parables in Roemer, *Who in the World Was Jesus?* and a refutation of Meier's fantastic claim.

579. See Roemer, *Tantalizing Teacher*, 136–38.

580. Meier, *Marginal Jew*, 2:699–700. See the discussion above on leprosy in connection with the miracle story of the leper in the synagogue and the end notes related to it. Meier points out in a little discussion on the pages referred to that it is not certain what the exact meaning of "leprosy" is as it occurs in these gospel stories. "Leprosy" today refers to "Hansen's disease" caused by the bacillus *mycobacterium leprae*. The descriptions in Lev 13 are not clear enough to be precise about the nature of these infections. The Hebrew word צרעת (Ōaraʻat) probably includes psoriasis, eczema, and vitiligo. It is questionable if Hansen's disease even existed in the ANE. However it is possible that by Jesus' day "leprosy" did include this disease. But the NT reflects the terminology of the OT and so may well refer to the types of skin diseases that are described there.

581. Plummer, *Luke*, 404. Cf., Luke 7:9, Mark 6:6, 8:10.

582. Meier, *Marginal Jew*, 2:702. He concludes that the story is a miracle story fused with an apothegm. I suppose that Jesus' three questions can be interpreted as a pronouncement. But are they? They really seem to be an expression of Jesus' surprise at the nine's non-response and that the one responder is a Samaritan. So his surprise has to do with the miracles emphasizing that both parts of the story are focused on the miracle. Furthermore, characterizing it as the fusion of two forms ignores the conclusion where Jesus tells the man to go his way for his "faith has saved" him rounding out the whole narrative as a miracle story. Of course, I recognize this duality since I have discussed it as a pronouncement story in Roemer, *Tantalizing Teacher*, 81–82.

583. I'm reading διὰ μέσου (*dia mesou*, the preposition *dia* with the genitive) with the codices Alexandrinus, Washingtonius, and Koridethian, and lectionaries over against the reading in the Nestle text of διὰ μέσον (dia meson, the preposition with the accusative) although that reading is supported by Sinaiticus and Vaticanus. (See below on the occurrence of διὰ μέσου in the Greek literature.) The English versions all correctly translate "through the midst" (KJV), "between" (NAS, NRS, RSV), "in the borderlands" (NJB). Meier, *Marginal Jew*, 2:704 finds the phrase "unintelligible" and

"a geographical mess" and translates it with "he was passing through the middle of Samaria and Galilee." Arendt, *Lexicon*, 508b also struggles with the meaning and says it can probably only mean "through Samaria and Galilee" which he goes on to say, "raises a practical difficulty, since we should expect to find the provinces mentioned in the opposite order" and suggests that the text might be damaged. The easiest solution to this conundrum is that Luke inserted this notice before the story of the miracle to account for a Samaritan being included in the group. The evangelists have basically created the narrative framework of their gospels. But Meier, *Marginal Jew*, 2:752, n127 rejects this idea. Why would Luke, he asks, "with no impetus from the tradition... have invented such a strange and indeed unintelligible phrase..."? It must have made sense to him, of course, and it can only mean he meant to say Jesus and his disciples were traveling along an area which would include both Jews and a Samaritan. Plummer, *Luke*, 403, however, has no problem understanding the phrase. His literal translation is "through what lies between" which he then understands as "along the frontier," or simply, "between." He finds this little phrase also in Xenophon, (*Anabasis*, i.4.4) where the author describes "a river flowing between two walls" and in Plato where he refers to "an intermediate course." Plummer also observes that if Jesus is going along the border and moving eastward (which accords with Luke's understanding that he is on his way to Jerusalem) Samaria would be on his right so Samaria would naturally be mentioned first. See also Geldenhuys, *Luke*, 435.

584. The number is large. Perhaps they had all gathered together because they heard that Jesus was passing that way. Plummer, *Luke*, 403.

585. See Roemer, *World of Jesus*, 502–6.

586. Plummer, *Luke*, 404.

587. Plummer, *Luke*, 404.

588. See Roemer, *Who in the World Was Jesus?*, 148–51. I mention there the certain narcissism that attaches to the finder of the treasure.

589. The counter story to this Samaritan is the parable of the rich fool who narcisstically reserves the treasure with which he is blessed exclusively for himself. See Roemer, *Who in the World Was Jesus?*, 165–68.

590. Contra Meier, *Marginal Jew*, 2:703 and the commentators he mentions in n117, 750. The faith that has "saved" the Samaritan applies also to the nine. That is the nature of the kingdom ala the parable of the Treasure in a Field. He essentially accedes to this point in n88, 750.

591. Meier, *Marginal Jew*, 2:703 and n122. On 750 he reproduces the arguments of those who understand the story as a creation of the church based on Mark 1:40–45 and the story of Elisha and his cure of Naaman 2 Kgs 5:1–27. There are parallels between this OT story and Jesus' own cleansing of the lepers: an Israelite holy man cures a foreigner, the healing is delayed, and the foreigner returns to give thanks. Meier points out, however, that parallels would arise from the form-critical category the stories share. He also correctly points out the differences: although the story of Elisha is mentioned elsewhere in Luke 4:27 that does not occur in this story and though Jesus is hailed elsewhere as an Elisha-like prophet that is not mentioned either in this story. Also the delay in healing is for different reasons and there is no punitive transfer of the leprosy as in the Elisha story. He further notes that there are two other miracle stories (13:10–17, 14:1–6) where the narratives have apothegm-like characteristics. There are other commentators who attribute the whole story to Luke's own creative hand based on the Naaman story.

592. Caird, *Luke*, 195.

593. Meier, *Marginal Jew*, 2:705. It certainly points to the fact that Jesus' person was well known and recognized as a miracle worker upon whom a sick person could rely

on to be healed. The word occurs frequently in the LXX and is used particularly of the people external to Israel: Exod 12:43, 29:33, Lev 22:10.

594. Meier, *Marginal Jew*, 2:705.

595. I have also dealt with this pericope in Roemer, *Tantalizing Teacher*, 110-11 as a controversy pronouncement story. "Dropsy" is the accumulation of fluid, an endemic condition, and a symptom of a serious illness such as heart failure.

596. Roemer, Tantalizing Teacher, 110.

597. Suggested by Meier, *Marginal Jew*, 2:710.

598. Plummer, *Luke*, 354 finds it probable that he had come hoping to be healed. The "behold" of vs 2 he says implies that the man was unexpected. But that he was invited is implied by the "let him go" of vs 4 which can also mean "permit to leave."

599. Cf., Matt 14:31 where Jesus "takes hold of Peter" "with his hand" (or "arm" cf., Ps 91:11) who, after having left the boat and was walking to him on the water starts to sink because he takes his eyes off of Jesus." Implied is that Jesus wrapped his arm around him to pull him out of the water.

600. Or perhaps a member of the body of Sadducees which formed a synhedrion. The word is used of Jairus, the president of a synagogue (Luke 8:41). John 3:1 uses the same terminology as here when Nikodemus is called a Pharisee and a ruler. In John 7:26 it refers to the "authorities" in general. In Luke 23:13, 35, 24:20 Pilate refers to the "chief priests and rulers." So it is possible this "ruler" in Luke 14:1 refers to member of the ruling class which was associated with the Sadducees. Sadducees and their colleagues interpreted the Torah strictly so it would not be surprising that this "ruler," if a member of the Sadducean class, would carefully observe Jesus' behavior. Perhaps he invited Jesus to this Sabbath meal for that very purpose (see Geldenhuys, *Luke*, 386). However, to assume that this ruler was of the ruling class the story would have to be placed in Jerusalem. Suggestive of that location is that Jesus immediately preceding this story (Luke 13:34-35) delivers his lament over Jerusalem which Matthew explicitly places in Jerusalem (Matt 23:37). If the story is associated with the Galilee then the "ruler" was perhaps the president of a synagogue. Such a person would also tend to interpret the Torah quite literally. See Luke 13:14 where the president of the synagogue is explicitly so named and adheres to a strict and literal interpretation of Torah. For the various officers of the synagogue see Roemer, *World of Jesus*, 571-3.

601. Plummer, *Luke*, 354 can even understand it as "interested and sinister espionage" and refers to Luke 6:7.

602. The oldest reading is "a son or an ox" supported by a great variety of manuscripts including especially Vaticanus and Freerianus. Other important manuscripts including Sinaiticus read "ass." Bezae reads "sheep." Several others combine all three. Copyists may have found the conjunction of ox and son as incongruous and altered "son" to "ass." Metzger, *Textual Commentary*, 164. The inclusion of "son" is the most difficult text and so the most likely the original. The son and ox are mentioned in Deut 5:14 as part of the explication of the 3rd commandment "in which the son stands first among the rational creatures possessed, and the ox first among the irrational." Plummer, *Luke*, 355 n1.

603. Rather than from the lesser to the greater (*a fortiori*, or Hebrew, *Qal VaChomer*) as I contended in Roemer, *Tantalizing Teacher*, 110.

604. The tendency in the process of textualizing the tradition by the evangelists is to add the Pharisees as frequent opponents of Jesus. The Mishnah lays down the general rule that where human life is involved that takes precedence over the Sabbath. For example, mYom 8,6-7 stipulates, that if a building fell upon a man the stones could be cleared away and that a physician can minister to a person if his life is in danger. However, the Mishnah places restrictions on the treatment of minor illnesses without

forbidding it completely. mShabbath 14, 6 reads "If his teeth pain [a person] he may not suck vinegar through them but he may take vinegar after his usual fashion [at meal times]." This rule of saving life was adopted during Maccabean times when a group of Hasideans had refused to fight on the Sabbath and were consequently slaughtered (1 Macc 2:34-8). Thereafter it was ruled that defensive measures could be taken but not offensive ones. See Schürer, *History* 2, 473-74. Moore, *Judaism*, 30 refers to the persecution under Hadrian when the rabbis at Lydda decreed that a Jew to save his life might yield on any point save three, idolatry, incest, and murder. The concession is based on Lev 18:5 where it says that the laws were given that a "man might live by them not die by them." The Essenes, on the other hand, did not allow the saving of an animal that happened to drop into a pit on the Sabbath (CD 11:13-14).

605. The Pharisaic oral tradition was based on the traditions and practices of the people. This oral tradition was made equal to and as authoritative as the written Torah and understood as also having been handed down by Moses. Jesus, it should be noted, was stricter on the law of divorce (Mark 10:2-12). So in general it can be said that Jesus intensified the moral law and relaxed the ritual law (e.g., see Matt 5:21-32).

606. Plummer, *Luke*, 355.

607. Meier, *Marginal Jew*, 2:757, n146 observes that φρέαρ (phrear, well) can also mean a pit or shaft and that the Hebrew גב (GeB, pit or ditch) is usually rendered βόθυνος (bothynos, ditch, hole) in the LXX and once is translated with φρέαρ. A well, of course, is a pit dug for the purposes of finding water and retaining it.

608. Souter, *Pocket Lexicon*, 25.

609. Cf., Rom 9:20, "But who are you, a man, to answer back (ἀνταποκρίνομαι) to God? Will what is molded say to its molder, 'Why have you made me thus?'" The word implies hostility and suggests that the usual translation of the English versions, "they could not reply" is too weak and does not catch the nuance of hostility. The use of this word may be Lucan redaction.

610. The fact that the precise medical condition producing the edema is not indicated and the fact that this is a singular occurrence of the condition mentioned in the NT is no argument against the historicity of the account. Just how could anyone know, except a modern physician, what produced the edema? The obvious symptom, on the other hand, could be observed by anyone. *Pace* Meier, *Marginal Jew*, 2:711. Meier's insistence (711) that Jesus' mere touch would be considered a violation of the Sabbath as improbable. But see note 604 above quoting the Mishnah where even running vinegar through the teeth was considered a violation of the Sabbath law!

611. In vs 1 some important manuscripts add the definite article to "feast" but the evidence favors its non-inclusion. The tendency in the tradition is to distinguish the feast with the definite article rendering it as "*the feast*" which identifies it as Tabernacles. (In fact one manuscript actually adds "Tabernacles"). In vs 2 various manuscripts add a definite article before "pool" which has to be supplied in order to make sense of the reading: "there is in Jerusalem at the sheep gate ("a" or "the") pool." Various manuscripts obligingly provide the name. Metzger, *Textual Commentary*, 208, n1 surmises that the original text repeated "pool" twice which would read "In Jerusalem near the sheep pool, there is a pool . . . ." There is also a plethora of variant readings for the name of the place, "Bethesda," "Bethsaida," "Bedsaida," Bedsaidan," and "Belzdetha." The least unsatisfactory reading is "Bethdzatha" from which other spellings may have derived. The western text adds "paralytic" in vs 3 and a variety of witnesses add "waiting for the stirring of the water" in order to prepare for the "troubling of the water" in vs 7. Verse 4 is a gloss clear from its absence in the earliest manuscripts including Sinaiticus and Vaticanus. It is marked as such in a number of later Greek witnesses. It reads (NKJ), "For an angel went down at a certain time into the pool and stirred up the water; then

whoever stepped in first, after the stirring of the water, was made well of whatever disease he had." (However, this ancient gloss, though not a part of John's gospel, may reflect with some precision a popular notion about the pool. The intermittent stirring of the water could have been caused by the occasional gushing of water by a spring.

612. Finegan, *Archaeology*, 227a–b. He also notes that in p⁶⁶ (Bodmer Papyrus 2, 2ⁿᵈ to 3ʳᵈ century) προβατική (probatikē) is set off between punctuation dots which would support the definition adopted here.

613. Finegan, *Archaeology*, 228a.

614. Read by Codex Alexandrinus and Ephremi (5ᵗʰ century), a majority of the Byzantine manuscripts, and adopted by KJV, NAS, NJB, and NKJ.

615. These names have been erroneously introduced. They are the name of a well-known town. Phillip, Peter, and Andrew came from there (John 1:44).

616. Finegan, *Archaeology*, 228b–29a. He gives the example of this kind of merging of two Hebrew letters into one Greek letter in the transliteration of the Greek Azōtos which renders the Hebrew "Ashdod." He also notes that Josephus in *War*, 4, 2, 148–51 in describing the third wall built north of Jerusalem says there was a hill opposite the Fortress Antonia called "Bezetha" which corresponds to the name "Bethzatha" implying that the pool gave its name to this new district of Jerusalem.

617. Finegan, *Archaeology*, 231a. Based on the archaeological evidence he says the dimensions of the northern pool were 174 feet on its south side and 131 feet and the east and west, and 164 feet on the north; the southern pool measured 189 feet on the north, 162 feet on the east, 157 feet on the west, and 215 feet on the south. So the water surface of the two pools measured about 5,000 square yards. Sirach 50:1–3 might refer to the construction of the pools sometime in the late third century early second century B.C.

618. Meier, *Marginal Jew*, 2:680. Note all the differences which he adduces.

619. The five porticos (vs 2) previously were thought to be only symbolic by scholars representing the five books of the Torah. But see von Wahlde, "Puzzling Pool of Bethesda," 41–47 who describes the history of the archaeological investigations. Beginning in the 1880's archaeologists exposed a rectangular pool with a wall that divided it and porticoes in the four sides and on the central wall. This was indeed a five-sided pool. It is, however, a complex site because a Byzantine church was built there and later a Crusader chapel which overlapped the Byzantine structure (43b–3a). There is evidence that the pool was a mikveh because of the steps that extend across the southern end of the pool and that they are interspersed with landings. These landings would allow a person to stand securely while immersing in the waters (45a). At the bottom of the dam separating the two pools is a large opening permitting water from the northern pool to enter into the southern pool. This northern pool is therefore a reservoir. The law required natural water from rain or a stream, differentiated from drawn water, to be used in a mikveh. (On mikveh see the so-named tractate in the Mishnah, Danby, *Mishnah*, 732–45.) This reservoir guaranteed that the waters of the mikveh remained ritually clean. Meier, *Marginal Jew*, 2:681 also references the Copper Scroll (probably written between AD 25 and 68) which mentions this pool. (11, 57 "next to them [referring to the preceding line] at Bet-Eshdatain בית אשדתי׳ (i.e., "Bethesda"), in the reservoir where you enter the small pool: vessels of offering of aloes, offering of . . ." Vermes, *Dead Sea Scrolls*, 588.) The Hebrew for "pool" is written in the dual which would suggest the translation "the House of the Twin Pools." (See Finegan, *Archaeology*, 228b.) Jesus performs a healing at another pool, the Pool Siloam in John 9:1–7. This pool was archaeologically identified in 2005.

620. Meier, *Marginal Jew*, 2:730, n11.

621. Bultmann, *Evangelium des Johannes*, 177, n4 enumerates the following Semitic characteristics of the story: the placement of the verb at the beginning of the sentence in

vs 7 ("he says") and the phrase in vs 5 which literally says "having in his illness" (translated by the versions such as the RSV "who had been ill thirty-eight years.") Also un-Greek-like is the phrase in vs 9 which literally says "And it was a Sabbath on that day."

622. The word ἀποσυνάγωγος (*aposynagōgos*, "excluded from the synagogue") is a hapaxlegomenon (occurring only once) in the NT perhaps a neologism invented by John.

623. Meier, *Marginal Jew*, 2:743, n82.

624. By the time of the evangelists the Pharisees have become a convenient foil in their gospel narratives since after the war they had become so prominent and the church was involved in controversies with them. Judaism on its side anathematized Christians at this time. The so-called Eighteen Benedictions (Heb., *Shemoneh Esreh*) bears witness to this strife between Christians and Jews. This prayer was the chief prayer of Judaism. Its final form was established only after the destruction of Jerusalem. It had to be recited three time a day including by women, slaves, and children. Its "Palestinian" form (found in the Cairo Geniza) perhaps comes closest to its form in the period AD 70—100. Its origin, however, is much older and can be traced back to some time in the Second Temple period. Josephus, for example, asserts it came from Moses, *Ant.* 4.8.13. (In the Hebrew text of Sirach following 51:12 there are a series of blessing that bear a remarkable parallels to this prayer.) The 12th benediction in the Palestinian form curses heretics including Christians, reading in part "And may the Nazarenes and the heretics perish quickly; and may they be erased from the Book of Life." However, the older reading may have read "Minim" (heretics or apostates in general). Schürer, History, 455-63.

625. "Works" are a prominent theme of John's theology and understanding of Jesus. (John 5;36; 6:28; 7:3-7; 10:25) as is the phrase the "light of the world," and the concept of "light." (John 1:4-9; 3:19-21; 5:35; 8:12; 11:10; 12:35-46).

626. An obvious Johannine interpolation explaining the Hebrew name.

627. Jesus uses spittle in the healing of the deaf mute in Mark 7:31-37 and with the blind man at Bethsaida (Mark 8:22-26). The difference here is that the spittle is a first step in the healing of the blind man. The washing in Siloam finally accomplishes the return of his sight. So the use here is discontinuous with the use in other traditions of Jesus' healings. Meier, *Marginal Jew*, 2:697.

628. In the story of the healing at Bethsaida (above) the mikveh plays no role. The stepped remains of the pool of Siloam was uncovered near the city of David (south of the Temple mount). During construction work to repair a water pipe the archaeologists Ronny Reich and Eli Shukron identified two ancient stone steps. Further excavation revealed they were part of a monumental pool. It was 225 feet long with a trapezoidal shape with the wider end on the east side. The pool was fed by waters from the Gihon Spring which would qualify the pool as a mikveh. It was Hezekiah (late eight century BC) who had a 1748-foot tunnel dug from the Gihon spring to bring water behind the walls of Jerusalem in anticipation of a siege by the Assyrian monarch Sennacherib (2 Kings 20:20). Instead of carving the tunnel from scratch, these engineers resourcefully modified natural crevices, caves, shafts, and fissures under Jerusalem. Natural forces created these formations thousands of years earlier. Since the builders utilized these natural formations, the tunnel meanders and covers 1,748 feet instead of the direct distance of 1000 feet. This, however, does not minimize the masterful craftsmanship utilized in the construction. The workers had to widen these passages and seal the walls and floor with plaster to prevent water from escaping. They also cut steps from the tunnel up natural shafts which connect to the surface. Propelling water through the tunnel was the builders next challenge. Impressively, they managed to slope the tunnel only 12.5 inches over the length of 1,748 feet allowing the water to flow through at a gentle pace. Siloam is mentioned in Isa 8:6.

ENDNOTES

629. At this point John's reference to the Sabbath occurs. The Sabbath has no function anywhere else in the story and probably was John's addition (vs. 14). Meier, *Marginal Jew*, 2:744, n87. The Pharisees do not appear in this proposed reconstruction since they probably would not question Jesus performing a miracle on the Sabbath.

630. John has added these reference to "Pharisees" and the "Sabbath." The two are connected in the Gospels reflecting conditions after the destruction of Jerusalem and the controversies between Jews and Christians in that period. "Sabbath" occurs in contexts of controversy in the gospel of John as in this narrative (John 5:9–18; 7:22–23). "Prophet" is one way John has characterized Jesus' person and ministry (John 4:19, 44; 6:14; 7:40, 52).

631. "The Jews" is the chief way John identifies Jesus' opponents occurring some 58 times in his gospel.

632. These last words reflect the theme of rejection of Jesus and expulsion from the synagogue and therefore I judge them to be John's further interpolation emphasizing the break between Judaism and Christianity.

633. That the disciples have not been present since chapter 6 of John and do not appear again until chapter 11 does not imply that John has inserted them here with their question but rather they were part of the tradition which was handed down to him. Meier, *Marginal Jew*, 2:743, n84 lists a number of commentators who agree with this assessment and that John has re-shaped vss 2–4. Furthermore, they also think that the traditional material even continued through the rest of the chapter.

634. Josephus, *War*, 6,7,2 [The day after the Romans had breached the walls of the city they drove] "the rebels from the Lower city burned the whole place as far as Siloam." See Roemer, *World of Jesus*, 324–54. The Pool of Siloam is mentioned elsewhere only in Luke 13:4 but nowhere else in the NT. See Roemer, *Tantalizing Teacher*, 135–36.

635. Meier, *Marginal Jew*, 2:697.

636. Meier, *Marginal Jew*, 2:697.

637. Marsh, *John*, 378.

638. Marsh, *John*, 379.

639. "I am the bread of life," 6:35; "light of the world," 8:12; "the door," 10:7; "the Good Shepherd," 10:11; "the resurrection and life," 11:25; "the way, the truth, and life," 14:6; "the true vine," 15:1; "before Abraham I am," 8:58; and absolutely in 18:4.

640. Exod 31:14 even decrees who profanes the Sabbath should be executed!

641. Marsh, *John*, 385.

642. E.g., mNedarim 2,5, "If the vow was of undefined Terumah (the portion of the harvest that had to be given to the priests), in Judea the vow is binding; but in Galilee it is not binding, since the men of Galilee know naught of the Terumah of the Temple-chamber." mYadim 4, 8, "A Galilean heretic said, I cry out against you, O Pharisees, for ye write in a bill of divorce the name of the ruler together with the name of Moses [giving him equal importance to that of Moses]." (Such a Galilean was no doubt a nationalist opposed to Roman rule.) What Finkelstein, *Pharisees*, 97 writes of the Galilean attitude toward the Pharisees could well apply also to their attitude toward urbanites. "To the blunt and ingenuous villager, Pharisaic amenity and politeness seemed more dissembling and chicanery; and their love of book-learning nothing more than pedantry. He could not realize that the ease of manner and conversation which was characteristic of the townsmen, as well as their polish and self-control, was so much a part of them as to be almost instinctive. He was as insensitive to the Pharisee's delight in abstruse discussion of the Law, as the modern uninitiate is to the universes of multiple dimensions. The ancient Galilean was amazed when he discovered the Pharisee spending hours in a discussion of whether mint and rue ought to be tithed." (See e.g., Mark 12:38–40; Matt 6:5, 12:2–7.)

643. See Roemer, *World of Jesus*, 235-37 for a detailed description of Pilate and his time in office.

644. It was a "one company town," so to speak.

645. I regard John's chronology of placing the cleansing of the Temple early in Jesus' ministry as the correct one.

646. So Jesus and his proclamation of the Kingdom and doing its works sets before the people a choice: Moses and the Torah or the new Moses through whom the grace of God is active.

647. This contradicts what the Jerusalemites said at the Feast of Tabernacles in 7:27. But their assertion is ironic: what they don't know is the true origin of Jesus in the Father.

648. Παρά (para) is a preposition which strongly emphasizes close relationships. It is used as a description of Jesus' own family, "those from his own" (Mark 3:21). It can mean "one's agent" or "representative."

649. The story is in the form of a miracle story: the coming of the miracle worker; the appearance of the petitioner; a description of the affliction; the petitioner's request and expression of trust; marveling (here not by a crowd but by Jesus himself) the dismissal of the petitioner; the promise that the healing has taken place; and the confirmation of the miracle. See Meier, *Marginal Jew*, 2:763, n178.

650. Bultmann, *History*, 38, n4 thinks that it "unquestionably is to be understood as child" and that Luke's "slave" is an "error in reproduction." I think rather that Luke's rendition is simply an interpretation of the word παῖς.

651. Capernaum lay at the boundary of Herod Antipas' tetrarchy and his brother Phillip's. It was the site of a toll station (see Mark 2:14). Royal officials and military officers would have been a natural part of the scene in Capernaum. So John's reference to a "royal official" is perfectly natural. There is not much difference between designating someone a centurion or a "royal official." The latter often refers to an ambassador, a scribe, or a courtier. Josephus uses it frequently for soldiers or troops of various monarchs including Herodians and the Roman emperor (see *War*, 1, 1, 5). Cf., Peddie, *Roman War Machine*, 10-11, 29-30. It is important to keep in mind that Capernaum was situated in the Galilee and so part of Herod Antipas' tetrarchy so no Roman military would have been situated there. Antipas had his own military. Roman legions would intervene only if necessary. So the "centurion" in this story would not have been Roman but either a Jew or a Syrian. (Even in the case of procurators his Roman military unit was not made up of Romans but Syrians. See Roemer, *World of Jesus*, 229-30.) It is obvious that the centurion mentioned in this story, however, was a Gentile.

652. Bultmann, *History*, 38 who finds the story to be a variant of the healing of the Syrophoenician woman's daughter is highly unlikely considering the huge differences between them. In the following I am following Meier, *Marginal Jew*, 2:766, n182.

653. The story of Peter entering the centurion's house in Acts 10:27-28 suggests itself. See particularly 10:22 where justification is made for doing so.

654. As suggested by Meier, *Marginal Jew*, 2:766, n182.

655. Meier, *Marginal Jew*, 2:767, n182.

656. Meier, *Marginal Jew*, 2:767, n183 and 184.

657. His encounter with the Samaritan woman in chapter 4 cannot be countered as such even though the Samaritans were not accepted by the Jews as faithful people of God. Even when Gentiles ask to see Jesus conveyed through two of Jesus disciples (John 12:20-26) he does not grant the request.

658. Meier, *Marginal Jew*, 2:724 who notes that the original Aramaic was תלי (*talyi* see *The New Covenant*, 9 *ad loc*) which is also ambiguous and means either "boy" or "servant."

659. Meier, *Marginal Jew*, 2:724 feels that John was dependent on an independent

tradition he received from his own source material perhaps oral tradition. He agrees that the core tradition meets the criterion of multiple attestation and that in a unique way: that two diverse sources with little in common agree on the core of a miracle story is a "striking datum." He further notes that trimmed of John's additions the story reaches back to pre-Gospel traditions which presupposes that the alternate version in Q was likewise not a creation of the writer(s) of Q.

660. Meier, *Marginal Jew*, 2:726.

661. Which even Meier, *Marginal Jew*, 2:726 agrees with!

662. This expression is indeed a mouthful! It is used by Tyson, *Christian Theology of Science*, which he defines as "The view according to which the locus of knowledge is the human knower. The knowledge of the human knower is the only valid foundation for truth."(185) So this standpoint can easily dismiss as false or outside the scope of science the Christology which holds that Jesus was God incarnate, that he was born of a virgin, physically rose from the dead, and ascended into heaven. He cautions against assuming it and then using it to defend Christian truth which leads to the loss of truth itself and consequent inability "to see knowledge and the world through Christian theology as a primary truth lens." (37)

663. See Roemer, *World of Jesus*, 228–54.

664. Moreland, *Simple Guide to Experience Miracles*.

665. See Wright, *People of God*, 246–72 and my summary of his description of Israel's experience and understanding of its vocation in Roemer, *Who in the World Was Jesus?*, 34–44.

666. For example, male Jews were exempt from Roman military service, the practices of Judaism were legally protected, and the temple and its cultus was protected from profanation. The synagogues also fell under this protection. Jews were exempted throughout the empire from appearing before a magistrate on the Sabbath or any Feast Day. Coins minted in the land did not have to bear any images. Roman troops were also not allowed to bring their standards into the temple precincts. See Roemer, *World of Jesus*, 228–33.

667. See Roemer, *World of Jesus*, 32–36. Prov 8.

668. See Roemer, *Who in the World Was Jesus?* 17–18.

669. See John 3:29, 4:36, 5:35, 15:20–22, 15:11, 16:20–22, 24, 17:13. So the theme of joy is pretty well scattered throughout the Gospel.

670. "Look! Your house will be left to you." (Luke 13:35, New Jerusalem Bible)

671. See above, chapter 2.

672. John may indeed have supplied the reaction to Jesus in 5:16–23 but it actually represents history by both what the miracle portrays and the historical fact of Jesus' rejection, persecution, and final execution on the cross because of his claims and kingdom activity.

673. I outlined in detail the animosity between the "rubes" of the Galilee and the sophisticated Jerusalemites in the exposition in this chapter.

674. This careful planning on Jesus' part also underscores his intention and ability to choose the time of his death (John 10:18). He is not subject to the decisions of others.

675. See my *World of Jesus*, the first volume in this series where I describe this first century milieu in terms of five dynamic features: historical memory of Israel beginning with the conquest of Alexander, religious competition, ecological divisions, social tensions, economic inequality, and political injustice.

676. In what follows in this paragraph I am summarizing the analysis of Wright, *People of God* which I've also recapped in Roemer, *Who in the World Was Jesus?*, 34–35.

677. See Roemer, *World of Jesus*, 417–27 on messiahship and David as the model of the messiah which included suffering and death.

678. There are also two such reports in the book of Acts: the raising of the woman Tabitha by Peter in 9:36–41 and the raising of Eutychus by Paul in 20:7–12 although it may be that the boy had not actually died (vs 10) although his fall appeared to have killed him. Cf., also the raisings by Elijah in 1 Kgs 17:17–24 and Elisha in 2 Kgs 4:8–37. See also Glynn, *God: The Evidence*, chapter 4 "Intimations of Immortality," 99–137 on his reports of so-called near death experiences.

679. Matthew's and Luke's version are obvious redactions of Mark's original story and so provide no independent witness to the story. See Meier, *Marginal Jew*, 2:777 and n 17, 841. I have dealt with Meier's insistence that the two stories of the hemorrhaging woman and Jarius's daughter were originally separate stories and were brought together either by a pre-Marcan redactor or Mark himself in chapter 3 where I discussed the healing of the hemorrhaging woman.

680. The name "Jarius" is not included by Codex Bezae (referred to by the siglum "D") making it, what textual critics call, a "western non-interpolation." This particular manuscript is notorious for expanding and adding ("interpolating") to the normal text of the NT. For example, its text of the book of Acts is one tenth longer. So when it omits words or phrases those omissions have a strong claim to reflecting the original text. See Metzger, *Text of the New Testament*, 50–51. However, Metzger, *Textual Commentary*, 85–86 presents four points supporting its retention the strongest of which is the impressive textual evidence. So I follow Metzger in maintaining the name as part of the original text.

681. The name is found e.g., in Num 32:41, Deut 3:14. The Hebrew form of the name is יאיר (Ya'ir "he [God] will enlighten").

682. "The lively vividness which distinguishes this narrative refers back again to an eyewitness (Peter)." Schmid, *Markus*, 112. (Translation mine.)

683. Meier, *Marginal Jew*, 2:843 n 26.

684. Taylor, *Mark*, 286.

685. See Roemer, *World of Jesus*, 571–72 for a description of this office. The word "one" is a Semitism, an indefinite pronoun equivalent to "a" or "a certain primate of the synagogue." Meier, *Marginal Jew*, 2:845, n 30.

686. At play here may be the idea of requital because the death of a child meant punishment and judgment on parents for some particular sin of which they were guilty. That would have been particularly pressing for Jairus because he might have been relieved of his position for that reason. So the life of the child, the reputation of the parents, and the father's position were all at risk. Little wonder then that Jairus was full of anxiety! Grundman, *Markus*, 114.

687. Haenchen, *Weg Jesu*, 208 finds the report of the deputation to Jairus as "business-like, cold, and strange" and the prescription not to bother Jesus any further as unique. So for him the whole expression is "unrealistic." But I wonder. Is he judging it on the basis of what one would expect in our contemporary society? The ancients may have not had such reticence and would just blurt out what had happened and advise Jairus to give up since Jesus, they would think, could hardly raise the dead. He further finds the whole notion of sending a deputation to Jairus as only the literary means of the story teller who seems to treat their message of the death of the girl as a matter of secondary importance after the concern for not bothering Jesus with coming to the house anymore. But wouldn't Jesus' presence in the face of a hopeless case only exaggerate even more the grief of this household? Wouldn't his presence be a distraction since certain hospitable actions would be required of the family? See Roemer, *Who in the World Was Jesus?*, 230–34: the parable of the shameless neighbor on the obligation to extend hospitality to a visitor. Again, so many commentators do not take the historical realities of Israelite society of the time into consideration but deal only with literary

considerations.

688. Meier, *Marginal Jew*, 2:786 takes the lack of any exalted Christological titles in the story to imply the antiquity of the tradition.

689. Taylor, *Mark*, 294 observes that the seven occurrences of the word in the LXX all mean "refuse to hear" (cf., also Matt 18:17).

690. These three form an inner circle of the twelve and Mark always names them in this order (see 13:3, 14:33). Why would this detail be added if it were not part of a historical report?

691. Luke adds at this point "seeing that she was dead" confirming that the child had really died.

692. See Roemer, *Who in the World Was Jesus?*, 74.

693. Taylor, *Mark*, 295. See Ps 87:6, Dan 12:2, 1 Thess 5:10.

694. Meier, *Marginal Jew*, 2:844, n 26. However, for him, this is a mere symbolical story that derived from an earlier miracle of healing so Mark can edifying his Christian readers with the assurance of an eschatological resurrection. However, he does demolish the idea that the story was originally of a healing and was transformed into a raising from the dead. 783–84.

695. Grundmann, *Markus*, 117.

696. Taylor, *Mark*, 295. But he does not follow through on this insight. He avers "... it would still remain an open question whether the restoration was a case of resurrection. It is clear that the saying is one of great ambiguity ... [which] ambiguity ... suggests that the case was one of apparent death." But then he has to admit that all three evangelists regarded the action of Jesus as a raising from death, a "resurrection." See Meier, *Marginal Jew*, and his long note 26 (2:843–44), disallowing Taylor's "ambiguity" discerning, as I do, that the text itself is describing a raising from the dead.

697. Taylor, *Mark*, 296. The word used there (ἐκβάλλω, ekballō) is the word employed in the exorcisms for "casting out" demons.

698. Taylor, *Mark*, 296. As Meier, *Marginal Jew*, 2:785, observes, "... our Greek Gospels do not attempt to create an artificial air of ancient tradition by regularly inserting Aramaic phrases into gospel narrative in general or miraculous stories in particular."

699. In fact by the age of twelve girls was considered of age and capable of marriage and so well along in their life span. Many children in that age were dead before six. Malina, *Social Science Commentary*, 211 gives the following statistics: 60% of people would die in their teens, 75% in their twenties, 90% in their forties, and maybe 3% would reach their sixties. I suspect. However, that these statistics apply to the Graeco-Roman world and are not descriptive for the Jewish community in which the Torah promoted healthy habits, children were treasured and protected, and human life was considered of great value. According to Ps 90:10 the average life span extended into the 70's. The death ages that are recorded for Israel's heroes of the past, though sometimes exaggerated, would support this number. See e.g., Gen 35:28, 50:22, Nmb 33:39, Deut 34:7, Josh 24:29, I Sam 4:15, 2 Sam 19:32, 2 Kgs 14:2, 15:2 21:1.

700. Cf., 4:41 "They feared with a great fear" which the versions translate with "feared exceedingly." See Meier *Marginal Jew* 2, 849, n 57 for other possible Semitisms.

701. Nineham, *Mark*, 160.

702. See Meier, *Marginal Jew*, 2:779.

703. See chapter 2 on "metaphysical Naturalism."

704. Schweizer, *Mark*, 121.

705. See above chapter 3, #2 "cleansing a leper." Plummer, *Luke*, 198 notices that almost all raisings from the dead were performed for women: 1 Kgs 17:23, 2 Kgs 4:36, John 11:22, 32, Acts 9:41, Heb 11:35.

706. Meier, *Marginal Jew*, 2:791 and 854–55, notes 78–81 finds parallels with the

story of the raising of Jairus' daughter: the dative of possession (Luke 7:12, 8:42); each is an "only child;" the weeping attendant on the deaths, and Jesus commanding the weeping to stop; the words Jesus uses in each case to raise the dead offspring; the "sitting up" which follows the raising.

707. Strange, "Nain," 1001a also agrees with the arguments in Meier, *Marginal Jew*, 2:795 who remarks that the specificity in naming the town and that it had a gate and thus a wall weighs against any idea that Luke has created the story to say nothing of the fact that Luke himself says he is setting forth what he has received (Luke 1:2). It seems irrational to suppose he made up anything that appears in his gospel which Meier himself asserts when he supposes that the parables of Jesus which are peculiar to his gospel came from his hand (see Roemer, *Who in the World Was Jesus?*, 30-31 and Meier, *Marginal Jew*, 5:189-229).

708. Egeria, Etheria, or Aetheria was a Western European Christian woman, widely regarded to be the author of a detailed account of a pilgrimage to the Holy Land about 381/2-386. The long letter dubbed *Peregrinatio* or *Itinerarium Egeriae*, is addressed to a circle of women at home. Historical details it contains set the journey in the early 380s A.D., making it the earliest of its kind. It survives in fragmentary form in a later copy lacking a title, date and attribution.

709. Plummer, *Luke*, 198.

710. Meier, *Marginal Jew*, 2:795 and 897 n 94: the widow's "only son" agrees with the Hebrew text of 1 Kgs 17:12 and not the Greek text; the clause καί αὐτή ἦν χήρα (*kai autē ēn chēra*, "and she was a widow") corresponds to a circumstantial clause in Aramaic and the paratactic construction (sentences joined by "and"). Meier, 857, n96 also observes that Luke does not eliminate parataxis in his L source whereas he often does when he includes a text from Mark. He further observes that Q material in Luke has a more Semitic flavor than it does in Matthew's version of the same material. Of course, one would expect Q to bear a greater Semitic cast having been recorded early in the 50's in the Holy Land. Another Semitism is the use of the word ἐξέρχομαι (*exerchomai*, lit.,"go out") in vs. 17 does not usually carry the meaning of a report "spreading." However, in biblical Greek it is used to translate Hebrew words that have that meaning (Meier, 795).

711. Arendt, *Lexicon*, 536a, says that the word can refer to a young man between the ages of 24 and 40.

712. Plummer, *Luke*, 199.

713. Luke refers to Jesus with this term 14 times in his gospel while it occurs elsewhere in his gospel 17 times. Cf., Matthew who has 23 verses where Jesus is called "Lord" out of a total of 79 occurrences.

714. Danker, *Jesus and the New Age*, 94.

715. The verb "sit up" (ἀνακαθίζω *anakthidzō*) occurs only here and in Acts 9:40. The intransitive form of this verb is rare in Greek except among medical writers. Stuhlmueller, *Gospel According to Luke*, 137a. Arndt, *Lexicon*, 54a

716. So Luke's reference to Jesus as "the Lord" (vs. 13) stands out.

717. Plummer, *Luke*, 200 appropriately notes that ". . . a writer of fiction would rather have given us the frantic joy of the mother and of those who sympathized with her."

718. In the OT the verb פאקד (PAQD) is usually translated in the LXX with ἐπισκέπτομαι (*episkeptomai*, "visit, look upon, have regard for, care for"). So it describes God's action in history drawing near in judgment of sin or in in favor by relieving distress for individuals or for Israel as a whole. It is God manifesting himself as the Lord of history. Luke uses the Greek verb seven times out of its 11 occurrences in the NT and makes God the subject. The acclamation then reproduces the LXX theological usage. So Jesus here is understood as the one who embodies God's gracious presence

among his people. But when Jesus weeps over Jerusalem, because God's "visitation" was not recognized, it now turns into judgment (Luke 19:41–44). See Roemer, *Beloved Son*, 104–5.

719. Meier, *Marginal Jew*, 2:852–53, n72.

720. Eusebius, *Ecclesiastical History* IV, 3, 309.

721. Marsh, *Saint John*, 415 considers this story as confronting "the reader with the problem of historicity in its acutest forms, historical, philosophical and theological." But he observes later in his exposition that "[t]he story does not read like a myth or an allegory, but like an actual transcript of something that once happened to real men and women . . ." (432).

722. "Signs" in the fourth gospel are all physical occurrences that enhance the earthly lives of the people involved. But they are "signs" in the sense that they point beyond themselves to the fulfillment of life with God. Meier, *Marginal Jew*, 2:799.

723. Meier, *Marginal Jew*, 2:798.

724. Meier, *Marginal Jew*, 2:862, n118.

725. Meier, *Marginal Jew*, 2:805, 1.The story circulated as an independent unit so that references within the now altered text that refer back and forth to other material in the gospel derive from John. 2. Most likely from the hand of John are the theological themes found in a more developed way in other discourses of Jesus in the gospel. 3. John is a writer of "suspenseful narratives" as evident in the dramas of the woman at the well (chapter 4) and the blind man (chapter 9). So literary seams, interruptions in the flow of the story, repetitions suggest that John is wrestling with the reworking of the tradition. 4. The vocabulary and style of John must come from his hand. This criterion is especially apropos where it is supported by the other criteria. I have used these criteria in making my judgments about which material is due to John's hand.

726. Meier, *Marginal Jew*, 2:813.

727. See Meier, 810–11 and his exegesis of vss 21–27 which he judges to be a "theological masterpiece in miniature." See also 864, n130 which corroborates his understanding (and mine) that these verses come from John's own hand. An example of John at work is vs 22 when Martha says she "knows" that what Jesus asks of God will be given to him and that Jesus is a miracle worker who can achieve miraculous results at least this side of the grave. "Knowing" in John's gospel has a special meaning. It actually means ignorance (cf., 9:24, 29, 41). That "knowledge" (= ignorance) continues in her reaction to Jesus' promise of resurrection which she takes to mean the eschatological one. So we are dealing with Johannine conceptions and vocabulary. "While keeping to the pattern of his great revelation discourses (I am + metaphor + promise of saving benefit to those who believe), John sums up everything he has to say in those discourses in a mini-discourse of two verses."

728. Meier, *Marginal Jew*, 2:815.

729. Meier, *Marginal Jew*, 2:821–22. He notes that the blind man in John 9 is one of the most "realized" individuals and developed personalities in all of the gospel stories and yet remains anonymous.

730. Those who deny historicity to the story have to explain why the names that occur in the story were chosen. They usually point to the stories that Luke derived from his special source that contained the story of the visit to Mary and Martha (Luke 10:38–42), the anonymous woman who anoints Jesus' feet (Luke 7:36–50), and in the parable of Lazarus and the rich man (Luke 16:19–31). On this relationship with this parable see the discussion below. They also point to the apparently special relationship between "L" (Luke's special material) and John. But the similarities occur mostly in the narratives of the passion and resurrection. Meier, *Marginal Jew*, 2:823, 867 n152.

731. Verse numbers are in bold preceding the sentences that are so numbered.

732. Meier, *Marginal Jew*, 2:816–18 argues for the excision of the reference to Martha and for him that "makes good dramatic sense." I would argue since the text that I propose as something close to the original tradition speaks for its historicity simply because it doesn't make for a literarily more dramatic text.

733. This "weeping" is not a quiet sobbing but a loud and uninhibited wailing obligatory according to the custom of the time.

734. For the translation in brackets see below.

735. See Meier, *Marginal Jew*, 2:818–19 for his reconstruction which is close to mine. I agree with Meier we are only capable of producing a rough approximation of the wording of the original tradition. No doubt too, the tradition was developed in the course of its life within the community.

736. Some commentators reduce the story extremely severely. See Meier, *Marginal Jew*, 2:867, n147 for examples. One commentator, for example, includes only vss 1, 3, 17, 38–39, 41, 43–44!

737. Meier, *Marginal Jew*, 2:807 thinks that "the Jews" in vs 8 are redactional but not in vss 18–19 because the use there seems more "neutral" as compared to the former which bears a "hostile" meaning. However, the original wording of the story would not refer to "Jews" at all, but as I argue, would simply refer to" the people" as in the synoptic gospel tradition. Why would Jews refer to their compatriots as "Jews"? Identifying the people as "Jews" is part of the redactional work of John.

738. Meier, *Marginal Jew*, 2:808–9.

739. Meier, *Marginal Jew*, 2:820. However, on the basis of similar wording in Acts 9:42 he does not find that the word is impossible in the original tradition.

740. Souter, *Pocket Lexicon*, 80. Arndt, *Lexicon*, 254a says it is an expression of anger and displeasure; Rienecker, *Sprachlicher Schlüssel*, 226 adds "to scold or censure, warn sternly, to speak with indignation, resentment, displeasure, animosity, exasperation."

741. Rienecker, *Sprachlicher Schlüssel*, 226. ". . . der Geist Gottes, als die treibende Kraft bezeichnet, welche die zornige Aufwallung seines Gemütes bewirkte und seinen Willen in eine entsprechende Bewegung versetzte." "That means that the Spirit of God is the motive force which caused his temper to flare up in anger, and caused his will to move accordingly." (Translation mine.) This is saying too much. Coordinating the two parts of the sentence as Luther does gives the meaning that it was Jesus' own (subjective) spirit that was involved here.

742. As Marsh, *Saint John*, 433 does. ". . .some deeply felt righteous indignation is what the word may well mean, and the rendering 'angry' rather overstates, and 'deeply moved' rather understates what seems to be in mind."

743. Bultmann, *Evangelium des Johannes*, 310, n4. Bultmann judges that the whole of vss 33–34 came from the so-called signs source and in that source the expression in 33a represents the pneumatic agitation of the "divine man." The whole verse then is used as expressing the voice of the mystagogue. Of course the whole idea of the "divine man" is now highly questioned as a concept. Also that gnosticism existed in the first century has been discredited. It was a second century development. Gnosticism taught that man is entangled in himself, helpless in a hostile, world that has inextricably permeated him. To become free of it and from his own physical self was the longing of the age as well as being free of the world which estranged him from his real self. So one had to pass through and get out of one's physical nature which, for the gnostic, is the meaning of redemption. The way of salvation to extricate oneself from this boundedness in the physical body and world was knowledge ("gnosis"). See Jonas, *Gnosis und Spätantiker Geist*, especially 199–210, ("Erlösung," "redemption").

744. See Matt 11:25–27. This prayer appears also in Luke 10:21–22 and so was a part of Q whose provenance was the early 50's in the Holy Land, that is, very close to

the time of Jesus having therefore a claim to authenticity. See also the frequent references to Jesus in prayer Luke 6:12, 22:46 and giving thanks Matt 15:3, Mark 6:41, 8:6.

745. Marsh, *Saint John*, 439. So all the Johannine additions to this story are his reflections on this reality and true to the intentions of Jesus as expressed in his prayer of thanks.

746. Marsh, *Saint John*, 438 seeing the story in the context of John's gospel comments that the real miracle though "bringing Lazarus back to his family and friends was indeed wonderful enough, but it is far more wonderful when he, dead in the tomb, is in that condition brought to the only life that is life indeed, viz. where a man, dead or alive, hears the voice of the Son of God and lives. It is in this sense that the story of Lazarus is the *crux interpretationis* of the whole gospel, for it compels the reader to decide whether he will take John's view of the miracle, that it is always in essence the gift of eternal life understood as knowing the one whom God has sent and obeying him..."

747. Meier, *Marginal Jew*, 2:822–31. For the exposition of the parable see Roemer, *Who in the World Was Jesus?*, 306–16.

748. Meier, *Marginal Jew*, 2:826–27 elaborates on the differences between the two parts of the parable. The first part has no reference to morality and Abraham does not explain the reason for the reversal of the status of the rich man and Lazarus. In the second half there is an explicit moral tone.

749. Meier, *Marginal Jew*, 2:824 who also notes that the name is commonplace in Jesus' day and is a shortened from of Eleazar. He also correctly disparages the whole idea that because the name means "God helps" in Hebrew it was added to the parable. But the Greek speaking readership of Luke's gospel would not know that and if it were so Luke would have provided a translation (as in Acts 1:19). He also makes a good case for vs 31 in the parable being a Lucan construction (828–30) which would then make it highly unlikely that John used Luke in reproducing the story of the raising of Lazarus since Luke also wrote late in the first century.

750. Meier, *Marginal Jew*, 2:830.

751. Or for that matter even longer. So much of the gospel traditions, perhaps especially the parables, have been shortened into the bare essentials of what is reported which makes them resemble the whole of Scripture which is written in a sort of shorthand.

752. See Roemer, *What Was the World of Jesus?*, 574–76.

753. The "sword" prefigures a terrible destruction see Ezek 14:17. In Christian art Mary is called the *Mater Dolorosa*, "the mother of sorrow."

754. The tomb is extant today in Bethany. When I visited there on October 24, 1994 I was able to climb into the entrance of the tomb and down its stairs to the crypt below.

755. The detailed analysis of Jewish culture, history, religion, economy, and social realities you will find in the first book of this series, Roemer, *What Was the World of Jesus?* The details of Jesus' counter-kingdom is explicated in books two and three of the series, Roemer, *Who in the World Was Jesus?* (the parables) and *The Beloved Son as Tantalizing Teacher* (the pronouncement stories).

756. In these passages Jesus is obviously speaking to the whole nation (Matt 5:1 "the multitudes"). And the twelve disciples are representative of the nation.

757. This is nothing new in Judaism as I've pointed out. The men who met Pilate's infringement on the sanctity of Jerusalem and the Temple with peaceful passive resistance is evidence that Jesus' kingdom ethics were well known to the people. He was only calling them to practice what they already knew and that these ethics were not pie-in-the-sky idealism but actually worked out in practice. See Josephus, *War* 2, 2, 169–74.

758. See the parable of the tower and preparation for war, Roemer, *Who in the World Was Jesus?*, 259–60.

ENDNOTES

759. Hiebert, "Theophany in the OT," 506a.
760. Other mountains are mentioned but Sinai and Mt Zion are prominent. Cf., Deut 33:26-29, Judg 5:4-5, Hab 3:3, 7, Psalm 68. So YHWH is identified as the "One of Sinai" (Judg 5:5) and "El Shadday" "God of the Mountain" (Ps 68:14).
761. Hiebert, "Theophany in the OT," 507b.
762. Hiebert, "Theophany in the OT," 507b.
763. Hiebert, "Theophany in the OT," 508b.
764. Hiebert, "Theophany in the OT," 510a.
765. Hiebert, "Theophany in the OT," 510b.
766. Alsup, "Theophany in the NT," 899a.
767. Taylor, *Mark*, 272.
768. Bultmann, *History*, 215-16. But Taylor, *Mark*, 273 holds that such additions are not characteristic of Mark.
769. So Schmidt, *Gospel of Mark*, 71 and Haenchen, *Weg Jesu*, 186. See the study of a first century boat found in the lake in *BAR*, 14:5, September-October 1988.
770. Smith, *Historical Geography*, 286. The moist air combined with the cold air currents from the west contribute to these storms "for which the region is notorious."
771. Taylor, *Mark*, 275.
772. Pace Meyer, *Marginal Jew 2*, 1005, n164. Cf., Grundmann, *Markus*, 104 ". . . wind and sea cannot be against him because storm and waves are in God's hand as he also is."
773. Taylor, *Mark*, 275-76 who notes that the verb φιμώθητι (phimōthēti, "be quiet!" an imperative perfect passive from φιμόω, phimoō, "muzzle") denotes its use in magical text to bind a person so as to render him powerless and then being able to harm him.
774. "Nature is not in independent, closed within itself, quantity but is part of evil which wrestles with the power of God." Grundmann, *Markus*, 105. In this way Grundmann expresses the biblical idea that all of nature participates in the fall perpetrated by Adam and Eve and so also yearns for "the deliverance from the bonds of corruption" (Rom 8:19-22).
775. Meyer, *Marginal Jew 2*, 927. He finds Jesus rebuking question Marcan redaction because it correlates with Jesus censure of the disciples in Mark 8:17-21 a certain Marcan insertion. (930) If that is so he further asserts that the disciples question in v 38 is also Marcan redaction. So if the Marcan redaction added rhetorical questions on the part of the disciples he opines that the question that the disciples ask themselves in vs 41 is also the Marcan hand at work. For him and most commentators the lack of understanding on the part of the disciples is a theme of Mark's depiction of the disciples. In this way he has basically eviscerated the story and we're left with a skeleton of the tradition. The commentators assume that Mark's portrayal of the disciples is his invention rather than part of the tradition that was handed down to him. The disciples' opacity to the person of Jesus is totally congruent with Peter's denial at the time of the Jesus' trial. Mark hardly made up the story of the denial!
776. Taylor, *Mark*, 273.
777. Grundmann, *Markus*, 105.
778. See the note below.
779. "In Jesus, as a stranger to the disciples' fear, the nearness of God appears so that the event becomes for them in one stroke a theophany." Grundmann, *Markus*, 105.
780. Freedom from anxiety is a major theme in Jesus teaching (see Matt 6:25-34; Luke 10:41, 12:22-29). The opposite, of course, is boldness in the faith (cf., 2 Cor 3:12; Phil 1:14; Phm 1:8).
781. Taylor, *Mark*, 273.

782. See also Job 38:8-11 where God has control of the chaos sea and in the creation sets its limits (cf., Prov 8:29); Ps 77:16-20 where the chaos sea fears God and in a theophany he makes a pathway through the waters to rescue Israel from Egypt. Here God's power over the sea is revealed though he himself cannot be seen. He is in control of the raging sea to save his people; his saving his people at the sea is depicted again in Is 51:9-10 where the sea is described as the chaos monster "Rahab" whom he cuts apart and "dries up" so that the "redeemed could cross over" (cf., Is 43:16). Personified Wisdom is also depicted as being in God's place and so held sway over the sea (Sir 24:5-6) and led Israel through the water (Wisd 10:17-18). So in theophanic language these passages depict God brandishing his power over the chaotic power of water at creation and at the time of the exodus.

783. Taylor also refers to a story quoted by Paul Fiebig, in his study of Jewish miracle stories in the Jerusalem Talmud, Berakoth 9, 1 which I reproduce here:

> "It happened concerning a heathen ship that was making a trip on the great sea (i.e., the Mediterranean) which had on board a Jewish child. A great storm arose on the sea and each individual stood up and began by raising his hands called upon his god. But it was of no use. When they saw that their prayers were of no use they said to the Jew, 'My son, stand up and call upon your God since we have heard that he will answer you when you cry to him for he is strong.' Immediately the child stood up and with his whole heart cried out, and the Holy One—praise be to him—accepted his prayer and the sea was silenced."

Fiebig, *Jüdische Wundergeschichten*, 61. (My translation.) The story is told by Rabbi Tanchuma who lived in the 4th century A.D. Bultmann, *History*, 235 thinks on the basis of similarities between the Gospel story and the story of Jonah and with this Jewish story that "an alien miracle story has been transferred to Jesus." Taylor disagrees and says that the Jonah story may only have influenced the phrasing. Taylor, *Mark*, 272-73 cites Wellhausen, *Marci*, 39 who straightforwardly says the story "ist nicht der Widerhall der Geschichte von Jonas." ("The story "is not an echo of the story of Jonah.")

784. Meyer, *Marginal Jew* 2, 928, 1006 n173. Meier prefers the former because for him the essential element of an epiphany must "include either the absence or invisibility of the divine or heavenly figure at the beginning of the story" and the "frightening appearance" of the same in power later within the story. His conclusion is that it is not "strictly" an epiphany for this reason.

785. See also note 20 and Dibelius, *Formgechichte*, 91 He references the miracles as "Epiphany stories in which the divine power of the miracle worker appears visible." Grundmann, *Markus*, 203 in agreement with Dibelius also calls the storm stilling an "Epiphany narrative" and also as the recasting of a very old resurrection report.

786. Meyer, *Marginal Jew* 2, 932.

787. Meyer, *Marginal Jew* 2, 933 gives as examples Peter's rescue from prison (Acts 12:6-9) and Paul's survival of shipwreck (Acts 27:13-44).

788. Meyer, *Marginal Jew* 2, 933

789. Roemer, *Tantalizing Teacher*, 18-27.

790. Cf., Acts 2:22 the beginning of Peter's Pentecost speech, in which he recalls Jesus' ministry by saying that Jesus was "a man designated by God with deeds of power, wonders, and signs that God did through him."

791. Wright, *Victory of God*, 193-94.

792. Meyer, *Marginal Jew* 2, 933.

793. Meyer, *Marginal Jew* 2, 933 underscoring his conclusion that the story as a

product of early Christian theology is not absolutely certain cites the story of the revivalist preacher, Aimee Semple McPheron who ordered a wind storm that threatened a tent meeting in August 1915 in Mount Forest, Ontario, Canada to cease which it immediately did. He also cites the experience of Joseph Klausner, a historical Jesus scholar, who in the spring of 1912 experienced a similar sudden storm on the Sea of Galilee which was followed by a sudden calm.

794. See Plummer, *Luke*, 227. "The fear which accompanies [the disciples' question] is not that which the storm produced, but that which was caused by a sudden recognition of the presence of supernatural power of a kind that was new to them."

795. Most commentators regard this Matthean addition as a homiletical expansion of the original narrative. Taylor, *Mark*, 330b.

796. It is part of what is called Luke's "great omission" (Mark 6:45–8:26). Meyer, *Marginal Jew 2*, 994, n111 presents all the various ideas as to why Luke made this omission. The simplest explanation is that this section was missing in the manuscript of Mark's gospel that he had available to him. The break occurred at Mark 6:46 with the reference to Jesus praying. Luke picks this up in 9:18 referring to this activity of Jesus. The defective manuscript then continued at Mark 8:27 where Jesus' disciples are obviously with him and he asks how the crowds identified him. Luke 9:18 thus contains contradictory statements that Jesus is alone praying but the disciple are in his company and Jesus puts to them this question which combines Mark 6:46 with 8:27. See Haenchen, *Weg Jesu*, 303–4 who gives a physical example of this happening to a text in the manuscript p75 where a thread held the manuscript together and caused the inner pages to rub against one another which eventually wore off the text on those pages. See also https://sites.google.com/site/inglisonmarcion/home/luke/lukes-great-omission?pli=1

797. Meyer, *Marginal Jew 2*, 906. This is hardly surprising given that Mark is writing around the time of the Jewish war, A.D. 70, i.e., the first generation of Christians. Mark further binds the two stories together by adding vs 52 describing the disciples' hardness of heart because they do not understanding the import of the multiplication of loaves. Thereby he creates an *inclusio* (6:30–52). Bultmann, *History*, 216 sees the story developing out of the calming of the sea adding the walking on the water. The final development then was John's version which dropped any reference to a storm and the walking on the water and coming to land are now central.

798. Taylor, *Mark*, 319b quotes Gustaf Dalman when he was at the mouth of the Jordan where it enters the lake in October 2021 reports that the water was so low due to the dry season he could almost go over it dry-shod and that an "absolutely dry bar lay before the mouth."

799. This observation supports the interpretation that the walking on the sea could have occurred after Jesus' resurrection. The introduction to the walking are so different in Mark 6:45 and John 6:15 it has to be concluded they come from the hand of each evangelist respectively. Each evangelist, however, has Jesus on a mountain before the walking takes place. That, of course, would enable him to see the disciples as they struggled against the wind on the lake. I suspect too that this reference to the mountain was part of the secondary connection of the story to the preceding miracle of the loaves. So the tradition history of the two stories is complicated.

800. Meyer, *Marginal Jew 2*, 916 and 1000 n141 gives a number of possible interpretations all of which he finds wanting.

801. Meyer, *Marginal Jew 2*, 917. He also refers to Gen 32:31–32 and 1Kgs 19:11 underscoring this interpretation.

802. Nineham, *Mark*, 184.

803. Meyer, *Marginal Jew 2*, 907, 914. The Job passage in the LXX describes God

in the same language as the gospels that "he walked on the sea as on the ground." This passage emphasizes that God walked on the water "as if it were dry land" while the MT describes him as "trampling the waves of the sea." The sea for Israel represented chaos, disorder, death, and evil, all the powers opposed to God. God had to bring them under control. In this respect it is to be noted Israel never became a sea-faring nation. In Ugaritic mythology Baal conquers the god Yamm (i.e., the ocean).

804. Meyer, *Marginal Jew 2*, 907, 914.

805. There are attempts to explain the walking on the water in naturalistic terms by noticing that the phrase "on the sea" (ἐπί τῆς θαλάσσης, epi tēs thalassēs) in John 21:1 means "by the sea." So this explanation goes, the disciples in their boat did not realize, because of the wind and darkness, that they were not in the middle of the lake but closer to land where Jesus was walking along the shore, "by the sea." So when they take him into the boat they found they were at once at land. See Marsh, *John*, 288–89. ἐπί is a preposition notorious for its variety of meanings that have to be supplied by the context. (Some examples: in Matt 3:7 it means "for"; in Matt 3:13 it means "to"; in Matt 3:16 it means "upon"; in Matt 4:4 it means "by" or "from.") So that if it means "by" in John 21:1 that meaning has nothing to say about its meaning in John 6:19. (In John 6:16 it obviously means "to.")

806. The "fourth watch" (around 3;00 a.m.) is Roman time reckoning. Jewish chronological reckoning divided the night into three watches. Taylor, *Mark*, 329a. If the story were a creation of the church what would be the point of specifying the time, particularly so precisely. More likely, in that case, the story teller would want the story to have universal application and not be confined to a particular time and place.

807. Arndt, *Lexicon*, 56a.

808. Arndt, *Lexicon*, 812b–13a.

809. See Job 20:8, "He will fly away like a dream, and not be found; he will be chased away like a vision (φάσμα phasma, apparition, phantom) of the night." Since the Torah forbids the consultation of the dead (Deut 18:11) the disciples would have been terrified to think they were confronting the apparition of the dead. Cf. 1 Sam 28 and the consultation of Saul with the dead Samuel by the work of the witch at Endor.

810. Meyer, *Marginal Jew 2*, 918.

811. Meyer, *Marginal Jew 2*, 919 rightly points out that Jesus' divinity was not some idea that developed over time out of a "low Christology" but was there right from the beginning. I would add that it was recognized in his resurrection that he was no ordinary man but was the incarnation of God. I would disagree with him that there was a sort of "grab bag" of Christologies both low and high. What the gospels see is that during his earthly ministry Jesus was "emptied" of his divinity (of course not in those explicit terms) but in his resurrection that "emptiness" came to an end and now he reclaimed it. This later became known as Jesus Christ's humiliation and exaltation. See, Pieper, *Dogmatics* 2, 280–330 for a thorough-going analysis of these states.

812. The text literally reads "they wanted to take him into the boat" (NRS). Luther translates similarly, "Da wollten sie ihn in das Schiff nehmen." ("They wanted to take him into the boat.")

813. Meyer, *Marginal Jew 2*, 996, n118 calls it an "epiphany" which he defines as "a striking, extraordinary, and temporary appearance of a divine or heavenly figure in the earthly realm, often to a select individual or group of people for the purpose of communicating a message." I find this definition totally adequate for defining a theophany. He does make a difference, however, between a "christophany" (an appearance of Christ) and a "theophany" (an appearance of God). In the latter, he emphasizes, that God's appearance is only indicated indirectly such as by earthquakes, lightening, and thunder. However, here Jesus in his appearance walking on the sea and declaring he is the "I

ENDNOTES

am" the disciples are experiencing a true theophany, God's manifestation among men.

814. So the point of the story is not the rescue of the disciples from danger but Jesus' revelation of himself in his divine nature. Of course, even from the standpoint of the disciples they are not in any grave danger (the wind is only against them which makes for slow going as the disciples row, vs 48). There is simply no dire need or mortal danger as in the story of the stilling of the storm. The disciples are only filled with fear when they see Jesus walking on the water. They think it is a ghost. See Meyer, *Marginal Jew 2*, 908 and especially n120, 996–97.

815. Meyer, *Marginal Jew 2*, 908.

816. But see Meyer, *Marginal Jew 2*, 998, n 123. This "miracle within a miracle" again ascribes to Jesus the power of YHWH (Ps 107:23–32 where sailors are "brought to their desired haven" by the wonderful works of YHWH). See Marsh, *John*, 290.

817. Meyer, *Marginal Jew 2*, 910.

818. Meyer, *Marginal Jew 2*, 911.

819. Meyer, *Marginal Jew 2*, 912.

820. Taylor, *Mark*, 326.

821. Meyer, *Marginal Jew 2*, 920–21. He comes up with an elaborate theory which has the primitive Christian community inventing the story along with the feeding of the 5000 with its Eucharistic symbolism. The walking on the water then "reflects the fact that, for the early church, the eucharist was the ritualized experience of an epiphany of the risen Jesus, coming to a small group of believers laboring in the night of this present age" giving courage and calming fears by his presence with them (923). The stories were not just totally speculative but based on reflections on the relevant OT passages. But even then, how made up stories could accomplish such profound effects is indeed "miraculous"! I think he has turned the whole community-Jesus tradition upside down. It was the "Word," i.e., the work and words of Jesus that molded the community and its theology, not the community generating and molding a Jesus-tradition. However, it must be said in agreement with most commentators that the two stories of the feeding and the walking were connected in the tradition which also then suggests historicity. It certainly may well be that the two stories were then connected with the church's Eucharistic celebrations and elaborated on its significance and meaning.

822. See Meier, *Marginal Jew*, 2:1023–24, n257 for an enumeration of the voluminous literature that has developed on this story.

823. Taylor, *Mark*, 318.

824. See the story of the inauguration of Joshua as successor to Moses and as leader of Israel and her shepherd (Num 27:14–23). The phrase ""like sheep who have no shepherd" occurs in vs. 17 of this passage, in 1 Kgs 22:17, and cf., also 2 Sam 5:1–3, 7:7, 1 Chr 11:2, 17:6, Ps 78:71. Cyrus, the first emperor of the Persian Empire is designated both anointed one (i.e., Messiah) and shepherd of Israel (Is 44:28, 45:1). Note also the figure of the shepherd in Zech 11.

825. Taylor, *Mark*, 318 strongly supports its original connection with the feeding narrative. See also the discussion concerning these verses above in my examination of the story of the walking on the water.

826. See Meier, *Marginal Jew*, 2:952–55 for a chart that compares all six renditions of the story which he has adapted from Brown, *Gospel According to John*, I, 240–43.

827. Meier, *Marginal Jew*, 2:1024, n262.

828. Meier, *Marginal Jew*, 2:950–51.

829. Meier, *Marginal Jew*, 2:955–56.

830. See the pronouncement story of the healing an official's household member in Roemer, *Tantalizing Teacher*, 98–100. The versions of the story in Matthew, Luke, and John differ as much as the two Marcan stories of the feeding and yet the healing story

is obviously referring to one event. However, as Meier, *Marginal Jew*, 2:1027, n273 observes there are those scholars who maintain the two versions refer back to two distinct events in Jesus' ministry.

831. See Meier, *Marginal Jew*, 2:1026, n 277 where he lists the following hapaxlegomena in Mark: vs 2 προσμένω (*prosmenō*, "remain"), vs. 3 νῆστις (*nēstis*, "hungry"), ἐκλύομαι (*eklyomai*, "grow weak, weary, faint") and ἥκω (*hēkō*, "come"), vs 4 ἐρημία (*erēmia*, "desert place"), vs 7 ἰχθύδιον (*ichthydion*, diminutive for fish, "little fish"), vs 8 περίσσευμα (*perisseuma*, "excess, left over"), vs 10 (a transitional verse leading to a the passage in which Pharisees ask from Jesus a sign.), μέρος (*meros*, here meaning "region"), and Δαλμανουθά (Dalmanoutha). Nothing is known of this name or place; some manuscripts read Mageda, Magdala, or Melegada). So five out of the eight verses of the passage contain words that occur nowhere else in Mark's gospel.

832. Meier, *Marginal Jew*, 2:958 comes to the same conclusion.

833. That John's version contains resonances with the version in Mark 6 also tells against the theory that the Mark 6 version was created by Mark on the basis of the story in Mark 8 (five thousand people fed with five loaves and two fish, the mentioning of the amount of two hundred denarii, twelve baskets of leftover crumbs, and the same word is used for "baskets," κόφινος, kophinos as opposed to σπυρίς (spyris "fisherman's basket" in Mark 8:8.)

834. In this discussion I am following Meier, *Marginal Jew*, 2:959 and the accompanying notes.

835. Dividing the crowd into groups would, of course, make it easy to count them.

836. See Roemer, *World of Jesus*, 391–437 for a detailed description of the many rival divisions within Jewish society of the first century.

837. Grundmann, *Markus*, 137.

838. Grundmann, *Markus*, 137.

839. Marsh, *John*, 285 suggests the gathering of fragments anticipates in fulfillment of Jesus' sacrificial death by "gathering into one the children of God who are scattered abroad" (John 11:52).

840. The desire to make him king reflects the actual historical evolutionary atmosphere in which Jesus lived and against which his whole ministry was opposed. Schweizer, *Mark*, 137. Also see Roemer, *World of Jesus*, 228–56. "King" implies messianic and messianic implies revolutionary ideology.

841. Grundmann, *Markus*, 137. He observes among the images found in the catacombs the baskets point to the Lord's Supper: so much remains over that many others can still be satisfied. The early church, as John 6 makes clear, saw the feeding in connection with the Lord's Supper. So there's also an internal connection with the huge amount of water turned into wine (John 2). Both stories come under the confession of John 1:16, "And from his fullness have we all received, grace upon grace."

842. Taylor, *Mark*, 323.

843. Taylor, *Mark*, 324.

844. Taylor, *Mark*, 326 who points out that Matthew (14:20), Luke (9:17), and John (6:13) all alter the Marcan phraseology.

845. See e.g., 1 Kgs 17:8-16, 2 Kgs 4:1-7, 42-44. Schweizer, *Mark*, 137 because of the plethora of these stories facilely dismisses this miracle as a "roving legend which has been transferred to Jesus."

846. Meier, *Marginal Jew*, 2:1030, n294.

847. Meier, *Marginal Jew*, 2:960-61.

848. John's identifying the bread as made from barley (κρίθινος, *krithinos*) is perhaps his addition to bring the story close to the Elisha story. Also the barley harvest was around the time of the Passover. But it could also have been part of the tradition

he received which wanted to reproduce the motif found in the Elisha story. Meier, *Marginal Jew*, 2:961-62 suggestion that the words of institution of the eucharist as a source for the feeding stories is highly unlikely since they were not repeated, as he supposes, in the early liturgies. This little historical report was added to the church's liturgies only much later. It was considered just that by the synoptic writers and Paul and for centuries was understood only as rubrics for the church's celebration. See Meier, *Marginal Jew*, 2:1030-31 n301 for those who find a relationship between the Eucharistic action of Jesus and the feeding stories. The giving thanks and breaking of bread was simply usual Jewish practice in the home at daily meals and the inclusion of both blessing of bread and wine has its roots in the Passover Hagaddah. It would have been unusual for there not to be a thanksgiving. Jesus was just simply following Jewish practice but at the same time giving directions for what should be included in future celebrations, namely, thanksgiving and memorial. So any one reporting a meal in a Jewish context would use similar words as are used in both the feeding stories and in the account of the first eucharist. Meier then refers to the double blessing which according to the Mishnah need not occur (mBer 6,1-6) but in fact does occur in the Passover Hagaddah. Even though there are only these two reports of Jesus giving thanks while presiding at a meal his practice of open commensality is referred to repeatedly in the gospels and we have to assume that Jesus would act as any Jew and give thanks over the food at these common meals he held with "sinners." That only references to Jesus giving thanks appear in these two stories has to do with the importance of the feeding stories as a witness to Jesus who feeds the people as God did ancient Israel in the wilderness. It is a theophany therefore and these details undergird the theophanic nature of the story. Cf., Acts 2:42, 46 where the earliest Christians "broke bread" together which action was coordinated with "prayers." So they understood themselves as simply following in the footsteps of their Master as their bread was multiplied in holding all things in common (Acts 2:44). Meier (964) thinks that hearing the words of institution proclaimed every week caused the feeding story to "reverberate with eucharistic echoes." But as I have already emphasized above, there was no such repetition in the celebration of the Eucharist. The words of institution are not a liturgical formulation but a historical report. He further insists that the references to fish recede into the background of the feeding stories (especially in Mark 8 where fish are only referred to once in vs 7) because the bread provides a direct reference to the institution narrative. However, in the Matthean parallel they are mentioned twice and he also refers to Jesus as giving thanks for both and breaking both to be distributed to the crowd. In the first rendering of the story in Mark 6 there is no such "receding:" Jesus takes both and blesses them; both are set before the people and fragments of both are gathered (So "fish" are mentioned three times. In the parallel in Matt 15 they are only mentioned twice. So Matthew appears to enhance them in one account and they seem to "recede" in the other. Luke's rendition of the first feeding there is also no "receding" of the presence of fish.) However, John does emphasize the bread but that coordinates with the whole discussion in his chapter 6 and Jesus as the bread of life. Thus a definite pattern of a supposed "receding" does not exist. Meier could have spared himself a lot of ink by recognizing these simple historical facts of Jewish and Christian practice and the function of the story as theophany. But Meier does admit that though the Elisha and the institution narrative influenced the feeding story that it was not so massive so that they explain its origin. He uses a felicitous metaphor to explain the relationship between the Elisha story and the institutional narrative when he writes that the feeding story was "refracted through the[ir] lenses." (965)

849. Meier, *Marginal Jew*, 2:966 and 1037 n319.

850. Meier, *Marginal Jew*, 2:966. Taylor, *Mark*, 321 finds the best explanation that the numbers are exaggerated. How that is supposed to render the event more acceptable

by the modern mind escapes me. What's the difference between multiplying the loaves to feed a dozen people or 5000?

851. Think of the crossing of the Reed Sea: Exodus reports that it was both a miraculous event but also there was some natural forces taking place: it was wind that caused the sea to part (Exod 14:21).

852. Taylor, *Mark*, 321. But he finds motifs that suggest that the incident was non-miraculous: there is no surprise registered on the part of the disciples or the people and the difficulty of understanding that Jesus, who was subject to human limitations, possessed creative power over natural processes.

853. Schweizer, *Mark*, 139.

854. Marsh, *John*, 284.

855. Charlesworth, Old Testament Pseudepigrapha I, 43–44.

856. Nineham, *Mark*, 179.

857. I have also dealt with this story in my previous book Roemer, *Tantalizing Teacher*, 143–44.

858. Stuart, "Curse," 1218b.

859. On the Holy War see Roemer, *World of Jesus*, 13–16.

860. See Roemer, *Who in the World Was Jesus?*, 146–48.

861. I have dealt briefly with Luke's call of the disciples in Roemer, *Tantalizing Teacher*, 59–61.

862. Meier, *Marginal Jew*, 2:898.

863. Meier, *Marginal Jew*, 2:899 finds nine words used in common by the two stories: embark, disembark, follow, net, fish, a large number of fish, and the sons of Zebedee, night, and boat. The phrase "sons of Zebedee" never appears anywhere else in John's gospel.

864. Meier, *Marginal Jew*, 2:900–901.

865. Meier, *Marginal Jew*, 2:900–904.

866. As I've argued in Roemer, *Tantalizing Teacher*, 59–61.

867. Plummer, *Luke*, 141.

868. Plummer, *Luke*, 143. "Not often," he writes, "do we find so many marks of [Luke's] style in so small a compass." Particularly prominent is Luke naming Peter as "Simon Peter" (vs 8) which appears nowhere else in Luke but fifteen times in John and in John 21 five times.

869. The "after six days" Mark 9:2 is another analogous temporal reference which commentaries connect with the six days that Moses was on the mountain (Exod 24:16) so the day when the divine voice came it was on the Sabbath. The presence of Moses in the transfiguration scene would coordinate with this story. But the connection seems somewhat superficial and difficult to make the relationship meaningful.

870. See my discussion of the meaning of the phrase in my exposition of the demoniac in the synagogue, chapter 2. Also see Meier, *Marginal Jew*, 2:1014–15, n217.

871. Smith, *Johannine Christianity*, 77 who identifies the story along with 2:12–22 and 6:16–21 as "epiphany" stories. However, along with John's high Christology it is more theophanic ("the Word was God" 1:1 i.e., God revealing himself) than epiphanic (manifesting something of the divine). The distinction is subtle. Bultmann, *Johannes Evangelium*, 77 underscores its theophanic character when he characterizes the subsection of the gospel, chapter 2–12 as "the revelation of the δόξα (*doksa*, "glory") before the world" (cf., 1:14).

872. At the Galilean site of 'Einot Amitai near Nazareth in northern Israel archaeologists discovered a 2,000-year-old quarry and workshop that produced stone vessels. Located on the western slopes of Har Yonah near Nazareth, 'Einot Amitai features a massive cave hewn into a chalkstone hill. The archaeologists discovered in their

inaugural excavation chalkstone vessels at different stages of production, suggesting that the cave functioned as a workshop. It made sense to purchase a vessel that could not become unclean, for once a vessel became ritually unclean, it had to be taken out of use. An impure pottery vessel, for example, had to be broken. However, the excavation has only found small vessels—mugs and bowls.

873. Meier, *Marginal Jew*, 2:936.
874. Meier, *Marginal Jew*, 2:938. When Jesus commends his mother to the care of the "beloved disciple" (19:25–27) it seems that John is thinking of her in terms of the mother of the faithful.
875. Meier, *Marginal Jew*, 2:939.
876. Meier, *Marginal Jew*, 2:940 finds this pattern in two other miracles in his gospel: the official who asks Jesus to heal his son and Mary and Martha pleading for his intervention with Lazarus's illness. Jesus at first seems to refuse, the petitioners accept this challenge of faith, and Jesus in response to that faith that will not give up accedes finally to the request.
877. Meier, *Marginal Jew*, 2:941.
878. Meier, *Marginal Jew*, 2:943. So also the parable of the wise and foolish virgins (Matt 25:1–13). See Roemer, *Who in the World Was Jesus?*, 296–98.
879. Shepherd, "Gospel According to John," 713b.
880. Meier, *Marginal Jew*, 2:944.
881. Meier, *Marginal Jew*, 2:945 finds that Jesus in John's gospel in chapters 2–4 replaces the Temple with his body, in chapters 5–10 Jewish observances and feasts are replaced: the Sabbath, Passover, and Hanukah. He also rightly interprets vs 11 as John's work (946) and how it relates to the rest of the gospel and the whole of John's theological enterprise. He concludes, ". . . from start to finish, John 2:1–11 is pervaded with Johannine theological concepts and literary patterns. It fits snugly and functions smoothly within the overarching literary and theological structure of the Gospel. Certainly, the impression one gets is that the pericope seems to be for the most part, if not entirely, the creation of the Evangelist or—as some would claim—of the Johannine 'circle' or 'school' whose work he inherited."
882. Meier, *Marginal Jew*, 2:948.
883. See Roemer, *World of Jesus*, 564–66.
884. Meier, *Marginal Jew*, 2:1021–22, n255 puts to the rest the narrative was built on a story about the wine god Dionysus creating wine from water.
885. However, cf., Shepherd, "Gospel According to John," 712a recognizes that "The incident is an excellent example of the author's ability to tell an interesting story, with details that are inherently plausible but at the same time full of symbolic meaning."
886. Vawter, "Gospel According to John," 428a is correct in recognizing that Christians would be sensitive to the sacramental association of the miracle with the Eucharist, the new testament Passover in which early Christians experienced the presence of Christ. In his Gospel John explicitly brings the story of the miracle into relationship with the OT Passover.
887. Meier, *Marginal Jew*, 2:880. He does not go so far, however, to assert that it therefore is a creation out of whole cloth by the evangelist. But he is at a loss characterizing it with any form critical category. Others characterize it as a pronouncement story, personal legend, a disputation, or a "norm" or "rule miracle" (a miracle that supports or grounds some rule, 974, n15). If the teaching of Jesus is the freedom of "the sons" from the temple tax the teaching is not substantiated by the predicted, but never reported, miracle.
888. Josephus, *Ant.* 18.9, *War* 7.6.6 and the tractate Shekalim in the Mishnah.
889. Schürer, *History* 2, 272.

890. See Roemer, *Who in the World Was Jesus?* 88–98 for a discussion of *mashal* and parable.

891. It was probably so that Paul derived his principle from the principle that Jesus enunciates here.

892. Grundmann, *Markus*, 178–79 provides a list of commentators and the analogues they come up with e.g., a myth; the "oldest" resurrection narrative; a vision of Peter; a sort of primitive story out of which other resurrection appearances developed; a gnostic myth of the soul which by two heavenly messengers is reminded of its real home; an epiphany narrative or an enthronization declaring Jesus messiah. Grundmann himself understands that behind the narrative stands a vision of Jesus which had an effect on him, a process that is known to us from the history of religions.

893. Nineham, *Mark*, 234. Or as in the Exodus passage preparation for a divine revelation. Priestly purification also took six days.

894. Grundmann, *Markus*, 180 who observes that in Mark 3:13–19 Jesus creates "the eschatological people of God."

895. See Roemer, *Tantalizing Teacher*, 18–27. What follows here is a summary of these pages.

896. Paul in Rom 8:32 refers to the *aqueda* "the binding [of Isaac]" and that, though God spared Isaac, he did not spare his own son.

897. Luke catches this reality by reporting that Jesus talks about his "exodus" in Jerusalem with his interlocutors. See below.

898. Grundmann, *Markus*, 181.

899. Grundmann, *Markus*, 181 refers to the fact that the priests while serving at their duties wore white and to Josephus, *War* 2, 8, 3 which describes the Essenes wearing white as symbol of heavenly purity. The Essenes' white clothing also symbolized for them that they were already living in the heavenly, eschatological reality.

900. Nineham, *Mark*, 234. Grundmann, *Markus*, 181 observes that the reference by Mark to the "whiteness that no fuller on earth could achieve" (vs 3) gives us a little insight to the kind of people who told and passed on this story in the tradition: they were village folk, the peasants, the Galilean poor familiar with the customs of daily life.

901. Grundmann, *Markus*, 181.

902. Cf., also 2 Cor 3:18 where the same word is used. "And we all, with unveiled face, beholding the glory of the Lord, are being changed ($\mu\epsilon\tau\alpha\mu\rho\phi\delta\omega$, metamorphoō) into his likeness from one degree of glory to another; for this comes from the Lord who is the Spirit."

903. Nineham, *Mark*, 234.

904. Grundmann, *Markus*, 181.

905. Nineham, *Mark*, 236.

906. See Zech 14. Moore, *Judaism*, 298.

907. See Roemer, *Tantalizing Teacher*, 89–98. The change was basically from that of the Sukkoth-eschatology found in Zech 14 and according to which the "cleansing" of the temple was preparing it for the eschatological influx of the Gentiles to the eschatological destruction of the Temple the eschatology outlined in Mark 13. That is why I judge John's placing the "cleansing" early on in Jesus ministry to be the correct chronology.

908. Matthew eliminates the remark finding it inappropriate. Fenton, *Matthew*, 275 also calls the story an epiphany.

909. Caird, *Luke*, 132

910. So the conversation Luke reports, the voice from heaven, and the narrative's resonance with the story of the prayer in the garden of Gethsemane all combine to point to Jesus as the suffering servant and give reason for the disciples' alarm contra

ENDNOTES

Schmid, *Markus*, 172.

911. Caird, *Luke*, 132 refers to research that reports intense devotions are often accompanied by physical transformation and a luminous glow.

912. Schweizer, *Mark*, 180 points out that that there is no Easter story that tells of a divine voice, heavenly companions, or the visible glory of Jesus. Also Easter stories always include sayings of Jesus.

913. See Schweizer, *Mark*, 183 who makes these points. However, I do not agree they are some kind of revelation of Jesus' divinity and of the disclosure of the so-called "messianic secret" (see above).

914. See the You Tube video "Mathematical Challenges to Darwin's Theory of Evolution."

915. See the temptation story (Luke 4:1–13; Matt 4:1–11). See also my exposition of this story in Roemer, *Tantalizing Teacher*, 43–51.

916. See the parable of the Unjust Steward in Roemer, *World of Jesus*, 247–59.

917. Roemer, *World of Jesus*, 249–54. Note particularly the depredations of the last procurator, Florus, and the outrages and affronts he perpetrated.

918. Historically, it finally occurred when Constantine proclaimed Christianity the state religion in 323. The mission to the Gentiles effected God's sovereignty. Norwich, *Byzantium* I, xxiv reflects this victory of God when he observes, "never in the history of Christianity or one is tempted to add, of any other of the world's religions–has any school of artists contrived to infuse so deep a degree of spirituality into its work. Byzantine theologians used to insist that religious painters and mosaicists should seek to reflect the image of God . . . in the churches and monasteries of the Empire we see it, again and again, triumphantly accomplished." However, the negative to Christian subjection of the Empire was Christian antisemitism when the church should have been the great supporter and protector of the Jews.

919. Josephus, *War*, 5, 9, 363–68. Josephus is writing for a Roman audience and so speaks in terms they could identify with and understand.

920. See Roemer, *World of Jesus*, 228–56.

921. See Roemer, *World of Jesus*, 13–16.

922. Theissen, *Miracle Stories*, 35.

923. See note 666 above and Roemer, *World of Jesus*, 228–33.

924. See Roemer, *Who in the World Was Jesus?*, 15–17.

925. Cf., Paul's epistle to the Galatians and the freedom of the Christian which is emphasized there. "For freedom Christ has set us free; stand fast therefore, and do not submit again to a yoke of slavery" (Gal 5:1).

926. See the ideologies of the various revolutionary groups in Roemer, *World of Jesus*, 401–37.

927. I outlined in detail the animosity between the "rubes" of the Galilee and the sophisticated Jerusalemites in my exposition of this miracle in chapter 3.

928. Although the Lucan and Matthean renditions are quite different from one another.

929. Which is not to say that the nation was not harassed, provoked, and even purposefully baited to revolt by some of the procurators and their incompetent and brutal regimes. See Roemer, *World of Jesus*, 228–56 especially the summary and analysis of the war 374–85. There were many of a "quietistic" attitude who were willing to wait on God to save the nation. Jesus differs from them because he is not pacifistic, merely sitting back waiting for a divine intervention. He proclaims and established the kingdom by his open commensality, his miracles of healing, exorcisms, and raising the dead. He established a community of the new age which was understood to be at the door and gave structure to this proleptic appearance of the kingdom by calling the twelve and sending

them out to reach out to the whole nation with the good news of the presence of the kingdom already established among them. One might say Jesus was an "active quietist."

930. Jesus' sudden appearance among the disciples in these incidents evokes the same reaction as here: they are terrified and think they are seeing a (punishing) spirit.

931. Cf., Rev 1:14, the glorified resurrected Christ is described and revealed in his divinity as compared to the saved in their white garments Rev 3:5, 4:4, 6:11, 7:14, 19:14.

932. The theophany at Sinai is no exception. They are only external displays (Exod 19:18-19, cf., Heb 12:18-19). It is only Moses who encounters God on the mountain but even then not face to face (Exod 33:20-3).

933. See, for example, Horsley, *Bandits, Prophets, and Messiahs*.

934. See Roemer, *Tantalizing Teacher*, 145-49.

935. Roemer, *World of Jesus*, 558-62.

936. From Roemer, *World of Jesus*, 512.

937. See the parable of the Rich Fool, the Rich Man and Lazarus, A Neighbor Comes at Midnight, the Unforgiving Servant, and the Good Samaritan. Roemer, *Who in the World Was Jesus?* 165-68; 306-16; 230-34; 201-7; 303-6.

938. Roemer, *Who in the World Was Jesus?*, 198-201.

939. Roemer, *Who in the World Was Jesus?*, 148-51, 294-96. See also 1 Cor 12, and Rom 12:4-8.

940. Roemer, *Who in the World Was Jesus?*, 241-47.

941. Roemer, *Who in the World Was Jesus?*, 247-59.

942. The parable of the Prodigal Son, Roemer, *Who in the World Was Jesus*, 241-47.

943. The fact that there were so many Gentiles who accepted Judaism because of its morality and its one God shows that Gentile hearts could be won to the true faith of Israel. Many a Gentile became a "proselyte" (προσήλυτος, "one who has come to [us]"): was circumcised and observed the Torah. So the kingdom demanded a new standard of obedience. Not the legalities of the Torah but the obedience of faith in Israel's God of love and forgiveness who sacrificed his own honor to include the outsider.

944. Roemer, *Who in the World Was Jesus?*, 247-59.

945. Roemer, *Who in the World Was Jesus?*, 350-56.

946. Roemer, *Who in the World Was Jesus?*, 316-23.

947. Roemer, *Who in the World Was Jesus?*, 230-34.

948. Roemer, *Who in the World Was Jesus?*, 323-30.

949. Roemer, *Who in the World Was Jesus?*, 306-16.

950. See Roemer, *Tantalizing Teacher*.

951. That the love of enemy did not just refer to one's fellow Jew but extended to Rome is shown by Jesus' other demand to go the extra mile. The Roman soldier had the power to impress a civilian to carry his baggage for one mile. By going the extra mile a brother would be spared having to lug his luggage.

952. So my interpretation of the Unjust Steward (Luke 16:1-8) understands it as creating a Jubilee in which everyone wins. See Roemer, *Who in the World Was Jesus?*, 247-59.

953. See the parable of the Returning Demons, Roemer, *Who in the World Was Jesus?*, 347-50.

954. See Roemer, *Tantalizing Teacher*, 76-80.

955. Witherington, *Jesus Quest*, 185.

956. Roemer, *World of Jesus*, 1-16.

957. Matt 14:5, 21:11, 21:46, Mark 6:15, Luke 7:16, 13:33, 24:19, John 4:19, 6:14, 7:40, 9:17, Acts 3:22, 7:37.

958. The reign of David, essentially the first real messianic king and the beloved of God, already portended the suffering aspect of God's royal son, see 2 Sam 15:13-16:14.

959. In this regard Jesus asserted that Israel was the "light of the world" and the "salt of the earth." But it had to realize that in its attitudes and practice (Matt 5:13–14). Jesus' saying here contains both an indicative assertion and a subjunctive warning: if salt loses its savor then is will be discarded.

960. There were those scholars who thought of early Judaism as a degeneration from the "pure" religion of Israel's past (if such conditions ever existed). Rather, Israel had come through the trauma of the exile absolutely determined to be faithful to the covenant by faithful adherence and observance of Torah. (Cf., Neh 8:1–10:39 where Ezra reads the Torah to the people, they confess their sins, and agree to abide by it.) And it succeeded at that. Judaism had eschewed every last vestige of pagan practice and faithless syncretism. Because the Jews were salt and light they could have no fear of falling back again into the old ways of the past. So with no possibility of back sliding, Jesus asserts they are able to be open to the Gentile world especially because the God of Israel was at work and active there too.

961. Rome's mismanagement of its client state by the mostly corrupt procurators makes it completely understandable why the people were so zealous to rid themselves of Roman rule.

Bibliography

Ackroyd, Peter R. *Exile and Restoration: A Study of Hebrew Thought of the Sixth Century B.C.* Philadelphia: Westminster, 1968.
Alsup, John E. "Theophany in the NT." In *IDB Supplement*, 898–900.
The Aramaic Scriptures Research Society in Israel. *The New Covenant Commonly Called The New Testament: Peshitta With a Hebrew Translation*. Jerusalem: The Bible Society, 1986.
Arendt, William F., and F. Wilber Gingrich. *A Greek-English Lexicon of the New Testament and Other Early Christian Literature*. Chicago: University of Chicago Press, 1952.
Barr, Stephen. *Modern Physics and Ancient Faith*. Notre Dame, IN: University of Notre Dame Press, 2003.
Blackburn, Barry. *Theios Aner and the Marcan Miracle Traditions*. Wissenshaftliche Untersuchungen zum Neuen Testament. Tübingen: Mohr, 1991.
Bourguignon, Erika. *Possession*. San Francisco: Chandler and Sharp, 1976.
Brown, Raymond E. *The Gospel According to John I–XII: Introduction, Translation, and Notes*. Garden City, NY: Doubleday, 1966.
Bultmann, Rudolf. *Das Evangelium des Johannes*. Göttingen: Vandenhoeck & Ruprecht, 1964.
———. *The History of the Synoptic Tradition*. New York: Harper & Row, 1963.
———. *Jesus Christ and Mythology*. New York: Scribner's, 1958.
Bartsch, H. W. *Kerygma and Myth*. London: SPCK, 1953.
Caird, G. B. *The Gospel of St Luke*. Harmondsworth: Penguin, 1963.
Carter, Warren. "Cross-Gendered Romans and Mark's Jesus: Legion Enters the Pigs (Mark 5:1–20)." *JBL* 134 (2015) 139–155.
Charlesworth, James H., ed. *The Old Testament Pseudepigrapha* 1. Garden City, NY: Doubleday, 1983.
Clifford, Richard J. "Isaiah 40–66." In *Harper's Bible Commentary* 571–96. San Francisco: Harper & Row, 1988.
Cohen, A. *Everyman's Talmud*. New York: E. P. Dutton, 1949.
The Complete Dead Sea Scrolls in English. Translated by Geza Vermes. New York: Penguin, 1995.
Dahl, M. E. *The Resurrection of the Body: A Study of 1 Corinthians 15*. Naperville, IL: Alec R. Allenson, 1962.

BIBLIOGRAPHY

Danker, Frederick W. *Jesus and the New Age: According to St. Luke*. St. Louis: Clayton, 1972.

Dibelius, Martin. *From Tradition to Gospel*. New York: Charles Scribner's Sons, 1935.

Draper, William. *History of the Conflict between Religion and Science*. New York: D. Appleton, 1874.

Evans, Michael. "The Lord Has Helped Us!" *foz* (2022) 10–13.

Finegan, Jack. *The Archaeology of the New Testament: The Life of Jesus and the Beginning of the Early Church*. Princeton: Princeton University, 1992.

Elledge, Roderick. *Use of the Third Person for Self-Reference by Jesus and Yahweh: A Study of Illeism in the Bible and Ancient Near Eastern Texts and Its Implications for Christology*. Library of New Testament Studies 575. London: T & T Clark, 2017.

Emerson, Ralph Waldo. *Selected Essays*. New York: Penguin Classics, 1982.

Eusebius. *The Ecclesiastical History* 1. Translated by William Whiston. 1926. Reprint, Loeb Classical Library. London: Harvard University Press, 1992.

Eve, Eric. "Meier, Miracle and Multiple Attestation." *Journal for the Study of the Historical Jesus* 3 (2005) 23–45.

Fenton, J. C. *The Gospel of St. Matthew*. London: Penguin, 1963.

Fiebig, Paul. *Jüdische Wundergeschichten des Neutestamentlichen Zeitalters*. Tübingen: J. C. B Mohr, 1911.

Finkelstein, Louis. *The Pharisees: The Sociological Background of Their Faith*. Philadelphia: The Jewish Publication Society of America, 1938.

Gallagher, Richard. *Demonic Foes*. New York: HarperOne, 2020.

Geldenhuys, Norval. *Commentary on the Gospel of Luke*. The New International Commentary on the New Testament. Grand Rapids: Eerdmans, 1956.

Glynn, Patrick. *God: The Evidence: The Reconciliation of Faith and Reason in a Postsecular World*. Rocklin, California: FORUM, 1997.

Grebe, Paul, et al., eds. *Duden: Stilwörterbuch der deutschen Sprache*. Mannheim: Dudenverlag, 1963.

Greivett, R. Douglas and Gary Habermaas, eds. *In Defense of Miracles*. Downers Grove, IL: InterVarsity, 1997.

Grundmann, Walter. *Das Evangelium nach Markus*. Theologischer Handkommentar zum Neuen Testament. Berlin: Evangelische Verlagsanstalt, 1965.

Haenchen, Ernst. *Der Weg Jesu*. Berlin: Walter de Gruyter, 1968.

Hiebert, Theodore. "Theophany in the OT." In *ABD* 4:505–11.

Horsley, Richard A. *Bandits, Prophets, and Messiahs: Popular Movements at the Time of Jesus*. San Francisco: Harper & Row, 1985.

———. "Can Study of the Historical Jesus Escape its Typographical Captivity?" *Journal for the Study of the Historical Jesus* 19 (2021) 265–329.

Hume, David. *Enquiry Concerning Human Understanding*. Edited by Eric Steinberg. Indianapolis: Hackett, 1977.

Jaffee, Martin S. *Early Judaism*. Upper Saddle River, NJ: Prentice Hall, 1997.

Jeans, James. *The Mysterious Universe*. Cambridge University Press, 1930.

Jeremias, Joachim. "Theophany in the OT." In *IDB* Supplement, 896–98.

Jonas, Hans. *Gnosis und Spätantiker Geist*. Göttingen: Vandenhoeck & Ruprecht, 1964.

Keener, Craig. *Miracles: The Credibility of the New Testament Accounts*. Grand Rapids: Baker, 2011.

BIBLIOGRAPHY

Kemp, Kenneth W. *The War That Never Was: Evolution and Christian Theology*. Eugene, OR: Cascade, 2020.

Kingsbury, Jack Dean. *Conflict in Mark: Jesus, Authorities, Disciples*. Minneapolis: Fortress, 1989.

Kübler-Ross, Elizabeth. *On Children and Death*. New York: Collier, 1983.

Levenson, John D. *The Death and Resurrection of the Beloved Son*. New Haven: Yale University Press, 1993.

Lewis, C. S. *Miracles*. New York: Macmillan, 1960.

Lyell, Charles and James A Secord. *Principles of Geology*. London: Penguin, 1997.

Mack, Katie. *The End of Everything*. New York: Scribners, 2020.

Malina, Bruce J. and Richard Rohrbaugh. *Social Science Commentary on the Synoptic Gospels*. Minneapolis: Fortress, 1992.

Malinowski, Bronislaw. "Magic, Science and Religion." In *Science, Religion and Reality*. Edited by Joseph Needham, 19–84. New York: Macmillan, 1925.

Marsh, John. *The Gospel of St. John*. Middlesex, England: Penguin, 1968.

McCurley, Foster R. *Genesis, Exodus, Leviticus, Numbers*. Philadelphia: Fortress, 1979.

McKnight, Edgar V. *What is Form Criticism?* Philadelphia: Fortress, 1969.

McRay, John. "Gerasenes." In *ABD* 2:991–92.

Meier, John P. *A Marginal Jew: Rethinking the Historical Jesus 2: Mentor, Message, and Miracles*. New York: Doubleday, 1994.

Metzger, Bruce M. *A Textual Commentary on the Greek New Testament*. London: United Bible Societies, 1971.

———. *The Text of the New Testament: Its Transmission, Corruption, and Restoration*. New York: Oxford University Press, 1992.

Meyer, Steven. Review of *Darwin's Doubt* by David Gelernter. *Claremont Review of Books* 19 (2019) 54–69.

Meyer, Stephen C. *Darwin's Doubt: The Explosive Origin of Animal Life and the Case of Intelligent Design*. New York: HarperOne, 2013.

———. *Return of the God Hypothesis: Three Scientific Discoveries that Reveal the Mind Behind the Universe*. New York: HarperOne, 2021.

The Mishnah: Translated from the Hebrew with Introductory and Brief Explanatory Notes. Translated by Herbert Danby. Oxford: Oxford University Press, 1933.

Moody, Raymond A. *Life After Life*. New York: HarperOne, 1975.

Moore, George Foot. *Judaism in the First Centuries of the Christian Era 1–2*. New York: Schocken, 1927.

Moreland, J. P. *A Simple Guide to Experience Miracles: Instruction and Inspiration for Living Supernaturally in Christ*. Grand Rapids: Zondervan, 2021.

Needham, Joseph. "Mechanistic Biology and the Religious Consciousness." In *Science, Religion and Reality*. Edited by Joseph Needham, 219–58. New York: MacMillan, 1926.

Nineham, D. E. *The Gospel of Mark*. Middlesex, England: Penguin, 1963.

Norwich, John Julius. *Byzantium: The Early Centuries*. London: Folio Society, 2003.

Ortland, Gavin. *Why God Makes Sense in a World that Doesn't*. Ada, MI: Baker Publishing Group, 2021.

Peddie, John. *The Roman War Machine*. Gloucestershire, UK: Alan Sutton, 1994.

Pelikan, Jaroslav. *The Melody of Theology: A Philosophical Dictionary*. Cambridge, MA: Harvard University Press, 1988.

Pieper, Franz. *Christian Dogmatics* 2. St. Louis: Concordia, 1951.

Plummer, Alfred. *The Gospel According to S. Luke*. The International Critical Commentary. Edinburgh: T & T Clark, 1913.
Pritchard, James ed. *The Ancient Near East: A New Anthology of Texts and Pictures* 1–2. Princeton: Princeton University Press, 1958.
Price, Neil. *Children of Ash and Elm*. New York: Basic, 2020.
Richardson, Alan. *The Miracle Stories of the Gospels*. London: SCM, 1941.
Rienecker, Fritz. *Sprachlicher Schlüssel zum Griechischen Neuen Testament*. Gieszen-Basel: Brunnen-Verlag, 1960.
Roemer, Carl E. *The Beloved Son as Tantalizing Teacher: Jesus Encounters His World*. Eugene, OR: Wipf & Stock, 2021.
———. *What Was the World of Jesus: A Journey for Curious Pilgrims*. Bloomington, IN: True Directions, 2014.
———. *Who in the World Was Jesus: An Encounter for Brave Hearts*. Lanham, MD: Hamilton, 2019.
Roth, Wolfgang. *Hebrew Gospel: Cracking the Code of Mark*. Oak Park, IL: Meyer Stone, 1988.
Schilling, Govert. *The Elephant in the Universe: Our Hundred-Year Search for Dark Matter*. Cambridge, MA: Belknap, 2022.
Schmidt, Daryl D. *The Gospel of Mark: With Introduction, Notes, and Original Text Featuring the NEW Scholars Version Translation*. Sonoma, CA: Polebridge, 1990.
Schmid, Josef. *Das Evangelium nach Markus*. Regensburg: Verlag Friedrich Pustet, 1958.
Schürrer, Emil, et. al., eds. *The History of the Jewish People in the Age of Jesus Christ*. 4 vols. Edinburgh: T & T Clark, 1979.
Schweizer, Eduard. *The Good News According to Mark*. Atlanta: John Knox, 1976.
Shepherd, Massey H. "The Gospel According to John." In *The Interpreter's One-Volume Commentary on the Bible*. Nashville: Abingdon, 707–28.
Smith, D. Moody. *Johannine Christianity*. Columbia, SC: University of South Carolina, 1984.
Smith, George Adam. *The Historical Geography of the Holy Land*. New York: Harper Torchbooks, 1966.
Souter, Alexander. *A Pocket Lexicon to the Greek New Testament*. Oxford: Clarendon, 1916.
Strange, James F. "Nain." In *ABD* 4:1001.
Strauss, D. F. *The Life of Jesus*. Philadelphia: Fortress, 1973.
Stuhlmueller, Carroll. *The Gospel According to Luke*. In *Jerome Biblical Commentary*, 115–64. Englewood Cliffs, NJ: Prentice Hall, 1968.
Stuart, Douglas. "Curse." In *ABD* 1:1218–19.
Suetonius, Gaius. *The Twelve Caesars*. Translated by Robert Grant. London: Penguin, 1979.
Sullivan, J. W. N. *Limitations of Science*. Oxford: Oxford University, 1961.
Taylor, Vincent. *The Gospel According to St. Mark*. London: Macmillan, 1966.
Theissen, Gerd. *The Miracle Stories of the Early Christian Tradition*. Philadelphia: Fortress, 1983.
Thurman, Howard. *Jesus and the Disinherited*. Boston: Beason, 1976.
Tuckett, C.M. "Messianic Secret." In *ABD* 4:797–800.
Twelftree, Graham H. *Jesus the Exorcist: A Contribution to the Study of the Historical Jesus*. Peabody, MA: Hendrickson, 1993.

———. "The Miracles of Jesus: Marginal or Mainstream?" *Journal for the Study of the Historical Jesus*, 1 (2003) 104–24.
Tyson, Paul. *A Christian Theology of Science*. Grand Rapids: Baker Academic, 2022.
Vawter, Bruce. "The Gospel According to John." In *The Jerome Biblical Commentary* 414–66. Englewood Cliffs, NJ: Prentice Hall, 1968.
von Rad, Gerhard. *Old Testament Theology: The Theology of Israel's Historical Traditions* 1. New York: Harper & Row, 1962.
von Wahlde, Urban C. "The Puzzling Pool of Bethesda." In *Biblical Archaeology Review* 37 (2011) 41–43.
Waetjen, Herman C. *A Reordering of Power: A Sociological Reading of Mark's Gospel*. Minneapolis: Fortress, 1989.
Weeden, Theodore J. *Mark: Traditions in Conflict*. Philadelphia: Fortress, 1971.
Wellhausen, Julius. *Das Evangelium Marci*. Berlin: Georg Reimer, 1903.
White, Andrew Dickson. *A History of the Warfare of Science with Theology in Christendom*. New York: D. Appleton, 1807.
Witherington, Ben, III. *The Jesus Quest: The Third Search for the Jew of Nazareth*. Downers Grove, IL: InterVarsity, 1995.
Wrede, William. *The Messianic Secret*. Cambridge: T & T Clark, 1971.
Wright, David P., and Richard N. Jones. "Leprosy." In *ABD*, 4:277–82.
Wright, N. T. *Jesus and the Victory of God*. Minneapolis: Fortress, 1996.
———. *The New Testament and the People of God*. Minneapolis: Fortress, 1992.

Index

abandonment of the transcendent, 3
Abba, 54, 214
acts of salvation, 29
Aelia Capitolina, 127
Aesculapius, 91
An Official's Servant at the Point of
    Death, 135
ancient Near Eastern mythologies, 22
anger 51, 74
anthropic principle, 9, 10
anthropology, 3, 25
antidote to Roman occupation, 76
antipodes "natural" and "supernatural,"
    26
anti-supernaturalism, 85
approaches to and interpretations of
    the miracles, 83
astrology, 94
astronomy, 2, 3, 8
authenticity of the miracles of Jesus, 30
autoscopic perception, 17

Babylonian creation myth, 21, 211
bandits, 152, 227
baptism, 214
biblical account of creation, 20
biblical cosmology, 22
big bang, 2, 11
biographical and controversy and
    scholastic dialogues, 237
biology, 8
blasphemy, 108, 110
body-mind connection, 53

Boyle, 4

Caesarea Maritima, 134
Caiaphas, 117
Cambrian explosion, 13, 16
Canopus, 91
Capernaum, 55
Catching a Shoal of Fish, 193
causality, 6
characteristics of magic, 91
charismatic miracle worker, 92
cherubim, 174
Christ is wedded to his people, 197
Christian freedom from all law, 226
classical Deists, 82
cloud is a symbol of God's presence, 203
coin in a fish's mouth, 200
command to be silent, 104
competition between various
    revolutionary movements, 228
complementarity, 88
components of a miracle story, 31
conquest of the east by Alexander, 40
constellation miracle, 87, 141. 217
contemporary culture's philosophical
    and scientistic posture, 140
contemporary miracles, 98, 142
convergence, 12–13, 20, 25, 210
covenantal nomism, 41, 73
created universe, 23
Creation Account in Genesis 211, 213
creation of the human being, 23
creation out of nothing, 199

INDEX

creator and the creation, 27
crisis of faith, 152
criteria for establishing the occurrence of a miracle, 217
criticism of miracles, 143
critique of the "metaphysical naturalist" understanding of history, 86
cursing of a fig tree, 34, 192
cursing as divine prerogative, 192
Cynicism, 42
Cyrus the Persian, 78

dark matter, 11–12
Darwin, 1, 2, 4, 13, 15, 16, 210
Darwinism, 14–16, 210
data of the soul, 19
degrading aspects of the Roman occupation, 93
deistic scientific worldview, 3
demise of the temple, 77
demon possession in the Gospels, 52
demonic possession, 19, 46–47, 51-2, 94, 116, 148, 210, 214
descent of the Spirit, 202
designer, 3. 7, 14–16, 24
deus absconditus, 54
diachronic analysis, 27
diagnosis of possession, 47
disciples' obtuseness, 182
distinction between illness and demon possession, 70
divine warrior, 63, 173, 224
DNA points to a designing intelligence, 210
Doppler effect, 11
double aspect of the kingdom, 108
dove imagery, 202

ecological location of the miracle stories, 93
Eddington, 6
egocentric epistemological foundationalism, 141
Eliezer ben Hyrcanus, 95
Elisha miracle, 190
elites and the peasants, 228
encoded information, 14
enlightenment, 4, 25–6

entropy, 9
Enuma Elish, 21
enumeration of the miracle stories, 36
Epidaurus, 91
eschatological battle, 33, 1152, 228
eschatology and politics, 148
Essenes, 152, 228, 241
ethic of non-retaliation, 154
Euclid, 8
evil in the world, 141
existential function of texts, 89–90, 97
exorcisms, 30, 36, 143, 239, 245,
experience of a theophany, 33

Feeding of the Five Thousand, 186
Feeding of the Four Thousand, 186
feeding stories, 32, 34, 187, 190
figure
   of Satan, 51
   of the "son of man," 108
   of Moses and Elijah, 203
finger of God, 76
foreign words in miracle stories, 94
forgiveness, 30, 103, 107, 109–110, 145–46, 170–71, 212, 219, 232–36, 242–44, 249
forgiveness of sin, 103, 206–9
form critics, 89, 124
forms
   of Israel's political existence, 245
   of miracle activity, 91
   of miracle stories, 30
free will, 6, 10, 21, 84, 141
freedom of the created order, 24
freedom of the kingdom, 207
Freud, 4
function of the miracle stories, 95, 97
functionalism, 89
functionalist models, 89

gaps in the fabric of natural causation, 89, 142
Gehenna, 60
genome, 2, 8, 16, 25, 210
ghost, 181, 185, 206, 224
God "the most high," 60
God's mercy, 77, 146, 193, 2234, 241–2
Graeco-Roman world, 91, 95

INDEX

great shoal of fish, 34, 194, 206, 225
Greek Magical Papyri, 44, 95

half-sheqel tax, 201
Hanina ben Dosa, 42, 92
healing, 42, 63, 73, 79, 91, 95, 101–107, 112, 115–23, 127, 132–33, 144–51, 186, 197, 211, 220, 234, 238, 241, 145
healing and magical practices, 91
healing at a distance, 67, 131, 130, 139, 151
healing
   of Blind and Dumb Demoniac, 71
   of Blind Bartimaeus, 119
   of a Blind Man, 117
   of a Crippled Woman, 120
   of a Daughter of the Syrophoenician Woman, 53, 64
   of a Demoniac Boy, 68
   of a Demoniac in the Synagogue, 54
   of a Dumb Demoniac, 71
   of a Gerasene Demoniac, 46, 58–9, 76, 154
   of an Ill Man by the Pool Bethesda, 125
   of a Man Born Blind, 127
   of a Man with a Withered Hand, 108
   of a Man with Dropsy, 124
   of a Paralytic, 107
   of a Woman with a Hemorrhage, 106
   of Ten Lepers, 121
   of the body politic, 213
healing sanctuaries, 91
healings and raisings from the dead, 249
Heisenberg, 8, 209
Hellenistic Judaism, 40
Hellenistic urban lifestyles, 40
Hellenization, 41
Herod Antipas, 55, 147
Higgs boson, 12, 108–109
Higgs field, 12, 209
historical context of the miracles, 151
historical intention of the miracle stories, 96

holy one of God, 56–7
Holy War, 71, 77, 192, 240. 244, 248
hospitality, 223, 228, 223, 234, 238–39
Hume, 4, 28, 83–5, 140, 208
Hume's definition of a miracle, 83

illeism, 108–109
image of God, 23, 49, 87
incarnation is the new wine, 197
indeterminacy, 6, 209
indeterminism, 10
indissoluble character of marriage, 236
infestations, 48, 74
intelligent agent principle, 98
intelligent design, 15–16, 20, 210
interiority and the purity of intention, 240
International Association of Exorcists, 48
Israel's sufferings, 152
Israelite monotheism, 173
Israelite theology, 32

Jeans, 5, 10
Jeremiah, 75, 215, 241
Jesus
   as Elijah redivivus, 56
   as the good shepherd of Israel, 225
   as the messianic priest, 203
   as founder of a new family of kinsmen, 240
   at the turning point of holy history, 227
   heals on the Sabbath, 241
   marked for humiliation and exaltation, 195
   never sets himself above the people, 223
   recapitulates Israel's history, 245
   refuses to be identified with the judges of old, 230
   reveals his identity, 107
   reverses the law of purity, 219
   self-consciousness, 117, 213
   walks on water, 179
   not an ascetic, 244
   not forming a sect, 241

INDEX

Jesus (*continued*)
    his baptism as the beginning of the new creation, 202
    invades the demonic realm, 75
    humanity, 140. 167, 202, 223–24
    revises his eschatology, 204
    self-understanding, 106, 244
    strong displeasure with himself, 167
Jewish worldview, 152
Jews of the diaspora, 73
Johanan ben Zakkai, 42
John the Baptist, 796, 109, 152
Jonah, 177–78
Josephus, 31
joy, 121, 79–80,123, 145, 149, 169, 171, 217
Jubilee, 31, 79, 121, 124, 148, 220, 230–241, 245, 248
judges, 151, 228, 230, 236

Kepler, 4
kingdom
    as a culture of new life, 170
    as the new creation, 117, 240
    demands a re-ordering of one's priorities, 115, 240
    invades the realm of disease, 241
    not a static reality, 244
    not based on a strict justice, 232
    not defined by legalities, 233
    not something earned, 240
    life and faith, 170, 222
    restorative power, 78, 245
    requires action, 232
    requires total self-surrender, 240
    reverses roles, 233
kraspedon ("fringe"), 111

Laplace, 2, 4, 208
large landholders, 133
latifundia, 228
law and anti-nomianism, 153
law of gravitation, 7
laws of logical inference, 84, 88
laws of probability, 6
leader of the synagogue, 121
leprosy, 102, 218
levels of magic, 92

limited good, xv–xvi, 206, 229
literary nature of the miracle stories, 89
loss of the land, 239
love commandment renders superfluous the Temple sacrifices, 242
love of enemies, 237

Maccabean revolt, 41
magic, 91–2, 115, 142
Marx, 4
materialist philosophy, 2, 4
materialist spirit, 85, 140
mathematical problem of Darwinism, 14
mathematics does not have transcendental significance, 7, 209
Maxwell, 5
mechanical view of the universe, 209
mechanistic determinism, 209
message of the miracle stories, 97
messianic banquet of the kingdom, 249
messianic leaders, 228
Messianic Secret, 60, 106–107
metaphors for the body politic, 61
metaphysical naturalism, 84–5, 99–100
metaphysical naturalist, 84, 86–9
military aspect to Jesus' behavior, 244
miracle, definition 26
miracles and kingdom proclamation, 35–6
mission to be a light to the nations, 242
molecular biology, 14
Moses and Elijah, 145, 203, 205, 207
Mount Zion, 33, 173–4
multiverse, 10
mutations, 14, 16, 210
mysterium tremendum, 174
mythological language, 181

natural selection, 2, 4, 8, 209
naturalistic thinking, 88, 141
nature miracles, 32, 36, 172
near death experiences, 16, 24–5, 210
new creation, 78, 80, 117, 132, 146, 150, 176, 182, 199, 202, 216, 218
new exodus, 78–9, 1145, 235
Newton, 1–5, 7
non-Euclidian geometries, 6, 209

INDEX

numinous presence of God, 122, 148, 162, 218, 222, 235

open commensality, 76, 80, 102, 190, 206, 238–39
oracles, 91
order of things, 85
out-of-body perceptions, 18

Parables
    Lazarus and the Rich Man, 168
    Great Assize, 233
    Neighbor Who Comes at Midnight, 234
    Pharisee and the Tax Collector, 234
    Treasure in a field, 123, 232
    Unforgiving Servant, 239
parables, 43, 66, 145, 152, 231–32, 134–35, 245, 147–49
paradox of the kingdom, 232
patron-client relationship, 229, 237
personified wisdom, 220, 245
Pharisees, 41, 44, 72–3, 95, 103, 113, 124–25, 128, 133, 146, 148, 150, 153, 161, 213, 215, 228, 231, 240–1, 243, 248
Physics, 6, 7–8, 12–13, 20, 24, 29, 209
Pilate, 134
possession and oppression, 46, 74
primate of the synagogue, 156
proleptic presence of the kingdom, 72, 159, 117, 221, 227
pronouncement stories, 30–1, 152, 227, 237, 247–49
prophets, 34, 55, 91–2, 152, 167–68, 216, 228, 230, 234, 241, 247
psychological aspects of demon possession, 51–2
purity and impurity, 103
purity laws, 66, 153

quality of matter, 5
Qumran, 35, 42, 44, 126, 213

raisings
    of a dead man at Nain, 159
    of Jairus's daughter, 155
    of Lazarus, 162
    of the dead, 103, 155, 169, 170–71, 200, 217, 245
realized eschaton, 197
reason and faith, 3, 5, 49, 74
reconstituted twelve tribes, 78
restoration of the creation, 132, 182
restored Israel, 154
revanchism, 171, 234, 246
revolutionaries, 77
revolutionary fantasies, 77

Sabbath
    creation's restoration, 147, 219
    intimately connected with creation, 219
Sadducean leadership, 152, 228
Sadducees, 231, 243
Samaria, 95, 122
Satan, 29, 31, 36, 43, 51–3, 55–7, 63, 72, 75–7, 79–80, 96, 107, 120, 143, 153–54, 211–12, 214–16, 236, 240, 244
Schrödinger, 7
science and religion, 5, 49
scientific historiography, 1
scientific materialism, 24–25
scientific worldview, 3–4
scientism, 49, 191
scribes, 55, 68, 108–10, 113, 145–46, 179, 197, 241
Second Isaiah's prophecy, 78
Serapis, 91
servant, 78–80, 108, 110, 201, 236, 239, 245, 247
sheep gate, 125–26
signs as enacted parables, 28, 199
Siloam, 129, 131–32, 149–50, 221
Simeon ben Yose, 42
Simon Magus, 95
Simon of Cyrene, 119, 243
sin, 3, 30, 51, 79, 88, 103, 108–10, 112, 127, 131, 141, 149, 170, 193, 204, 208, 211–12, 219, 222, 227, 235
situation in life ("Sitz im Leben"), 89–90, 95
situation in life of the miracles, 95
social intention of miracle stories, 95

INDEX

social milieu of the miracle stories, 91
sociology of literature, 89–90, 217
Solomon as a miracle worker, 147
son of man, 107–9, 145, 192, 197, 202, 219, 235, 245
sons of the kingdom are free, 226
soothsaying, 91
soul, 18–19
St. Augustine, 3
Stammering Man, 115–16, 146–47, 219
Stilling of a Storm, 175
stilling of the storm as exorcism, 206
stone vessels, 196
structural analysis, 64, 68, 89
Sukkoth, 2204, 207
synchronic analysis, 27

table fellowship, 102, 189, 190, 206, 217
table fellowship and kinship, 206
taxes, 228, 241, 243
taxonomies of the different demonic states, 46
teleological, 10, 88
temple of Jupiter Capitolinus, 201
tensions between urban and rural, 133–34
tent of meeting, 33
the "I am," 181–82, 225
the "void," 12, 22, 211
the ark, 174
the existential function of the miracle stories, 96
the inclusion of "Gentile sinners," 145, 190, 215
"Torah" of the kingdom of God, 246
the sacred, 20, 25, 97
Theophanies, 3, 30, 32–34, 171, 174–75, 207, 227, 249
theios anēr ("divine man"), 54
themes of Jesus' ministry, 63
theological and scientific knowledge, 22

theophanic sites, 33
theophany in the OT, 173
theophany stories, 34
this world as a closed system of cause and effect, 84
Torah, 33, 113–15, 122, 124, 132–34, 146–47, 151, 153, 215, 228, 238, 240–422, 246
transfiguration, 34, 117, 201, 203–4, 207, 226–27
trust, 53–54, 64, 206, 214, 224, 239, 241
twelve disciples, 237
types for the practice of exorcism, 44
Tyre, 65–66

uncertainty principle, 8, 209
universal constants, 209
universality of the kingdom, 66
universe as designed, 2, 36, 87, 141, 209
unresponsiveness of Israel, 220

variety of oppressions, 47
violation miracle, 87, 141, 217

walking on the water,, 32, 179, 182, 206, 224
Water Changed into Wine, 195
water of Jewish purification, 198
why evil exists, 50, 74
wine of the new covenant, 198, 207
women, 102, 144, 169
world of the spirit, xviii, 2, 10, 13, 18, 20, 24–28, 31, 36, 40, 49–50, 91, 98, 143, 174, 208, 210–12,
worldview, 3–4, 15, 86–88, 141, 152, 158

YHWH's servant, 78

Zechariah, 76
Zecharian eschatology, 77
Zoroastrianism, 51

www.ingramcontent.com/pod-product-compliance
Lightning Source LLC
Chambersburg PA
CBHW061424300426
44114CB00014B/1523